Edited by

Sandra Buckley

Michael Hardt

Brian Massumi

THEORY OUT OF BOUNDS

Methodology of the Oppressed

Chela Sandoval

Foreword by Angela Y. Davis

Theory out of Bounds *Volume 18*

University of Minnesota Press

Minneapolis • London

Shorter and different versions of chapter 2 were published as "U.S. Third World Feminism:
The Theory and Method of Oppositional Consciousness in the Postmodern World,"
Genders 10 (spring 1991), copyright 1991, reprinted by permission of the University of Texas Press;
and as "Feminist Forms of Agency and Oppositional Consciousness," in
Provoking Agents: Gender and Agency in Theory and Practice, edited by Judith Kegan Gardiner
(Chicago: University of Illinois Press, 1995), reprinted by permission of the University of Illinois Press.
A different version of a section of chapter 5 was published as "Theorizing White Consciousness for a
Post-Empire World: Barthes, Fanon, and the Rhetoric of Love," in *Displacing Whiteness:
Essays in Social and Cultural Criticism*, edited by Ruth Frankenberg
(Durham: Duke University Press, 1997), 86–106; reprinted by permission of Duke University Press.
Condensed, earlier versions of the second half of chapter 7 appeared as
"New Sciences: Cyborg Feminism and the Methodology of the Oppressed,"
The Cyborg Handbook, edited by Chris Hables Gray (New York: Routledge Press, 1995), 407–21,
copyright 1995 from *The Cyborg Handbook*, reproduced by permission of Routledge, Inc.; and as
"Re-Entering CyberSpace: Sciences of Resistance," *Dispositio/n: Journal of Cultural Histories and Theories* 19,
no. 46 (1994 [1996]): 75–93, published by the Department of Romance Languages and Literatures at the
University of Michigan, reprinted by permission of *Dispositio/n*.

Published by the University of Minnesota Press
111 Third Avenue South, Suite 290
Minneapolis, MN 55401-2520
http://www.upress.umn.edu

Printed in the United States of America on acid-free paper

LIBRARY OF CONGRESS CATALOGING-IN-PUBLICATION DATA
Sandoval, Chela, 1956–
Methodology of the oppressed / Chela Sandoval.
p.   cm. — (Theory out of bounds ; v. 18)
Includes bibliographical references and index.
ISBN 0-8166-2736-3 (alk. paper) — ISBN 0-8166-2737-1 (pbk. : alk. paper)
1. Postmodernism—Social aspects.   2. Feminist theory.   3. Postcolonialism.
4. Culture—Study and teaching.   I. Title.   II. Series.
HM449 .S27 2000
303.4—dc21
00-009294

The University of Minnesota
is an equal-opportunity educator and employer.

11 10 09 08 07 06 05 04   10 9 8 7 6 5 4

For Pearl Sandoval, my mother,
whose courage and love
inspired this work.

We seek a world in which there is room for many worlds.

Subcommander Marcos
Zapatista Army of Liberation (EZLN), Mexico

Contents

Foreword

Angela Y. Davis

CHELA SANDOVAL has always grappled with the dilemmas confronting scholars and activists who work to make a difference in the world. With the publication of her pioneering essay "U.S. Third World Feminism: The Theory and Method of Oppositional Consciousness in the Postmodern World," Sandoval emerged as an important thinker known for her rigorous critiques of feminisms that fail to acknowledge the complicated ways race, class, and sex inform the category of gender. Sandoval argued for an emancipatory potential in women-of-color formations and strategies precisely because, unlike in neoliberal conceptions of diversity, difference could be embraced in these formations and strategies not as an objective in itself, but rather as a point of departure and a method for transforming repressive and antidemocratic social circumstances.

  In placing U.S. third world feminism at the center of her work, Sandoval theorized a social movement in which she herself had played a major role as organizer and theorist. As she revisited the work of Cherríe Moraga, Audre Lorde, Gloria Anzaldúa, Barbara Smith, Lorna Dee Cervantes, Paula Gunn Allen, Barbara Noda, and many others, Sandoval engaged with texts that enacted the collaborative strategies she also helped to shape. This legendary article, "U.S. Third World Feminism: The Theory and Method of Oppositional Consciousness in the Postmodern World," developed Sandoval's theory of differential consciousness, and revealed her ability to directly confront some of the most vexing questions facing contemporary social activists.

The groundwork for her analysis was set in a report she wrote on the 1981 National Women Studies Association Conference, where she examined the limitations of a women's movement that "forced a false unity of women." Differentially acting feminists of color, by virtue of their multiple positionalities, Sandoval argued, not only controverted the notion of a homogeneous (white) women's movement, but they also could not harbor aspirations for a separate, unitary third world women's movement. In this formation Sandoval identified the potential for a "self-conscious flexibility of identity and political action," and for the development of competent critiques of the movement of power along axes of race, gender, class, and sexuality that could in turn serve as ingredients for a new methodology of liberation.

In her new work, *Methodology of the Oppressed*, Sandoval designs a method for emancipation that builds bridges across theoretical chasms and creates strategies for globalizing resistance from below. This book provides us with a series of methods, not only for analyzing texts, but for creating social movements and identities that are capable of speaking to, against, and through power. Her theory and method of oppositional consciousness in the postmodern world joins with the "methodology of the oppressed," and together these methods create the mode of social action, the hermeneutic she calls "love in the postmodern world." Sandoval argues that this is the mode of social action and identity construction that is necessary for understanding ourselves, each other, and the nature of being and collectivity itself under economic and cultural globalization. Rooted in her knowledge of activism, Sandoval's book is a map for understanding how to effect dissidence within twenty-first-century cultural conditions.

In *Methodology of the Oppressed*, Sandoval initiates a monumental task of resituating and reinterpreting the work of major Western theorists such as Fredric Jameson, Roland Barthes, Michel Foucault, Donna Haraway, and Hayden White in relation to the insights of those U.S. women-of-color feminisms that insist on international solidarity, and resistance to racism, class bias, and homophobia. Here, Sandoval identifies important ways in which critical and cultural theorists have worked under the philosophical and political influences of subordinated communities in pursuit of liberation. Sandoval's work is a decolonizing theoretical and political enterprise arguing that oppositional consciousness is not a lost utopian ideal, and that with a differential form of consciousness, derived from women-of-color feminisms and the alliance-building strategies they demand, it is possible to avoid culs-de-sac in theory and political practice. The utopian impulse that informs *Methodology of the*

Oppressed, and the obstinacy (in the Marcusean sense) of Sandoval's new critical theory, lead her and the reader on a quest for new vocabularies that can help to decolonize the imagination.

        Methodology of the Oppressed is concerned with creating a place for significant interventions in the social world; it can be described as a prolegomenon that critically examines the conditions and possibilities for contemporary radical movements in this era of global capitalism. Emerging scholars who want to link their work to pursuits for social justice will be inspired by the way Chela Sandoval refuses to abandon her belief in the possibility of revolutionary resistance. As this book troubles traditional ways of thinking about social activism, it simultaneously subverts the idea of the social passivity of theory. By focusing on prospects for psychic emancipation, Sandoval summons a new subject capable of love, hope, and transformative resistance.

Acknowledgments

METHODOLOGY OF THE OPPRESSED was born in the intellectual crucible that was the History of Consciousness program at the University of California at Santa Cruz. My mentors there were Hayden White, Donna Haraway, James Clifford, and Teresa de Lauretis. The book was also influenced by the many colleagues and friends I have been fortunate to know, especially Emma Pérez, Elizabeth Marchant, Caren Kaplan, Katie King, Zoe Soufoulis, Sandra Azaredo, Ronaldo Balderrama, Antonia Casteñeda, Aida Hurtado, Norma Alarcón, José Saldívar, Lisa Lowe, Bettina Aptheker, Marge Franz, Nancy Stoller-Shaw, Catherine Angel, and Helene Moglan. Friendship, ongoing conversations, published and unpublished exchanges over the years with admired allies and colleagues Gloria Anzaldúa, Angela Davis, Noel Sturgeon, Tim Reed, Gayatri Spivak, Fredric Jameson, Vivian Sobchack, Constance Penley, Barbara Ige, Shirley Flores-Muñoz, Yolanda Broyles-Gonzalez, Audre Lorde, Roz Spafford, Marge Franz, James "the Computer Wiz," Ellie Hernandez, Charles Long, Osa Hidalgo, Stephen Heath, and Michel Foucault everywhere inform these chapters.

    Methodology of the Oppressed was completed with the support of the University of California Humanities Research Institute located on the Santa Barbara campus. I am especially grateful to Rafael Pérez-Torres, Lata Mani, Ruth Frankenberg, and Katie King, who, aside from having read parts of the manuscript in process, have been critically astute, supportive, and generous colleagues and friends.

I greatly appreciate my students in the Chicano Studies Department at Santa Barbara, whose participation and engagement advanced and grounded this book in unexpected ways. *Methodology of the Oppressed* would not have been completed without the devoted help of Lisa Biddle and Janet Sandoval. Lisa generated the graphics, illustrations, and helped me copyedit the book. My sister Janet contributed expert organizational and editorial advice above and beyond the call of duty. Heartfelt thanks go to the spiritual activists who provided encouragement, support, and affection during the book's completion, especially Nancy Giulliani. Finally, I want to acknowledge those dear friends whose love, generosity, and friendship have sustained me: Billie Harris, Jim Vieth, Pam Springer, Tish Sainz, Susana Montaña, Michael Angelo Nocera, and Rosa Villafañe-Sisolak and her children (my stepchildren) Almanda, Jason, Ariel, Adam, Nina, and Aaron.

Methodology of the Oppressed is lovingly dedicated to Pearl Antonia Doria-Sandoval and José Machlavio Lucero-Sandoval, my philosopher mother and social activist father; to my sisters Janet, Robin, Sandy, and Julie; and to our aunts, uncles, and *primos/as*—the Luceros, Serranos, Sandovals, Archluletas, Naranjas, and Dorias in honor of the new pasts and futures we are weaving.

Introduction

Where there is power there is resistance.

                                      Michel Foucault

The range of contemporary critical theories suggests that it is from those who have suffered the sentence of history—subjugation, domination, diaspora, displacement—that we learn our most enduring lessons for living and thinking.

                                        Homi Bhabha

Give name to the nameless so it can be thought.

                                        Audre Lorde

MANIFEST LANDMARKS in theory transfigure when the foundational underplate that makes their very existence possible shifts upward. *Methodology of the Oppressed* follows this theory uprising—this ascendance of the latent force that once had inspired, energized, and made possible the U.S. intellectual geography of the late twentieth century. What surfaces is the forgotten, an underlayer of oppositional consciousness that quietly influenced the history of U.S.-Euro consciousness throughout the twentieth century. Exposed is a rhetoric of resistance, an apparatus for countering neocolonizing postmodern global formations. Here, this apparatus is represented as first, a theory and method of oppositional consciousness: the equal rights, revolutionary, supremacist, separatist, and differential modes; second, as a methodology of the oppressed (which cuts through grammars of supremacy), and which over the course of the book transforms into a methodology of emancipation comprised of five skills: semiotics, deconstruction, meta-ideologizing, democratics, and differential consciousness; and finally, the book argues that these different methods, when utilized together, constitute a singular apparatus that is necessary for forging twenty-first-century modes of decolonizing globalization. That apparatus is "love," understood as a technology for social transformation.

This theory uprising moves through and with the works of Fredric Jameson, Donna Haraway, Michel Foucault, Hayden White, Jacques Derrida, Frantz Fanon, Gloria Anzaldúa, Audre Lorde, Barbara Noda, Paula Gunn Allen, and Roland Barthes, among others, drawing from and transforming their bodies of work in order to identify and prolong that which inspires them. The goal here is to consolidate and extend what we might call manifestos for liberation in order to better identify and specify a mode of emancipation that is effective within first world neocolonizing global conditions during the twenty-first century. This book is divided into four parts: (I) "Foundations in Neocolonial Postmodernism"; (II) "The Theory and Method of Oppositional Consciousness in the Postmodern World"; (III) "The Methodology of the Oppressed: Semiotics, Deconstruction, Meta-ideologizing, Democratics, and Differential Movement II"; and (IV) "Love in the Postmodern World: Differential Consciousness III."

Part I engages in a close textual analysis of Fredric Jameson's investigations of capitalist, socialist, repressive, and emancipatory developments as they occur within the transnational order known as postmodernism.[1] The central problem encountered in Part I is Jameson's assertion that forms of resistance, oppositional consciousness, and social movement are no longer effective under the imperatives of the neocolonizing mode of globalization he calls postmodernism. Part II, "The Theory and Method of Oppositional Consciousness in the Postmodern World," counters Jameson's assertion by tracking the U.S. women's social movement from 1968 to 1988, and identifying the oppositional practices adapted and utilized by U.S. feminists of color, who advanced one of the first essentially "postmodern" resistance movements of the twentieth century, U.S. third world feminism.[2] In the analysis of U.S. third world feminism, a cultural topography emerges by which oppositional forms of theory, practice, identity, and aesthetics can be, in Jameson's terms, "cognitively mapped." This topography reveals five different sites through which oppositional consciousness is expressed, and these become dialectically linked when viewed through a "differential" mode of oppositional consciousness and social movement.[3] In identifying the practices that constitute the differential mode of resistance, it is necessary to stipulate the inner and outer technologies, the psychic and social processes required of the practitioners of differential social movement. By doing this one constructs an alternative and dissident globalization in place of the neocolonizing forces of postmodernism. These efforts comprise the heart of Part III, and of the book itself. Parts I and II lay the groundwork and prefigure what comes next, while Parts III and IV contain the central precepts of this book.

Part III, "The Methodology of the Oppressed," lays out the primary inner and outer technologies that construct and enable the differential mode of social movement and consciousness: (1) semiotics; (2) deconstruction; (3) meta-ideologizing; (4) differential movement; and (5) democratics. In so doing, Part III is detailing the technologies necessary not only for generating a dissident and coalitional cosmopolitics,[4] but for revealing the rhetorical structure by which the languages of supremacy are uttered, rationalized—and ruptured. These technologies are carefully delineated in the close textual analysis of the body of work left by one of the central theorists of the twentieth century. Roland Barthes's work first as a structuralist and then as a poststructuralist, his analyses of social, cultural, and aesthetic representations, and especially his work on semiology, function in *Methodology of the Oppressed* as a litmus for testing the relationship between Western metaphysics and decolonizing cultural and psychic formations.[5] Barthes's work is located at a unique historical juncture where postcolonial, postmodern, poststructural, feminist, ethnic, and queer theoretical schools converge. His work can be seen to prefigure, and in many cases go beyond, the critical categories and contradictions that are central to the intellectual processes of decoloniality.[6] Utilizing U.S. third world feminist criticism as a means of analysis, my engagement with Barthes allows me to identify new decolonizing apparatuses for intervening in postmodern globalization— among these, the methodology of the oppressed. Part III reveals how the technologies of this methodology of the oppressed are the skills necessary for accomplishing sign reading across cultures; identifying and consciously constructing ideology; decoding languages of resistance and/or domination; and for writing and speaking a neorhetoric of love in the postmodern world.[7] The methodology of the oppressed provides what Barthes calls a "punctum" not only to the differential form of social movement enacted by U.S. feminists of color, but also to a mode of consciousness that Gloria Anzaldúa calls "soul" or *amor en Aztlán,* Jacques Derrida calls *différance,* Hayden White calls "the sublimity of the historical process," and Barthes calls "prophetic love."[8]

Part IV of this book, "Love in the Postmodern World," demonstrates that the forms and contents of the methodology of the oppressed are deeply imbricated throughout the works of many influential writers who are thinking our way into the twenty-first century. This part synthesizes the work of theorists Jacques Derrida, Hayden White, Michel Foucault, Frantz Fanon, Donna Haraway, Roland Barthes, Audre Lorde, Gloria Anzaldúa, Merle Woo, Janice Gould, Paula Gunn Allen, Barbara Smith, Emma Pérez, and others. Across disciplines, these works similarly agitate for a revolutionary consciousness that can intervene in the forces of neocolonizing postmodernism. The forms and contents of this dissident consciousness arise variously in and through my discussions of (1) the principles of political love and desire; (2) love as a political apparatus; (3) the end of academic apartheid; (4) the bases for creating interdisciplinary knowledge; (5) radical *mestizaje*; (6) *différance*; (7) the grammatical position of subjugation; (8) the middle voice as the third voice; (9) technoscience politics; and (10) decolonizing cyberspace.

Part IV reviews the methods that were developed in previous chapters in order to clarify that which is spoken so rarely in critical, cultural, and social movement theory, yet it is what underlies and connects all disciplinary endeavors. In Part IV, "love" is defined as the form and content prescribed through the entire assembly of methods and materials from previous chapters. Here, love is reinvented as a political technology, as a body of knowledges, arts, practices, and procedures for re-forming the self and the world. This affirmative practice and interpretive strategy, this hermeneutics of love easily bypasses the usual order of perception, insofar as it expresses the difficult-to-discern consciousness that Cornel West calls "prophetic vision," while activating the operations of the now extinct middle voice of the verb.[9] *Methodology of the Oppressed* argues that a diverse array of thinkers are agitating for similarly conceived and unprecedented forms of identity, politics, aesthetic production, and coalitional consciousness through their shared practice of a hermeneutics of love in the postmodern world, and it demonstrates that the apartheid of theoretical domains dividing academic endeavors by race, sex, class, gender, and identity is annulled when this fundamental linkage is discerned. In so doing, the book seeks to analytically reconcile the tensions and boundary disputes that threaten to shatter contemporary academic life and intellectual production. Together, the theories and methods, practices and procedures detailed in this book comprise a cognitive map for guiding practitioners toward a dissident and coalitional consciousness effective in making a place for creative forms of opposition to the neocolonizing cultural imperatives of postmodern globalization.[10]

My intent in choosing theoretical writings to analyze signifies my belief that such writings are cultural productions that can be scrutinized archaeo-logically just as any literary, filmic, or other cultural artifact can be examined to identify the meanings, hopes, aims, and desires contained within them. In this I fol-low literary theorist Terry Eagleton's advice, which is that "it is most useful to see 'literature' as a name which people give . . . to certain kinds of writing within a whole field of what Michel Foucault has called 'discursive practices,' *[and that] if anything is to be an object of study it is this whole field of practices* rather than just those some-times rather obscurely labeled 'literature.' "[11] In choosing critical and cultural theory, including postmodern, poststructuralist, global feminist and ethnic schools of thought to decode, I am looking for the lines of force and affinity such writings share that link them with the theories, hopes, desires, and aims of decolonizing sex, gender, race, ethnic, and identity liberationists. The book's aim thus is to contribute to a re-defined "decolonizing theory and method" that can better prepare us for a radical turn during the new millennium, when the utopian dreams inherent in an interna-tionalist, egalitarian, nonoppressive, socialist-feminist democracy can take their place in the real.

Methodology of the Oppressed pursues these decolonial lines of force and affinity through a selection of the so-called canon of Western theory to demon-strate the shared desire for a postcolonial twenty-first century. This study shows that no canonical Western thought is free of de-colonial effects. Whether we read the work of Fredric Jameson, Roland Barthes, Hayden White, Donna Haraway, Jacques Derrida, or Judith Butler, we will see how each writing contains the decolo-nizing influences of what is defined in this book as postcolonial U.S. third world feminist criticism—in other words, these works contain lines of force and affinity necessary in matrixing a decolonizing globalization that is no longer necessarily "postmodern." Questions such as What is Western? What is "third world"? What is "first"? deconstruct under the weight of this analysis—which reconstructs theory and method to create a new vision and world of thought and action, of theory and method, of alliance. But are these still "Western" writers? Or have Western writers been so influenced by decolonizing forces during the twentieth century that they contain a certain utopian postcoloniality—an accountability from the beginning to what I call "U.S. third world feminism"? Part IV of this study asserts that the work of such thinkers contains the postcolonial U.S. third world feminism necessary for decolonizing the twenty-first century. If so, their work can be seen as partially composing the prehistory of a coming third millennium.[12]

An important note on terminology: there are three uses of the term *differential* in this book; each use is technically distinct from the others, yet all are aligned in the conceptualization of a theory and method of oppositional consciousness, the methodology of the oppressed, and the hermeneutics of love. The first use of the word refers to the differential form of *social movement* identified and described in Part II as the theory and method of U.S. third world feminism. The second use, described in Part III, identifies a specific *technology* of the methodology of the oppressed that produces the differential movement of consciousness through meaning. The third use of the term is identified in Part IV. Here "differential consciousness" refers to a process Derrida describes as "unnameable" even as he interprets its processes. But this third form of differential consciousness also has been defined by Anzaldúa as the workings of the "soul," and by Audre Lorde when she describes the mobile "erotic" as a place where "our deepest knowledges" are found[13]: three uses of the same word for three different but connected processes and procedures. My commitment to the development of a neologism such as that represented in this nexus of terms reflects my belief that we need a new, revitalized vocabulary for intervening in postmodern globalization and for building effective forms of understanding and resistance. New terminologies help bring unprecedented modes of consciousness, agency, and collective action into being that (coactive with all other political formations) will provide us access to a *liberatory* global space as country people of the same psychic terrain.

The Season of De-coloniality

By nineteenth century's end the Western European will to know had consolidated in the expansionist exploration and attempted colonization of the globe. This drive to final mastery incited the great battles for self-determination that, by the mid-twentieth century, culminated in a far-reaching and deep-seated disavowal of Western rationality.[14] Among its other effects, this disavowal also galvanized whole new expressions of consciousness, politics, and aesthetic production — until the impulses that had initially propelled Western expansionism were no longer easily retrievable. The paradoxical successes of the West's imperial project meant becoming subject to the speech of the colonized other; this expanding access to other "third" world language-scapes functioned to make ever more obvious the historically constructed limits by which Western thought, psychology, and culture were bounded.[15]

Western colonial explorations opened up other world geopolitical regions, making available vastly different languages, cultures, and riches for Western consumption. These new terrains of language possibility enflamed transformative scholarship by dominant philosophers whom we can perhaps no longer identify *as* "Western." The twentieth-century season of de-coloniality thus was introjected inside the most solid ranks of Western being from where—during the century's latter half—it was to reemerge as passionate renunciation. It is important to discern how theorists such as Roland Barthes, Hayden White, Jacques Derrida, Gilles Deleuze, and Michel Foucault align with each other in their desires to defy and remake the most traditional and sacred forms of Western thought and organization. But it is even more crucial to understand how their thinking also aligns with that of de-colonial theorists such as Frantz Fanon, Aimé Césaire, Eldridge Cleaver, Gloria Anzaldúa, Haunani-Kay Trask, Merle Woo, Donna Haraway, Leslie Marmon Silko, and Audre Lorde, thinkers who rose from myriad populations but who similarly survived conquest, colonization, and slavery in order to develop insurgent theories and methods for outlasting domination. Recognizing the alignments between these ideational forces becomes critical to the project of identifying citizen-subjects and collectivities able to negotiate the globalizing operations of the twenty-first century. There is a juncture where the thinking of these philosophers aligns, and from where a decolonizing theory and method accelerates. This theory and method are the subject of this book.

The other world knowledges that transformed twentieth-century Western thought were generated not only in the west's imperial confrontations with difference, but during the season of anti- and de-coloniality that followed. This season of de-coloniality is a transitive zone in which conversion from older modes of colonial domination was made necessary. It was during this season that the modes of resistance that are effective against contemporary neocolonizing global forces were first lived out, identified, and defined. U.S. peoples of color have long acted, spoken, intellectualized, lived out what Cherríe Moraga calls a "theory in the flesh," a theory that allows survival and more, that allows practitioners to live with faith, hope, and moral vision in spite of all else.[16] *Methodology of the Oppressed* reclaims that theory from the halls of the academy where it has been intercepted and domesticated. A central argument of this book is that the primary impulses and strains of critical theory and interdisciplinary thought that emerged in the twentieth century are the result of transformative effects of oppressed speech upon dominant forms of perception—that the new modes of critical theory and philosophy, the new modes of reading and analysis that have emerged during the U.S. post–World War II period, are fundamentally linked to the voices of subordinated peoples. One purpose of this book is to lift dominant forms of repression, to allow us to remember.[17]

Thus, the period from the last half of the nineteenth century through the 1970s can be seen as a cultural breach replete with myriad forms of de-colonial events. Within this cultural breach, new self-conscious sciences were developed that can be said to typify and express a Western de-colonial era: psychoanalysis can be understood as the naming and delimitation of the Western psyche; Marxism as the delimitation of capitalist economic processes; semiotics as the demarcation of meaning itself; feminism identifies the functions through which gender and sex are differentiated and bound by power—the list goes on.[18] Jean-Paul Sartre is often considered the first twentieth-century thinker to signal the historical moment when the Euro-American self is able to turn a painful gaze back to the construction of its own body, its own psychology, the rationality of its own cultural milieu. But whether one cites the work of Sartre—or of Frantz Fanon, Simone de Beauvoir, Roland Barthes, Angela Davis, or of any of the other examples at hand—the rationality of Western thought can be said to have found its limits in the twentieth century, where the unsettled and out-of-kilter visions of nineteenth-century Western thinkers such as Nietzsche and Heidegger can be said to have at last found a home.

The twentieth-century season of reproachment shook the Western will to know in all its settling points, permitting a release of new knowledges in the sciences, arts, and humanities.[19] This decolonizing period cultivated knowledge formations that defied and transgressed the traditional boundaries of academic disciplines: ethnic studies, women's studies, global studies, queer theory, poststructuralism, cultural studies, New Historicism, and the critique of colonial discourse developed as intellectual movements that similarly understood Western rationality as a limited ethnophilosophy—as a *particular* historical location marked by gender, race, class, region, and so on.[20] Their shared aim was to generate new analytic spaces for thought, feeling, and action that would be informed by *world* historical conditions.

During this same period Euro-U.S. societies became subject to an onslaught of additional transformative forces, including an increase in human populations, the generation of totalitarian political regimes (unique to the twentieth century), growing urbanization, space exploration, nuclear power and weapons, the development of new media for the indoctrination and education of the masses, and the globalization of capitalist economies and cultures.[21] What many called the "cultural crisis" of the West—the "breakdown" of traditional institutions, values, beliefs, attitudes, morals, and so on—was symptomatic of the overwhelming recognition by many peoples that they were no longer capable of making sense of or giving meaning to the practices that life in "advanced" industrialized societies required its members to observe. The season of de-coloniality ended with the growing recognition that the West had entered a necessarily "posttraditional" era.[22]

      This unprecedented period in Western history was identified and named according to myriad political and intellectual stakes that variously described first world societies as "postindustrial," "consumer," "high-tech," "multinational," "transnational," "postcolonial," "postmodern," and/or "global." Although the precepts of these separate terminologies often contradict one another in the expression of their theoretical and methodological practices, each conceptual domain seeks to identify that which is agreed upon across all differences: that a new cultural dominant has overtaken the rationality of the old. During the 1980s, the term *postmodernism*, and, in the 1990s, the term *globalization*, were most widely utilized.[23] Within the theoretical boundaries of such terms it is agreed that Western societies have undergone a series of cultural mutations that parallel the economic transformations linked to late-capitalist transnational expansionism. Interesting to scholars is the coalescing relationship between these transformations and a mode of oppositional consciousness that has been most clearly articulated by the subordinated. The juncture examined in this book is that which connects the disoriented first world citizen-subject (who longs for the postmodern cultural aesthetic of fragmentation as a key to a new sense of identity and redemption, or who longs for the solidity of identity possible only—if at all—under previous eras) and a form of oppositional consciousness developed by subordinated, marginalized, or colonized Western citizen-subjects who have been forced to experience the so-called aesthetics of "postmodern" globalization as a precondition for survival. It is this constituency that is most familiar with what citizenship in this realm requires and makes possible.

Millennial Time: The Fifth Sun

At the turn of the millennium, it was easy to recognize the imperializing nature of transnational capitalism: it crosses all borders, it colonizes and subjectifies all citizens on different terms than ever before. It is imperative to recognize the profound transformations in first world cultures that Fredric Jameson points to in his diagnosis of postmodernism as neocolonial and imperialist in function. It is also imperative not to lose sight of the methods of the oppressed that were developed under previous modes of colonization, conquest, enslavement, and domination, for these are the guides necessary for establishing effective forms of resistance under contemporary global conditions: they are key to the imagination of "postcoloniality" in its most utopian sense.

Methodology of the Oppressed is not organized as a history that re-counts stages text by text while demonstrating forms of exchange that occur within each era. Rather, it is concerned with a general economy of consciousness in its op-positional forms. The book ranges over feminist, postcolonial, poststructuralist, eth-nic, global, critical, and cultural theory in order to provide ways of thinking, acting, and conceptualizing under the postmodern imperatives of globalization, with the aim of supporting the lines of engagement necessary for the encouragement of de-colonizing global forces. There are several primary projects here. The book devel-ops a theory and method of oppositional consciousness in the postmodern world; identifies the methodology of the oppressed; and maps out rhetorics of resistance, domination, and coalitional consciousness. It describes how these theoretical meth-ods comprise a hermeneutics for identifying and mobilizing love in the postmodern world as a category of social analysis—an outsider methodology that makes visible a particular U.S. form of criticism developed during 1970s and 1980s U.S. third world feminism. Moreover, the book maps the relationship of critical, poststructural, cul-tural, and feminist theory to de-colonial and postcolonial theorizing in order to il-lustrate a model for the decoding of cultural artifacts—including theory—through an alternative apparatus for analysis. It renders that approach in all its specificities, locating its activity in "U.S. third world feminism," and argues that this alternative mode of criticism can point the way to the analysis of any theoretical, literary, aes-thetic, social-movement, or psychic expression.

The methodology of the oppressed is a deregulating system: it represents a lapse in the sovereignty, training, and laws that regulate disciplines. This book encourages the intensification of its play in our classrooms, by practicing on cultural artifacts of every kind—from film, television, and computer representa-tions to architectural environments, literature, theory, and science. Friends have sug-gested that the label for the process I call "the methodology of the oppressed" is a misnomer, that this process is better described as a postmodern decolonizing activ-ity, a methodology of renewal, of social reconstruction, of emancipation—or per-haps better—a methodology of love in the postmodern world.[24] The four parts of this book interactively function as a weaving: U.S. social reality is etched by the op-positional forms of consciousness expressed through differential social movement. This form of social movement is guided by the methodology of the oppressed and its technologies: semiotics, deconstruction, meta-ideologizing, democratics, and differential movement. The methodology of the oppressed provides access to a dif-ferential consciousness that makes the others possible. Together, these interwoven categories comprise the forms and contents that enable a hermeneutics of love in the postmodern world.

This book crosses the stubborn apartheid of theoretical domains by insisting on the de-colonial linkages that prepared and produced late-twentieth-century critical theory. It demonstrates how so-called poststructuralist theory is de-colonizing in nature, prepared during a decolonizing Western cultural breach, developed by those with a stake in increasing that breach—Eastern empires, third world exiles, lesbian and gay theorists, the alienated, the marginalized, the disenfranchised: Kristeva, Barthes, Foucault, Derrida, Fanon, Lorde, Goek-Lim, Lipsitz, Haraway, hooks, Moraga, Gunn Allen, Butler, Alarcón, Pérez-Torres, Yarbro-Bejarano, West, the list increases. It is imperative that we see their work in this de-colonial light—only then can we unsettle the apartheid of theory that threatens vocabulary, language, connection, and hope under late-capitalist, postmodern, neocolonial, global systems of exchange.[25] In the expediencies of this examination, we will discover new ways of reading, thinking, behaving, hoping, imagining, from the simplest activity—reseeing Fredric Jameson's model of postmodernism—to the most obtuse, understanding the differential form of oppositional consciousness and social movement as the methodology of the oppressed that can generate a hermeneutics of love in the postmodern world.

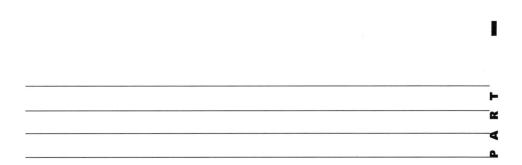

PART I

Foundations in
Neocolonial Postmodernism

O   N   E

Fredric Jameson: Postmodernism Is a Neocolonizing Global Force

I have proposed a "model" of postmodernism ... but it is the construction of such a model that is ultimately the fascinating matter. Alternate constructions are desirable and welcome, since the grasping of the present from within is the most problematical task the mind can face.

Fredric Jameson

We are concerned with structures of consciousness. We are acquainted with those structures only as they are manifested in discourse.

Hayden White

This latest mutation in space—postmodern hyperspace—has finally succeeded in transcending the capacity of the individual human body to locate itself, to arrange its immediate surroundings perceptually, and cognitively to map its position in a mappable external world.

Fredric Jameson

Chicanos, as *los de abajo*, know all too intimately the reality of decentered subjectivity and the violence that results from the pursuit of master narratives—progress, expansion, Manifest Destiny. This is not to say that Chicanos have formed a postmodern culture *avant la lettre*. It is to say that Chicanos have lived and survived (which is a form of triumph over) the disparities made plain by the critical light of postmodernism.

Rafael Pérez-Torres

Postmodernism Is a Globalizing Neocolonial Force

NO INTELLECTUAL proclamation better augured potential changes to come, no science-fiction fantasy—from *Neuromancer* to *Blade Runner*—better presaged the aura and particulars of late-twentieth-century global transformations than Fredric Jameson's 1984 manifesto on the theme "postmodernism."[1] Like that other infamous manifesto, by Marx and Engels, which warned of the social changes endemic to the transition of capital from its market to its monopoly stage,[2] "Postmodernism, or the Cultural Logic of Late Capital" similarly portends an original, powerful, dangerous, and now global transformation of capital from one stage to another. Unlike its earlier counterpart, however, Jameson's manifesto offers little hope that a new subject of history can rise from the rubble of the old order to forge another, more liberatory. What his essay does offer is a palpable grasp on the current crisis, a crisis that is a peculiarly superstructural affair, profoundly affecting consciousness and culture. Jameson's manifesto renders a declaration: it functions as a clear public warning (especially to all the first world, its "North American" site, he clarifies) that the transmutation of economic, political, cultural, and psychic formations, under the influence of unprecedented forms of global exchange, are coalescing into dangerous neocolonial conditions. Jameson's endeavor is to identify principles on which ethical and politically effective opposition to such conditions can be mobilized. As such, Jameson's essay has earned its status as a manifesto. Without the hopeful tone of its antecedent, however, without recognizing the new subjects of history who have ascended out of colonization, Jameson's manifesto has yet to inspire the "new radical cultural politics" and alternative forms of globalization for which its author longs (89).

Jameson argues that first world culture has undergone a shift, a transformation of immense proportions to be imagined "in terms of an explosion, a prodigious expansion of culture throughout the social realm" (87). His manifesto names and defines (what we might apprehend but yet not fully comprehend): an entirely new, all-encompassing form of "dominant cultural logic or hegemonic norm" that increasingly determines the environment of the contemporary first world (55). Postmodernism, he continues, is "not merely a cultural ideology or fantasy:" It is the "genuine historical and socio-economic reality" of the "third great original expansion of capitalism around the globe" (88). At the same time, Jameson asserts, this transnational reality should be recognized as a "*particularly North American space*" (ibid.; my emphasis). Those who fail to recognize the postmodern dimensions of globalization, writes Jameson, are contributing to the evolution of a human consciousness that is incapable of evaluating and affecting its present-in-history. Jameson warns that "if we do not achieve" the recognition of this specific, globalizing cultural space, if our perceptions are not transformed enough to take it in, to understand it, then human consciousness shall fall "into a view of present history as sheer heterogeneity, random difference, a co-existence of a host of distinct forces whose effectivity is undecidable" (57). Perceiving the present as random difference leads to ethical, moral, geographic, and situational undecidability. Such undecidability dangerously short-circuits the switch points through which egalitarian and democratic social, political, economic, cultural, and individual powers can be routed.

Jameson's manifesto predicts that first world and especially U.S. cultural orders are attaining an original epoch wherein consciousness is becoming threatened with an irrevocable and tragic fall into despair; this despair can be tempered, but only with a hysterical and addictive form of exhilaration. Such an exciting decline is caused, Jameson thinks, by a breakage in our diachronic sensibilities, the sense of history that links a civilization's comprehension of itself to its past and future. This breakage has disrupted the boundaries within which traditional values and meanings find safe haven, and rendered dominant forms of consciousness incapable of making sense of "reality" as it unfolds. Incapacities such as these reappear across history. They are resurgent at either the beginning or the end of a civilization's comprehension of itself: it is to this kind of historical moment that Jameson alerts his readers. His prescription is for citizen-subjects to face and name the dynamics of the present epoch in order to generate strategies and tactics that can effectively confront them. To these ends, he sets his manifesto's aim, which is "to project some conception" of the new "systemic cultural norm and its reproduction, in order to reflect more adequately on the most effective form of any radical cultural politics today" (ibid.).

Other efforts have been made to define and name this new global world order. So-called multinational late capitalism is identified and defined in works ranging from Daniel Bell's *The Cultural Contradictions of Capitalism*, to Lyotard's *The Postmodern Condition*.[3] But such works are flawed, their authors little more than "apologists" (71), Jameson asserts, for what is a devastating and *neocolonial* global transformation. Rather than confronting or challenging postmodern neocolonizing forces, such intellectual workers are stubbornly producing "alarming new kinds of literary criticism, based on some new aesthetic of textuality or *écriture*" (54). Or they are generating and even welcoming "news of the arrival and inauguration of a whole new type of society, most famously baptized 'post-industrial society' (Daniel Bell)," he writes, but often also designated "transnational society," "consumer society," "media society," "information society," "electronic society," "cyber society" or "high tech, and the like" (55). Scholarly approaches such as these to name, define, and grapple with globalizing first world cultural conditions must be challenged as sadly ineffective responses to the dangers and specificities of a neocolonizing cultural condition that Jameson suggests we name "post" or even "hyper" modernism. But this globalizing cultural force paradoxically generates, inspires, and demands these very same intellectual "analyses" of it. This scholarship must be repudiated, Jameson writes, and understood to be a "complacent (yet delirious) camp-following celebration" of the aesthetics of the neocolonial world of postmodernism, even and "including its social and economic dimension." For Jameson, it is "surely unacceptable" (85). For the perversity of postmodern socio/political/economic culture must be courageously confronted and opposed in all its neocolonial dimensions and originality.

Such opposition is difficult to achieve, for what we face, Jameson writes, is a "prodigious expansion of culture throughout the social realm to the point at which everything in social life — from economic value and state power to practices and to the very structure of the psyche itself can be said to have become 'cultural' in some original and as yet untheorized sense" (86). The central question Jameson leaves us with is this: How does one go about thinking, talking, living, theorizing, or resisting an original, prodigious, and ongoing first world cultural expansion, indeed, this imperial neocolonization of all citizen-subjects, when the nature of this very expansion functions to take in any thought about it?

Postmodern Entrapment

The preceding modernist Euro-American cultural epoch was, in part, eclipsed through its own proliferation. Modernist aesthetic forms once were capable of engaging, parodying, and reproducing life. They worked by creating and inspiring resistant and oppositional responses to dominant cultural forms. But today, modernist works can no longer similarly stimulate or engage a first world sensibility. Instead, such works sit "cobwebbed" in museum corridors, Jameson writes, their formerly challenging messages long absorbed into everyday U.S. advertising culture. Moreover, within the postmodern neocolonial cultural machine, even new, dissident, and emergent aesthetic formations are continuously made obsolete, cannibalized into the system's need for novelty. Today, Jameson despairs, the production of oppositional forms is encouraged, but these are soon used up and thrown away like any other commodity of which we have grown tired.

Picasso and van Gogh are two modernist artists among Jameson's examples who produced effectively oppositional and parodic aesthetic expressions (58). Jameson argues that the power of their works derived from the artists' alienation and distance from dominant cultural mores and forms. Under globalizing postmodernism, however, this kind of "critical distance" from the dominant has been erased (85). In its place, the citizen-subject has become submersed in an "exhilaratory" but superficial affect, "schizophrenic" (61) in function, which perceives aesthetic representations as just continuing examples of a plethora of differences available for consumption under advanced capitalist social formations. Parody, the art form that under modernism mimicked the dominant in order to challenge it, has become extinct. It has been replaced by a new aesthetic whose manifestation is replication, varying example after example, fragmentation that Jameson names "pastiche." Jameson asserts that the pastiche postmodern aesthetic has invaded and taken over all cultural forms, even intellectual production itself; in this way, knowledge, scholarship, and the academy itself are caught up in the imperatives of postmodernism.

For all these reasons, the ending of the modernist period, of its conquests, slavery, colonizations, and resistances, is not perceived by Jameson as the foundation on which a higher, morally evolved, and "postcolonial" order can evolve. Instead, for Jameson, modernism's limit is a tragic ending. His manifesto provides the spectacle of the death of this more virtuous time, a time when, although forms of oppression were more obvious, the ability to construct a moral and oppositional stance was easier to locate and defend. The advent of postmodernism means that the first world citizen-subject has become caught in a strange, new, tragic antinarrative, escape from which requires fresh forms of perceiving and acting. But Jameson fears that new, promising modes of seeing and representing the world have become unachievable, that they "cannot be generated under present postmodern conditions." This is because historical situations can evolve "in which it is not possible" for citizen-subjects to break through the net of ideological lines that make us subjects in culture. This postmodern entrapment, Jameson asserts, comprises "our situation in the current crisis" (91).

Jameson's essay goes on to design an original and hopeful activity he calls "cognitive mapping" and that he thinks may be capable of identifying,

Fredric Jameson

negotiating, and challenging postmodern cultural conditions. But this effort also dissipates under the weight of his discouragement, until Jameson's manifesto congeals into a eulogy to passing modes of Western consciousness. These textual dynamics demonstrate what can become of the radical utopian impulse when disillusioned, cynical, and hopeless. But the urgency of the present demands that our scholarly responses not be limited by the confines of imagination.

Textual Mutations

The limits in the Jamesonian imaginary are made clear as it travels across texts. Jameson provides the painting *Peasant Shoes* by van Gogh (1884) as an archetypal example of the now-abolished modernist era and ethos, yet this modernist painting, he argues, is still able to sustain itself across historical periods. *Peasant Shoes* generates a sense of "immortality," Jameson writes, capable of crossing epochs because it produces a mirage of life itself in its work upon perception. In Jameson's view, van Gogh's

> peasant shoes slowly re-create about themselves the whole missing object world which was once their lived context.... The work of art...draws the whole absent world and earth into revelation around itself... [by way of] insistence on the renewed materiality of the work, on the transformation of the one form of materiality — the earth itself and its paths and physical objects — into that other materiality of oil paint offered and foregrounded in its own right and for its own visual pleasures. (59)

But if this modernist painting *Peasant Shoes* stands on the side of life, compare its activity with Jameson's next example. This is a painting of a similar object, but it is accomplished during a different era. The 1965 painting by Andy Warhol, *Diamond Dust Shoes*, represents for Jameson a *postmodern* aesthetic, which, we shall say, stands on the side of death. Jameson writes that these shoes are "shorn of their earlier life world...it is as though the external and colored surface of things — debased and contaminated in advance by their assimilation to glossy advertising images — has been stripped away to reveal the deathly black-and-white substratum of the photographic negative which subtends them" (60). The difference between these two paintings, Jameson emphasizes, is "not a matter of content any longer but of some more fundamental mutation" in the world (a world that, under postmodern globalizing cultural conditions, has become transfigured into "a set of texts or simulacra"). The effect this fundamental mutation in culture has upon consciousness — or on what Jameson calls the "disposition" of the nationalist first world subject — is one of the primary concerns of Jameson's essay (60). Under postmodern cultural conditions, he warns, we can observe "a shift in the dynamics of cultural pathology" such that "the alienation" of the citizen-subject as generated under previous social eras, has been "displaced" by what he calls the "fragmentation of the subject" (63). This fragmentation brings about "the end of the bourgeois ego or monad" of previous times, and will undoubtedly bring about "the end of the psychopathologies of that ego as well." It is important to recognize that, in Jameson's view, there is nothing to celebrate in these "wanings," "fragmentations," or endings of the modernist Western and first world psyche.

The death of the bourgeois ego, the individual monad, the centered citizen-subject, in Jameson's estimation, only makes way for the mutated birth that is postmodern subjectivity—*a neocolonial psychic condition*. With this birth comes the death of much, much more. The expiration, for example, he regrets, of "style—in the sense of the unique and personal, the end of the distinctive individual brush stroke (as symbolized by the emergent primacy of mechanical/technological reproduction)," and the end of "feeling, since there is no longer a self present to do the feeling." Or rather, I should qualify, for Jameson, "feelings" are now replaced by "intensities," which "are free-floating and impersonal, and tend to be dominated by a peculiar kind of euphoria" (64). But, in the face of all these terminations, what kind of euphoria can inhabit this no-longer-present postmodern self? Have contemporary cultural conditions brought about the opportunity for the evolution of a higher, more liberatory form of being? On the contrary, Jameson asserts, this euphoria marks the onset of a new form of mass cultural pathology. It is "schizophrenic" in nature—charged with all the hallucinogenic intensity of a state of being that is unique to the cultural logic of the first world at the beginning of the third millennium.

The West is a science-fiction world come to life: its characters trapped inside an unmapped city, drifting inside a transnational space wherein "the subject loses its capacity to extend its pro-tensions and re-tensions across the temporal manifold" (71). Western subjectivity is wedged between a past that has abandoned it and a nonexistent future, nonexistent because one of the features of postmodern hyperspace ("a space whose baleful features are only too obvious" [88]) is that we are already living a mirage of its possibilities. The first world subject can experience profound pain and anxiety, Jameson believes, or exhilaration in being disconnected from history; for this is a Lacanian world in which signifiers are severed from their signifieds, inducing in the once-centered first world subject a sense that all meanings have been set free. Such "freedom" generates a form of historical amnesia—hence the hallucinatory euphoria that is peculiar to postmodernism. But the teasing euphoria of postmodernism can quickly turn to horror, for the euphoria

Figure 1. Three modes of aesthetic representation: *(a)* modernism, *(b)* post-modernism, and *(c)* decolonial U.S. third world feminism—a dissident globalization. *(a)* Vincent van Gogh, *A Pair of Boots (Les Souliers),* from the Cone Collection in the Baltimore Museum of Art.

is generated by the citizen-subject's proximity to the edges and abysses of meaning, a location that allows consciousness glimpses "in astonishment, stupor and awe" of what is so "enormous as to crush human life altogether" (77). This is a world in which all perceptual space is cluttered by the presence and rationality of technology and by perpetual images of the simulacrum, in which happiness is euphoric and de-pendent on a schizophrenic affect constantly cracking in the shadows of what is the postmodern sublime. For Jameson, the exhilaration and horror of what first world subjectivity must face is "the limits of figuration" and "the incapacity of the human mind to give representation to such enormous forces" (ibid.).

Under the shadow of the postmodern sublime as conceived in Jameson's text, Andy Warhol's *Diamond Dust Shoes* becomes a microevent that makes it possible to glimpse the exciting yet superficial euphoria that marks first world

Figure 1. *(b)* Andy Warhol, Diamond Dust Shoes. Copyright 1999 Andy Warhol Foundation for the Visual Arts/ARS, New York.

cultural pathology as it comes embedded in the very surface of the paint itself; "this is the glitter of gold dust, the sparkling of gilt sand, which seals the surface of the painting and yet continues to glint at us." Think, however, Jameson suggests longingly, of now archaic modernist texts, such as "Rimbaud's magical flowers that look back at you, or of the august premonitory eye-flashes of Rilke's archaic Greek torso which warns the bourgeois subject to change his life: nothing of that sort here, in the gratuitous frivolity [of Warhol's] final decorative overlay" (61). I thus read much of Jameson's manifesto as eulogy, a funeral dirge for a lost time and place where it was once possible to know exactly who you were and where you stood; a time when it was possible to map your position in social space and to consider from what Archimedean point you could court the possibility of action. This positioning is necessary for comprehending the place in the social order from which one is expected to speak. For a political conservative, liberal, radical, even anarchist (who moves against *any* order), such comprehensions are essential.[4] This is why many political intellec-

Figure 1. *(c)* Still from *Jumpin' Jack Flash* (1986).

tuals lament the ending of the modern era, when it was possible to apprehend clearly who were the rulers and who the ruled and to look clearly into the face of one's enemy. Instead, according to Jameson, such clarity is traded, under first world postmodern conditions, for a disorientation that permeates every body, regardless of social caste. For Jameson, there is no center to indict, no enemy to accuse, no new revolutionary subject of history to rise and support; there are only "faceless masters" to imagine, masters who are themselves the slaves of postmodern neocolonial globalization (66).

The nature of Jameson's distinction between the two cultural dominants, modernism versus postmodernism, should be clear by now. In contests over meaning, the new cultural dominant, postmodernism, has triumphed, and first world culture has traded depth for surface, the possibility of egalitarian transformations for the excitement of constant but superficial change, feeling for an indeterminate sense of euphoria and intensity, alienation for fragmentation, style for technological reproduction, and life for death. For Jameson, the vision is bleak: "What we must now affirm is that it is precisely this whole extraordinarily demoralizing and depressing original new global space which is the 'moment of truth' of postmodernism" (88).

Aesthetic and Culture Crimes:

The Amputation of Oppositional Consciousness

Under postmodern globalization, art no longer functions as an instrument of social criticism and change. Parody, for example, is an art form that requires the coexistence of inherited and dominant cultural norms and traditions, which it mimics, ridicules, and transforms. But, under the legacy of the West's high-modern period, Jameson explains, an onslaught of difference replaced normality and parody, the West's aesthetic of resistance. In their place, a panoply of heterogeneous aesthetic forms, *ethoi*, and possibility burdened and collapsed their internal structures, creating the new, postmodern aesthetic form "pastiche." In Jameson's terms, both parody and pastiche are similar insofar as both are the "imitation" of a mask, but in its metamorphosis from parody, pastiche has become the "*neutral* practice of such mimicry, without any of parody's ulterior motives" (65; my emphasis). Postmodern aesthetic forms (such as punk culture, the songs of Laurie Anderson, and the performance pieces of Guillermo Gómez-Peña or Monica Palacios) may *appear* to parody social norms. But functionally, Jameson asserts, this work can be understood as pastiche in function, that is, as "amputated... of any conviction that alongside the abnormal tongue," which is "momentarily borrowed, some healthy linguistic normality still exists" (ibid.). For Jameson, this loss of "healthy" normality is not a liberatory condition; it is, rather, a grim symptom.[5]

Advanced capitalist territories today are being linked, writes Jameson, into varying fields of "stylistic and discursive heterogeneity without a norm" (ibid.). This new territorialization disables all formerly dominant languages or understandings that might have been used to define the present diffusion of social reality; there are no controlling codes capable of mapping this mobile terrain. This means that U.S. citizen-subjects live in an era of postliteracy, Jameson writes, that operates beyond older notions of language, writing, and imagination itself. In the place of these past skills for negotiating reality, postmodern citizen-subjects become mesmerized, engaged, and charmed by the schizophrenic, metonymic psychic and material conditions around them, in which the citizen-subject lights from experience to experience, object to object. In this new world, all aesthetic formations, experiences, even being itself become merely part and parcel, a simple technology, of the globalizing cultural dominant, postmodernism.

Contemporary first world cityscapes provide Jameson's panoramic model of these psychic, social, and aesthetic devolutions. Once grand and unique downtown areas of 1950s USA (whether they are today maintained, dilapidated, or renovated) were transformed during the 1980s into simply more examples of a global plethora of shopping areas, city centers, and malls that compete to offer their services, he writes. Buildings are constructed without any single main entrance (there are usually several) and without any central meeting place (but rather, many small areas, any of which can temporarily serve as stopping point for separated travelers who are similarly displaced and disoriented). These new urban areas and architectural innovations demonstrate how our very living spaces reproduce the larger organization of multinational capitalism; they exhort human consciousness to replicate in its own structures the same decentering and disorganization modeled in the city's concrete and glass realities. Postmodern cityscapes, Jameson asserts, stand before us "as something like an imperative to grow new organs." In order for perception to locate itself, we must "expand our sensorium and body," to some new "unimaginable" and "ultimately impossible dimensions" (80).

This desperate view is magnified and distorted by Jameson's own (modernist and first world) alienation as it is projected onto the spectacle before him. He sees the decentered city, his perception punctuated by the glitter of mirrored skyscrapers, "Yuppie renovations," high-rise malls, the dissolution of "formerly grand hotels," and the "ruins of both the idea and reality" of public housing as products of the pastiche-aesthetic-crime of the postmodern first world. The only defense against such aesthetic fragmentation, Jameson thinks, is to permit ourselves to fully perceive the abundance of manifold meanings that surround us. This means that we take them in as what he calls "radical difference"—difference, that is, which is composed of separate pieces, but whose aggregate is, in sum, meaningless. Within this perceptually deforming structure of postmodernism that can only generate ultimate meaninglessness, Jameson concludes, the human ability to organize and unite in a great dissident and oppositional "collective project" has been shattered, leaving human consciousness trapped in an exhilarating form of hopelessness (85).

The Differential Method for Cognitive Mapping

But if Jameson is correct in his premise that first world subjects have lost their "positions as individual and collective subjects" in the social order, lost their capacities to "act and struggle," to speak a single language, to represent through parody, if such citizen-subjects have become immobilized by "spatial as well as social confusion" (92), then it becomes imperative to identify yet another "moment of truth" under globalization. If, as Jameson argues, the formerly centered and legitimated bourgeois citizen-subject of the first world (once anchored in a secure haven of self) is set adrift under the imperatives of late-capitalist cultural conditions, if such citizen-subjects have become anchorless, disoriented, incapable of mapping their relative positions inside multinational capitalism, lost in the reverberating endings of colonial expansionism, and if Jameson has traced well the psychic pathologies brought about in first world subjectivity under the domination of neocolonial drives in which the subject must face the very "limits of figuration," then the first world subject enters the kind of psychic terrain formerly inhabited by the historically decentered citizen-subject: the colonized, the outsider, the queer, the subaltern, the marginalized. So too, not only are the "psychopathologies," but also the survival skills, theories, methods, and the utopian visions of the marginal made, not just useful but imperative to all citizen-subjects, who must recognize this other truth of postmodernism—another architectural model for oppositional consciousness in the postmodern world.[6]

This other truth shimmers through Jameson's own text the moment he quotes from Michael Herr's book on Vietnam, *Dispatches*. It is on this quotation, which is, he writes, about "the first terrible postmodern war," that Jameson's text swerves, and it becomes possible to gain what might be called a postmodern access to it through a different entrance than those through which he has invited us.[7] The permeability of this entrance is partially permitted by what should be seen as Jameson's own ambivalence about postmodernism: his revulsion for its "terrible" workings is combined with a grudging admiration for all it implies—its "extraordinary linguistic innovation" or the "eclectic way" in which the language of Herr's book "impersonally fuses a whole range of contemporary collective ideolects" (84). Jameson is not seduced by this movement beneath the glitter, for this phony life, he thinks, is only illusion that further disguises the death drive of neocolonial first world postmodernism. The following passage describing a scene from the war in Vietnam is exemplary, Jameson argues, for it sensuously concentrates something of the mystery of postmodernism as it reproduces the psychic condition it develops in all citizen-subjects:

He was a moving-target-survivor subscriber...except for the rare times when you were pinned or stranded the system was geared to keep you mobile, if that was what you thought you wanted. As a technique for staying alive it seemed to make as much sense as anything, given naturally that you were there to begin with and wanted to see it close...the more you moved the more you saw, the more you saw the more besides death and mutilation you risked....Some of us moved around...like crazy people...we'd still be running around inside our skins like something was after us, ha, *La Vida Loca.*

In the months after I got back the hundreds of helicopters I'd flown in began to draw together until they'd formed a collective meta-chopper, and in my mind it was the sexiest thing going; saver-destroyer, provider-waster, right hand-left hand, nimble, fluent, canny and human; hot steel, grease, jungle-saturated canvas webbing, seat cooling and warming up again, cassette rock and roll in one ear and door-gun fire in the other, fuel, heat, vitality and death, death itself, hardly an intruder. (85)[8]

This life-inside-war, writes Jameson, reveals the forms of consciousness developed under globalizing postmodernism, the schizophrenic perceptual schema demanded by survival under its rationality, the hallucinogenic excitement of experience, the addictive intensity that feels like euphoria, and the drive for new experiences, even when these ultimately lead to death. Jameson thinks that this expression of *la vida loca*, the crazy life that is composed of mobile and exhilaratory survival skills deployed under warlike conditions, is an expression that permits his readers to comprehend the damages to subjectivity that occur under postmodernism. But what Jameson does not recognize is that this quotation describes a third location as well, which is the space neither of war nor of postmodernism. The psychic and physical spaces in which subjugated citizen-subjects live is also understood to be an at least metaphoric, if not real, "war zone."[9] it is from this place that oppositional consciousness under neocolonial postmodernism has been generated.

It is no accident that the passage above, and much of the book *Dispatches* itself, is composed of what are working-class, bricolage, *caló*, Chicano/a, and African-African speech forms — "nonstandard languages" that have developed in the interstices, through, over, under, and beyond regularized forms of English. What Jameson's account neglects to mention is that a life lived metonymically from experience to experience is also a course of action demanded of those who hold out against conditions of hunger, deprivation, humiliation, colonization, and social subjection. Such citizen-subjects often do not lay claim to any *single* "healthy linguistic normality" from which to speak and act, because doing so might impair one's chances for survival. This process of taking and using whatever is necessary and available in order to negotiate, confront, or speak to power—and then moving on to new forms, expressions, and ethos when necessary—is a method for survival that has vital links to Jameson's version of "cognitive mapping" (we will examine the forms this method takes in Parts II, III, and IV of this book).

Jameson believes that the first step to developing an effective form of resistance to neocolonizing postmodernism requires that citizen-subjects heighten their competencies at making their way through society, at crossing its scattered distances and central spaces, at negotiating through, over, and around its complex crevices and openings. Jameson describes this form of skilled dissidence as a "cartographic" proficiency; it requires the skill of knowing how to chart or map social and cultural territories in consciousness or imagination as one is moving across them. Citizen-subjects must develop this cartographic knowledge, Jameson writes, in order to better map and determine our psychic and material relations with the new "local, national and international realities" produced by globalizing postmodernism (91). This skill, which Jameson calls "cognitive mapping," should endow "the individual subject with some new heightened sense of its place in the global system" (92). Empowerment occurs when the citizen-subject coordinates its existential data "(the empirical position of the subject)," with "unlived abstract conceptions of the geographic totality" (90), comes to a decision, and moves from there. But coordinating these two dimensions (existential, everyday experience, on the one side, with abstract conceptions or scientific knowledge, on the other) requires the inventiveness of ideology.

The ability to creatively link and articulate living ideologies fluctuates during different historical periods. Contemporary first world human societies have entered a unique historical condition under postmodernism, Jameson warns, in which it is no longer "possible at all" for individuals to cognitively map or coordinate their positions between lived experience and the larger world. It is this inability to coordinate, in Lacan's terms, the relationship between the imaginary and the real, to map in our own minds the relation between our individual positions and the urban totality in which we find ourselves, that leads to postmodern forms of crises in consciousness, ideology, culture, and history (89, 91). For Jameson there is no doubt: the end of well-functioning ideologies means the end of their liberatory and oppositional expressions as well, and this *is* "our situation in the current crises" (91). His conclusion prepares the grounds for his understanding of contemporary North America as a postmodern "dystopia." In his view, postmodern cultural conditions literally offer "no place" for the subject to stand in ideology: no oppositional consciousness allowed. Jameson's failed search to identify an effective mode of resistance and oppositional consciousness in relation to postmodernism returns us to the perceptual and political skills developed out of other modes of disorientation.

I discussed earlier survival skills developed under subordination that revolve around the *manipulation of ideology.* These skills juggle, transgress, differ, buy, and sell ideologies in a system of production and exchange bent on ensuring survival. The war zone of *Dispatches* thus stands as a metaphor not only for describing the psychic zone of postmodernism, but also for describing the metaphoric space where survival against all odds and the creativity of revolt under domination take place. Out of this other, third kind of war zone in which bodies and minds are shattered into so-called nonstandard forms, practices, identities, and worldviews develop that are unique to a new kind of rationality. This rationality can be translated as a theory, method, and practice that provides the kind of cognitive mapping for which Jameson longs. The oppositional consciousness it generates travels differentially but with literacy across and through cultural spaces: it is a mobile, flexible, diasporic force that migrates between contending ideological systems.

This differentially moving force expresses a whole new coordinate in Jameson's knowledge of and charting of social space. It operates as does a technology—a weapon of consciousness that functions like a compass: a pivoting center capable of drawing circles of varying circumference, depending on the setting. Such a differential force, when understood as a technical, political, aesthetic, and ethical practice, allows one to chart out the positions available and the directions to move in a larger social totality. The effectivity of this cultural mapping depends on its practitioner's continuing and transformative relationship to the social totality. Readings of this shifting totality will determine the interventions—the tactics, ideologies, and discourses that the practitioner chooses in order to pursue a greater good, beginning with the citizen-subject's own survival. Reading signs to determine power relations is its principal technique, the readings obtained are the indications that guide all movement. This differential form of oppositional consciousness is a field with no specific content until such readings are produced. Within this zone, the subject maps and remaps its positions along mobile and alternative trajectories (91). It is this differential mode of oppositional consciousness that constitutes the mode of radical cognitive mapping that Jameson seeks. His own version of cognitive mapping is inadequate within the context of postmodern globalization because its processes require older, outmoded forms of consciousness and ideology in order to function. In Jameson's model, cognitive mapping can only be accomplished in Althusser's terms, where the citizen-subject attempts to represent in some *realistic, believable, cohesive, meaningful way* its "imaginary relationship" to its "real conditions of existence,"[10] an operation that is, however, hopelessly interrupted by postmodernism's engulfing cultural processes.

Differential cognitive mapping would engage consciousness, ideology, citizenship, and coalition as masquerade. It requires a consciousness that perceives itself at the center of myriad possibilities all cross-working—any of which is fodder for one's loyalties.[11] Such loyalties, once committed, can be withdrawn and relocated depending on survival, moral, and/or political imperatives. This was surely the aim of Jameson's version of cognitive mapping: to provide a *"situational representation"* on the part of the individual citizen-subject "to that vaster totality...which is the [social] ensemble (90; my emphasis). Differential resistance thus functions very much like Althusser's hoped-for but unachieved 1960s "science of ideology," but when the differential form of cognitive mapping is used it is the citizen-*subject* who interpellates, who calls up ideology, as opposed to Althusser's formulation, in which it is "ideology that interpellates the subject." To deploy a differential oppositional consciousness, one can depend on no (traditional) mode of belief in one's own subject position or ideology; nevertheless, such positions and beliefs are called up and utilized in order to constitute whatever forms of subjectivity are necessary to act in an also (now obviously) constituted social world. (This is the form of identity, social movement, and "cognitive mapping" examined in this book. The structures of this method, who utilizes it, and how and why it is practiced are the subjects of Part III.)

New Subjects of Global History and the "Death of the (Previous) Subject"

U.S. critical and cultural theorists appear unable to criticize their own sociocultural realm, Jameson thinks. At best, they analyze postmodern neocolonialism only to become its defenders—these are its "apologists," he writes. At worst, critical thinkers produce more symptoms of it: increasing theories of "textuality," "*écriture*," or "schizophrenic writing," he thinks, only add up to "heaps of fragments" (71). The postmodern-pastiche-effect has thus infiltrated every aspect of academic production. But such tendencies are rarely criticized or challenged by scholars themselves, Jameson complains; they are, rather, welcomed or defended as "exciting," "aleatory," "randomly heterogeneous," "mestiza," "fragmentary," "hybrid," "mobile," "nomad," and so on. Such "critical responses" are a sign that contemporary scholars have become so "deeply submerged" in postmodern space that they are incapable of any "indignant moral denunciation" of it (88). This disappearance of the ability to find a political and moral stand among academics, of critical distance, of parody, and of effective oppositional consciousness, coupled with the influence of a pastiche brand of intellectual and creative work, all conform to another distinctive disappearance that Jameson demands we confront: the "death of the subject."

It is necessary to point out that this death mourned by Jameson is of a particular *modernist* incarnation of subjectivity. Jameson forgets, however, that there *are* other forms of being. But his very definition of "the subject" is trapped in a view of the human structured and defined by a historical understanding of the modernist experience. This means that, for Jameson, "a once existing centered subject (in the period of classical capitalism and the nuclear family) has today in the world of organization and bureaucracy, dissolved" (63). This is what Jameson calls a modernist or "historicist" definition of the subject, and it is at odds with the different understanding of the subject utilized by the "radical poststructuralists," for whom, Jameson writes, the subject never existed in the first place. Both the modernist-historicist and radical poststructuralist schools agree that under postmodernism "the bourgeois subject is dead," but, Jameson posits, each camp differs fundamentally on the causes and meanings of its disappearance. Jameson's (modernist) historicist challenge to poststructuralism is that its radical approach is at one with the psychopathologies of postmodernism itself: radical poststructuralism, he challenges, exists as only another symptom and unconscious accomplice of its machinations.

But in detailing what appears to be two opposite definitions of the subject as the only two that matter, and by conflating radical poststructuralist theory with the cultural dynamics of an ever-proliferating postmodernism, Jameson consigns himself to what he describes as an "unhappy paradox" (ibid.): if poststructuralist celebrations of the fragmentation and death of the subject are "at one" with the cultural imperatives of postmodernism, then he has left himself with a choice between a radical poststructuralist/postmodern subjectivity that is diffused and nowhere, on the one side, and, on the other, a horrifyingly claustrophobic modernist/historicist subjectivity, which he himself describes as a "self sufficient field and a closed realm...shut off from everything else." This is because modernist/historicist beings, he grieves, live in the "windless solitude of the subject, buried alive and condemned to a prison cell without egress" (ibid.). Self-expression momentarily breaks through this alienation effect by putting the inside outside, but also, through a kind of loop—re-creating an isolated inside once again as payment for "expression." In the conflated modernist/historicist view of the subject, then, as against the conflated poststructuralist/postmodernist view, Jameson's dilemma is his understanding that the *alienation* and *isolation* of the Western subject is necessary for the concomitant presence of life expression, creativity, what he calls "unique and personal style," and of dissident forms of expression—an "unhappy paradox" indeed (ibid.). One might think that the evolution of a new cultural dominant and the subsequent possibility of new forms and possibilities for subjectivity arising from its influence would signal the end of this dilemma that paralyzes. Instead, Jameson's despair is that the ability to move or see "outside the massive being of capital" (a movement and vision that once made modernist individuality and oppositional cultural acts possible) has been abolished. Instead of entering into a new moment of liberatory human evolution as citizen-subjects, "we are submerged," he despairs, "to the point where our now postmodern bodies are incapable of distantiation," creativity, coalitional alliances, and effective oppositional forms of consciousness (87).

There is another way out of this unhappy paradox that sets a modernist/historicist view of an isolated but "real" subject now under erasure against a poststructuralist/postmodernist view that the subject never existed in the first place—a third view of the citizen-subject for which Jameson's essay does not account. In order to perceive this third view, it is necessary to extend the so-called modernist/historicist position and the poststructuralist/postmodernist position in order for them to similarly recognize that "fragmentation" is neither an experience nor a theoretical construct peculiar to the poststructuralist or postmodern moments. Indeed, the fragmentation or split subjectivity of subjection is the very condition against which a modernist, well-placed citizen-subject could coalesce its own sense of wholeness. Such wholeness of being became the modernist "solid identity" that now has the opportunity to move toward a "critically distant" relation to the dominant. This means that the moves of the modernist citizen-subject away from the dominant and toward "critical distance" and the forms of oppositional consciousness that Jameson mourns as lost were paradoxically made possible only through the concomitant presence of shattered minds and bodies, often beyond survival. Indeed, the condition recently claimed as the "postmodern splitting of the subject" is one of the conditions that conquered and colonized Westerners were invited to survive under modernist and previous eras, if survival were a choice. The citizen-subject's postmodern despair over experiencing this condition can be released when the practitioner looks to the survival skills and decolonizing oppositional practices that were developed in response to such fragmentation under previous cultural eras.[12]

Freedom from the Prison House: A Dissident Form of Globalization

Jameson's two understandings of the subject make invisible what I identify as an anticolonial, mestiza, U.S. feminist of color, queer, and differential conceptualization of the subject. To comprehend this other conceptualization, one cannot fully inhabit either the modernist/historicist or the poststructuralist/postmodernist position, but rather inhabit each and partially; for to conceptualize the subject as either present under modernism, or fragmented, schizophrenic, and absent under postmodernism, is to once again evade the differential practice of "cognitive mapping."[13] Under this third form of subjectivity, the citizen-subject is understood to exist, just as it is understood as always capable of dissipating, but both in quotients measured in order to bring about forms of being that will be capable of intervening in power. This articulation between the self and its absence is a shifting place of mobile codes and significations, which invokes that place of possibility and creativity where language and meaning itself are constituted.

The end of the twentieth century found the emotional ground tone of the once centered, modernist, first world citizen-subject shot through with intensities so that it resembled the emotional territory of subordinated peoples.[14] If Jameson is right, that first world citizen-subjects are increasingly "unable to unify the past, present and future" of their own psychic lives (66), then citizen-subjects are entering the emotional state of peoples whose native territories were replaced, their bodies subordinated to other dominants, their futures unclear; those colonized by race, class, sex, gender, culture, nation, and power who developed a "schizophrenic" relation to dominant languages—referents "never what they were supposed to be." This violently fragmented condition and all its intensities, like the confined yet interminable war zone of *Dispatches*, calls up a psychic positioning that reproduced itself first as necessity, then as aesthetics, and finally as politics.

The contemporary U.S. cultural conjuncture Jameson identifies as late capitalism exposes all citizen-subjects to novel conditions of power that encourage a hypersensitivity to the ongoing constitution and disintegration of subjectivity; it is no longer the "outsider" who bears the burden of such recognitions. In this sense, under postmodern cultural and economic conditions, citizen-subjects undergo a shared democratization of oppression. This new circumstance not only brings about the "death" of the modernist subject for which Jameson laments. First world subjectivity is crossing fractured, postmodern thresholds to an unprecedented mode of life that is capable of, among other things, igniting whole new collective ideals, styles, knowledges, politics, and being (from U.S. third world feminism to the methodology of the oppressed, from rap to Tex-Mex music, from deconstruction to cultural and global studies). To extend and connect Jameson's theoretical positions regarding postmodernism to the third, differential form of consciousness makes visible a new collective subject (decentered, yes—but not schizophrenic) and writes U.S.

third world feminism, subaltern, queer, and de-colonial resistance back into history, theory, and consciousness.[15] In his 1984–94 meditations on postmodernism, Jameson cannot quite grasp the dialectical movement of subjectivity that disallows, yes — but at the same time allows — individual expression, style, and personality. For these attributes do not necessarily disappear under postmodernism; rather, they undergo another level of tactical and strategic conversion.

When Jameson mounts an attack on the cultural critics of our time, the so-called apologists or celebrants of postmodern globalization, he forgets that neither they — not Lacan, Lyotard, Deleuze, or Guattari — nor he are the first to experience or conceptualize schizophrenia as unexplored cultural pathology or as a liberatory mode of hypermodern consciousness. The scapegoated, marginalized, enslaved, and colonized of every community have also experienced and theorized this shattering, this splitting of signifieds from their signifiers.[16] In the sane, these episodes are thought of as opportunities for re-cognition, as turning points in one's life history. Those not destroyed by this kind of schizophrenic effect, the war zone that shatters one's sense of self into hysterical exhilaration or depression beyond scope, those who survive the discovery that "freedom and triumph" are "forbidden to them" and so turn toward "something else to be,"[17] develop modes of perceiving, making sense of, and acting upon reality that are the basis for effective forms of oppositional consciousness in the postmodern world. The first world is in full transformation, replete with mobile and "sheer images of itself, pseudo events, spectacle, simulacrum," a neocolonizing postmodernism that fills every body (66). Yet effective forms of resistance are also moving to reappoint egalitarian forms of power.

In attempting to repossess identity and culture, U.S. feminists of color during the 1960s and 1970s, U.S. punks during the early 1980s, peoples of color and queers during the 1990s developed survival skills into technologies for re-organizing peoples and their collective dreams for empowerment into images-turned-fact. Jameson's manifesto is blind to such "facts" where they remain invisible as effective modes of postmodern resistance and dissident globalization, which leaves him and others to despair that "if there is any real left" it is only derived from the horrible "shock of grasping" the limits of our shared "confinement" under postmodernism (71). It is understandable that the once centered citizen-subject, in reaching toward freedom, becomes demoralized when finding only shimmering restraint at the end of its grasp — upon which it is only possible to, in Jameson's words, "trace our mental images" of freedom (ibid.); for historically, the centered form of subjectivity for which so many peoples long is not accustomed to sensing the structurally powerless position within which all citizen-subjects under the influence of postmodernism struggle. Dominated populaces realize their subjection to power (that people are the words the social order speaks). The radical form of cognitive mapping that differential consciousness allows develops such knowledge into a method by which the limits of the social order can be spoken, named, and made translucent: the body passes through and is transformed.

The hyperspace of multinational postmodernism expands through the physiologies of all first world subjects regardless of social, racial, sex, or gender class, in the transformation of such classes into bureaucratic and technocratic entities whose function is to shift power through, and give life to, the transnational social body. All citizen-subjects are becoming strangely permeated, transformed, — and marginalized.[18] In this respect, the industrial working class, the so-called proletariat, can never again be viewed as the only revolutionary "subject of history" any more than can the indomitable and transforming presence of the third world, of peoples of color, of lesbians, gays, queers, women, or the subordinated. There has been an upheaval under neocolonizing postmodernism that has transferred a potentially revolutionary apparatus into the body of every citizen-subject, regardless of social caste. As previously legitimated centers unravel from within, cityscapes degenerate, consciousness and identity splinter, the revolutionary subject who rises from the rubble is mutant: citizen-subject of a new, postmodern colonialism — and de-colonialism — active all at once.

In part, Jameson's worst fears are true: the first world is undergoing a democratization of oppression that none can escape. It crosses all class, race, gender, sex, and culture boundaries to shift in some previously impossible way the differences that once defined the very structure of political hierarchy. Although inequities of material resources and subordinations by race, class, nation, gender, and sex continue to operate under the protection of law and order, a new kind of psychic penetration evolves that respects no previous boundaries. Under modernism, the centered citizen-subject, challenged by ethical considerations, could step out of its social positioning in order to find a critical moral and distant vantage point, and there take a resistant, oppositional stand. If Jameson is right, neocolonial postmodernism has rendered this move ineffective — and this is the source of his despair. Indeed, all older forms of morality in this new first world dissipate in the face of a meaninglessness that is, Jameson writes, no longer a matter of content anymore, "but of some more fundamental mutation, both in the object world itself — now become a set of texts of simulacra — and in the disposition of the subject" (60). What Jameson is unable to detect is that this mutation in culture, which affects all political, social, ethical, and cultural relations and institutions (which is an "explosion of culture throughout the social realm," he writes), also makes accessible, to oppressor and oppressed alike, new forms of identity, ethics, citizenship, aesthetics, and resistance.

The skills, perceptions, theories, and methods developed under previous and modernist conditions of dispossession and colonization are the most efficient and sophisticated means by which all peoples trapped as inside-outsiders in the rationality of postmodern social order can confront and retextualize consciousness into new forms of citizenship/subjectivity. The next chapter examines the differential mode of cognitive mapping as it developed during 1970s and 1980s U.S. social movements. What emerges is a utilitarian theory and method of oppositional consciousness through which twenty-first-century global forms of social movement, consciousness, aesthetics, and culture can be recognized, evaluated, analyzed, and enacted.

The Theory and Method of Oppositional Consciousness in the Postmodern World

T W O

U.S. Third World Feminism:
Differential Social Movement I

Caminante no hay puentes, se hace puentes al andar (Voyager there are no bridges, one makes them as one walks).

Gloria Anzaldúa

What "feminism" means to women of color is different from what it means to white women. Because of our collective histories, we identify more closely with international Third World sisters than with white feminist women. . . . A global feminism, one that reaches beyond patriarchal political divisions and national ethnic boundaries, can be formulated from a new political perspective.

Alice Chai

The vision of radical Third World feminism necessitates our willingness to work with people—the colored, the queer, the poor, the female, the physically challenged. From our connections with these groups, we women on the bottom throughout the world can form an international feminism. We recognize the right and necessity of colonized peoples throughout the world, including Third World women in the United States, to form independent movements toward self-government. But ultimately, we must struggle together. Together we form a new vision which spans self-love of our colored skins to the respect of our foremothers who kept the embers of revolution burning.

Cherríe Moraga and Gloria Anzaldúa

Definition of Womanism: "... Committed to survival and wholeness of entire people, male and female. Not a separatist, except periodically, for health."

Alice Walker

Feminists of Color and Postmodern Resistance

THE SOCIAL movement that was "U.S. third world feminism" has yet to be fully understood by social theorists. This social movement developed an original form of historical consciousness, the very structure of which lay outside the conditions of possibility that regulated the praxes of 1960s, 1970s, and 1980s U.S. social movements. In enacting this new form of historical consciousness, U.S third world feminism provided access to a different way of conceptualizing not just feminist consciousness but oppositional activity in general: it comprised a formulation capable of aligning U.S. movements for social justice not only with each other, but with global movements toward decolonization.

Both in spite of and because they represented varying internally colonized communities, U.S. third world feminists generated a common speech, a theoretical structure that remained just outside the purview of 1970s feminist theory, functioning within it—but only as the unimaginable.[1] Even though this unimaginable presence arose to reinvigorate and refocus the politics and priorities of feminist theory during the eighties, an uneasy alliance remained between what appeared to be two different understandings of domination, subordination, and the nature of effective resistance—a shotgun arrangement at best between what literary critic Gayatri Spivak characterized in 1985 as a "hegemonic feminist theory"[2] on the one side, and what I call "U.S. third world feminist theory" on the other.[3] I do not mean to suggest that this perplexing situation can be understood in merely binary terms. On the contrary, what this investigation reveals is the way in which the theory and method of oppositional consciousness and social movement documented here—and enacted by an original, eccentric, and coalitional cohort of U.S. feminists of color—was contained and made invisible through the means of its perception and appropriation in the terms of what became during the 1970–80 period a hegemonic feminist theory and practice.

U.S. third world feminism rose out of the matrix of the very discourses denying, permitting, and producing difference. Out of the imperatives born of necessity arose a mobility of identity that generated the activities of a new citizen-subject, and that revealed yet another model for the self-conscious production of resistance.[4] This chapter lays out U.S. third world feminism as a model for oppositional political activity and consciousness in the postmodern world. In mapping this model, a design is revealed by which social actors can chart the points through which differing oppositional ideologies can meet, in spite of their varying trajectories. This knowledge becomes important when one begins to wonder, along with late-twentieth-century cultural critics such as Jameson, how organized oppositional activity and consciousness are possible under the co-opting nature of so-called postmodern cultural conditions.[5]

The model put forth in this chapter transcodes the great oppositional social movement practices of the latter half of the twentieth century, especially in the United States — those of the civil rights movement, the women's movement, and ethnic, race, sex, gender, class, and human liberation movements. During this period of great social activity, it became clear that oppositional social movements, which were weakening from internal divisions over strategies, tactics, and aims, would benefit by examining philosopher Louis Althusser's theory of "ideology and the ideological state apparatuses."[6] In this fundamental essay, Althusser lays out the principles by which humans are called into being as citizen-subjects who act — even when in resistance — in order to sustain and reinforce the current dominant social order. In this sense, for Althusser, all citizens endure ideological subjection. Althusser's postulations, however, suggest that "means and occasions"[7] do become generated whereby individuals and groups in opposition are able to effectively challenge and transform oppressive aspects of identity and social order, but he does not specify how or on what terms such challenges might be mounted.

In supplementing Althusser's propositions, I apply his theory of ideology to the particular concerns raised within North American liberation movements of the 1968–90 period, in order to develop a theory of ideology that considers consciousness not only in its subordinated and resistant yet appropriated versions — the subject of Althusser's theory of ideology —[8] but in its more effective, persistent, and self-conscious oppositional manifestations. In practical terms, this extended theory focuses on identifying forms of ideology in opposition that can be generated and coordinated by those classes self-consciously seeking affective liberatory stances in relation to the dominant social order. The idea here, that the citizen-subject can learn to identify, develop, and control the means of ideology, that is, marshal the knowledge necessary to "break with ideology" while at the same time *also* speaking in, and from within, ideology, is an idea that lays the philosophical foundations enabling us to make the vital connections between the seemingly disparate social and political aims that drive, yet ultimately divide, social movements from within. In Althusser's terms, the model I propose would be considered a "science" of oppositional ideology, one that apprehends an effective oppositional consciousness igniting in dialectical engagement between varying ideological formations.

This study identifies five principal categories around which oppositional consciousness is organized, and which are politically effective means for transforming dominant power relations. I characterize these as the "equal rights," "revolutionary," "supremacist," "separatist," and "differential" forms of oppositional consciousness. These ideological positions are kaleidoscoped into an original, eccentric, and queer sight when the fifth, differential mode is utilized as a theoretical and methodological device for retroactively clarifying and giving new meaning to any other. Differential consciousness represents a strategy of oppositional ideology that functions on an altogether different register. Its powers can be thought of as mobile—not nomadic, but rather cinematographic: a kinetic motion that maneuvers, poetically transfigures, and orchestrates while demanding alienation, perversion, and reformation in both spectators and practitioners. Differential consciousness is the expression of the new subject position called for by Althusser—it permits functioning within, yet beyond, the demands of dominant ideology. This form of oppositional consciousness was enacted during the 1968–90 period by a particular and eccentric cohort of U.S. feminists of color who were active across diverse social movements. This cohort enacted the differential mode of social movement, which was subsequently developed under the aegis of "U.S. third world feminism."

This chapter identifies and investigates the primary modes of oppositional consciousness that were generated within one of the great oppositional movements of the late twentieth century, the second wave of the women's movement. What emerges in this discussion are the dominant ideological forms that worked against one another to ultimately divide the movement from within. I trace these ideological forms as they were manifested in the critical writings of some of the most prominent feminist theorists of the 1980s. In their attempts to identify a feminist history of consciousness, many of these thinkers detected four fundamentally distinct evolutionary phases through which activists pass in their quest to end the subordination of women. But, viewed in terms of another paradigm, "differential consciousness," here made available for study through the activity of U.S. third world feminism, these four historical phases are revealed as only other versions of the very forms of consciousness in opposition also conceived and enacted within every post-1950s U.S. liberation movement.

These diverse social movements were simultaneously seeking affective forms of resistance outside of those determined by the social order itself. My contention is that the feminist forms of resistance outlined in what follows are homologous to five fundamental forms of oppositional consciousness that were expressed within *all* U.S. liberation movements active during the latter half of the twentieth century. This chapter systematizes a political unconscious whose presence structured U.S. feminist theoretical tracts, in order to make manifest a generally applicable theory and method of oppositional consciousness in the postmodern world.

The recognition of the fifth form, differential consciousness and social movement, is crucial for shaping effective and ongoing oppositional struggle.[9] The application of differential consciousness generates grounds for making coalitions with decolonizing movements for emancipation in global affinities and associations. It retroatively provides a structure, a theory, and a method for reading and constructing identity, aesthetics, and coalition politics that are vital to a decolonizing postmodern politics and aesthetics, and to hailing a "third-wave," twenty-first-century feminism. My answer to the perennial question asked by hegemonic feminist theorists throughout the 1980s is that yes, there *is* a particular U.S. third world feminist criticism: it is that which provides the theoretical and methodological approach, the "standpoint," if you will, from which this evocation of a theory and method of oppositional consciousness has been summoned.

Situating History

From the beginning of what was known as the second wave of the women's movement, U.S. feminists of color have claimed feminisms at odds with those developed by U.S. white women. Already in 1970 with the publication of *Sisterhood Is Powerful*, black feminist Frances Beale was determined to name the second wave of U.S. feminism a *"white* women's movement" because it insisted on organizing along the binary gender division male/female alone.[10] U.S. women of color have long understood, however, that especially race, but also one's culture, sex, or class, can deny comfortable or easy access to any legitimized gender category, that the interactions between such social classifications produce other, unnamed gender forms within the social hierarchy. As far back as the middle of the nineteenth century, Sojourner

Truth found it necessary to remind a convention of white suffragettes of her "female" gender with the rhetorical question "Ain't I a woman?"[11] American Indian Paula Gunn Allen has written of Native women that "the place we live now is an idea, because whiteman took all the rest."[12] In 1971, Toni Morrison went so far as to write of U.S. women of color that "there is something inside us that makes us different from other people. It is not like men and it is not like white women."[13] That same year, Chicana Velia Hancock concluded: "Unfortunately, many white women focus on the maleness of our present social system as though, by implication, a female-dominated white America would have taken a more reasonable course" for people of color of *either* gender.[14]

These signs of a lived experience of difference from white female experience in the United States appear repeatedly throughout 1980s U.S. third world feminist writings. Such expressions imply the existence of at least one other category of gender, reflected in the very titles of books written by U.S. feminists of color during that period. *All the Women Are White, All the Blacks Are Men, but Some of Us Are Brave* (1982); and *This Bridge Called My Back* (1981) indicate that feminists of color exist in the interstices between normalized social categories.[15] Moreover, in the title of bell hooks's first book, the question "Ain't I a Woman" becomes transformed into a defiant statement, while Amy Ling's feminist analysis of Asian American writings, *Between Worlds* or the title of the journal for U.S. third world feminist writings, *The Third Woman*, also insist on the recognition of a third, divergent, and supplementary category for social identity.[16] This in-between space, this third gender category, is also recognized in the early writings of such well-known authors as Maxine Hong Kingston, Gloria Anzaldúa, Audre Lorde, Alice Walker, and Cherríe Moraga, all of whom argued that an eccentric coalition of U.S. third world feminists is composed of "different kinds of humans," new "*mestizas*," "Woman Warriors" who live and are gendered, sexed, raced, and classed "between and among" the lines.[17] These "sister outsiders" (1984), it was argued, inhabit an uncharted psychic terrain that Anzaldúa in 1987 named "the Borderlands," "*la nueva Frontera*." In 1980, Audre Lorde summarized the U.S. white women's movement by saying that "today, there is a pretense to a homogeneity of experience covered by the word SISTERHOOD in the white women's movement. When white feminists call for 'unity,' they are misnaming a deeper and real need for homogeneity." We begin the 1980s, she writes, with "white women" agreeing "to focus upon their oppression as women" while continuing "to ignore the differences" that exist among us as women.[18] Chicana sociologist Maxine Baca Zinn rearticulated this position in a 1986 essay in *Signs*, saying that though "there now exists in women's studies an increased awareness of the variability of womanhood," in the view of U.S. third world feminist criticism, "such work is often tacked on, its significance for feminist knowledge still unrecognized and unregarded."[19]

How did the hegemonic feminism of the 1980s respond to this other kind of feminist theoretical challenge? The publication of *This Bridge Called My Back* in 1981 made the singular presence of U.S. third world feminism impossible to ignore on the same terms as it had been throughout the 1970s. But soon the writings and theoretical challenges by such feminists of color were marginalized into the category of what Allison Jaggar characterized in 1983 as mere "description,"[20] and their essays deferred to what Hester Eisenstein in 1985 called "the special force of poetry,"[21] while the shift in paradigm referred to here as "differential consciousness," and which is represented in the praxis of U.S. third world feminism, was bypassed and ignored. If, during the 1980s, U.S. third world feminism had become a theoretical problem, an inescapable mystery to be solved for hegemonic feminism and social theorists across disciplines, then perhaps a theory of difference — but imported from Europe in the conceptual forms of "*différance*" or "French feminism" — could subsume if not solve it.[22] How did this systematic repression occur within an academic system that is aimed at recognizing new forms of knowledge?

Feminism's Great Hegemonic Model

1980s hegemonic feminist scholars produced the histories of feminist consciousness that they believed typified the modes of exchange operating within the oppositional spaces of the women's movement. These efforts resulted in systematic studies that sought to classify all forms of feminist political and aesthetic praxis. These constructed typologies fast became the official stories by which the women's movement understood itself and its interventions in history. In what follows, I decode these stories and their relations to one another from the perspective of U.S. third world feminism: from this critical perspective they are revealed as sets of imaginary spaces, socially constructed to severely delimit what is possible within the boundaries of each narrative. Taken together, these narratives legitimate certain modes of culture, consciousness, and practice, only to systematically curtail the forms of experiential and theoretical articulations expressed by an eccentric cohort of oppositional activists. In what follows, I demonstrate how manifestly different types of hegemonic feminist theory and practice are, in fact, unified at a deeper level into a great structure that sets up and organizes the logic of an exclusionary U.S. hegemonic feminism.

This logic of hegemonic feminism is organized around a common code that shaped the work of a diverse group of feminist scholars, including

Julia Kristeva, Toril Moi, Gerda Lerna, Cora Kaplan, Alice Jardine, Judith Kegan Gardiner, Gayle Greene, Coppélia Kahn, and Lydia Sargent. Its influence encrypts some of the key texts of the 1980s, including the influential essay by literary critic Elaine Showalter, "Toward a Feminist Poetics,"[23] the introduction to the now-classic set of essays on the "future of difference" edited by theorists Hester Eisenstein and Alice Jardine; the historicist essay by Gayle Greene and Coppélia Kahn on "the social construction of woman";[24] and political scientist Allison Jaggar's *Feminist Politics and Human Nature*, a foundational dictionary of feminist consciousness and social movement. In what follows, we can watch scholarly consciousness as it transcodes political practice to reproduce exclusionary forms of knowledge.

Showalter's work identifies a three-phase "taxonomy, if not a poetics, of feminist criticism."[25] This three-stage structure is reiterated throughout the 1980s text of hegemonic feminist theory and criticism, and it is always conceptualized as proceeding temporally. For Showalter, these three stages represent suceedingly higher levels of historical, moral, political, and aesthetic development. For example, Showalter's schema advises literary scholars to recognize a first-phase "feminine" consciousness when they identify in their readings women who write "in an effort to equal the cultural achievement of the male culture." In another place, theorist Hester Eisenstein concurs when she similarly identifies the movement's first stage as characterized by feminist activists organizing to prove that "differences between women and men are exaggerated," and should be "reduced" to a common denominator of sameness.[26] So too do Gayle Greene and Coppélia Kahn identify this same first-phase feminism in their historicist essay "Feminist Scholarship and the Social Construction of Woman." In its first stage, they write, feminist history and theory were organized "according to the standards of the male public world and, appending women to history" as it has already been defined, scholars left "unchallenged the existing paradigm."[27] This first stage is similarly replicated in Jaggar's monumental *Feminist Politics and Human Nature*. Within her construction of what she identifies as four "genera" of feminist consciousness (which, she asserts, are "fundamentally incompatible with each other"), first-phase "liberal feminism" is fundamentally concerned with "demonstrating that women are as fully human as men."[28]

In the second phase of what can be recognized as a feminist history of consciousness, the literary critic Showalter argues that women stopped trying to equal the achievement of men. Under second phase feminism, women "reject the accommodating postures" of the first "feminine" phase, and instead engage, criticize, and write "literature" in order to "dramatize wronged womanhood."[29] Eisenstein puts it this way: a second "assumption about difference evolved" out of the first, "specifically that women's lives WERE different from men's," and that "it was precisely this difference that required illumination."[30] So too, in Greene and Kahn's view, did feminist scholars turn away from first-phase feminism's "traditional paradigm." Second-phase feminism, they believed, encourages scholars to extend "their inquiries to the majority of women unaccounted for by traditional historiography." In search of "the actual *experiences* of women in the past," second-phase scholars ask questions about the specifics of women's daily lives, about its "quality," about "the conditions in which they lived and worked, the ages at which they married and bore children; about their work, their role in the family, their class and relations to other women; their perception of their place in the world; their relation to wars and revolutions."[31] It was in such specificities, Greene and Kahn assert, that the realities comprising women's lives, and not men's, would be revealed. Jaggar too argues for the recognition of second-phase feminism, describing it as the moment when feminists turn to Marxism as the way to undermine the feminism of the liberal first phase. Rather than integration or assimilation, second-phase feminists want to restructure the old society, she writes, so that it becomes incapable of subordinating the differences that the class of women represent.[32]

In the third, "female," and final phase for Showalter, "the movement rejected both earlier stages as forms of dependency" on masculinist culture, and instead turned "toward female experience as a source of a new, autonomous art."[33] According to Eisenstein, it is in this third phase that women seek to uncover the unique expression of the essence of woman that lies beneath the multiplicity of all her experiences. Eisenstein asserts that "female differences originally seen as a source of *oppression* appear as a source of enrichment." Third-phase feminism is thus "woman-centered," a phase within which maleness — not femaleness — becomes "the difference" that matters.[34] In this phase, she concludes, it is men, not women, who become "the Other." Greene and Kahn argue for a comparable third-phase feminism within which "some historians of women posit the existence of a separate woman's culture, even going so far as to suggest that women and men within the same society may have different experiences of the universe."[35] Jaggar's typology characterizes her third-phase feminism as an "unmistakably twentieth-century phenomenon": it is the first approach to conceptualizing human nature, social reality, and politics "to take the subordination of women as its central concern." Her version of third-phase feminism contends that "women naturally know much of which men are ignorant," and takes as "one of its main tasks . . . to explain why this is so." In the women's movement, Jaggar points out, third-phase feminism was actualized under the names of either "cultural" or "radical" feminisms.[36]

These three different forms of feminist practice, the "liberal," the "Marxist," and the "cultural" forms, construct different modes of oppositional aesthetics, identity, and politics. But are these forms of oppositional consciousness and praxis "fundamentally incompatible with one another," as Jaggar asserts? And what makes these forms of consciousness necessarily "feminist" in nature? Can they not also be understood as the forms of oppositional consciousness that come into operation whenever any social movement begins to coalesce? The answers that the differential praxis of 1970s–1980s U.S. third world feminism provided to these questions fundamentally transformed not just our understandings of feminist theory and practice, but our understandings of social movements and consciousness in resistance under neocolonizing postmodern global conditions.

Throughout what can now be clearly viewed as a three-phase feminist history of consciousness, as white feminist Lydia Sargent comments in her 1981 collection of essays *Women and Revolution*, "racism, while part of the discussion, was never successfully integrated into feminist theory and practice." This resulted in powerful protests by feminists of color at each phase of what became exclusionary, yet oppositional, feminist practices. U.S. feminists of color, writes Sargent, stood against what they understood to be "the racism (and classism) implicit in a white feminist movement, theory and practice."[37] But the movement's inability to reconcile in any meaningful way the challenges lodged by U.S. feminists of color indicated a structural deficiency within feminist praxis, and this prompted activists and scholars to agitate for a fourth, final, and "antiracist" phase they defined as "socialist feminism."

Socialist feminism became the added-on phase of a hegemonically constructed four-category taxonomy of feminist consciousness, the unachieved category of possibility wherein the differences represented by race and class could be (simply) accounted for. In Eisenstein's typology, because it is above all a chronology, the differences represented by U.S. feminists of color become visible only at this last stage. In the eighties, as the women's movement "grew more diverse," it "became '*forced*' (presumably by U.S. feminists of color, though she does not say) "to confront and to debate issues of difference—most notably those of race and class."[38] In this regard, Jaggar's book has much to say. She typifies first-phase "liberal feminism" as "tending to ignore or minimize" racial and other "difficult" differences, second-phase "Marxist feminism" as tending to recognize only differences of class, and third-phase "radical feminism" as tending to "recognize only differences of age and sex, to understand these in universal terms, and often to view them as biologically determined." But fourth-phase "socialist feminism," she hopes, will be capable of recognizing differences among women "as constituent parts of contemporary human nature." For Jaggar, this means that the "central project of socialist feminism" must be "the development of a political theory and practice that will synthesize the best insights" of second- and third-phase feminisms, those of the "Marxist and radical traditions," while escaping the "problems associated with each."[39]

Socialist-feminist theorist Cora Kaplan agrees with Jaggar, indicting the earlier three forms of feminism (the liberal, Marxist, and cultural forms) for failing to incorporate an analysis of power beyond gender relations in their rationality. Such limited comprehensions of gender, insofar as they seek a unified female subject, she argues, construct a "fictional landscape." Whether this landscape is then examined from liberal, Marxist, cultural, psychoanalytic, semiotic, or some other feminist perspective, "the other structuring relations of society fade and disappear," leaving us with the "naked drama of sexual difference as the only scenario that matters." According to Kaplan, socialist feminism will become transformative and liberatory when it "comes to grips with the relationship between female subjectivity and class identity."[40] Socialist feminism has not yet developed a theory and method capable of achieving this goal, however, or of coming to terms with race, culture, nation, class, or even sex or gender differences between female subjects. Although Jaggar continues to claim socialist feminism as "the most comprehensive" of feminist theories, she allows that socialist feminism has made only "limited progress" toward these goals. For her, socialist feminism remains only the "*commitment* to the development" of such "an analysis and political practice," rather than a theory and practice "which already exists."[41] She admits that insofar as socialist feminism stubbornly "fails to theorize the experiences of women of color, it cannot be accepted as complete" (11). Yet she asserts that "socialist feminism" remains the "ultimate" and "most appropriate interpretation of what it is for a theory to be impartial, objective, comprehensive, verifiable and useful" (9).

We have just charted our way through a ubiquitously cited four-phase feminist history of consciousness, a cognitive map consisting of "liberal," "Marxist," "radical/cultural," and "socialist" feminisms. We can schematize these phases as "women are the same as men," "women are different from men," "women are superior," and the fourth catchall category, "women are a racially divided class." The presumption of theorists throughout their analyses was that each of these political positions contradict one another. We shall see that this shared comprehension of feminist consciousness is unified, framed, and buttressed with the result that the expression of a unique form of U.S. third world feminism became invisible outside its all-knowing logic. Jaggar's contribution illustrates the problematic effect brought about by this hegemonic structure when she claims that a specific U.S. third world feminist theory, method, and criticism "does not exist." This dismissal is based on her understanding of the written works produced by feminists of color during the 1970s and 1980s (authors such as Paula Gunn Allen, Audre Lorde, Nellie Wong, Gloria Anzaldúa, Cherríe Moraga, Toni Morrison, Mitsuye Yamada, bell hooks, the third world contributors to *Sisterhood Is Powerful*, or the contributors to *This Bridge Called My Back*), which, she claims, operate "mainly at the level of description." Those that *are* theoretical, she continues, have yet to contribute to any "unique or distinctive and comprehensive theory of women's liberation" (ibid.). Jaggar's four categories subsume the expressions of U.S. third world feminism into either the "liberal," "Marxist," cultural," or "socialist"-feminist categories. She warns her readers not to assume that U.S. third world feminism has been "omitted" from her book—it has only been included within one of the dominant "four genera" of feminist consciousness outlined above. The differential form of U.S. third world feminism, however, functioned just outside the rationality of Jaggar's four-phase hegemonic structure. But to recognize the differential would require of Jaggar, and of hegemonic feminism, a distinctive shift in paradigm.[42]

Throughout the 1980s, U.S. third world feminism was sublimated, both denied and spoken about incessantly. Or, as African-American literary critic Sheila Radford-Hill put it in 1986, the fifth, outsider form of U.S. third world feminism was "used" within hegemonic feminism as a "rhetorical platform" from which "white feminist scholars" could "launch arguments for or against" the same four basic configurations of hegemonic feminism.[43] It is thus not surprising to find that the activist writings produced by women of color theorists between 1968 and 1990 are laced with bitterness; for, according to bell hooks in 1984, the stubborn sublimation of U.S. third world feminist thought was understood as linked to "racist exclusionary practices" that made it "practically impossible" for new feminist paradigms to emerge. Although, she wrote, "feminist theory is the guiding set of beliefs and principles that become the basis for action," the development of feminist theory has become a task permitted only within the "hegemonic dominance" and approval "of white academic women."[44] One year later, Gayatri Spivak stated that "the emergent perspective" of "hegemonic feminist criticism" tenaciously reproduces "the axioms of imperialism." Although hegemonic feminism has produced enlightening and liberating spaces, these spaces coalesce into what Spivak characterized as a "high feminist norm." This norm reinforces the "basically isolationist" and narcissistic "admiration" of hegemonic critical thinkers "for the literature of the female subject in Europe and Anglo America," as if such fascination can lead to liberation.[45] Under the strain of these kinds of ideological divisions, the 1980s women's movement buckled from within.

During the 1968–90 period, the four-phase hegemonic typology just outlined was commonly utilized and cited (self-consciously or not) by social theorists across disciplines as the way to understand oppositional praxis. But this conceptual model, this typology for organizing history, identity, criticism, and theory, is useful for oppositional actors only insofar as it is understood as the mental map of a given time and place, in this case, the cultural territory that U.S. feminists of color ironically renamed the "white women's movement." From the perspective of a differential U.S. third world feminist criticism, this four-category structure of consciousness interlocked into a symbolic container that had its own political purposes—both hoped for and achieved—but that also set limits on how feminist consciousness could be conceptualized and enacted. Its four-phase structure obstructed what could be perceived and even imagined by agents thinking within its constraints. What must be remembered is that each position in this typology is an imaginary space that, when understood and enacted as if self-contained and oppositional to one another, rigidly circumscribes what is possible for social activists who want to work across their boundaries. Movement activists became trapped within the rationality of its structure, which sublimated and dispersed the specificity of a differential U.S. third world feminist theory, method, and practice.

Despite the fundamental shift in political objectives and critical methods represented by feminist and other social movements, there remained in their articulations a traditional reliance on what can be recognized as previous and *modernist* modes of understanding and enacting oppositional forms of consciousness. But the recognition of U.S. third world feminism demanded that activists and scholars extend their critical and political objectives further. During the 1970s, U.S. feminists of color identified common grounds on which to make coalitions across their own profound cultural, racial, class, sex, gender, and power differences. The insights gained during this period reinforced a common culture across difference comprised of the skills, values, and ethics generated by a subordinated citizenry compelled to live within similar realms of marginality. This common border culture was reidentified and claimed by a particular cohort of U.S. feminists of color who came to recognize one another as countrywomen—and men—of the same psychic terrain. The theory and method of differential U.S. third world feminism they de-

veloped is what permitted the reengagement with hegemonic feminism that follows—
on its own terms—and beyond them.

The Theory and Method of Oppositional Consciousness in the Postmodern World

The following alternative typology was generated from the insights born of oppositional activity that occurred beyond the inclusive scope of the 1970s–80s women's
movement. The form of U.S. third world feminism it represents and describes was
influenced not only by struggles against gender domination, but by the struggles
against race, sex, national, economic, cultural, and social hierarchies that marked
the twentieth century. It is a mapping of consciousness organized in opposition to
the dominant social order that charts the feminist histories of consciousness I have
just surveyed, while also making visible the different grounds from which a specific
U.S. third world feminism advanced. This new typology is not necessarily "feminist" in nature. Rather, it comprises a *history of oppositional consciousness.*

This new cartography is best thought of not as a *typology*, but as
a *topography* of consciousness in opposition, from the Greek word *topos* or place, for
it represents the charting of psychic and material realities that occupy a particular
cultural region. This *cultural topography* delineates a set of critical points within which
individuals and groups seeking to transform dominant and oppressive powers can
constitute themselves as resistant and oppositional citizen-subjects. These points
are orientations deployed by those subordinated classes who seek subjective forms
of resistance other than those determined by the social order itself. These orientations can be thought of as repositories within which subjugated citizens can either
occupy or throw off subjectivities in a process that at once enacts and decolonizes
their various relations to their real conditions of existence. This kind of kinetic and
self-conscious mobility of consciousness was utilized by U.S. third world feminists
when they identified oppositional subject positions and enacted them *differentially.*

What hegemonic feminist theory was identifying over and over
again, and from across disciplines, were only feminist versions of four forms of consciousness that appear to have been most effective in opposition to modernist modes
of capitalist production insofar as these same four responses appear again and again
across social movement theory and action of every type. But, as Jameson points out,
under postmodern transnationalization new forms of resistance and opposition must
be recognized. Hegemonic feminist scholarship was unable to identify the connections between its own understandings and translations of resistance, and the expressions of consciousness in opposition enacted among other racial, ethnic, sex, cul-

tural, or national liberation movements. Doing so would have required a paradigm shift capable of transforming all notions of resistance and opposition, and not only within feminist social movements, but across all social movement boundaries.

All social orders hierarchically organized into relations of domination and subordination create particular subject positions within which the subordinated can legitimately function. These subject positions, once self-consciously recognized by their inhabitants, can become transfigured into effective sites of resistance to an oppressive ordering of power relations. From the perspective of a differential U.S. third world feminism, the modes of consciousness identified by U.S. hegemonic feminist theorists were viewed as examples of subordinated consciousness in opposition, but they were not viewed as particularly *feminist* in function. In order to transfigure subordination into resistance, and to make the differential visible as a critical apparatus not only within U.S. feminist theory but within the fields of critical and cultural studies in general, a new topography was necessary that would be capable of mapping the ideological spaces wherein oppositional activity in the United States has taken place (a cognitive mapping, if you will). The mapping that follows identifies the modes that the subordinated of the United States (of any sex, gender, race, or class constituency) have claimed as the positions that resist domination. Unlike its previous and modernist hegemonic version, however, this alternative topography of consciousness and action is not historically or teleologically organized; no enactment is privileged over any other; and the recognition that each site is as potentially effective in opposition as any other makes visible the differential mode of consciousness-in-resistance that was developed within a particular school of U.S. third world feminism since the 1960s and that is a particularly effective form of resistance under global late-capitalist and postmodern cultural conditions.

The following five-location topography of consciousness demonstrates hegemonic feminist political strategies to be expressions of the forms of oppositional consciousness that were utilized also by profoundly varying subordinated constituencies under earlier modes of capitalist production. The addition of the fifth and differential mode of oppositional consciousness to these has a mobile, retroactive, and transformative effect on the previous four, setting them all into diverse processual relationships. The cultural topography that follows thus compasses the perimeters for a theory and method of consciousness-in-opposition that can gather up the modes of ideology-praxis represented within previous liberation movements into a fifth, differential, and postmodern paradigm. This paradigm makes clear the vital connections that exist between feminist theory in general and other theoretical and practical modes concerned with issues of social hierarchy, marginality, and dissident globalization. Because this is a topography, it is perhaps best represented if visually demonstrated, for it maps transiting relationships set in motion by the fifth, differential form. For analytic purposes, I describe its locations categorically here as the "equal rights," "revolutionary," "supremacist," "separatist," and "differential" forms of consciousness-in-opposition. U.S. third world feminism, considered as an enabling theory and method of differential consciousness, thus brings the following five ideological forms into view:

The Equal-Rights Form

Within the first equal-rights enactment of consciousness-in-opposition, the members of the subordinated group argue that the differences for which they have been assigned inferior status lay in appearance only, not in "reality." Behind what they maintain are only *exterior* physical differences from the most legitimated form of the human-in-society is a content, an essence that is the same as the essence of the human-in-power. These oppositional actors argue for civil rights based on the philosophy that all humans are created equally. Practitioners of this particular ideological tactic demand that their humanity be legitimated, recognized as the same under the law, and assimilated into the most favored form of the human-in-power. Aesthetically, the equal-rights mode of consciousness seeks duplication; politically, it seeks integration; psychically, it seeks assimilation. Its expression can be traced throughout U.S. liberation movements of the post–World War II era as manifest in the early National Organization for Women (NOW), the League of United Latin American Citizens (LULAC), or the praxis of the civil rights movement as articulated by the young Martin Luther King. Hegemonic feminist theorists claimed this form of oppositional consciousness as "liberal feminism."

The Revolutionary Form

If the previous ideology-as-tactic insists on a profound resemblance between social, cultural, racial, sexual, or gender identities across their (only) external differences, then this second ideology identifies, legitimizes, claims, and intensifies its differences—in both form *and* content—from the category of the most human. Practitioners of the revolutionary form believe that the assimilation of such myriad and acute differences is not possible within the confines of the present social order. Instead, they reason, the only way that society can affirm, value, and legitimate these differences will be if the categories by which the dominant is ordered are fundamentally restructured. The aim of such radical transformation is to lead society toward the goal of functioning beyond all domination/subordination power axes. This revolutionary mode of oppositional consciousness was enacted within social movement groups across every difference, including the Black Panther Party, the American Indian Movement, the Brown Berets, as well as in the theories and practices of U.S. Marxist and socialist feminisms.

The Supremacist Form

Under "supremacism" the oppressed not only *claim* their differences, but they also assert that their differences have provided them access to a higher evolutionary level than that attained by those who hold social power. Whether practitioners understand their superior differences to have biological origin, or to have developed through a history of social conditioning, is of little practical concern. What matters is the consequence: the subordinated group understands itself to function at a higher state of psychic and social evolution than does its counterpart. The mission of supremacist practitioners of oppositional consciousness is to provide the social order a higher ethical and moral vision, and consequently more effective leadership. The precepts above guide any subordinated group that argues for its superiority over the dominant—from cultural and radical forms of feminism to "nationalisms" of every racial, ethnic, gender, sex, class, religious, or loyalist type.

The Separatist Form

This is the final tactic of resistance of the four most commonly mobilized under previous modes of capitalist production. As in the previous three forms, practitioners of separatism recognize that their differences are branded as inferior with respect to the category of the most human. Under this fourth mode of agency, however, the subordinated do not desire an "equal-rights" type of integration with the dominant order. Neither do they seek its "revolutionary" transformation, nor do they stake a supremacist position in relation to any other group. This form of political resistance is organized, rather, to protect and nurture the differences that define its practitioners through their complete separation from the dominant social order. The separatist mode of oppositional consciousness is beckoned by a utopian landscape that stretches from Aztlán to the Amazon Nation.

The maturation of a resistance movement means that these four ideological positions emerge in response to dominating powers. Such ideological positions become more and more clearly articulated, to eventually divide the movement of resistance from within; for each of these four sites generates its own sets of tactics, strategies, and identity politics that have appeared, as Jaggar asserts in the example of hegemonic feminism, as "mutually exclusive" under previous and modernist understandings of resistance. The differential practice of U.S. third world feminism undermines this appearance of the mutual exclusivity of oppositional practices of consciousness and social movement, however, and allows their re-cognition on new terms.

The Differential Form of Consciousness and Social Movement

U.S. feminists of color, insofar as they involved themselves with the 1970s white women's liberation movement, also enacted one or more of the four ideological positionings just outlined—but rarely for long, and rarely adopting the kind of fervid belief systems and identity politics that tend to accompany their construction. This unusual affiliation with the women's movement was variously interpreted as disloyalty, betrayal, absence, or lack: "When they *were* there, they were rarely there for long" went the usual complaint. Or, "they seem to shift from one type of women's group to another, and another." They were the mobile (yet ever-present in their "absence") members of this, as well as of other race, class, and sex liberation movements. It is precisely the significance of this mobility that most inventories of oppositional ideology and agency do not register.[46]

It is in the activity of what Anzaldúa calls weaving "between and among" oppositional ideologies as conceived in this new topographical space, where another and the fifth mode of oppositional consciousness and activity is found.[47] I think of this activity of consciousness as the "differential," insofar as it enables movement "between and among" ideological positionings (the equal-rights, revolutionary, supremacist, and separatist modes of oppositional consciousness) considered as variables, in order to disclose the distinctions among them. In this sense, the differential mode of consciousness functions like the clutch of an automobile, the mechanism that permits the driver to select, engage, and disengage gears in a system for the transmission of power. The differential represents the variant; its presence emerges out of correlations, intensities, junctures, crises. Yet the differential depends on a form of agency that is self-consciously mobilized in order to enlist and secure influence; the differential is thus performative. For analytic purposes, I place differential consciousness in the fifth position, even though it functions as the medium through which the equal-rights, revolutionary, supremacist, and separatist modes of oppositional consciousness became effectively converted, lifted out of their earlier, modernist, and hegemonic activity. When enacted in dialectical relation to one another and not as separated ideologies, each oppositional mode of consciousness, each ideology-praxis, is transformed into tactical weaponry for intervening in shifting currents of power.

These differences between a processual and differential five-location *topography* of consciousness-in-opposition and the previous four-category *typology* of hegemonic feminism became available for analysis through U.S. third world feminist theory and practice. The 1970s–80s social movement called U.S. third world feminism functioned as a central locus of possibility, an insurgent social movement that shattered the construction of any one ideology as the single most correct site where truth can be represented. Indeed, without making this kind of metamove, any "liberation" or social movement eventually becomes destined to repeat the oppressive authoritarianism from which it is attempting to free itself, and become trapped inside a drive for truth that ends only in producing its own brand of dominations. What U.S. third world feminism thus demanded was a new subjectivity, a political revision that denied any one ideology as the final answer, while instead positing a *tactical subjectivity* with the capacity to de- and recenter, given the forms of power to be moved. These dynamics are what were required in the shift from enacting a hegemonic oppositional theory and practice to engaging in the differential form of social movement, as performed by U.S. feminists of color during the post–World War II period of great social transformation.

In 1985, Chicana theorist Aida Hurtado identified U.S. third world feminism as a differential form of social movement in these terms: "by the time women of color reach adulthood, we have developed informal political skills to deal with State intervention. The political skills required by women of color are neither the political skills of the White power structure that White liberal feminists have adopted nor the free-spirited experimentation followed by the radical feminists." Rather, she continues, "women of color are more like urban guerrillas trained through everyday battle with the state apparatus." As such, Hurtado asserts, "women of color's fighting capabilities are often neither understood by white middle-class feminists" nor leftist activists and at the time of her writing, "these fighting capabilities are not codified anywhere for them to learn."[48] In 1981 Cherríe Moraga defined U.S. third world feminist "guerrilla warfare" as a "way of life," a means and method for survival. "Our strategy is how we cope" on an everyday basis, she wrote, "how we measure and weigh what is to be said and when, what is to be done and how, and to whom . . . daily deciding/risking who it is we can call an ally, call a friend (whatever that person's skin, sex, or sexuality)." Moraga defines feminists of color as "women without a line. We are women who contradict each other." This radical form of U.S. third world feminism functions "between the seemingly irreconcilable lines — class lines, politically correct lines, the daily lines we run to each other to keep difference and desire at a distance." She interpellates a constituency of "U.S. third world feminists and their allies" when she writes that it is *between* such lines that "the truth of our connection lies."[49]

That same year, Anzaldúa described the "truth of this connection" as one linking women who do not share the same culture, language, race, sexual orientation, or ideology, "nor do we derive similar solutions" to the problems of oppression. But when the differential form of U.S. third world feminism is deployed, these "differences do not become opposed to each other."[50] Instead, says Audre Lorde, each and every difference, all tactical positionings are recognized as "a fund of necessary polarities between which our creativities spark like a dialectic. Only within that interdependency," each ideological position "acknowledged and equal, can the power to seek new ways of being in the world generate," along with "the courage and sustenance to act where there are no charters."[51] The "truth" of differential social movement is composed of manifold positions for truth: these positions are ideological stands that are viewed as potential tactics drawn from a never-ending interventionary fund, the contents of which remobilizes power. Differential consciousness and social movement thus are linked to the necessity to stake out and hold solid identity and political positions in the social world.

The differential mode of social movement and consciousness depends on the practitioner's ability to read the current situation of power and self-consciously choosing and adopting the ideological stand best suited to push against its configurations, a survival skill well known to oppressed peoples.[52] Differential consciousness requires grace, flexibility, and strength: enough strength to confidently commit to a well-defined structure of identity for one hour, day, week, month, year; enough flexibility to self-consciously transform that identity according to the requisites of another oppositional ideological tactic if readings of power's formation require it; enough grace to recognize alliance with others committed to egalitarian social relations and race, gender, sex, class, and social justice, when these other readings of power call for alternative oppositional stands. Within the realm of differential social movement, ideological differences and their oppositional forms of consciousness, unlike their incarnations under hegemonic feminist comprehension, are understood as tactics — not as strategies.

This theoretical and methodological design was developed, utilized, and represented by U.S. feminists of color because, as Native American theorist Paula Gunn Allen put it in 1981, so much was taken away that "the place we live now is an idea" — and in this place new forms of identity, theory, practice, and community became imaginable. In 1987, Gloria Anzaldúa specified that the practice of a radical U.S. third world feminism requires the development of a differential consciousness that can be both applied and generalized: "*la conciencia de la mestiza.*" This is the consciousness of the "mixed blood," she writes, born of life lived in the "crossroads" between races, nations, languages, genders, sexualities, and cultures, an acquired subjectivity formed out of transformation and relocation, movement guided by *la facultad*, the learned capacity to read, renovate, and make signs on behalf of the dispossessed. So too the philosopher Maria Lugones claims that the theory and method of U.S. third world feminism requires of its practitioners nomadic and determined "travel" across "worlds of meaning." African-American feminist theorist Patricia Hill Collins describes the skills developed by U.S. feminists of color who, through exclusion from male-controlled race liberation movements and from white-controlled female liberation movements, were forced to internalize an "outsider/within" identity that guides movement of being *according to an ethical commitment* to equalize power between social constituencies. And Gayatri Spivak suggests "shuttling" between meaning systems in order to enact a "strategic essentialism" necessary for intervening in power on behalf of the marginalized. This, in order to practice the political method Alice Walker names "womanism":[53] the political hermeneutic for constructing "love" in the postmodern world.[54]

It is now easier to comprehend the utopian element insinuated throughout 1970s and 1980s writings by U.S. feminists of color, as in this address by African-American literary critic Barbara Christian: "The struggle is not won. Our vision is still seen, even by many progressives, as secondary, our words trivialized as minority issues," our oppositional stances "characterized by others as divisive. But there is a deep *philosophical* reordering that is occurring" among us "that is already having its effects on so many of us whose lives and expressions are an increasing revelation of the INTIMATE face of universal struggle."[55] This "philosophical reordering," referred to by Christian, the "different strategy, a different foundation" identified by hooks, can be recognized as, in the words of Audre Lorde, a "whole *other* structure of opposition that touches every aspect of our existence at the same time that we are resisting." Recognizing this fundamentally different paradigm for engaging in social movement would, according to Barbara Smith, "alter life as we know it."[56] In 1981, Merle Woo asserted U.S. third world feminism as a new paradigm. She described it as an edifice of resistance that does not "support repression, hatred, exploitation and isolation," but which is a "human and beautiful framework," "created in a community, bonded not by color, sex or class, but by love and the common goal for the liberation of mind, heart, and spirit."[57] It was the differential mode of oppositional consciousness that inspired and enabled this utopian language throughout the 1960s, 1970s, and 1980s among U.S. feminists of color across their own boundaries of race, culture, ethnicity, class, and sexual differences.

Differential Coalitional Consciousness: The End of Domination

In 1991, East Indian feminist theorist Chandra Talpade Mohanty reminded feminists of color that it is not enough to be "a woman," "poor," "Black or Latino" to "assume a politicized oppositional identity." What is required, as Fredric Jameson has insisted, is a specific methodology that can be used as a compass for self-consciously organizing resistance, identity, praxis, and coalition under contemporary U.S., late-capitalist cultural conditions.[58] Differential consciousness and social movement comprise the radical form of cognitive mapping that Jameson seeks. This theory and method understands oppositional forms of consciousness, aesthetics, and politics as organized around the following five points of resistance to U.S. social hierarchy: (1) the equal-rights ("liberal," and/or "integrationist") mode; (2) the revolutionary ("socialist" and/or "insurgent") mode; (3) the supremacist (or "cultural-nationalist") mode; (4) the separatist mode; and (5) the differential (or "womanist," "*mestiza*," "Sister Outsider," "third force," U.S. third world feminist . . . it has generated many names) mode of oppositional consciousness and social movement. It was this last, differential mode that enabled a specific cohort of U.S. feminists of color to understand and utilize the previous four, not as overriding strategies, but as *tactics* for intervening in and transforming social relations.[59] Viewed under the auspices of U.S. third world feminism understood as a differential practice, the first four modes are performed, however seriously, only as forms of "tactical essentialism." The differential praxis understands, wields, and deploys each mode of resistant ideology as if it represents only another potential *technology of power.* The cruising mobilities required in this effort demand of the differential practitioner commitment to the process of metamorphosis itself: this is the activity of the trickster who practices subjectivity as masquerade, the oppositional agent who accesses differing identity, ideological, aesthetic, and political positions. This nomadic "morphing" is not performed only for survival's sake, as in earlier, modernist times. It is a set of *principled conversions* that requires (guided) movement, a directed but also a diasporic migration in both consciousness and politics, performed to ensure that ethical commitment to egalitarian social relations be enacted in the everyday, political sphere of culture. As we shall see in the chapters to follow, this ethical principle guides the deployment of all technologies of power that are utilized by the differential practitioner of a theory and method of oppositional consciousness.

Early in this chapter I suggested that Althusser's 1969 notes toward a "science" of ideology could fruitfully be extended into a theory and method of oppositional consciousness in the postmodern world. Such a theory and method are composed of recognizing the structures around which consciousness disperses and gathers in its attempts to challenge social powers. The equal-rights, revolutionary, supremacist, and separatist forms of consciousness in opposition are made visible and more useful under the kaleidoscopic activity of the differential mode of consciousness in opposition. Differential consciousness re-cognizes and works upon other modes of consciousness in opposition to transfigure their meanings: they convert into repositories within which subjugated citizens either occupy or throw off subjectivity, a process that simultaneously enacts yet decolonizes their various relations to their real conditions of existence. This dialectical modulation between forms of consciousness permits functioning within, yet beyond, the demands of dominant ideology: the practitioner breaks with ideology while also speaking in and from within ideology. The differential form of oppositional consciousness thus is composed of narrative worked self-consciously. Its processes generate the other story — the counterpoise. Its true mode is nonnarrative: narrative is viewed as only a means to an end — the end of domination.

A differential oppositional consciousness recognizes and identifies oppositional expressions of power as consensual illusions. When resistance is organized as equal-rights, revolutionary, supremacist, or separatist in function, a differential form of criticism would understand such mechanisms for power as transformable social narratives that are designed to intervene in reality for the sake of social justice. The differential maneuvering required here is a sleight of consciousness that activates a new space: a *cyberspace*, where the transcultural, transgendered, transsexual, transnational leaps necessary to the play of effective stratagems of oppositional praxis can begin.[60] I have stated that the differential mode of resistance represents a new form of historical consciousness, and this is the case on both diachronic and synchronic levels. It is itself the product of recent decolonizing historical events and produces an ever-new historical moment out of the materials of ideology at hand.[61]

Differential praxis was utilized by an irreverent cadre of feminists of color within seventies and eighties U.S. women's movements.[62] In acknowledging this praxis, a space was carved for hegemonic feminism to become aligned with other spheres of theoretical and practical activity that are also concerned with issues of marginality. Adjustments thus have occurred within feminist theory that have recalibrated its dimensions and gauge. Donna Haraway's manifestos and manuals for a "situated subjectivity" and a "cyborg feminism" wherein the category of women "disappears," Teresa de Lauretis's contributions that extend fundamental feminist tenets into "eccentric" and differential forms, and Judith Butler's theorization of "performativity" all transcode and extend the bases and principles of 1968–90 U.S. third world feminist praxis. Today, the differential remains an extreme juncture. It is a location wherein the aims of feminism, race, ethnicity, sex, and marginality studies, and historical, aesthetic, and global studies can crosscut and join together in new relations through the recognition of a shared theory and method of oppositional consciousness. The differential occurs when the affinities inside of difference attract, combine, and relate new constituencies into coalitions of resistance. The possibilities of this coalitional consciousness were once bypassed when they were perceived as already staked and claimed by differing race, gender, sex, class, or cultural subgroups. But global transcultural coalitions for egalitarian social justice can only take place through the recognition and practice of this form of resistance that renegotiates technologies of power through an ethically guided, skilled, and differential deployment.

The Methodology of the Oppressed

Semiotics, Deconstruction, Meta-Ideologizing, Democratics, and Differential Movement II

T H R E E

On Cultural Studies: An Apartheid of Theoretical Domains

Subjugated knowledges are those blocs of historical knowledge which were present but disguised.... [These are] differential knowledge[s] incapable of unanimity, and which owe [their] force only to the harshness with which [they are] opposed by everything surrounding [them].

> Michel Foucault

The only home/is each other/they've occupied all/the rest/colonized it; an/idea about ourselves is all/we own.

> Paula Gunn Allen

She is willing to ... make herself vulnerable to foreign ways of seeing and thinking. She surrenders all notions of safety, of the familiar. Deconstruct, construct. She becomes a *nahual*, able to transform herself into a tree, a coyote, into another person.

> Gloria Anzaldúa

My "method" is not fixed . . . it is based on what I read and how it affects me, that is, on the surprise that comes from reading something that compels you to read differently. . . . I therefore have no method, since every work suggests a new approach.

Barbara Christian

It was a while before we came to realize that our place was the very house of difference rather than the security of any one particular difference.

Audre Lorde

A constant that changes is by definition paradoxical, and therefore messy. The idea of an inconsistent constant so bothers some physicists that they proposed a new kind of funny stuff in the universe, called quintessence. The term comes from the fifth essence that ancient philosophers believe permeated the universe — in addition to the four fundamental essences of earth, air, fire and water.

"Quintessence," said University of Pennsylvania astrophysicist Robert Calwell, "is shorthand [for a cosmological constant that varies]. It's dynamic, it's real, it's substantive. But it's not like any other kind of matter."

Los Angeles Times, "Missing Pieces of the Cosmic Puzzle," Monday, June 15, 1998, p. 1

WHEREAS THE aim of the preceding chapter was to develop a rhetoric of oppositional consciousness and social movement, the aim of Part III is to develop the language, terminologies, and technologies of its most unusual practice, the differential form, to sharpen the methodological, theoretical, and political underpinnings necessary in order to describe and advance the utility of differential consciousness as a practice of social intervention. Foucault has admonished us that this cannot be done, however, without identifying and honing what can be thought of as the "inner technologies" that are indispensable for the development of its being in the psychic and material lives of its practitioners. The process of mapping the technologies of the differential form of social movement is accomplished in the next chapter, which reveals the psychic/material/spiritual but repressed being of what will be argued is the "methodology of the oppressed." The methodology of the oppressed is a set of processes, procedures, and technologies for decolonizing the imagination.

During the 1970s, this methodology became explicit in the location of theoretical and political insurgency that was U.S. third world feminism. But it is important to recognize that this methodological form has also arisen from many locations during the post–World War II period, including from within the academic domains of feminist, poststructural, postcolonial, queer, postmodern, and globalization studies, as well as from within popular U.S. cultural representations from Hollywood films such as *Repo Man* (1982), *Brother from Another Planet* (1984), *Total Recall* (1990), *Thunderheart* (1992), *Pulp Fiction* (1994), and *Matrix* (1999). To comic books that feature a new mutant citizenry such as the *X-Men*.[1]

More obvious for contemporary cultural theorists in the human and social sciences, though, is the commitment to this mode of differential and oppositional consciousness that has emerged in the writings of a diverse array of scholars, including Stuart Hall, Audre Lorde, Donna Haraway, Cornel West, Judith Butler, Homi Bhabha, Jacques Derrida, Michel Foucault, Gloria Anzaldúa, Gayatri Spivak, Ernesto Laclau, Chantal Mouffe, Hayden White, Patricia Hill Collins, José Esteban Muñoz, Emma Pérez, and Trinh T. Minh-ha. They all have developed separate terminologies for a theory and method of oppositional consciousness, or at least explored and specified the varying dimensions of its differential form. It is no accident that over the last twenty years of the twentieth century new terms such as "hybridity," "nomad thought," "marginalization," "*la conciencia de la mestiza*," "trickster consciousness," "masquerade," "eccentric subjectivity," "situated knowledges," "schizophrenia," "*la facultad*," "signifin'," "the outsider/within," "strategic essentialism," "*différance*," "*rasquache*," "performativity," "*coatlicue*," and "the third meaning" entered into intellectual currency as terminological inventions meant to specify and reinforce particular forms of resistance to dominant social hierarchy.[2] Taken together, such often seemingly contending terms indicate the existence of what can be understood as a cross-disciplinary and contemporary vocabulary, lexicon, and grammar for thinking about oppositional consciousness and social movements under globalizing postmodern cultural conditions. Oddly, however, the similar conceptual undergirding that unifies these terminologies has not become intellectual ground in the academy for recognizing new forms of theory and method capable of advancing interdisciplinary study.[3] This divisive and debilitating phenomenon plagues intellectual production, and it is not unlike the division that plagues the rest of the social world, the academic manifestation of which can be recognized as a "racialization of theoretical domains," itself another symptom of the twenty-first century biopolitical race and gender wars predicted by Foucault. Let us examine this apartheid in more detail before we investigate its remedy, which the subsequent chapters begin to unravel in the works of Roland Barthes and Frantz Fanon, among many others.

The Racialization of Theoretical Domains—an Apartheid of Academic Knowledges

Critical and cultural studies in the U.S. academy, and the theoretical literature on oppositional forms of consciousness, difference, identity, and power, have been developed as divided and racialized, genderized, and sexualized theoretical domains. Throughout the latter half of the twentieth century, these studies often looked something like this: "white male poststructuralist theory," "Euro-American white feminist theory," "ethnic studies" or "postcolonial cultural theory," "U.S. third world feminist theory and method," and "queer theory," a newly coalescing intellectual domain that is claiming its own place in this structure that regulates academic canon formation.[4] In spite of the profoundly similar theoretical and methodological foundation that underlies such seemingly separate domains, there is a prohibitive and restricted flow of exchange that connects them, and their terminologies are continuing to develop in a dangerous state of theoretical apartheid that insists on their differences. It is easy to outline the territories of this theoretical imaginary: the domain of "white male" poststructuralist theory (primarily concerned with power, subjectivity, and class) has been challenged for ignoring the theoretical contributions developed out of Euro-American/white feminist, postcolonial, and/or third world feminist theoretical domains. Euro-American white feminist theorizing, on the other hand (conceived as primarily interested in power, subjectivity, and sex/gender issues), has been criticized for reluctantly drawing from the domain of white male poststructuralism (except when transcoded through "French" feminisms), postcolonial, or U.S. third world feminist theoretical domains. "Postcolonial criticism" (focused primarily on issues of power, subjectivity, nation, race, and ethnicity), unlike the others, is perceived as freely exchanging with the realm of white male poststructuralist theory (this cross-exchange has an old volatile history, as witnessed in 1940–60 Sartre/Fanon/Barthes relationships). Such generous attention also is criticized, however, for rarely extending to U.S. third world feminist scholarship, and even less to white feminist theory. Queer theory, for all its interdisciplinary innovation, is generally considered the primary domain of sex studies in relation to minoritarian and majoritarian behaviors. As I have argued earlier, however, the theoretical project of U.S. third world feminism insists on a standpoint, the theory and method of oppositional consciousness, Anzaldúa's "*la conciencia de la mestiza*," which is, I argue, capable of aligning such divided theoretical domains into intellectual and political coalition.

Insofar as academic disciplines generate division in this way, they continually reproduce an apartheid of theoretical domains. These divisions further demonstrate the articulation of knowledge with power inasmuch as what is being reenacted on a conceptual level are colonial geographic, sexual, gender, and economic power relations. Such divisions encourage what Cornel West describes as the appropriation of "the cultural capital of intellectuals of color" and women,[5] insofar as their contributions are folded into some "appropriate" category and there go submerged and underutilized, as we have witnessed in the relationship between U.S. third world and hegemonic feminist academic forms (or, as we shall see in chapter 4, in the scholarly relations between the Fanon of 1951 and the Barthes of 1957). Paradoxically, however, each of these divided (by race, gender, and sex) theoretical domains is also uniformly, fundamentally, and to all appearances unconsciously committed to the advancement of a similar deep structure of knowledge.

I want to briefly reconsider the example provided by the 1970s social movement of U.S. third world feminists, who argued that feminists of color represent a third term, another gender outside the regularized categories of male and female, as represented in the very titles of publications such as *All the Women Are White, All the Blacks Are Men, but Some of Us Are Brave, Ain't I a Woman?, This Bridge Called My Back,* and *Sister Outsider.* These books proposed that the social space represented by these "third-term" identities is that place out of which a politicized differential consciousness arises. It is this personal, political, and cultural configuration that permitted feminists of color from very different racial, ethnic, physical, national, or sexual identities access to the same psychic domain, where they recognized one another as "countrywomen" of a new kind of global and public domain, and as a result generated a new kind of coalition identity politics, a "coalitional consciousness," if you will. What in the past were survival politics at their most fundamental level became developed during the U.S. social movements of the 1960s and 1970s into theory and method of consciousness in opposition. This theory and method was enacted as praxis during the 1970s women's movement, when feminist activists of color identified the integrationist, revolutionary, supremacist, separatist, and differential modes of resistance as fundamentally linked to one another, in the form of a rhetorical structure when viewed through the differential form. This structure comprises a social-movement theory: U.S. third world feminism. But it also functions as a method for the analysis of aesthetic and political texts.

The connection that links each of the racialized, genderized, sexualized, in short, divided, theoretical domains in the academy to one another is that each is grappling with the hope—or despair—of globalizing postmodern first world cultural conditions by seeking, willing, or celebrating some aspect of the meaning or operation of a differential form of oppositional consciousness, whether this be in the form of the "hybrid," the "mobile, the "nomad," or any "radical *mestizaje*" form of "situated subjectivities." To recognize this equivalent and similarly constructed method across disciplines can work to undo the apartheid that divides theoretical domains, and redirect academic desire away from its tendencies toward intellectual colonialism. What this concurrent, symptomatic, and insistent emergence is enacting out of each theoretical domain is the academic expression of a stubborn methodology, examined in the next chapter, one that the cultural logic of late capital has made necessary to the survival of every first world citizen—what I call, for political reasons, the "methodology of the oppressed." My argument is that this emergence can be understood as part and parcel of an historical movement toward what is a new, truly global and "postcolonial" (that is, post-Western empire) condition.

Paradoxically, however, the generalized appearance of differential consciousness across cultural and academic territories must also be understood as symptomatic of the shape that politics also is *required* to assume in everyday life under present cultural conditions, given the demands of transnationalizing forces that are leveling new kinds of oppressions across all categories. Social actors committed to egalitarian social relations, who are seeking the basis for a shared vision, an oppositional and coalitional politics, and who seek new inner and social technologies that will ensure that resistant activity not simply replicate the political formations that are linked to transnational cultural expansion, must self-consciously recognize, develop, and harness a dissident globalization, a methodology of the oppressed, which is composed of the technologies that make possible differential social movement. This project is capable of developing oppositional powers that are analogous to but also homeopathically resistant to postmodern transnationalization, and can develop the kinds of human beings who are able to wield those powers.

The differential mode of consciousness in opposition can be productively read across many different kinds of texts, and across disciplines, to identify the instructions they contain for its generation. Indeed, this is the project that comprises the second half of this book, where we shall see Euro theories and U.S. theories converging and colliding, in a conflagration in which a new theoretical space appears, in which the previously repressed technologies of the methodology of the oppressed become undeniably visible, in an original and post-empire practical and theoretical domain.[6]

Power in Metaphors

Why does this book insist on detailing the technologies of the methodology of the oppressed? As we have seen, Jameson argues that the shift of capital to a transnational stage has brought about a mutation in the very structure of Western consciousness. Under new, globalized, postmodern organizations of power, he writes, oppositional forms of consciousness can only add up to a host of distinct forces that are equalized ultimately by their similar lack of effectivity. This is because these residual forms of resistance (that is, they were effective under previous *modernist* modes of capitalist social formation), can no longer find solid grounds from which to become mobilized under postmodern economic and cultural conditions. Here, Jameson's understanding of power is crucial. For him, under the imperatives of a global postmodern cultural dominant, power no longer gets generated out of a single source: the dominant master, king, class, race, sexual orientation, or gender, against which consciousness can then constitute itself as resistant. Indeed, Jameson argues, the singularity of this older notion of power, its organizations and its resistances, is in the process of being replaced. One of the perils in this replacement, or shift from power's previous historical vertical organization, is that new forms of hostility, antagonism, and dangers become directed "horizontally" between and within social classes, a dynamic symptomatic of the postmodern "democratization" of oppression.

This shifting away from a conception of power that Foucault has called its hierarchical "sovereign model"[7] means that, even for Marxist cultural critics such as Jameson, power can be perceived as doing something other than situating in a vertical, up-and-down, and pyramidal position, with white, male, heterosexual, capitalist realities on hierarchically top levels. Instead, global postmodern power is increasingly figured as a force that circulates horizontally, on a lateral and flattened plane, even if many-sided, with deviations occurring at every turn. This metaphoric respatialization images power, whether appearing in television ads, or theoretical tracts, as circulating in a sort of electronic pinball-game movement, as opposed to perceiving power as a pressure that forces up-and-down, or top-to-bottom, movement. As in the previous, sovereign, pyramidal model of power, the location of every citizen-subject can be distinctly mapped on this postmodern, flattened, horizontal power grid according to such attributes as race, class, gender, age, or sexual orientation, but this reterritorialized circulation of power redifferentiates, groups, and sorts identities differently. Because they are horizontally located, it appears as if such politicized identities-as-positions can equally access their own racial-, sexual-, national-, or gender-unique forms of social power. Such constituencies are then perceived as speaking "democratically" to and against each other in a lateral, horizontal—not pyramidal—exchange, although from *spatially* differing geographic, class, age, sex, race, or gender locations.

Movement on this postmodern grid, therefore, can be viewed as *equally* circumscribed, or made possible, by the similarly delimited circumstances of every citizen and its social group(s), as all equivalently contend for power on the matrix, a process that is felt to be—particularly by the once centered first world subject—a new kind of democratization of oppression. All positions are perceived as equalized by their relative potential for displacement on the grid, until previous colonial, race, class, gender, or sex differences become askew from their previous hierarchized meanings, to reappear in a new guise as horizontally positioned forms of neocolonial (postmodern) identities and proliferating coalition groups.

The postmodern understanding of power, then, is figured as a globalized, flattened but mobile, gridlike terrain. This terrain comes complete with power nodules inhabitable by collective subjectivities who are perceived as capable of accessing, with equal facility, their own peculiar quotients of power. It has been a late-twentieth-century shift in conceiving of power away from a vertical to a horizontal plane that has resulted in a new set of metaphors for organizing recent critical and cultural theory. Social change is described less through vertical and hierarchized metaphors that represent oppositional actors as "below," "under," "inferior," or "subordinate," who move "up," become "elevated," or "overcome" all obstacles. Instead, such metaphors are being replaced with horizontal alternatives that describe oppositional movement occurring from "margin to center," "inside to outside," that describe life in the "interstices" or "borderlands," or that center the experiences of "travel," "diaspora," "immigration," "positionality," or "location" on the grid. Contemporary scholarship in the humanities, then, becomes a painstaking, exacting attempt to find ways to speak about, to, or against any positionality across flattened social distances in a necessary transcoding, but the failure *or* success of any such effort only painfully leads to a greater apartheid: the racialization, genderization, sexualization of theoretical domains.

Following both Foucault and Jameson, this metamorphosis in how power is perceived and experienced creates different kinds of social being than did the previous "modern" depth conception of power as sovereign. In this regard, we know that under (still-residual) U.S. cultural formations, the pyramidal under-standing and enactment of power calls up into place certain kinds of confidences, arrogances, self-denigrations, inferiorities, moralities, resistances—in short, subjec-tivities. But the shift to a postmodern and horizontal perception of power displaces such fictions and their structures, undoing previous forms of subjectivity, morality, and resistance.

In this new world of superficially circulating postmodern pow-ers, even the confidences of citizen-subjects who reside at the highest levels of a pyramidal economic and ideological structure are shaken, and moral inducements to patronly or matronly compassion and social compunctions to demonstrate "gracious charity" in relation to "those less privileged" are weakened.[8] For the "underclasses" are perceived as having their own unsettling, ominous, and equal accesses to forms of power just as potentially threatening as those forms available to the capitalist up-per classes, white races, male genders, or dominant sexualities under previous hier-archical organizations of power. Within this new world order, this new global post-modern grid, "affirmative action" thus can be understood to only provide unfair advantage to some other, equally if not similarly positioned, neighboring constituency. This late-capitalist retranslation of difference allows hierarchical and material dif-ferences in power between people to be erased from consciousness, even while these same economic and social privileges are bolstered. The growing metaphoric domi-nance of this newly conceived horizontal grid networking the globe generates a kind of double-reality and double-consciousness of power, with new and old formations at work all at once.

A vertical-to-horizontal shift in how power is being experienced and understood charges human relations with a strange, perverse, new shimmer of "equality," which results in ever-new modes of democratically exchanged hostilities, competitions, antagonisms, and suspicions. This phenomenon appears in leftist pe-riodicals that describe the growing frictions between oppositional activists along lines of sexual orientation, gender, race, class, nation, or other differences as forms of "horizontal hostility." In these cases, differences perceived between constituen-cies are apprehended as evidence of an increasing need for *greater* division and re-mobilization in order that one's own power base is better secured. Success in aggregat-ing similar differences leads to greater fear and hostility toward other constituencies, insofar as all individuals and groups are perceived as equivalent contenders on the grid for the services of power. This dynamic renews tendencies toward "nationalist" and supremacist ideologies. The use of supremacy or nationalism, as we saw in the last chapter on differential social movement, can have expedient political results in a quest to challenge oppressive authorities, when self-consciously viewed and utilized as one tactic, among many others, rather than as an overall and compulsive strategy for living out identity, politics, and power.

Past organizations of Western capitalist powers have emphasized the vertical, pyramidal, or what we might call the paradigmatic axis over a syntagmatic, diachronic, and horizontal axis in encouraging the citizen-subject to take its place in the social order.[9] This paradigmatic emphasis demands that citizens concentrate on identity as it is arranged and articulated on a vertical, pyramidal structure, that is, according to what lies below and above it, in order to try to "better" or "secure" their own positions. A "Marxist return to history" can be considered the attempt to horizontally level such relationships, positioning the meanings of identity on a flattened axis with similarities to the postmodern global grid. But the Marxist horizontal axis functions *diachronically* to emphasize "what comes next" in order to retroactively affect what has come before, and will come after.[10] When power is conceived as if circulating on a lateral, (postmodern) horizontal plane, but without the hope generated by a Marxist sense of narrative and time, the Jamesonian postmodern sense of despair and exhilatory hope all mixed together is produced.

These dynamics, part and parcel of postmodern global cultural changes in the first world, contribute to ongoing racialization and apartheid of theoretical discourses in the academy. Such ongoing tensions and crises in representation are symptomatic of a new era, in which the nature of what comprises permissible human being is transforming. These ruptures are generating new, unexpected forms of social antagonisms between groups — even alliances based on hostility. Yet postmodern shifts in power are also revealing previous moralities as being nothing more than forms of ideological control — opening space in the order of the real for the previously unimaginable.

Multidimensional Powers

These two conceptions of power, the "sovereign," pyramidal understanding, and the postmodern, horizontal understanding, structure much of the theoretical and pedagogical debate in the humanities, informing such positions as Jameson's, who talks about an epistemic shift that figures the postmodern as inherently "superficial" or flat, and the modern as inherently deep. To recognize the activity of a differential form of oppositional consciousness, "*la conciencia de la mestiza,*" the activity of a "strategic essentialism" as Gayatri Spivak puts it, of "U.S. third world" or "third space" feminism, however, demands that power be recognized as a site of multidimensionality. To combine flat with deep deterritorializes the space of power one more time in a fashion that makes the journeys, paths, fields, and networks of differential consciousness representable.

      The theory and method of oppositional and differential consciousness is aligned with Foucault's concept of power, which emphasizes the figure of the very *possibility* of positioning power itself. This possibility depends on constant rearrangement in relation to a whole paradigm that includes mobile paradigmatic and syntagmatic dimensions, and that requires the perpetual reformatting of consciousness, and practice. Thus, subjectivity is continually redetermined by the fluctuating influences of those powers that surround and traverse us, as well as by the memory of those identities that might have taken, and may still take, "our" current places. It is in the shifting conjuncture between the paradigmatic and the syntagmatic that new combinatorials emerge, through an ongoing form of semiotic life reading that places the subject differentially inside power.

      My interest, then, as we will see in the following chapters, lies in the mobile interchange between the sovereign, Marxist, and postmodern conceptions of power, in the contrasts created by the inter-transferences between them, in *coordinating* the syntactical flat style and the paradigmatic depth style into original vectors, through emphasizing semiotic positioning and movement. Such activity, perception, and behavior requires the development of a form of consciousness that is capable of tactically projecting any vertical, pyramidal, or "deep" code onto a flat, horizontal, and superficial code in the way that Jakobson projected the paradigm onto the syntagm.[11] This understanding of power is not syntactical in nature, that is, is arranged in order of meanings that make "sense," insofar as power is viewed as continually regenerating, and intervened in differentially, according to the contingencies necessitated by social crisis. Power, thus, is viewed as performative. In chapter 4 we see that the methodology of the oppressed insists on the differential understanding and enactment of power, with the effect of something like what Jacques Derrida and Hayden White identify as the "middle voice" of the verb. The methodology of the oppressed is formulated and taught out of the shock of displacement, trauma, violence, and resistance, as I demonstrate in the studies of semiology, Roland Barthes, and Frantz Fanon in chapter 4.[12] In Part IV, we see the practitioners of the methodology of the oppressed recognizing their places and bodies as narrativized by and through the social body, and who are thus self-consciously committed to unprecedented forms of language, to remaking their own kinds of social position utilizing all media at their disposal—whether it is narrative as weapon, riot as speech, looting as revolution. In such activities, no legal boundaries are upheld as sanctified limits of the law, and their aim is chiseling out a new social body—one capable of acting justly on behalf of equality.

Against Intellectual Apartheid: Coalitional Consciousness

Jameson and others have maintained that neocolonial postmodern globalization has transformed the utility of previous modes of oppositional consciousness, bringing into question those forms of resistance that were effective under prior sovereign organizations of power. But, paradoxically, these same global cultural conditions are also driving the generation of an effective new form of consciousness that can puncture the postmodern illusion of a linear-homogeneous plane that typifies the new transnational space. The differential form of social movement and consciousness in opposition is that punctum. However, the very cultural dynamics that shatter, move, and transform identity, and that appear to horizontalize social positionalities, also serve to divide intellectual work in the university into the fragmented, postmodern, and racialized theoretical domains identified earlier, making a collectively shared vision and language of resistance difficult to identify and agree upon. Although a separate set of vocabularies and terminologies is developing within each of the theoretical domains in cultural studies for thinking about consciousness in opposition, there is as yet no agreed-upon interdisciplinary approach for bringing these languages together in the shared project that underlies their many articulations: a theory and method of consciousness-in-opposition that focuses on the citation and deployment of a differential form. Nevertheless, this "differential" mode of oppositional consciousness is being manifested in the academic world under varying terminologies, concomitantly and symptomatically from across disciplines as part and parcel of semiotics, poststructuralism, postmodernism, New Historicism, the critique of colonial discourse, and as represented in the cultural theory accomplished by feminist, ethnic, queer, film, and contemporary social, political, global, and historical studies across disciplines. These domains thus join in their efforts to understand, confront, and recommend new strategies for egalitarian social change at this juncture of human social organization.

I am proposing that a shared theory and method of oppositional consciousness and social movement is the strategy of articulation necessary to resolve the problematics of the disciplinization and apartheid of academic knowledges in the human and social sciences. Such a shared understanding of resistance would permit studies of domination, subordination, and their escapes to converge around a single and shared project. If centers of power, whether conceived as "communist," "capitalist," or something else are now attached to dislocation, the technologies of a differential mode of oppositional consciousness represent a concomitant microphysics of power capable of negotiating this newest phase of economic and cultural globalization. As we saw in chapter 2, people of color in the United States, familiar with historical, subjective, and political dislocation since the founding of the colonies, have created a set of inner and outer technologies to enable survival within the developing state apparatus, technologies that will be of great value during the cultural and economic changes to come. In the next chapter, we see that formerly marginal, subordinated, and polyform citizen-subjects are claiming a difficult coalitional psychic terrain, and in so doing an original postempire yet transnational citizenship is emerging, made possible through the decolonizing activities of what is defined as the methodology of the oppressed.

Theory, however staid and final, even when it situates identity in a desperate move toward final knowledge, is also capable of enabling the development of a common community of understanding that can, in its collective will, further politically oppositional goals. In the rest of Part III and in Part IV, in the interests of furthering the aim of mapping, negotiating, and reconfiguring the contemporary social landscape and its academic outposts, the terminologies developed by first world thinkers are transcoded in order to advance the differential mode of consciousness, and to make visible its guiding apparatus, the methodology of the oppressed. The idea here is to advance the possibility of connection, of a "coalitional consciousness" in cultural studies across racialized, sexualized, genderized theoretical domains: "white male poststructuralism," "hegemonic feminism," "third world feminism," "postcolonial discourse theory," and "queer theory." This advance requires a trespassing operation that will lead to a topography and poetics of theoretical space within which the methodology of the oppressed becomes freed from its repression in academic discourse: a "theory uprising" that is useful to all these theoretical domains.[13] Chapter 4 details the forms of subjectivity, processes, and procedures that compose the methodology of the oppressed. Chapter 5 examines the forms and contents that permit supremacism. Chapters 6 and 7 demonstrate how all that has passed, our studies of postmodern globalization and its resistances, oppositional consciousness, differential social movement and U.S. third world feminism, the methodologies of the oppressed and of supremacism, together makes visible the provisions of a hermeneutics of love in the postmodern world.

F   O   U   R

Semiotics and Languages of Emancipation

La facultad is the capacity to see in surface phenomena the meaning of deeper realities, to see the deep structure below the surface.... Those who are pushed out of the tribe for being different are likely to become more sensitized (when not brutalized into insensitivity).

Gloria Anzaldúa

When a people share a common oppression, certain kinds of skills and defenses are developed. And if you survive you survive because those skills and defenses have worked.... There was a whole powerful world of... communication and contact between people that was absolutely essential and that was what you had to learn to decipher and use.... You have to get it for yourself... it is a very difficult way to live, but it also has served me.

Audre Lorde

These... are survival strategies — maps, blueprints, guidebooks that we need to exchange in order to feel sane, in order to make sense of our lives.

Gloria Anzaldúa

Roland Barthes Is a De-Colonial Theorist

I HAVE referred to differential consciousness and social movement as "mobile," "flexible," "diasporic," "schizophrenic," "nomad," but it must be realized that these mobilities align around a field of force (aside from motion itself) that drives, inspires, and focuses them. This force is the methodology of the oppressed. Differential oppositional movement can be thought of as a process through which the practices and procedures of the methodology of the oppressed are enacted. Conversely, this methodology is best thought of as comprised of techniques for moving energy — or better, as *oppositional technologies of power*: both "inner" or psychic technologies, and "outer" technologies of social praxis. In Chapters 4 and 5 I track these oppositional technologies through their inscriptions in the theoretical works of two scholars who were poised on the cusp of the ending colonial era and the beginning of the postmodern. So situated, their writings contain many of the characteristics that theorists over the following fifty years across disciplines have sought to explain or decode.[1]

Today, Roland Barthes is rarely understood by academics as a "de-colonial" theorist, as a scholar whose work has contributed to the great world-historical movement toward decolonization that marked the twentieth century. Yet Barthes's 1957 work *Mythologies* represents one of the first attempts to encode in Western academic, technical, and "scientific" language what I refer to as "the methodology of the oppressed."[2] Still, semiotics, no matter how fundamental to the methodology of the oppressed, comprises only one of its five technologies. *Mythologies* represents an excerpt, a brief but important quotation from a great, ongoing succession of survival skills developed over time that compose the methodology of the oppressed. Barthes's excerpt can be understood as a gathering up, a methodical, synchronic compendium of what he views as the most profound skills that comprise semiology-as-resistance. I thus rely on Barthes's early work on semiotics, and on his emancipatory method for challenging dominant ideology, what he calls "mythology," as guides to the methodology of the oppressed — both recognizing and reclaiming Barthes's early contributions to de-colonial praxis, while also studying the ways his early "science" of semiotics depends on, articulates, and strays from the collective principles and procedures of this very methodology.

By way of orientation and introduction, what follows is a brief description (utilizing, whenever possible, Barthesian categories) of the five technologies that comprise the methodology of the oppressed. First, Barthes's semiology (what Anzaldúa calls "*la facultad*," or Henry Louis Gates Jr. calls "signifin'"), his "science of signs in culture," comprises one of the fundamental technologies of the methodology of the oppressed. The second, well-recognized technology is the process of challenging dominant ideological forms through their deconstruction, what Barthes calls "mythology." The third and "outer" technology is what Barthes calls "revolutionary exnomination," and what I call "meta-ideologizing" in honor of its activity: the operation of appropriating dominant ideological forms, and using them whole in order to transform them. This third technology is absolutely necessary for making purposeful interventions in social reality, whereas the previous two technologies, "semiology" and "mythologizing," are "inner" technologies that move initially through the being of consciousness itself. A fourth technology of the oppressed that I call "democratics" is a process of locating: a "zeroing in" that gathers, drives, and orients the previous three technologies — semiotics, deconstruction, and meta-ideologizing — with the intent of bringing about not simply survival or justice, as in earlier times, but egalitarian social relations, or, as third world writers from Fanon through Wong, Lugones, or Collins have put it, with the aim of producing "love" in a decolonizing, postmodern, post-empire world.[3] Differential movement is the fifth technology, the one through which, however, the others harmonically maneuver.[4] In order to better understand the operation of this mode of differential movement (which is of a different order than differential social movement and consciousness), one must understand that differential movement is a polyform on which the previous technologies depend for their own operation. Only through a differential movement can they be transferred toward their destinations, even the fourth, "democratics," which always tends toward the centering of identity in the interest of egalitarian social justice. These five technologies together comprise the methodology of the oppressed, and the methodology of the oppressed is what enables the enactment of the differential mode of oppositional social movement that I described in the example of U.S. third world feminism as interventionist praxis.

Chapters 4 and 5 examine how these five technologies encode the works of Roland Barthes and Frantz Fanon; the close analyses provided better enable the reader to identify the internal apparatuses of the technologies themselves. Part IV then identifies how these technologies also guide the works of many more late-twentieth-century theorists. But in order to remember how it is the experiences of colonization and decolonization that are the historical conditions under and out of which differential consciousness and the methodology of the oppressed emerge, our investigation of Barthes's contributions to the methodology of the oppressed begins with a detour through a book published six years before Barthes's *Mythologies*, a book written by a philosopher of a different sort, Frantz Fanon.[5]

Frantz Fanon and the Methodology of the Oppressed

The title of Fanon's 1951 work, *Black Skin, White Masks,* calls up an unsettling mode of perception, for the title disrupts the racial binary hierarchy between "black" and "white" by unifying these racial categories into a single body, a racially cyborg body, part technology (mask), part biology (skin).[6] But it also does something else, something more challenging. In considering this body of skin and mask, one experiences a kind of vertigo: if the skin is black, but the face one views, or wears, is only a disguise of white power—"black skin, white masks"—then physical, psychic, and cultural environs become unstable meanings: distinctions between insides and outsides, forms or contents, nature and culture, and between what is understood as superior or inferior are set askew. The metaphor "black skin, white masks" calls up, but also undoes, the very racial binary opposition that the metaphor also depends on in order to be spoken. A metaphor such as this operates through what is known as a "chiasmic" change of signification, a twisted trope that makes meaning by turning in on itself, by repeating while simultaneously inverting the relationship between two concepts.

In this metaphor, the "skin" comes to function as does a mask: both exterior coverings contain something other than what appears on the surface. Using another (Barthesian) terminology, one can say that the first form (the black skin) becomes "cannibalized" by a second form (the white masks). The first form, "black skin," is a material and bodily form that, though masked, concealed, and "consumed," cannot fully disappear. It remains present though disguised as a trans-form, a present/absence, which now means something other than that which its own past histories once permitted it. This transhistorization and -formation occurs because the physiologically real and social form, the black skin, is recast under the figurative and socially imposed "white mask," a process that refigures the black skin into another kind of disguise. The process is a chiasmic loop that creates a dual process of mimicry: when the mask fits, appearances are counterfeited on both sides.

In this way, Fanon's chiasmic metaphor reproduces the violent and sickening vertigo called up in the process of masking as survival under colonization by race, a disguise that, as dominant powers have it, conceals, represses, denies, deforms, or erases. Yet, what must be remembered in Fanon's metaphor is that this disguise also enables the tactical deception of the impostor who controls—between skin and masks, an interspace.[7] There is a living chiasmic intersection where the black skin and the white masks meet. It occurs in the space between these two different kinds of covering: here, something else, some other kind of social space, movement, and body can be discerned.

True, it is the violence of colonial invasion and subjugation by race that opens this border between skin and mask, where faces shatter into the wretchedness of insanity, capitulation, or death. But this location, which is neither inside nor outside, neither good nor evil, is an interstitial site out of which new, undecidable forms of being and original theories and practices for emancipation, are produced. For example, the concept of "split consciousness" articulated by third world thinkers including W. E. B. Du Bois, James Weldon Johnson, Fanon, Audre Lorde, Gloria Anzaldúa, Paula Gunn Allen, and Trinh T. Minh-ha arises out of this location.[8] These theorists see what they do as they do it from the dominant viewpoint as well as from their own, shuttling between realities, their identities reformatting out of another, third site. In this formulation, both the limits of insanity and the possibilities of emancipation are born out of the same horrors of subjugation. In both cases, movement—differential movement—is recognized as fundamental to advancing survival (or, as Bob Marley puts it, "exodus,"—the way out, liberation—is "movement of the people"). It is on such "movement" that the technologies that comprise the methodology of the oppressed depend: Fanon's 1951 imposition of the image "black skin/white masks" on a white colonizing culture provided one means by which to interfere with and move the colonial relations between the races; his aim was to deconstruct the kinds of citizen-subjects that colonialism produced. Indeed, the title *Black Skin, White Masks* suggests a "meta-ideological" operation: a political activity that builds on old categories of meaning in order to transform those same racialized divisions by suggesting something else, something beyond them. Fanon's metaphor also enacts and is driven by a moral code that demands equality where none exists (black = white, skins = masks). And all these operations of meaning—which are identified in this chapter as the technologies of (1) deconstruction, (2) meta-ideologizing, and (3) democratics—these combined efforts to press upon consciousness, are accomplished by depending on the profound capacities of consciousness to enact another technology of the method, (4) differential movement through perceptual domains...which is required in order to both understand and to enact these meanings.

To discern the last, semiotic technology that is built into *Black Skin, White Masks*, we need look no further than to Fanon's stated aim in writing the book: "to demonstrate to white civilization and European culture" that what it "often calls the black *soul*" is, rather, "a white man's *artifact*" (14; my emphasis). To describe the soul as an "artifact"—as the "white man's" manufactured, cultural invention—was viewed by the dominating cultures of the time to be a shocking, heretical act. For here Fanon is not only pointing out the proclivities of dominating cultures to treat racially different "souls" as commodities—objects or produce to be bought and sold; if *souls* too can be artifacts, then Fanon's challenge to the coloniz-ing culture is that the "white man" may have misread the "raced" and "cultured" na-tures of colonized peoples, that the image of the colonized cultivated by the colonizer may be only an artifact engineered by that imagination to serve its own needs for superiority. Even more threatening for the colonizing mind, Fanon's charge implies that dominant reality itself might be also a similar construction.[9] This is perhaps Fanon's primary political intervention: to claim that "the black soul is a white man's artifact" represents yet another intervention by the subordinated, a recurring de-mand throughout the period of Western imperial expansion, colonization, and de-colonization, to recognize dominant social reality as an *interested* construction, com-posed of peculiar symptoms that make up a specifically raced and cultured milieu. Fanon's challenge exemplified just one more insistently arising and transforming directive from varying and conquered cultures, races, genders, and nations to con-sider every aspect of colonial rule, including the most personal — even spiritual forms of being — as the distorted mirrors, the constructed "artifacts" of a dominating race, sex, and gender politics.

The semiotic technology of the oppressed that underlie this kind of challenge is not unfamiliar to the Western academic tradition. As Hegel had al-ready pointed out, the methodology that allows one to read forms of domination as "artifacts" is a familiar behavior among powerless subjects, who early on learn to analyze every object under conditions of domination, especially when set in exchange with the master/colonizer (what is his style of dressing? her mode of speaking? why does he gesture? when do they smile?) in order to determine how, where, and when to construct and insert an identity that will facilitate continued existence of self and/or community. Throughout the de-colonial writings of people of color, from Sojourner Truth to Tracy Chapman, this profound commitment to sign reading emerges as a means to ensure survival.[10] It is this semiotic technology of the oppressed that per-mitted Fanon to recognize the values, morals, and ideologies of dominant Euro-American cultures — from the "soul" through language, love, sex, work, violence, or knowledge — as "artifacts."

Fanon argues that subjugated classes must fully take in (must "semiotically" read, if you will) such "artifacts" and their meanings. But then (avoid-ing insanity), these artifacts are to be deconstructed in a fashion that can allow the social projection (the meta-ideologization) of new and revolutionary meaning sys-tems in order not only to ensure survival for the powerless, but to induce social jus-tice. Identifying and naming the dominant culture a "white society and European culture," and defining its construction of racial identities as a chiasmic relation between "black skin and white masks," are social interventions designed to challenge the legitimacy of dominant ideology as "natural"—for the sake of bringing about egalitarian social relations (the "democratic" technology). But Fanon's 1951 book was only one small symptom of the effect the methodology of the oppressed was to have in dominant intellectual life.

Resituating Roland Barthes

The ongoing and defiant demand of the colonized to recognize culture as artifact, as an interested construction reflecting the values of the most powerful social constituencies, rather than as productions of the white man's God, or nature, was a challenge that many twentieth-century Western philosophers of meaning could not ignore. Here I am especially interested in the semiotics of Peirce (1839–1914), Saussure (1857–1913), and, of course, Barthes (1915–80), one of the great inheritors of the white, male, and European philosophical tradition. If, as Fanon proposed in 1951, "every colonized people must at some point come face to face with the *language* of the civilizing nation" (18), then Roland Barthes's famous 1957 manifesto on "mythologizing," written six years later, represents one white man's attempt to speak back. Today, Barthes's groundbreaking work on semiotics can be understood as an important academic contribution to what has become a compelling worldwide movement toward decolonization. What must be recognized is that semiology developed simultaneously with the process of modernist derealization going on in the confrontation between Western imperial powers and the stubbornly resistant cultures and languages of conquered peoples of color, along with the development in conquered cultures of oppositional forms of consciousness and behavior that emphasize the trans-formality of reality itself. These simultaneous and codependent developments explain how Roland Barthes's works were so deeply influenced not only by the 1951 work of Frantz Fanon, but by the technologies of the methodology of the oppressed. I am suggesting that Barthes clearly apprehended the powers permeating cultures in the grasp of colonial and imperial interests. As Fanon already had pointed out, subjugated peoples of color were reading Western cultural forms very differently than were white Westerners themselves. The problem for Barthes in *Mythologies* became how to go about describing the methodology that permitted the colonized to see, hear, and interpret what appeared natural to the colonizer as the cultural and historical productions that they were.[11]

For Karl Marx, the proletariat was the social class most likely to develop the insight, consciousness, and collective political will necessary to challenge constructed social reality, the standards and conventions of social and economic hierarchies in the West. According to the Barthes of *Mythologies*, however, that location of political insurgency, of potentially emancipatory consciousness, and of moral, political, and collective will, had relocated to the site of non-European peoples of color, who for him represented a new transcultural and revolutionary social class. "Today," Barthes wrote in 1957, "it is the colonized peoples who assume *to the full* the ethical and political condition described by Marx as being that of the proletariat" (148). Barthes is here recognizing that Marx's emphasis on the centrality of labor alone to social self-creation would not lead to equality and to the emancipation of the oppressed, whether as "workers" or as "colonized" peoples of color. Rather, in the conceptual movement from the site of the "proletariat" to that of "colonized peoples," Barthes hoped to locate what he called the "ethical" and "political" sensibilities, that is, the specific *methodologies*, that might lead to the emancipation of consciousness from its slavery in and to the dominant order, and for everyone, in the same way that feminist theorist Nancy Hartsock hoped, some twenty years later, that the "feminist" standpoint could liberate consciousness from its strictures in masculinist order, or in the way Donna Haraway hoped that "cyborg feminism" would free citizen-subjects from every order.[12] My argument in the following chapters is that when Barthes recognized that an emancipatory consciousness is not necessarily linked to one's class, colonial, or racial location, he was freed to identify another form of consciousness and behavior, a standpoint, in short, a specific methodology which in 1957 he named the "science of semiology." In this chapter, we track just how effective Barthes was in achieving his aim of formulating a new liberatory method for freeing consciousness from the domination of social order, and of identifying grounds for coalition among the "subordinated." In doing so, it is possible to clearly identify the five technologies of what I call for purposes of political expediency "the methodology of the oppressed" and their mechanisms as they are encoded in Barthes's work.

Preliminaries, Preamble, Groundwork

Mythologies, the title of Barthes's book that is our primary guide, already signals a problematic code shift through which enough meaning escapes to leave Barthes's method for oppositional and emancipatory praxis overlooked and neglected by the very social movements toward self-determination of the sixties and seventies that could have best understood and utilized them. Should the term *mythologies* be understood in its traditional sense, thus referring to the myths of dominant society? Or does the term refer to examples of the liberatory *method* Barthes generates, advocates, and employs in order to *analyze* myth, consciousness, and dominant ideology? Unfortunate slippage occurs when Barthes utilizes this term to signify both concepts at once: "mythologies" in his text represents both the objects to be decoded and successful examples of his decoding method at work (156). Barthes does state in the "Preface" to *Mythologies* that he does not intend to use the term *myth* in any "traditional" sense, and he does promise that his final theoretical essay, "Myth Today," will clarify its meanings in a "methodical fashion" (11). But this unfortunate problem of nomination, indeed, of method itself, rather than becoming clarified in his text, remains opaque. Nevertheless, what the social exile Barthes accomplishes is a map for identifying the oppositional technologies necessary to a growing transnational class-in-resistance. It is this method that it is imperative to decode and understand under neocolonizing global postmodernism.

Notice the conflation of what are distinct conceptual domains through Barthes's use of similar terminologies to name them, such as "myth," "mythologies," "mythology," "mythologizing," and "mythologist." I can identify the commonly understood meanings of these Barthesian terms by saying that in his analysis, the term *myth* refers to "ideology," while *mythologies* refers to any ideology to be analyzed. These are easily understood meanings, and they make sense in any usual formulation. The terminological and conceptual confusion and elision occur, however, when Barthes chooses the *singular* of the term *mythologies* (i.e., mythology) to represent the new, semiotic, and emancipatory form of analysis he is introducing. This means that the semiotic *deconstructions* of ideology he is teaching us to produce are *also* called (like all ideologies to be analyzed) "mythologies." Thus, when practitioners are "mythologizing," they either can be naively reproducing dominant ideology, on the one side, or participating in a powerful, liberatory process of *deconstructing* those very ideologies, on the other. The meanings of the final term on this list are also ambiguously provocative: Barthes's "mythologist" refers to the heroic and lonely practitioner of "mythology" understood as liberatory practice, one who semiotically decodes, who "mythologizes."

These nominations smudge the differences between object, methodology, and practitioner, eliding the antagonistic relationship between one who acts *in concert* with dominant ideology and one who acts *in resistance* to that very ideology. It is a set of terminological connections and elisions that advance, but also delimit, the liberatory possibilities of Barthes's conception of semiology, while making the methodology of the oppressed difficult to differentiate among his other discoveries. Such elisions are symptomatic of the reception of Barthes's important contribution, which has slipped away from the very moorings that might have helped sustain and advance scholarship in ethnic, feminist, postcolonial, queer, or global studies. Moreover, such unfortunate slippages are one of the reasons that Barthes's revolutionary methods for understanding and transforming culture have been so little recognized or understood by cultural workers interested in social change.

As we shall see in the rest of Part III, in the hurtle between the speech of the "colonized," across to the normative Western language of academic speech and thinking (that which Barthes was challenging) from one realm of signification to another, an important loss of meaning occurs. The methodology of the oppressed becomes recoded in Barthes's work as a "general science" (111), semiology, which today is apprehended as dehistoricized, deracinated: it is a method made "general" and not constantly resituated, as Barthes would have wanted. Or, as we shall see in the analysis of Barthesian semiology that follows, the methodology of the oppressed is confined, not to the status of the imaginary or the symbolic, but to the status of the Real, where it is ultimately dismissed for being incapable of effectively handling the Symbolic.[13] In such encodations, the emancipatory praxes developed by colonized peoples of color and utilized by Barthes evaporate under the individual expression of Barthes's own genius as originator of a method for decoding and decolonizing dominant order. Barthes's great manifesto on semiology thus can be seen as both advancing de-colonial interests and inadvertently extending relations of cultural center and periphery in the formation of the canon of literary theory.[14]

Barthes is thus trapped on the very surfaces of the dominant reality that he also views as "mask." Nevertheless, he staunchly maps its contours, identifying, exploring, and claiming the aporia that opens between it and the forms beneath. In this realm of the "undecidables," Barthes becomes a cartographer of what is identified in the pages that follow as the methodology of the oppressed, "discovered" and claimed by him and which, though identified in his work, remains curiously absent, present—but in cannibalized form. In his version, this coalitional site is fully present yet curiously deserted of its constituencies, except for Barthes himself and any other lone heroic figure who might hold on, however tenuously, to the proposed identity that Barthes calls the "mythologist." We watch the problems these positions create for Barthes in his being unable to fully identify the possibilities of coalitional consciousness for which he longs, but which will be laid out in Part IV of this book, "Love in the Postmodern World."

What follows is a close reading of Barthes's analysis and its terminologies, with two already important deviations that I want to emphasize: in order to clarify the textual elisions and confusions in "Myth Today," I transcode Barthes's term *myth* as "ideology"—from the Greek word for "form"—and his "mythologist," the activist who decodes ideologies, is trans-formed in what follows into the "practitioner of the methodology of the oppressed."[15] These changes will help clarify the primary point, which is the crucial position that Barthes's manifesto on sign reading and ideology reconstruction must hold for those interested in the ongoing development of twenty-first-century modes of liberatory globalization.

By way of introduction to the methodology of the oppressed, let me say that semiology can be understood as a sensitivity, after all, a mode of perceiving that Western thinkers such as Peirce, Saussure, and Barthes encoded for our academic understanding. This discriminating sensibility is a hermeneutic with content, and it has other names, such as "signifyin'" in U.S. black culture, or "*la facultad*" in Chicano/a culture,[16] but no version has been as methodically specified as a form of resistance as Barthes's own; his work on semiology comprises a technical act, an attempt at Western science on which many of the great and influential late-twentieth-century theorists of poststructuralism, postmodernism, and postcoloniality base their work. Even more obvious (as Fanon has demonstrated), Barthes's version of semiology as mode of perception and decipherment comprises one of the fundamental skills necessary to differential consciousness understood as political intervention. Indeed, the close analyses of Barthes's work that follow will reveal all five of the technologies of the methodology of the oppressed.

We begin with this guarantee: social meanings (i.e., ideologies) can be recognized as *forms*, not contents (109).[17] As such, like any form, ideology can be perceived, identified, distinguished, and reproduced when necessary. Barthes wants his readers to recognize that ideology is a *pattern*: indeed, it is a structured pattern of meaning, of feeling, of consciousness itself. Barthes's 1957 radical effort seeks to un-form this socially produced consciousness by traversing and revealing the very patterns that trap and contain meaning in those that Fanon referred to as the "white man and European culture." Barthes's analysis is thus a study of consciousness that, in its movement from perception to meaning, becomes grounded in a system of being that determines the formation of his own cultural and racial milieu, his own people. This courageous and self-conscious analysis depends heavily for its success on the (unmarked) technologies that comprise the methodology of the oppressed.

Barthes resolutely diagrams out the containers that structure consciousness in order to propose a praxis for breaking meaning and mind free out of their living yet frozen "mythical" (or rather, ideological) forms (these forms, he writes, are like "speaking corpses"), and return them to "life," that is, to a process that can occur beyond domination. His essay "Myth Today" is a manual for emancipating consciousness, proposing semiology as key to generating the liberatory mode of deconstruction that Barthes calls "mythology." Barthes's essay is a graspable, step-by-step outline of Western consciousness as it is expressed in its most reified, colonized, and supremacist forms, and a set of prescriptions for bringing these forms back to life. Chapters 4 and 5 of this book also comprise a handbook of sorts. These chapters can be read as a technical manual for comprehending and following the technologies of the methodology of the oppressed. As such, the analysis is technical, slow, and methodical as the substance and the structures of this methodology are introduced. These chapters will also identify the four kinds of consciousness produced under dominant systems of meaning, the speech of the oppressed, six ways to counter oppressive meaning systems, and, in chapter 5, the rhetoric of supremacism.

A Manual for Liberatory Globalization:

Sign Reading across Cultures

To grasp Barthes's procedure for emancipating consciousness, it is necessary to comprehend the three primary terms (borrowed from linguistics) that, when taken together, are used to describe the basic structure of any humanly generated system of meaning. These three terms are (1) the Signifier (Sr), which represents any shape — or form — that meaning can inhabit; (2) the Signified (Sd), which represents any concept capable of filling one — or more — of these forms; and (3) the Sign (S), a third object produced in the symbiotic relationship between a Signifier and a Signified (see Figure 2). For any object to enter into meaningful social exchange, it is first grounded in this basic level of "signification" — of meaning production: all Signs are comprised of a relationship between a form, the Signifier of meaning, and its detachable content, a Signified-concept. Barthes makes it clear that on the plane of experience Western human perception is usually unable to apprehend the Signified-concept as a separate entity, one that only finds temporary expression through some kind of material object, or form. Rather, "normal" perception in the West (and this is the source of its fundamental alienation) first grasps the *correlation* that unites Signifier and Signified: a third object, the "associative total of the first two terms" — the Sign itself (121).

Central to utilizing and applying this theory of meaning in what follows — and to understanding Western consciousness itself — is the ability to recognize the Signifier–Signified relationship as only *arbitrarily* connected. This means that it is the capriciousness of human history and its judgments that work to associate and link the forms that become "Signifiers" with any Signified-concept. The danger for consciousness here, Barthes despairs, is that this *historically* produced link between Sr and Sd is perceived as emanating from *nature*, rather than being

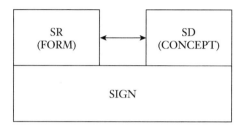

Figure 2. How human history in the West has structured meaning.

perceived as a cultural, historical, and human production. When consciousness shifts from perceiving human "history" and its contingencies to perceiving "nature" in this way, Barthes warns, the connection of consciousness to what he calls the "possibilities" of being becomes subdued, alienated, quieted — even erased. Here in this most fundamental formula for understanding the generation of meaning in the Sr/Sd/Sign relationship, the ground is prepared for Barthes's contribution to a new "de-colonial" form of consciousness and discourse, for Barthes hoped that the recognition of this model (even in this most fundamental form) would help enable citizen-subjects turn "nature" back into a material history of possibilities.[18] To summarize, then: first-level meaning-production occurs in the Sr/Sd/Sign relationship. This relationship can be understood as an inscription that generates the tissue of a meaning system: it is an ascription of meaning to objects that occurs at the most primary level of humanly produced signification.

Once set into place, however, this Sr/Sd/Sign relationship can easily form a new and second object. Human meanings easily proliferate, complicate, and rise to what Barthes called a "mythical" level of understanding, appropriation, and exchange. This "mythical" level is ideology, and ideology is what extends consciousness into an alienated "phony" social life, the everyday life of citizen-subjects that seems more real than real (115).[19]

Ideology Is Robbery by Colonization

We can now demonstrate how ideology and dominant forms of social consciousness are produced. It is at a "second" level, Barthes points out (see Figure 3), that the Sign is emptied out of its previous meaning-associations, and converted into form once again. Transmuted into a new Signifier, the old Sign is ready to be inhabited by an incoming and more powerful Signified-concept in a process that generates a second-level meaning system: ideology. This metamorphosis of the older Sign into a new Signifier-form means that the previous meanings, the histories and social us-

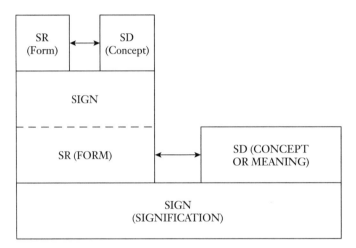

Figure 3. Barthes's model of how ideology is formed: its recognition enables a radical seminology.

ages associated with the Sign at its first level, are appropriated and colonized. The older Sr/Sd/Sign system now only serves as a form of seemingly "naturalized" evidence to ground and link some new and imposed meaning to an appearance only of "nature," "history," and "truth." In this process what Barthes calls a *phony* "real" nature, a "pseudo-physis," is produced (142). And it is at this level, Barthes insists, that people's access to material history, history's creation of forms-as-Signifiers, and history's relationship to consciousness itself are swept away from human apprehension.[20] This process has powerful ramifications insofar as it affects dominant cultures and consciousness. At this point in Barthes's argument, however, he simply wants to make the *form* by which meaning and consciousness are structured very clear: Ideology, he argues, is a *second*-order semiological system. That which *was* a Sign (namely, the associative total of a concept and a form) in the first system becomes a new Signifier—a mere emptied-out form—in the second. Because the second-order level of signification-in-ideology both hides and yet speaks in and through the first level of signification, Barthes describes ideology as a "metalanguage" (115), that is, as a second language in which one speaks about and through a first.

The realm of being *outside* its inscription in human modes of naming, categorizing, producing, and exchanging meaning, the world *exterior* to Signifier/Signified/Sign relationships, is named the "referent" in this theoretical domain. *Caló* and some forms of music, speech, and gesture, but especially poetry, represent the desire to regain that realm through the determination to use Signs by stretching, or breaking, the equation between Signifier and Signified insofar as this link has come to take on the appearance of "nature." Barthes thus calls poetry a "regressive semiological system" (133). This means that poetry reaches back through the levels of meaning production to try to lead consciousness out of its disciplinization and inscription in culture to a potential utopia existing between, around, and through language — that place, according to Barthes, is where the referent itself resides (ibid.). Semiologists assert that it has only been through Signifier/Signified and Sign relationships conceived as medium that the referent can be made available for conscious appropriation, exchange, and consumption.

To summarize this formula: *ideology* comes into being when there is an appropriation of a first-level Sign system in its entirety in a process that transforms it into *form* alone, a Signifier for a second and newly arrived Signified. The historical and arbitrarily linked meanings of the earlier Sr/Sd/Sign relationship are sublimated under the power of this incoming, imposed concept, the now hidden yet still present historically verifiable truths of the first-level meaning system, cannibalized to serve new purposes.

Indeed, Barthes writes, the first-level sign system even helps to give the second-order level of meaning-in-ideology the appearance and feel of a "natural" object, rather than of a historically produced and power-laden event. This occurs because the previous structure and its historically real links to culture appear and disappear, he writes, in a "turnstile" fashion. The historical links are still there, he stresses, but only as a present-absence (structurally similar to an "alibi"). Thus, they help permit a new, insolent, but authoritative Signified-concept to fully inhabit and claim its place in the body of the older form, and indeed, in the body of the cultural order itself. What must be understood is that "it is this constant game of hide-and-seek" between first-level historically provided meanings, and the new form as it uses them, "which defines" the hypnotic, reality-appearing powers of ideology (118).

Barthes's radical aim in *Mythologies* is to challenge this formation through which Western meaning, consciousness, and ideology are produced, and thus to rescue the irreproachably good, compliant citizen-subject of Western culture as she/he unerringly enters this sensuous experience, this living prison house of meaning. Barthes's strategy is to demonstrate how meaning is conjugal, erotic, and satisfyingly naturalized. Grasped "through my eyes," he writes, the new ideological Signifier "has a sensory reality...there is a richness in it" (117). Citizen-subjects submit to the work of ideological signification innocently, consuming its meanings whole in order to obtain the satisfactions they provide. But it must be understood that the processes of ideology are also inductive: they feel and appear to be intelligent, "objective" processes as well as sensuous ones. It is in these linkages between perception, bodily sensation, and intellectual comprehension that much of the power of ideology subsists.

Barthes is asking us to be conscious of this patterned motion of consciousness, to become a consciousness aware of the forms necessary to its satisfaction, to learn to study our own consumption of perceptual and intellectual gratification. The process of semiology, of semiotic-mythology, permits that same consciousness, searching the components of its pleasure, to discover the structure of "signification" itself, to identify the culturally produced meaning system that is providing a space for what is a circumscribed and particular subjectivity — one's own — to emerge.

For Barthes, there is no need to develop a theory of the "unconscious" in order to understand this socially and culturally produced consciousness, this consciousness-in-ideology. Because ideology hides nothing, he tells us, the ingredients of its meaning are on the surface: "there is no latency of the signified-concept in relation to the form of the signifier," he writes. Once they are part of the sign, both are clearly present (and not present) (123). Barthes's anguish is that it is in this defensively structured production of meaning as "alibi" — where material history is always elsewhere, somewhere beyond the (meta)language of ideology, yet also always present — that "bourgeois" citizen-subjects of 1957 (those whom Fanon refers to as "the white man and European culture") generate their predominant forms of being.

It is precisely because ideology deprives material and historicized forms of their meanings (emptying them out, transforming them into a "gesture" [122] reauthorizing and filling the forms with a new, incoming concept) that *a new methodology for emancipating consciousness must be founded.* This new method, Barthes hopes, will be capable of carrying Western consciousness across meaning differentially, in the interests of returning its connections to an egalitarian sense of human being and society. Barthes's proposal for this new method of perception and decipherment is semiotic "mythology." He insists that the only way to understand this new emancipatory method and the tissues of signification that comprise it is to first understand ideology as "a double system: its point of departure is constituted by the arrival of a meaning" (ibid.). And in that space between departure and arrival a lacuna appears, one that engenders our desire, disorients us, and beckons us — either to what Barthes calls the "zero degree of meaning" (132), that no-place from which substance arises, or to the comforting promise of security, solid meanings, grounded once again. Barthes emphasizes that the choice is between the liberation of "prophetic," "poetic," "revolutionary," semiotic or "mythologizing" forms of consciousness, on the one side, and, on the other, the trap of ideological forms of thinking.

Radical Semiology/Emancipatory Deconstruction

The structure of meaning thus laid out, Barthes provides his most famous example of the process of an emancipatory "semiology" in action (sign reading) through "mythology" as method when he deciphers a photo that appeared on the 1956 cover of a popular French magazine (see Figure 4).

Figure 4. The 1956 cover photo of *Paris Match* made famous by Barthes's semiotic analysis. Courtesy of *Paris Match*/Izis.

It is no accident that discussion of this photoimage of colonial, race, age, gender, and power relations recurs repeatedly throughout Barthes's essay "Myth Today." The photo is of a black youth who wears the full-dress uniform of the French colonial empire. His pose is altogether formal, palm open in a rigid salute, eyes fixed and lifted in a steady gaze. Barthes writes of this image that "there is no better answer" to white French citizens nervous about the moral benefits of conquest and colonization than the "zeal" that emanates from this image of the young soldier as he serves his "oppressors" (116).

Barthes chooses this photo to illustrate Fanon's old point that one's image, even one's "soul," can come to function as the constructed "artifact" of a particular social force, in this case a "white and European desire." Barthes points out that in the movement from historically contingent (Sr/Sd) Sign to ideological meaning, this image of the African/French youth can no longer emanate in a fashion that can represent his own life and the histories that brought him to this moment. Instead, the image and its (historically and materially situated) meanings are appropriated—to signify (unashamedly) something else. This image now represents an ideology, Barthes writes, "the greatness of the French colonial Empire" (125) for which, in this instance, the African/French youth becomes the fundamental prototype. As ideology, the image is sensuous, yet intellectual; it calls up a thinking consciousness in the viewer, who can remark ("naturally," casually to itself, Barthes warns): "Look at this good Negro" saluting "like one of our own" white boys (124).

This kind of ideological imagery and speech thus perpetrates an "arrest" Barthes says, "in both the physical and legal sense of the term," an arrest of the perceiving viewer, an arrest of every party involved:

> French imperiality condemns the saluting Negro to be nothing more than an instrumental signifier, the Negro suddenly hails me in the name of French imperiality; but at the same moment the Negro's salute thickens, becomes vitrified, freezes into an eternal reference meant to *establish* French imperiality. (125)

In this process of consciousness (and of form), material history, indeed, the Real itself, as humanly constructed is razed and transformed into a phony "nature." Barthes describes this disappearance of history as a "robbery by colonization" (132). It is not the young African/French soldier who disappears in this robbery, however. He remains, "half-amputated, deprived of memory," but "not of existence" (122). Barthes reminds us that a meaning such as this ideology could never evolve simply from "the nature of things." Ideological meaning is, rather, a paradoxical kind of "language" (a creation and exchange of meaning) that is at once *chosen* by history, even as ideology appropriates and erases that very history. Once the African is dispossessed of his own previous histories, he becomes transformed into a "gesture," an index that points toward another concept and a new history: the greatness of the empire, the "general history of France" (from its "colonial adventures, to its present difficulties"). This functioning of ideology (as language stolen, then returned) thus leaves intact the neuroses of the present dominant society, what Barthes refers to as a "threatened Empire" (131). There is yet another primary and horrifying denial inscribed in this image when it becomes ideology, Barthes writes. The "contingent, historical, in one word: *fabricated* quality of colonialism" itself—has disappeared (143).

Examples such as these demonstrate Barthes's reliance on the processes of colonization-by-race—as example—to drive the conceptual apparatus of his work. Barthes goes so far as to define ideology *as the process of colonization itself*: the occupation, exploitation, incorporation, and hegemonic domination of meaning—by meaning. Barthes's reliance on colonial power relations does not end here: his method, semiotic-mythology, is a careful map of the lacuna between meaning systems reminiscent of another kind of horrifying disjuncture. Barthes's method recalls (into being) the very schism in consciousness that occurs when one is ripped away from legitimized order—"reality"—to be placed as outsider in a process endemic to coloniality-by-race, a chasm Barthes's method invites all readers to enter.[21] Using (de)"colonization" as his central organizing metaphor, both thematically and methodologically, Barthes's commitments to the emancipatory processes of colonized peoples of color (and to all subordinated subjectivities) permit him to recognize these two technologies of the methodology of the oppressed. Indeed, Barthes's "scientific" schema has described a structured way to enter the aporia created by the pulling away of consciousness from dominant and grounded meanings, and a process by which to heal that chasm through new "technologies" for the reconfiguration of meanings. But semiology (Sr/Sd/Sign reading) and "mythology" (understood as the deconstruction of ideology) comprise only two of the technologies necessary for diversifying meaning and consciousness into new configurations. There are three others.

Consciousness and the End of Ideology

What makes human consciousness moral? Colonizing? Oppressed? Cynical? Dominating? Emancipatory? Revolutionary? Barthes thinks he knows, and his answers to these questions allow us to continue comparing the substance and structures of

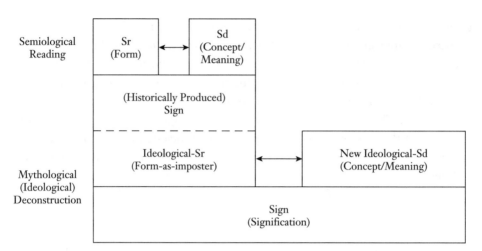

Figure 5. Four ways to decode the ideological signifier and sign.

his method for emancipating consciousness with the substance and structures of the methodology of the oppressed.

In Barthes's formulation, human consciousness is positioned according to how it takes in and decodes "the ideological-Signifier." As you remember, this ideological-Signifier is a structured *form*-as-impostor, insofar as the form contains previous histories (embedded in a latent Signifier/Signified/Sign relationship) that are disguised under the imperatives of an incoming and powerful new ideological concept (see Figure 5) (we saw this operation at work in the image of the black youth who becomes a French soldier saluting, and in the example of "white masks" that overtake "black skins"). By focusing differently on the ideological-Signifier (whose forms feel and look like "reality"), Barthes argues that Westerners produce four fundamental types of consciousness: (1) that of the "cynic" who focuses on the ideological-Signifier as a *potential* meaning; (2) that of Barthes's semiologist who focuses on the ideological-Signifier as an empty form; (3) that of the legitimized citizen-subject who focuses on both form and meaning at once; and (4) that of the citizen-subject who is *not* interested in receiving forms or meanings—only necessities: the consciousness of the subordinated.[22]

The first "cynical" passage through perception is accomplished when one strikes an indifferent pose in relation to the ideological-Signifier's plenitude. This form of consciousness views the full Signifier as *form* alone; it understands the Signifier's *potential* emptiness as given, and knowledgeably understands that the form can parasitically carry an *artificial* and imposed meaning. For this cynical mode of perception, there is no history (that matters) embedded in the form's previous incarnation as a full, first-level language-object, a Sign. This insensitivity to the historical complexity of the ideological-Signifier is born out of a hypersensitivity that recognizes all forms, regardless of their histories, as capable of carrying new, more instrumental meanings, created by contemporary forms of power that matter now. This cynical mode of focusing perception is that of the advertiser, the self-conscious producer of ideologies who, Barthes writes, coldly starts "with a concept" wedded to power, *then* begins to search for a useful form to represent it. The work of such a consciousness would be to constantly produce the new, but without any belief or stake in egalitarian movements of power.

From the perspective of this consciousness, the photo of the young African soldier saluting the French conquering flag is matter-of-factly viewed as a potential vehicle (the history of the image is inconsequential—the photo exists as an artless, empty Signifier, a form) for some useful concept, in this case, the greatness of the empire, one image among many that might have been chosen to represent and naturalize the legitimacy of colonization. A cynical producer of ideologies "can very well give to French imperiality many other signifiers besides a Negro's salute," writes Barthes; "a French general pins a decoration on a one-armed Senegalese, a nun hands a cup of tea to a bedridden Arab, a white school-master teaches attentive piccaninnies" (127). The cynical consciousness either generates or apprehends such images coldly, with nonchalance. The attitude here creates an efficient economy: any image can function as another potential example of some larger, more inclusive concept, which derives, in its obvious finality, from the political imperatives of power, rather than from the political possibilities of struggle. The cynical consciousness moves among power's images scornfully, but is capable of serving the dominant order well, even as it mocks it. This consciousness considers the appropriation of forms by power to be inevitable. Its loyalty is to the undeniable truth of power as it inhabits forms, rather than to forms themselves: this consciousness is thus "for sale."

Barthes's second mode of perception is the method for decolonizing consciousness claimed by Barthes for science, in the name of liberation as semiology/mythology. This mode of consciousness fully takes in the photo. But then the image is semiotically re-viewed, and clarified as deceivingly empty: pregnant with very particular histories... yet these are shot through with a greater, all-embracing, and imposed concept, which cannibalizes those histories—and thus the form itself—alive. Barthes insists that consciousness can distinguish the deformation imposed by the incoming ideological-Signified upon the older Sign, must learn to understand the nature of ideology-as-impostor. This is not just a technical feat, Barthes believes. It is a moral necessity, a particular accomplished sensitivity that can be learned. Barthes writes, "If I focus on a full signifier, in which I clearly distinguish" the difference between meaning and form, "and consequently the distortion" that the meaning imposes on the form, "I undo the signification" of the ideology, and "I receive it as an imposture: the saluting Negro becomes the ALIBI of French imperiality" (128).

Although the young soldier's image is resignified when it becomes taken by dominant ideology, Barthes reminds us that its older meanings also remain. The mythologist's analysis reveals these added meanings as an "appearance only." These older meanings have been appropriated in order to provide an "alibi" to help ground (in a phony nature) the *artificiality* of coloniality-by-race. The perception and deciphering of the mythologist is thus a de-ideologizing and emancipatory form of perception; it shatters any dominant ideology into these constituent parts. The consciousness that uses the technologies of semiology and deconstruction can no longer naturalize the legitimacy of the empire in the image of the young boy—thus the image is released from its use as another racist instrument of colonization. Barthes claims this decolonizing mode of consumption and deconstruction of dominant ideology as that of his technician, the mythologist, who uses semiology in order to create liberation of meaning through deconstructions of this sort. Literary and cultural theorists of *Mythologies* acknowledge Roland Barthes as one of the inventors of "semiology." But there are *two* methods that are distinguished here: Barthes's proposal for a form of consuming ideology through a "semiology" (a sign reading) that rises to the level of a "mythology" that deconstructs dominant ideology-become-reality represents *two* technologies. These two, along with three others, create the methodology of the oppressed and enable the differential form of consciousness and social movement (practices that the horrors of conquest, colonization, and domination forced the subordinated to develop in order to ensure their survival).

The seductive danger of the third form of perception is that it is the mode encouraged in any consciousness that longs for "normality," that is, which longs for the reality of dominant, legitimated, and middle-class status. This form of consciousness permits an uninterrupted consumption of ideology: following the law of the dominant social order, credulous in its consumption of what appears to be "reality," it proceeds by deciphering the ideological-Signifier as a whole made up of the dominant concept linked with its form as if they were inextricably united. As Barthes writes, "the saluting Negro is no longer an example or symbol," as it is to the cynical consciousness; "still less" is this image an "alibi" of anything, as it is to a practitioner of the methodology of the oppressed, Barthes's mythologist. Rather, for this third form of consciousness, the image of the saluting young soldier emanates "the very presence" of a great, French imperiality (ibid.). The dominant culture and its imperatives of power thus appear "naturalized" through the turnstile activity of the dominant Signifier as it almost reveals its absent histories, in the image of the uniformed young black male who salutes.

Barthes's first two modes of deciphering the Signifier-in-ideology, the cynical and the semiotic-mythologizing form, are formal, "static," and analytic, he writes (ibid.). Both cynicism and semiotic-mythologizing destroy dominant ideology insofar as they recognize that it is a *structured* appropriation of the image. Barthes writes:

> If I read the Negro-saluting as symbol pure and simple of imperiality, I must renounce the reality of the picture, it discredits itself in my eyes *when it becomes an instrument*. Conversely, if I decipher the Negro's salute as an alibi of coloniality, I shatter the myth even more surely by the obviousness of its motivation. But for the myth-reader, the outcome is quite different: everything happens as if the picture *naturally* conjured up the concept, as if the signifier *gave* a foundation to the signified. (129–30; my emphasis)

Ideology, Barthes insists, comes to exist at "the precise moment when French imperiality achieves the natural state" (130). The third and "dominant" mode of perceiving, Barthes argues, will decipher an ideology according to its own dynamics and imperatives. This last consumer thus joins the life of the ideology itself, becoming an uncorrupted living perceptual and intellectual machine of its work.

Yet, paradoxically, it is this very moment of original perceptual *jouissance*—a blissful seeing—that is what is required of the practitioner of the methodology of the oppressed, indeed, of Barthes's trained mythologist. They must permit perception to consume ideology innocently, in all the sensuous and deductive pleasure such consumption demands. Why allow oneself this dangerous kind of split consciousness?[23] How else, Barthes asks, can the analyst go on to demonstrate the ways in which ideology corresponds to the general needs and interests of dominant society, to demonstrate that what appears as "natural" is in fact ideology-as-construction? Only by permitting consciousness to grasp the ideology whole (the risk is crucial) can we go on to decipher, to deconstruct, and hopefully, to "reveal" the "essential functions" of ideology (129).

To enact the methodology of the oppressed (of which I have introduced two of its technologies, semiology and deconstruction), one voluntarily focuses on the very moves of consciousness that ideology demands of its host. The practitioner feels the work of ideology on perception and consciousness, but then replays those moments in order to interrupt "the turnstile of form and meaning" by focusing on each separately—thus interrupting the formation of identity itself as it is called upon by their movement. Suddenly, the activity of ideology is no longer alive; it is "static and formal" (ibid.) in this mode of deciphering that goes against ideology's own dynamics—its own life. In Barthes's terms, this form of consuming and deconstructing ideology comprises an "archaeological" dig through meaning and consciousness that can return meaning production to "its healthy" state: that of the arbitrariness of the sign and the resulting mobility that keeps history, language, meaning, and spirit alive.

The danger here, and the paradoxical truth, is that it is also this very life of language in motion that permits ideology *its own life activity* as a parasitical invader of meaning's Signifiers, cutting them away from history and regrounding them in the satisfyingly real but phony nature of ideology. To counteract this colonization of meaning by ideology, the practitioner of the methodology of the oppressed must utilize a third technology, must pierce through the phony nature created by ideology, by moving into and through the forms and meanings of signification in a systematic excavation that leads the consuming consciousness away from a sense of meaning-as-nature, toward the connections of meaning to history...or to something else. The flexibility of consciousness required to make these transits through meaning describes the third technology that I call "differential movement (II)."

To summarize: The shift from the condition of legitimized citizen and faithful consumer of ideology to another location (to the state of what Barthes himself despaired was marginal, for here live the colonized, people of color, sex and gender deviants, the oppressed, and his "mythologist") means that one must learn to take in, decipher, and deconstruct ideology using a formal mode of analysis. One willingly perceives the image, but then, removing oneself from its system of life, its composition is revealed as a structured appropriation of previous meanings and forms: the life of dominant ideology is thus undone. Barthes thinks that only a "mythologists'" scientific training can permit the colonial image of the young saluting soldier to be understood as an invasion and robbery of his previous meanings-in-history.

Yet social life under subjugation requires the development of this very process of semiotic perception and deconstruction; it provides moments when the deformations that the dominant concept imposes on any object-as-form (black faces/white masks) become all too clearly, and painfully, apprehended, when colonized or subordinated subjects perceive dominant ideology, and understand the distortion that power is capable of imposing on any form. Under conditions of colonization, poverty, racism, gender, or sexual subordination, dominated populations are often held away from the comforts of dominant ideology, or ripped out of legitimized social narratives, in a process of power that places such constituencies in a very different position from which to view objects-in-reality than other kinds of citizen-subjects.[24] The skills they might develop, if they survive, have included the ability to self-consciously navigate modes of dominant consciousness, learning to interrupt the "turnstile" that alternately reveals history, as against the dominant forms of masquerade that history can take, "focusing on each separately," applying a "formal method of reading," cynically but also uncynically, and not only with the hope of surviving, but with a desire to create a better world. These skills, which comprise the methodology of the oppressed, are the very technologies Hegel so surely recognized in his description of the insights available to the slave, but not to the master, when he wrote that it is in the consciousness of the slave that nature and God are unlinked from whatever images are proposed as law. It is important for twenty-first-century marginalized citizen-subjects to recognize and claim Barthes's academically theorized and named procedures of semiology, and the concomitant method of ideological deconstruction, "mythology," for what they are: two recognizable technologies of resistance that have been integral to the operation of the methodology of the oppressed. Under postmodern globalization, these technologies are now part and parcel of a necessary methodology of emancipation.

Barthes's failure, was that he understood the visions, perceptions, and activities of the oppressed to lie altogether elsewhere, in a realm that is outside "cynical," "semiotic-mythological," or "dominant" modes of perception.[25] His idea (which is partially right) is that the oppressed do not *theorize* what they see as do the cynic, the semiologist, or the dominant consumer: *they act*.[26] As we shall see, however, Barthes's version of the "speech of the oppressed" becomes unilateral and monotonous in its clarity of function; for Barthes's analysis reduces, then elevates, the so-called speech of the oppressed to the realm of the "real," which strangely places this speech outside all the culturally infiltrated methods and forms of consciousness outlined so far. Although Barthes recognizes the dynamics of colonization-by-race, and indeed, goes so far as to conceptually replace the "proletariat" with the "colonized" in his analysis of contemporary cultural conditions, he somehow still is unable to fully grasp the implications for coalition of the very replacement he suggests, which would link his own methodology with the methodology of the oppressed. The formation of Barthes's own aporia, however, permits us to identify and examine another important technology of this shared methodology of emancipation.[27]

Transforming the Speech of the Oppressed into the Language of Revolution: Seven Ways to Counter Ideology

It will be useful to examine Barthes's definition and use of the category of "the oppressed." In his early mid-twentieth-century view, those who inhabited this category are the working poor, the proletariat, on any citizen-subject who functions as worker (or slave) for the dominant order's maintenance. But this kind of oppression, Barthes argues, provides its constituencies a strange form of emancipatory language, for communication among such laborers occurs at what he identifies as the "zero degree of language" (132). At this degree, language only becomes nature at the very moment that worker speaks to transform nature, writes Barthes. This kind of transformative speech thus is emancipated from ideology (145). In this fashion the "speech of the oppressed" does not engage or become second-level metalanguage—ideology—in the same way as does the speech of the dominating classes.

This is because, in Barthes's example, the consciousness of a worker who must cut down a tree is "operational." This means, Barthes writes, that the worker is "transitively linked" to her or his object: between the tree cutter and the tree, there is nothing but action. It is this transitivity—the *connection of language to object through labor*—that creates the outright and specifically political "speech of the oppressed" that is *de*-ideologized and emancipatory, according to Barthes. If, on the other hand, one should speak about a tree while "*not a woodcutter*" who intends to cut it (146), he continues, then that person is consigned to the realm of ideology, cut off from what is real. Of this second consciousness caught in ideology, Barthes writes,

> I can no longer "speak the tree," I can only speak "about it, ON it." My language is no longer the instrument of an "acted-upon-tree," it is the "tree-celebrated" which becomes the instrument of my language. I no longer have anything more but an intransitive relationship with the tree; the tree is no longer the meaning of reality as a human action, it is an *image-at-one's disposal.* Ibid.

This is the very way in which "cynical," "mythological," "dominant," or "differential" forms of consciousness work, through a kind of reverse poetics that pulls awareness *away* from the referent rather than toward it, and which, in the case of dominant consciousness especially, blurs the relationship of action to material reality. Of the tree cutter who is a member of Barthes's laboring "oppressed," he writes that the tree is not an "image-at-one's-disposal," it is simply work-as-action: language passes over image and becomes transitively linked to its object. Barthes's speech of the oppressed thus generates a language intimately tied to the referent. Indeed, this speech is not separated from the work or object that must be effected to ensure survival: it functions more like a material act itself, inextricably linked to the material world—and, here I must point out, this speech is not fully "linguistic."

In Barthes's view, this language, the "speech of the oppressed," occurs at the "zero degree" of expression, and is thus exiled from the thick, ideological portions of the rich. The oppressed "speak the truth" in as homologously innocent a fashion as Barthes's dominant and legitimized classes consume ideology: both moves are parallel, insofar as placing the oppressed in the Real, outside analytic self-consciousness, is the same as placing the dominant myth-reader in the false-real of full Ideology. (In the semiological drama it is the "cynic" and "mythologist" as deconstructor who have the most agentic roles.) The naïveté of the oppressed in relation to their ability to exchange dominant ideological forms occurs because, writes Barthes, the oppressed are "unable to throw out the real meaning of things, to give them the luxury of an empty form, open to the innocence of a false nature." Or, if speaking a lie, their deception advances "pointing to its mask," the disguise of the oppressed an obvious masquerade donned for the sake of survival. Barthes writes:

> The oppressed is nothing, he has only one language, that of his emancipation, the oppressor is everything, his language is rich, multiform, supple, with all the possible degrees of dignity at his disposal: he has an exclusive right to metalanguage. The oppressed MAKES the world, he has only an active (political) language: the oppressor conserves it, his language is plenary, intransitive, gestural, theatrical. (149)

Does Barthes's own proposed method of semiotic-mythology generate an "in-between" form of consciousness, then—a language like that of the oppressed, which is active and political, but also able to engage with and through the languages of ideology? Not so, mourns Barthes, for semiotic-mythology is neither transitive nor political in the sense of the speech of the oppressed; nor, as we shall see, does it promote the analyst's connection to the social world. Is it possible, then, that Barthes's transitive speech of the oppressed might also include idioms for speaking in and through ideology where, if images are not "at-ones'-disposal," they are at least disposable? Unfortunately, again, not in Barthes's view. His own proposition fails to see anything more than this: a two-term binary opposition with the *illusion* of freedom in dominant ideology beckoning from the one side, versus the *reality* of freedom in the zero degree of language (under oppression) on the other, with the lone, heroic mythologist, armed with semiology, making up the terms in between as he goes.

Barthes is clear about the following: the language of the dominating classes *is ideology* and *depoliticized*, where the "de" is an active prefix, referring to a complicated activity of consciousness that undergirds the operation of the social world, fixes its forms of hierarchy and power, while undoing its connections to history. This language, it must be understood, aims at "eternalizing" the hierarchies of the dominant order. On the other side, Barthes writes, the language of the oppressed aims at "transforming" all it speaks (ibid.). The transformation of being effected through the speech of the oppressed is useless in the realm of ideology in all cases but one: the disruptive "language of revolution" (146).

We know that, in Barthes's formula, whenever humans are oppressed, acting as "producers," workers, or slaves to the dominant order, or, better put, whenever we speak in order to *transform reality* and no longer to preserve it as an image, wherever language is linked to the making of things and no longer naturalizing them, ideology becomes impossible. A *pure language of revolution*, Barthes argues, cannot be ideologized, then, if revolution is defined as "a cathartic act meant to reveal the political load of the world: it *makes the world*" (ibid.), in a fashion homologous to the way in which the speech of the oppressed is an act that "makes the world." While dominant classes hide the structures that ensure their domination—even from themselves—thereby producing ideology, Barthes asserts, the speech of the oppressed "announces itself openly," as must revolutionary language, thereby abolishing the blinding life of ideology (ibid.). It is this language of revolution Barthes hopes for but cannot reach, for it is allied to the "speech of the oppressed," and thus outside "cynical," "semiological," or "dominant" forms of speech. The speech of the oppressed thus can become fully linguistic only when it is lifted up into becoming a "language of revolution."

To summarize: I have identified so far six ways to counter the effects of dominant forms-as-ideology. The first is Barthes's "zero degree" of language, that is, the ability to speak outside the terms of ideology, as does the tree cutter whose speech is transitively linked to its object, in a process Barthes identifies as the "speech of the oppressed." The second is the language of "revolution," which is, as we have seen, also transitive, insofar as it is immediately linked to the simultaneous destruction and remaking of the world, spoken to "transform reality and no longer to preserve it as an image." A third is the method of semiotic-mythology, which works by reading the signs of power, and then self-consciously deconstructing them, through interrupting "the turnstile of form and meaning" that makes up dominant ideology, thereby releasing signification once again to its creative, "arbitrary" state. The fourth and fifth forms would be "antilanguages" in Barthes's vocabulary: silence as a form of resistance refuses to engage ideology at all, he writes, while "contemporary poetry" desires to reach back through the sign itself to find the "meaning of things" beyond their inscription in language. Poetry, according to Barthes, yearns for a "pre-semiological" state and reaches toward this place by "stretching" the link between Signifier and Signified until meanings diffuse, and "something like the transcendent quality" of the object, "its natural, (not human) meaning" begins to shimmer through the veil of human language (133).

Yet, none of these potentially oppositional languages, or anti-languages, writes Barthes, can counter the weight of dominant ideological signification as well as can one last intervention, another kind of language, or technology of resistance; and here is where it becomes possible to identify yet another technology of the methodology of the oppressed, "meta-ideologizing." This challenge to dominant cultural forms best occurs, writes Barthes, not by speaking *outside* their terms, as in his own version of the "speech of the oppressed," nor through manifestly setting new terms linked to the real, as in "revolutionary speech," but through the *ideologization of ideology* itself. This is what happens, Barthes insists, when revolutionary language "accepts [that] to wear a mask, to hide its name, to distance itself into a Nature," is necessary in order to advance its cause (146–47). This revolutionary strategy, what Barthes calls "exnomination" (which, he writes, "may or may not be tactical"), comprises yet another resistant language that functions both within and against ideology. It comprises another technology of the oppressed (or, perhaps we should specify another name, for this is in effect a technology for emancipation) that works by grafting a *third level* ideological system onto a dominant second-level system, and by using this resignification process as a tactic for challenging the dominant order of power (see Figure 6). Barthes explains: "Truth to tell, the best weapon against" ideology is to ideologize it in its turn, and to produce an "*artificial*" ideology. Because ideology "robs" one of something, why not rob ideology? "All that is needed is to use it as the departure point for a third semiological chain, to take its signification" as the first term of a second-level ideology (135). This self-conscious production of another level of signification parasitically based on the level of dominant ideology serves to either display the original dominant ideology as naive—and no longer natural—or to reveal, transform, or disempower its signification in some

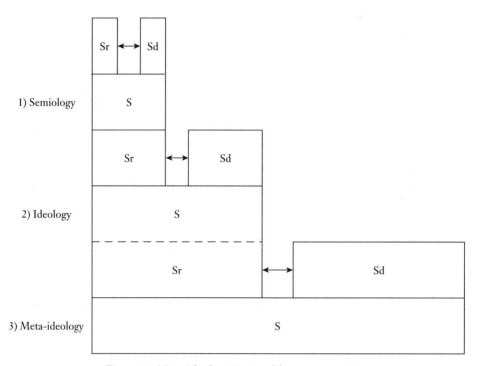

Figure 6. Meta-ideologizing is a liberatory practice.

other way. In opposition to Barthes's view, insofar as one is acting from a new, third, and self-consciously constructed system in order to transform the second level of dominant order, the practitioner of this kind of technology of what I have called until now the "methodology of the oppressed" is engaging in an emancipatory, or revolutionary, activity, which is like the "real work" of Barthes's oppressed, for the practice of this technology is *transitively* linked to the order of meaning that one intends to change.

The Methodology of ~~the Oppressed~~ Emancipation: Semiology, Deconstruction, Meta-Ideologizing, Differential Movement II, and the Ethical Technology: Democratics

The work of (1) "semiology" for reading the signs of power, concomitant with (2) the "mythology" used to *deconstruct* those sign-systems, while (3) creating new, "higher" levels of signification built onto the older, dominant forms of ideology in a radical process I call "meta-ideologizing" are three emancipatory technologies capable of restoring consciousness to history. This manipulation of one's own consciousness through stratified zones of form and meaning requires the desire and the ability to move through one layer of Sr/Sd/Sign relationship and into another, "artificial," or self-consciously manufactured ideology and back again, movement that is (4) differential. Indeed, it is this differential movement that comprises the fourth technology in resistance of the methodology of the oppressed (it is this differential movement, as I demonstrated in the example of women's liberation, that allows consciousness to challenge its own perimeters from within ideology). At the juncture where the technologies of "semiology" and "deconstruction" link with "meta-ideologizing," the differential technology of methodology of the oppressed becomes unavoidable; for it is through differential movement that the third technology, meta-ideologizing as political intervention, is made possible, insofar as meta-ideologizing depends on what I have called "flexibility"—of perception, consciousness, identity, and tactics in relation to power. Meta-ideologizing is the third technology of oppositional powers that moves in, through, then outside of dominant ideology. It is the strategy where Barthes's method of semiotic-mythology manifestly links with the methodology of the oppressed as its technologies move, differentially, toward survival of the people.[28]

Indeed, I can now fully propose that both technologies, meta-ideologizing and differential movement, are transitive in nature (in the "revolutionary" manner Barthes admired, but was not able to discern in his own semiology/mythology): practitioners enact any position only insofar as they are ultimately hoping to transform both the position they hold and the reality it acts upon. The differentially enacted process of meta-ideologizing functions at its best not necessarily where there is revolution, but rather where there is activity that seeks egalitarian relationships. Both technologies, meta-ideologizing and differential movement, are, in Barthes's terms, suited to "wear a mask, to hide" their names, "to generate an innocent metalanguage," and to distort themselves into a "phony nature" that, understood through the guiding force of the methodology of the oppressed, is always tactical (146). Self-consciously organized as an oppositional political activity, this kind of "revolutionary ex-nomination," however, is embarked upon in order to bring about revolutionary movement, the repoliticizing of language—the reconnection of language to action. Insofar as these technologies are born out of oppression of every sort, they, like Barthes's "speech of the oppressed" when it tries to speak in ideology, always tend toward producing what Barthes calls "artificial" ideologies. But, unlike Barthes's speech of the oppressed, this artificial ideologizing is not accomplished naively.

Indeed, the methodology of the oppressed and its technologies of resistance are constantly reorganized to self-consciously reappropriate and reapportion ideology, and in doing so, they serve to make the languages of emancipation more subtle, more rich, multiple, supple, and flexible, with "all possible degrees of dignity" at their disposal. This reappropriation of ideology insists on the ability of consciousness to meta-ideologize, to move in, through, and outside of dominant ideology through the technology of differential movement. Under the methodology of the oppressed, the flexible, improvisational, "differential" technology of consciousness permits the technologies of "semiotic reading," "deconstruction," and "meta-ideologizing" to occur as powers of reapportionment and of boundary change.[29] But these four technologies join with a fifth that guides them, and this is (5) an *ethical* ideological code that is committed to social justice according to egalitarian redistributions of power across such differences coded as race, gender, sex, nation, culture, or class distinctions. Whether the effort is to *semiotically* take in meanings, to transform those meanings through *deconstruction* or *meta-ideologization*, to reform them under an ethically *democratic imperative*, or whether, Barthes adds, the effort is to poeticize, to try to force "the sign back into meaning . . . to reach not the meaning of words but the meaning of things themselves" in their presemiological state (133), all of these movements through consciousness and through the social order depend on the technology of *differential movement*.

Our insistent recognition of the differential movement of consciousness demanded by meta-ideologizing as praxis—indeed, demanded by all the technologies of the methodology of the oppressed—creates a trope in Barthes's work, a turn that opens into the lacuna wherein "semiology," "deconstruction," "meta-ideologizing," "differential movement," "democratics," indeed, all the technologies that comprise the methodology of the oppressed, appear only to disappear from history, becoming the theoretically repressed forces that nevertheless guided the social movements of the 1960s, 1970s, and 1980s, as we have seen through their expression within the U.S. women's movement of that period. These technologies are what drove the movement through its various historical phases (the liberal, revolutionary, supremacist, separatist, and differential modes) and what positioned each phase in relation to power. Barthes's scholarly work on emancipatory forms of consciousness dropped out of social-movement history and theory at the moment his work failed to actualize its links with the methodology of the oppressed, thus abandoning contemporary theorists of social movement, from historical to social sciences, from ethnic studies to feminist theory, engaged in a process of rediscovery and renaming these technologies of oppositional powers, over and over again.

Barthes's scholarship crosses disciplinary borders. Indeed, we have seen how, disobeying the rules of authority and power that divide knowledge into academically separated categories, Barthes's commitment to the reality of freedom, and for all peoples (as opposed to the illusion of freedom in dominant ideology), allowed him to generate a theory of semiotics-as-weapon for emancipating consciousness—for decolonizing the imagination. But the range of his 1957 sedition against dominant authority was limited by his own personal commitment to that very authority. Barthes's three modes for perceiving and decoding dominant ideology—that of the "cynic," the "mythologist," the "dominant perceiver" of ideology—and that of "the oppressed," are a schema in which a coalitional form of consciousness among dominant citizen-subjects committed to the equal distribution of power, and those who have occupied outsider status, is made thinkable—and yet remains unthought. Barthes's control over naming and defining was that of a scholar, while his authority over the material rose from his position as renegade and outsider. Yet Barthes's territorial range of control ended at the location where his semiotic theory of resistance should have met in coalition with those theories of resistance that have been generated by oppressed and colonized peoples. Unable to negotiate that leap, Barthes constructed instead a view of semiotics, of "mythology," and of resistance where the individual practitioner can only act alone, isolated, and in despair. The border-crosser Barthes was not able to recognize the new kinds of warriors, the shape-shifters who comprised his allies in resistance.[30] Ironically, it was Barthes's very jurisdiction over interpreting and applying semiology or mythology to academic speech that limited his ability to recognize the possibilities of this coalitional consciousness. Instead, Barthes saw himself as discoverer of a new terrain that was, as yet, unpeopled.[31]

The fact is that by 1957, decolonization was simultaneously revealing and producing these technologies of oppositional consciousness across divisions of nation, race, ethnicity, sex, and gender. The irony represented in Barthes's work is that in it we can see the West coming to unconsciously assimilate that which it sought to annihilate, the methodology of the oppressed.[32] The encounter between Barthes's academic method and the methodology of the oppressed, made possible through Barthes's identification of "semiology/mythology," is of a very special type: the intellectual colonization and conquest of a methodology of subordinated peoples. If Barthes is right in saying that ideology cannibalizes forms of being, it does so in the same way that dominant societies have cannibalized the conquered.

Chapter 1 reviewed Jameson's argument that, in order to generate a "new cognitive map," we need new inner/psychic and outer/social technologies capable of locating ourselves within postmodern globalizing cultural conditions. In chapter 4, I have charted five technologies necessary for this new cartography. To summarize: the first technology is the semiotic perception of objects-in-culture as signs of power to be taken in, read, and interpreted. The second is the method for the decolonization of meaning through its deconstruction, what Barthes calls mythology. The third, "meta-ideologizing," like the previous two, requires *differential movement* for its existence, first in the movement through perception demanded by the "inner" technology of semiology, and then in the "outer" and differential movement of identity itself through social order in the effort to effect change. This last movement through the social order requires the utilization of meta-ideologizing, which, insofar as it depends on a differential enactment of consciousness, is the technology that unavoidably links Barthes's work with the methodology of the oppressed. Under the recognition of meta-ideologizing as a technology, poetry, silence, and all other technologies of resistance can be viewed as ideological weaponry. Each is reformatted as other possible techniques of resistance useful under postmodern cultural conditions, where Sr's are detached from Sd's, unsettling stable identity, indeed, making stable identity itself only one other mode of tactical response to the circulation of powers. The formation and use of these ideological weapons depend on the semiotic reading and deconstruction of power through signs, utilizing the differential ability to cruise, cross, intersect, shift, and "low ride" between such signs. These skills generate ever-new meta-ideological formations for the purpose not only of survival, as under previous utilizations by the oppressed, but of bringing about new ethical and political standards in the name of egalitarian and democratic social change: the technology of "democratics." Together, these five technologies comprise the apparatus that is the methodology of the oppressed, the methodology on which, I have argued, the oppositional mode of social movement theory and method I call the "differential" depends.

Resistant or oppositional activity, whether effective or ineffective, may not be linked to a moral or ethical aim. The technology of "democratics" is the purposive guiding strategy that is interested in challenging the institutionalization of dominant ideology, and the forms of social and psychological inequity it naturalizes. This technology permits, drives, and organizes the methodology of the oppressed: it is the moral and ethical commitment to enact any of its technologies with the aim of equalizing power between humans. This last aim, and technology, though not theorized by Barthes, is fully enacted by him, especially in his highly self-critical reading of Western forms of white European and colonizer consciousness, which is what we examine in the following chapter.

F   I   V   E

The Rhetoric of Supremacism as Revealed by the Ethical Technology: Democratics

Institutionalized rejection of difference is an absolute necessity in a profit economy which needs outsiders as surplus people. As members of such an economy, we have all been programmed to respond to the human differences between us with fear and loathing and to handle that difference in one of three ways: ignore it, and if that is not possible, copy it if we think it is dominant, or destroy it if we think it is subordinate. But we have no patterns for relating across our human differences as equals. As a result those differences have been misnamed and misused in the service of separation and confusion.

Audre Lorde

We must strive to "lift as we climb." . . . We must climb in such as way as to guarantee that all our sisters, regardless of social class, and indeed all of our brothers climb with us. This must be the essential dynamic of our quest for power.

Angela Davis

ANOTHER ENTRANCE to the methodology of the oppressed is provided by way of an investigation of the language of supremacy. In *Black Skin, White Masks*, Fanon ruthlessly outlined the forms of colonial consciousness encouraged in peoples of color who live under white supremacist rule. Seven years later, Barthes matched Fanon's effort, giving us a list of the primary ideological forms that structure consciousness for members of Euro-white colonizer classes. Barthes's account attempts to answer the question of how "innocent, well-intentioned citizens" can end up enacting the racism of a domineering class. The answers he provides are in the form of an inventory of the psychosocial forms around which consciousness is constituted as "white," Western, middle-class, but above all else, supremacist. My argument is that Barthes's inventory establishes and constitutes a *rhetoric of supremacy* that is comprised of seven "figures" or "poses" for the performance and dispersal of a legitimized human consciousness. When enacted by their practitioners, these poses are experienced as natural, normal, and neutral categories of being. Indeed, each pose for consciousness calls up possibilities and prohibitions for thought and behavior that typify the "good citizen-subject," one who is capable of functioning well under the imperatives of nationalist state formation. The danger of this rhetoric and its categories for behavior is that it encourages the development of authoritarianism, domination, suprema- cism — and even fascism — in its practitioners. At the same time, this rhetoric con- structs the most seemingly innocuous forms of personal and everyday life — of sub- jectivity, of citizenship itself.

In Barthes's analysis, Western consciousness disperses around seven principle poses, or figures, which he names after the processes of politics and identity they encourage. These are "the inoculation," "the privation of history," "iden- tification" ("exoticism" is a subset of identification), "tautology," "neither-norism," "the quantification of quality," and "the statement of fact." These categories consti- tute rhetorical figures, that is, they constitute a "set of fixed, regulated, insistent fig- ures" around which ideological-Signifiers (Sr's) become arranged in order to generate "reality" (150). Individual citizen-subjects relate differently to these rhetorical fig- ures, for the figures are themselves forms, and "each of us can fill in" a specific form according to our own particular nation, race, ethnic, sex, gender, or class inflections (ibid.). Yet what must be realized over any variation in content is that these seven forms generate a structure, a rhetoric for being that orders and regulates Western social space and consciousness. It is this rhetoric that animates the great ideological perversions, especially those that invite citizen-subjects to faultlessly consume ide- ology, and to guilelessly reproduce "depoliticized" and supremacist forms of speech, consciousness, morality, values, law, family life, and personal relations.

Barthes utilized the technologies outlined in chapter 4 in order to decipher and deconstruct certain objects in Western culture. Semiotic methodology, he asserts, is what allowed him to identify the seven figures identified in this chapter as the categorical poses within which the white middle classes of the 1950s disposed themselves in order to draw up, arrange, maintain, and regenerate a meaningful life in culture. What becomes called up and naturalized as the real, as history itself in this arrangement, is, to Barthes's horror, however, a "dream": the dream of the contemporary Euro-American world. Most striking about Barthes's figures is that they call up a consciousness capable of supremacy, regardless of the basis on which such supremacy arises, whether it be race, gender, culture, class, sex, nation, or a combination of these. Barthes's discovery of these seven poses is no small feat. In what follows, the lingering questions are, Why has this portion of Barthes's work been elided by contemporary cultural critics who also are concerned with discovering such "poses" themselves? Why have Barthes's fundamental contributions to anticolonial resistance, and to a quite contemporary and utopian postcolonial theory, and particularly his work on the rhetoric of white consciousness, been elided in contemporary cultural, critical, and literary theory, even by those scholars who are also concerned with identifying such "poses" for consciousness? The following analysis is positioned to answer these questions.[1]

The Rhetorical Figures

Each "figure" or pose for consciousness in the rhetoric that follows is easily recognizable; it emerges in every population. What hails this rhetoric into the real is difference. Paradoxically, however, once enacted, each figure becomes a machine—a deputy for the real that works to erase difference. Even at the beginning of the twenty-first century, the following figures are called on to tempt, inhabit, and shape not only the most obedient and deserving citizen-subject, but also the most rebellious agent of social change.

The Inoculation

The first figure in this rhetoric for being is fundamental to the maintenance of dominant identity. It is through the figure Barthes calls inoculation that consciousness surrounds, limits, and protects itself against invasion by difference. The inoculation works homeopathically: it provides cautious injections—in modest doses only—of dissimilarity (the affirmative-action approach). The outcome is that, by incorporating a small, tidy portion of difference, the good citizen-subject does not have to accept its depth or enormity, and thus s/he can remain as is. That is why middle-class citizen-subjects often can display an admirable tolerance for difference. But such "tolerance," Barthes notes, is only a medium for controlling its final impact, for through the figure of inoculation difference can be recognized, taken in, tamed, and domesticated. Inoculation is a form of consciousness that keeps its practitioners safe yet stimulated, for difference is treated as a controlled substance. It can be enjoyed in small doses, but always under conditions of moderation and restraint.

But inoculation is not only capable of immunizing individual consciousness, warns Barthes. Its force extends to immunize "the collective imagination" as well. For example, the inoculating figure can encourage the general recognition of "the accidental evil of a class-bound institution"—but only so that "its principal evil," that of class hierarchy itself, can be concealed (150). This figure, pose, or habit of consciousness thus protects not only the psyche, Barthes writes, but culture as well against any threatening difference that can cause the "generalized subversion" of what is. Inoculation performs as a preventative, securely buffering consciousness; it provides a sanitary precaution against the contamination of the same by difference.

The Privation of History
The second figure of this rhetoric works by distancing all objects in culture from the material history of what has made them what they are, an estrangement that deprives (Western) consciousness of any responsibility for what has and will become. The tragedy for the good citizen-subject is that this estrangement also creates a peculiar kind of passivity in consciousness. This is because "the privation of history" serves its populations as a kind of "ideal servant," Barthes warns: "it prepares all things, brings them, lays them out, the master arrives, it silently disappears: all that is left for one to do is to enjoy this beautiful object without wondering where it comes from." What happens, worries Barthes, to the colonizing and white consciousness after it accepts and submits to this work of ideology, this estrangement and privation of history, this luxury at a price? His answer is that this rhetoric of supremacy colonizes the colonizer's consciousness as well.

This figure that deprives us of history is "felicitous," Barthes writes; it provides us a happy but ignorant pose. His example is of a tour book designed to guide the first world consumer through third world countries by providing photos of exotic "primitives" preparing dances, food, clothing, and so on, seemingly for the camera's pleasure. In these photos, the intricate and profound differences (in both historical trajectories and present conditions) of the peoples depicted dissolve under their primary appearance as festive objects for Western consumption as entertainment. The privation of history thus inoculates consciousness—it procures a little tantalizing difference—but not too much; it protects and tames the colonizer's imagination as viewer. This pose for consciousness thus blithely turns its practitioners away from the very production of contemporary and past histories. But this ignorance also alienates citizen-subjects from recognizing their abilities to intervene in that which ever rages: the possibility of directing individual and social destinies. Instead, under the imperatives of this figure, all the participating citizen-subject must do is perceive, reach out, and "possess" any new object "from which all soiling trace of origin and choice" has been removed" (151). This "miraculous evaporation" of history covers the world with pleasurable magic, writes Barthes, and is thus one of the most determining figures in the rhetoric of supremacy, even as it seduces, shapes, and (neo)colonizes most middle-class forms of consciousness (ibid.).

Identification

When enacting this third pose, which Barthes calls identification, consciousness draws itself up, comforts itself, and identifies itself (or, as Fanon writes, constitutes itself as "human") through a comparing and weighing operation that seeks to equate all differences with itself—the better to either brush differences aside as unimportant or to assimilate them. This figure generates a colonizing consciousness incapable of viewing actual differences in others, for everything is recognized only as the self—but in other guises. Locations where "the Other threatens to appear in full view," Barthes warns, such as the "spectacle" or the "courthouse," are transformed through this figure into mirrors in which the good citizen-subject can see refracted only other versions of itself—though gone astray. Should the good citizen-subject inadvertently find itself face-to-face with what is sublimely and horifically other, Barthes predicts one of the four following responses: citizen-subjects will (1) blind themselves, (2) ignore the differences, (3) deny the other, or (4) transform the other into themselves (152). Possibilities for confrontation are thus undone and sabotaged, while perceptions of difference are reduced to sameness. At best, under the imperatives of the first world cultural order that Barthes inhabits, the other is recognized as a deceptive snare, a lure threatening to ambush with its duplicity the sense of self on which the citizen-subject secures its own forms of humanity. Barthes warns that from the point of view that becomes dominating in any culture, what is truly "other" becomes perceived as "a scandal which threatens" the very essence of one's being when, under the rhetorical pose of identification, that being has become supremacist in function.

There are emergency conditions when the other cannot help but appear in all its sublime dissimilarity, warns Barthes. In such emergency conditions, another figure related to identification can comfort and save dominant forms of subjectivity from the horror of confronting the abyss of absolute difference. Identification extends to a dependable emergency figure known as "exoticism," where the exoticized other can be perceived as pure (sex) "object," "spectacle," or "clown." Difference is then safely relegated to the limits of humanity and can no longer threaten "the security of the home" (ibid.).

The three figures of the rhetoric so far listed would permit the citizen-subject to situate and "identify" itself as living at the center and best of all that yet is. The "privation of history" extracts the colonizing consciousness from the imperatives of any history that might say differently. And the citizen-subject can be painlessly, effectively, and pleasurably "inoculated" against incorporating any unlikeness that might transform or subvert what is. Hope and faith draw the converted to inhabit and live out these figures—they provide entry to the first world promised land for Barthes, a 1950s Camelot of consciousness.

Tautology

Barthes's list continues with "tautology," a term for the metaphoric device that defines like by like. Tautology activates the previous three figures insofar as each operates by defining the dominant tautologically: what is other is only itself, but in other forms. Tautological reasoning enables citizen-subjects to believe that Western knowledge can be understood and justified as such: "History is history," "Truth is truth," and even "That's just the way it is—that's all." Tautology operates behind a badge of authority, where its rationality is hidden. The favorite (tautological) answer to anyone who questions that authority is: "Because I said so, that's why!" This figure of supremacy works like a magic act, Barthes thinks. The magic it produces? A "dead, motionless" world (153). This redundant, superficial figure depends for its influence on power itself,[2] which it uses to freeze meaning into place, thereby protecting and legitimizing what is. Any citizen-subject in a state of crisis can turn to tautology for protection. It acts as a stopgap. Is one speechless? Powerless? At a loss? In need of a quick answer or explanation for what is? Then take refuge in tautology, Barthes recommends, in the same way one takes refuge in fear, anger, or sadness.

Neither-Norism

Neither-norism is the pose that enables the citizen-subject to develop an independent "neutrality" or "objectivity" in behavior. Neither-norism generates the kind of noncommitted, detached, moderate, and nonextreme mode of being that is so highly valued in the West. In Barthes's estimation, this pose is exemplified by the phrase "I want *neither* this *nor* that" (153).[3] Here the citizen-subject is encouraged to reduce reality to two or more formal opposites, and each side is relieved of its historically produced differences. This activity provokes a "final equilibrium" for being that immobilizes "values, life, and destiny," Barthes writes. Although differences are registered, they are dismissed or ignored, so that the "rational" performer of neither-norism no longer has to choose between contending power-laden realities; s/he only has to to endorse what already is (108). To choose between contending realities would mean that one has judged the hierarchies determining what already is to be intolerable, states Barthes. But, under the influence of neither-norism, the citizen-subject can appear to take a "higher" moral ground by making no commitment to any alternative direction at all. This apparent neutrality, "objectivity," and levelheadedness creates an inflexibility of being that supports the order of the dominant rather than that of some other moral, or political, order.

The Quantification of Quality

To utilize the sixth figure in Barthes's rhetoric of supremacy would mean to value all images—indeed, reality itself—according to the quantity of effects they produce. The more, the better: more tears, increased emotion, added travel, hyperexperience, accumulated commodities, heaps of money, amassing collections, dwellings, books, knowledge—the measure is never finally enough. Hyperaccrual, more flamboyant effects are felt to equal the measure, degree, depth, and magnitude of meaning in life. A search for increase becomes connected to the search for a higher, better, more noble existence. In these efforts to motivate life, the *inexpressible goodness of quality* is reduced to quantity. For Barthes, this valuing of quality through the quantity of effects produced is a social and psychological dynamic not well analyzed in the university; for "the quantification of quality," quality disguised as quantity, economizes scholarly intelligence itself, and academic knowledge has come to "understand reality more cheaply" (ibid.).[4]

The Statement of Fact

This final rhetorical figure supports all those that came before. Under "the statement of fact" the citizen-subject is encouraged to speak and know with certainty, is trained to assert its own reality as if there were no other. Barthes explains that this performance operates through two central devices: the aphorism and the maxim. These conservative forms of speech stand in resistance to a radical way of speaking and knowing with certainty: the proverb, which, unlike the others, allows people to express the "revolutionary truth" of knowledge and power (154).

What distinguishes the proverb and bestows this radical possibility is the experimental and active engagement that it fashions between its speaker and some aspect of everyday life. Enacting its meaning as it is spoken, the proverb is transitively completed only by human encounter with the world. Insofar as the proverb expresses and demands human engagement with its surroundings, Barthes stresses that it represents a form of emancipatory speech, as opposed to the ideologically circumscribed forms of speech generated by the six figures defined above. Barthes's example of proverbial speech in action is the statement "The weather is fine." When spoken by a hopeful farmer concerned with the crops, this statement is not meant to direct others how to view or feel about the weather. Rather, it is meant to be a "technological statement," meaning that farmers must draw today's weather into their farming labor every hour, through speech, in order to successfully farm and cultivate their crops and livestock. This kind of technological statement represents the innovative side of the proverb, which sends forth speech as (uncompleted) action—the results of which are hoped for, but still unknown.

The innovative activity of a technological statement such as this differs profoundly from the activity produced by the other ways of knowing and speaking with certainty, the aphorism and the maxim. The aphorism is language gathered up with the express purpose of dividing and marking off boundaries and horizons of being: it is a speech act devised to make reality "hold." The essence and power of the aphorism are expressed fully, however, only when extended to become a transfigured but allied speech act called the "maxim." The maxim is the language device that asserts the greatest authority insofar as its meanings appear to rise out of some fundamental kind of philosophical or religious premise. Together, the aphorism and the maxim are tools for communication that support the ideological pose of the speaker who "knows for sure." The costs of this form of knowledge and its powers are high, for the statement of fact is "no longer directed towards a world to be made; it must overlay one which is already made, bury the traces of this production under a self-evident appearance of eternity: it is a counter-explanation, the decorous equivalent of a *tautology*, of this preemptory *because* which parents in need of knowledge hang above the heads of their children" (155).

The statement of fact is a form of authority supported by the structure of the dominant social order, but its confidence and knowledge are not spoken, heard, or experienced by its users as socially constructed, but as rising out of the nature of how things are and should be. Thus, this figure for knowing and power creates a peculiar certainty of being felt by its practitioners to be only the honest, straightforward expression of what is — of common sense. The term *common sense* as used here should be defined, Barthes points out, as "truth when it stops on the arbitrary order of him who speaks it" (153). This is why the statement of fact and its devices, the aphorism and maxim, wielded as though they are the most innocuous, innocent, and straightforward containers for common sense, contain all the force of supremacism. The powers of this form imbue and empower each of the previous six forms of colonial ideology outlined so far: the inoculation, which takes in quite small, controlled portions of difference, the better to assert essential truths; the privation of history and neither-norism, both of which entertain and solidify the self and social reality by overlooking specific situated histories (reality is already well under control!); identification, through which all differences can appear only as varying or deviant units of oneself; tautology, in which all knowledge necessary for living is circuited through some authoritative and centralizing power; and the quantification of quality, wherein differences are counted, added up, cataloged, and hierarchically displayed in order to demonstrate the depth and quality of existence as it already is.

Together, these seven figures comprise Barthes's 1957 postulation for a rhetoric that catalogs the poses for inhabiting white consciousness in its colonizing mode. This rhetoric circulates in innocuous yet, I have argued, supremacist modes. Barthes's warning is that this rhetoric of supremacism installs a phony nature as the real, and prohibits humans from "inventing" themselves (155). This prohibition is central to the damages of Western ideological formation, he thinks, and to any imperialist, racist, and colonial project, for the rhetoric of supremacism will not "rest until it has obscured the ceaseless making of the world, fixated this world into an object which can be forever possessed, catalogued its riches, embalmed it, and injected into reality some purifying essence which will stop its transformation, its flight towards other forms of existence" (ibid.).

The seven figures of this rhetoric of supremacy immobilize the world by nurturing and constructing a consciousness and culture that long for "a universal order" that can fixate "once and for all the hierarchy of possessions," of selfhood, of passion, of being (ibid.). This order is computed until dominant morality becomes "a weighing operation," writes Barthes. All socially constructed forms and essences are "placed in scales," and the successful, middle-class, colonizing citizen-subject in its illusion of power becomes "the motionless beam." The final computation of the rhetoric of supremacism freezes the world, for essentializing and weighing processes incapacitate difference and the unknown…so that after all is said and done, the dominant arrives at what is the same.

Fanon's earlier work had been written to point out "the various attitudes that the Negro adopts in contact with white civilization," whereas Barthes's own self-study of colonial psychology as it is effected in dominant consciousness reveals the horrifying effects of racism and colonialism on the perpetrators themselves (12). Indeed, Barthes's rhetorical forms of consciousness-in-ideology comprise an exposé of the forms of consciousness produced through the demands of a particular economic, political, and cultural order, and coalesce into what can be considered the psychopathology of Western culture. These possibilities for identity have their pleasures and their comforts; that is why they are enlisted, though they are supremacist exchanges of power. Moreover, to undermine the constitution of this rhetoric, as Barthes well knew, is also to challenge any final hope for an integrated, whole self capable of warding off the polluting effects of such differences as color, race, gender, sex, or nation. The expectation of writers such as Fanon and Barthes was that a different kind of society might emerge capable of dividing up and figuring consciousness differently than this rhetoric is able to, and thereby generating the possibility for new collective and political subjects.

Barthes's *Mythologies* represents one of the first efforts to critique and outline "white" forms of consciousness by a member of the colonizing class responding to the decolonizing processes going on at the time he was writing. His was the first critique of white consciousness to emerge from the imperatives of what was fast becoming a post-empire history.[5] In this sense, Barthes's early work can be seen as equivalent to the work on "white consciousness" accomplished, forty years later, most powerfully in work generated out of the volatile relations between the white and U.S. women of color feminisms of the 1960s, 1970s, and 1980s by thinkers such as Ruth Frankenberg, Vron Ware, Bernice Johnson Reagon, bell hooks, and Cherríe Moraga.[6] But investigations of "white" forms of consciousness are also being generated by other scholars of culture in disciplines ranging from biology, anthropology, and sociology to ethnic studies, cultural studies, and postmodernism. Thinkers from every vantage point are interested in the attempt to graph the various subject positions that are unconsciously structured—categories of psychosocial formation that comprise Barthes's "poses" (or "masks," as Fanon earlier called them), that embody supremacist forms of consciousness. Strangely, Barthes's attempt to theorize the structure of colonial and "middle-class" consciousness has been taken up by few contemporary theorists of culture. And this is so despite Barthes's reliance on a quite contemporary and de-colonial cultural criticism.

In finding the dominant social rhetoric that functions in the mode of a language, the poses for subjectivity available to dominating classes, Barthes hoped to undo the effects of being a citizen-subject in Euro-American culture, to undermine the subject positions of legitimate, middle-class citizens, to cite these poses, and their languages as comfortable masquerades for identity. Barthes's despair was that the innocent usage, consumption, acceptance, or production of these rhetorical figures consigned citizen-subjects to generating and accepting a multileveled, profound alienation-in-consciousness as a natural state of being. Barthes's pain over the recognition of this profound alienation as it determined psychic and social life brought him face-to-face with the languages and idioms of survival spoken by colonized peoples, and into contact with the methodology of the oppressed, which he at once affirms and asserts while blinding himself to its ongoing practices and practitioners. I am suggesting that the erasure from academic scholarship of Barthes's important contributions on the topic of supremacist and/or white consciousness is in part due to his own simultaneous recognition and repression of the methodology of the oppressed, a methodology that had been accounted for seven years earlier by Frantz Fanon.

Frantz Fanon before Roland Barthes:

Changing the Supremacist Mind

Long before Barthes methodically encoded semiology in "Myth Today," and conceived of listing the rhetorical figures that organize Western consciousness, Frantz Fanon had already mapped out the methodology of the oppressed. One result was that Fanon was able to identify his own version of the rhetoric of supremacy by which dominant cultures and consciousness were guided. Fanon's own map of this rhetoric of supremacy is based on the following (semiotic) assertion: "every dialect spoken," he begins, whether uttered by the "white man" or by the "oppressed," represents a specific "way of thinking" (25). He continues by arguing that most dominant ways of thinking are not developed with any "intention" to hurt or anger the subordinated. Yet (using language that parallels Barthes's), Fanon writes that "it is just this *absence* of wish, this lack of interest, this indifference, this automatic manner" of "classifying," "imprisoning," and "primitivizing" that injures both colonized and colonizer (32); for the structure of dominant speech stubbornly "fastens" those who are different to an "effigy" of themselves, "snaring" and "imprisoning" them in a dream, where they become "eternal victims" of an "essence" for which they are not responsible (35). The rhetoric of supremacy thus damages and enslaves the colonizer as well as the colonized, Fanon asserts, for the good citizen-subject is allowed entrance to dominant society, which in return provides rigidification "in predetermined forms, forbidding all evolution, all gains, all progress, all discovery" of difference (224). Legitimized citizen-subjects of dominant society, he warns, those "allowed to assume the attitude of a master," thus become unwitting "slaves" to an invisible, naturalized process of "cultural imposition" (117).

A society that freezes social hierarchy into place is a society in which equality and justice between humans are impossible to achieve, Fanon believes. Further, "justice" in a society that naturalizes hierarchy through domination is always constructed in a fashion that serves the needs of the dominating order. From time to time, writes Fanon, colonized peoples of color have been asked by members of a white colonizing class to fight for "Liberty and Justice, but these were always white liberty and white justice"—not liberty and justice for all. Such differences must be recognized, Fanon asserts, and dominant reality identified as comprised of specific "values secreted" by good citizen-subjects who are trying to live according to the meanings of a larger, dominating order. This is why, Fanon explains, former slaves watch "unmoved before" young white men who "sing and dance on the tightrope of existence" as they yearn for the forms of liberty and justice designed within the dominant cultural matrix (221). Their versions of liberty and justice, Fanon insists, are not the same as those that must be fought for by subordinated and revolutionary peoples.

Revolutionary liberty and justice, in the views of both Fanon and Barthes, are difficult to imagine for citizen-subjects shaped by the social and psychic categories of a (nation/class/sex/gender/race) colonizing state, for this state generates in consciousness an innocuous and everyday craving for supremacy. Although such cravings and their resultant knowledges and powers are "cultural, which means acquired," Fanon writes—and thus transformable—the colonizing mind becomes satisfied by what is, and senses supremacy as only a natural pose for being. How does one go about resisting this dominant rhetoric of supremacy and its forms of cultural imposition, thus making individual and social transformation possible? Fanon starts this way: "White society" (which is "based on myths of progress, civilization, liberalism, education, enlightenment, refinement") can be transformed precisely by forces, skills, methods, and techniques developed to oppose "the expansion and the triumph" of Western colonial ideologies, for these are tainted with supremacy (194). If such oppositional forces do not mobilize, Fanon warns, then the rhetoric of supremacy, its signs and meanings, "the movements, the attitudes, the glances" of the legitimized citizen-subject will assign and "fix" those who are different, the world, as well as the dominant citizen-subject practitioner itself, immobilize them all in "the sense in which a chemical solution is fixed by a dye" (109). This is the danger of the rhetoric of supremacism, write both Fanon and Barthes, that it works to "fix" all peoples into images that support and rigidify its own forms of being.[7]

Fanon exhorts every enslaved consciousness (those who have become dominant image) to "burst apart" all they have become—an eruption that will fragment the self, he warns. But these fragments can be put together again when another kind of transfomative self arises (ibid.). This new self can liberate citizen-subjects from any "archetype," free them from the dominant poses and figures that comprise the rhetoric of "civilized" consciousness.[8] Such emancipation requires citizen-subjects to "incarnate a new type" of subjectivity. Fanon describes this process as occurring through a "slow," painful, re-"composition of my self in an ongoing process of mutation" (111, 23, 51). The choice for Fanon is to speak in and along with "the white world (that is to say the real world)," he adds ironically, to become its consciousness by embodying its rhetoric, or to found a new, unhabituated real with its own concomitant language forms, meanings, psychic terrains, and countrypeople. Fanon claims to have made this shift: "in the world in which I travel, I am endlessly creating"—and re-creating—'myself'" (229).

This means that the psyche, as well as the categories by which the human becomes human, must be re-formed.[9] Fanon wants us to understand that if "whiteness" remains a set of learned behaviors called up within a specific social and psychic rhetoric, then any race, culture, class, sex, or gender can inhabit the supremacist categories of whiteness. His warning is that the "Negro problem" is not about the "problem of Negroes living among white men," but is, rather, the problem of "Negros exploited, enslaved, despised by a colonialist, capitalist society" that is "only accidentally white"—any race can utilize and inhabit the categories of supremacism. The race that does so creates a rhetoric-for-being that binds (in varying forms) all citizen-subjects. Such enslavement includes the white man in a white man's state, Fanon writes, for he has become "enslaved" by his own expressions of "superiority" (60; my emphasis). Thus, the speakers and the rhetoric of the dominant order must be transformed, in order to free up what both Fanon and Barthes agree are predetermined, rigidified, and immobilized states of being. Unlike Barthes, Fanon is hopeful about the consequences of becoming an agent for such transformations. One who "takes a stand against" the "death" of being in supremacism, he writes, joins a new, original, revolutionary cadre that is cross-racial, cross-class, and cross-nation: an alliance of countrypeople of the same psychic terrain (225). Fanon sees himself in elective affinity with this revolutionary community. He is just another member of a cadre of actors and potential actors committed to transforming the dominant according to principles derived from the methodology of the oppressed, whereas Barthes views himself as an isolated, lone hero of semiology/mythology. Yet both thinkers end their books by inviting readers to access a new world, by utilizing the tools of what I have identified as the methodology of the oppressed: sign reading; deconstruction and reconstruction of signs; an ethical commitment to justice; and the differential movement that keeps all aspects of being in motion and mutation.

There is a permeable boundary suggested here, between black skin and white masks, between Fanon's work and that of Barthes, between psyche and forms of social rhetoric, between the socially reinforced poses-for-being and new configurations of order and consciousness that, through its permeability, require a new kind of interfacing: the ability to tell another story, a differing version, facing the degree of difference between versions, while recognizing a function that recurs in spite of all disparities. This recurring function depends on correlations, conversions, and transfers of meaning. The methodology of the oppressed is that interfacing; it demands the recovery of meaning through movement called for by Fanon: the bursting of the self and its re-formation through mutation, and in the differential intervention of that self into social categories for the sake of their reapportionment and conversion. In this realm, previous categories of "race," the rhetoric of "supremacy," and its necessary colonizations of gender, sex, race, class, or any social identity or styles of analysis, transform under its recognition and enactment, which generates a differential form of social movement that is bent on coalition between subordinated constituencies, and which is capable of transforming the politics of power. These forms and contents can be recognized, in Barthes's terms, as another kind of rhetoric. I call this a neorhetoric of love in the postmodern world. In Part IV of this book, this rhetoric of love is identified as a means of social change.

Toward a Neorhetoric of Love

In 1972, Tzvetan Todorov observed that "semiotics" has "come to claim a dominant position within a *global restructuring of knowledge*."[10] This has happened because semiotics represents what is made invisible in most academic theorizing, a partial joining with and enactment of the methodology of the oppressed. Without recognizing this link, the Barthes of 1957 was left alone, abandoned, in despair. Moreover, in sublimating this methodology, the signifiers of Barthes's own writing call up the very bourgeois Western society and its imperializing impulses that Barthes is also trying to critique. What Barthes forgot is what Fanon defiantly cited much earlier, when he concluded his book *Black Skin, White Masks* by saying: "I want the world to recognize, with me, the open door of every consciousness" (123).

Fanon recognizes this "door" not simply as a location of access and departure. This "open door" of consciousness is a place of crossing, of transition and metamorphosis. At this threshold, meanings are recovered and dispersed through another rhetoric that transfigures all others, and whose movement is its nature. In the following chapter, we see that this rhetoric generates a hermeneutics of "love in the postmodern world." This neorhetoric operates differentially because it is guided by the terms of the methodology of the oppressed: the consciousness it requires reads the variables of meaning, apprehending and caressing their differences; it shuffles their (continual) rearrangement, while its own parameters queerly shift according to necessity, ethical positioning, and power. This coalitional consciousness is being coded under U.S. global, postmodern and postcolonial discourses, in hegemonic and U.S. third world feminisms, and in queer theory as a new kind of theory in revolution, and which has been represented in chapters 3, 4, and 5 as part and parcel of the methodology of the oppressed.

I have systematically followed the early work of Roland Barthes on semiology, aided by Fanon, in order to methodically describe the composition of what I call the "inner" and "outer" technologies of resistance that together comprise the body of the methodology of the oppressed. I have claimed semiotics as one technology of this methodology, and I have argued that those academic disciplines across the board, from feminist theory to ethnic studies, from history to sociology, which are now constructing theories of resistance and opposition, are doing so in disparate languages but under the auspices of a similar theory and practice, which can be summarized by calling up the methodology of the oppressed particularly as expressed in its "differential" aspect.

In tracing the flow of significance from one semantic field to another in Barthes's work, from the terminologies of semiology to that of his "mythology," I have demonstrated how what I call the methodology of the oppressed appears—and disappears—in turnstile fashion. The semiotic perception of signs in culture as structured meanings that carry power is a basic survival skill necessary to subordinated and oppressed citizenry. A related technology that I have tracked through Barthes's work details the moves necessary to deconstruct those perceptions and the signs linked to them through the method of "mythology," a method best understood as deconstruction. We have seen that all (ideological) meanings can be semiotically reconstituted through a third technology I call meta-ideologizing. Each of these technologies is accomplished in the interests of proposing egalitarian social relations in the technology of "democratics." And none of these processes can occur without the "differential" movement of meaning. I have called the sum total of these interrelated technologies the methodology of "the oppressed." But in 1957, Barthes was not able to fully link the academic "science" of semiology or mythology with that very population, those who, ironically, would have been for him a community of allies.

The Failure of Barthesian Semiology Is the Power of the Methodology of the Oppressed

Barthes's 1957 manifesto on semiology is structured around an odd trope—a twisted appropriation—which is also the model on which much academic work in the West is framed, and which is the source of Barthes's continuing despair, the "difficulties" he predicts in "feeling" (if not in method) for the semiologist as "mythologist" (156). Barthes unveils ideology as speech—stolen and restored—while also appropriating and denying the language of the colonized. (As Barthes himself ironically advises, "speech which is restored is no longer quite that" which was taken away: "when it was brought back, it was not put exactly in its place" [125].) Barthes's inability to recognize the language of the colonized leads to the demoralized demeanor that runs through the work of even this most sympathetic and resolute of allies in decolonization. Barthes writes that "semiology...knows only one operation: reading or deciphering" the signs that come before it (114). The next step, deciding what direction to take in order to ensure survival, was the misstep for Barthes that led to the precipice, as we shall see, of his disillusion, cynicism, and despair.

Barthes's optimism in regard to "semiology-mythology" is that (like his other optimistic form, his "speech of the oppressed") it will participate "in the making of the world." Practitioners of semiology, he writes, should "have no trouble in feeling justified" in their work as decoders of ideology, however excluded and isolated they may become from other people. This is because semiology, understood as a process of "unveiling," is fundamentally a political act. In Barthes's terms, this means that semiology creates transitivity—it enters and enacts the zero degree of meaning, it is "founded" on an enactment of language that "postulates" its freedom. De-ideologizing through semiology, he asserts, the process of the deconstruction of signs, serves to "harmonize" the world—"not as it is" but as it longs to become (156). It is in this location—where the practitioner of Barthesian semiotics seeks to enact a method for "harmonizing" what is with what might be—that Barthes's method links with what I have called the methodology of the oppressed, and especially with the form of oppositional power generated under colonization called differential social movement and consciousness; for both Barthes's method and differential social movement (or U.S. third world feminism) can be recognized to be, in Barthes's terms, "at once an understanding of reality and a complicity with it" (ibid.).

But while, for U.S. third world feminism, this location of simultaneous "understanding" and "complicity" represents a necessary standpoint for ensuring survival and social evolution as enacted through the technologies of the methodology I have identified, a site where the reapportionment, alchemy of identity, and potential metamorphosis of reality are made possible, this juncture is for Barthes the site of his guilt, his alienation, and his historical limits in modernism; for Barthes sees the "complicity" of semiotic analysis as one that exiles him from all true "revolutionary action," which he must live only at a distance — "vicariously," he writes. The speech of his semiologist is only a "metalanguage," he despairs: "it 'acts' nothing; at the most, it unveils — or does it? To whom?" Indeed, according to Barthes, the best work of his semiotic-mythology (and thus, I think Barthes would add, of the methodology of the oppressed) is always, in his view, "hampered" insofar as it is guided, and limited, "by its ethical origins," by its "moral" emphasis — by what I call the "democratic" technology of the methodology of the oppressed (ibid.). For Barthes, ethics are not a guiding technology of his method of semiology-mythology; ethics are rather the very reason for the semiologist's necessary but shamed "complicity" with the dominant, and the simultaneous cause of Barthes's separation and isolation from any community. Although the only link between Barthes's practitioner and the world of others can be the semiologist's "utmost morality," this link also disconnects and divides rather than connects; for this morality, in Barthes's view, provides relation neither to others nor to social being in history (ibid.).

Commitment to radical semiology only banishes Barthes from the very world he lives in, where he becomes "excluded," he writes, "cut off" from all other consumers of ideology, "estranged" from "the entire community," "condemned to live" in isolation from citizens of like stature. The "havoc" that semiotic-mythology brings to the language of the practitioner's community, Barthes warns, is "absolute," there is "no hope of going back," no "assumption of payment" (157). With this "loss of innocence" (the "tender open possibilities" — also an ideology), Barthes believes that the practitioner of semiotic-mythology ultimately is disjoined from all other consumers of ideology (ibid.). This is no small matter; for if Barthes can no longer perform as innocent consumer and user of ideology (as those who enact the methodology of the oppressed must), then his only alternative is to view himself as exiled from reality: the lone, heroic, solitary figure who voluntarily severs from dominant ideology. In this self-imposed estrangement from one's own people, the Barthesian semiotician as mythologist is, Barthes laments, "condemned to live in a theoretical sociality," exclusively. Allied to others in theory only, Barthes's life in society means, at best, "to be truthful." His self-imposed estrangement, however, brings him closer to a new kind of community—which already surrounds him, but which he can only partially perceive.

This is because Barthes paradoxically continues, in lucid agony, to long for community within the same dominant culture he is also committed to transform. As prophet for that community, he warns that Western citizens increasingly "cannot manage to achieve more than an unstable grasp of reality." This, he says, "gives the measure of our present alienation: we constantly drift between the object and its demystification, powerless to render its wholeness" (159). The community is thus suspended, increasingly barred from its own dominant realities, wavering in a state of uncertainty, and relegated to the mobile form of schizophrenia that is associated with subordination. Barthes predicts that connections will eventually be reestablished (though not in his own lifetime) "between reality and men, between description and explanation, between object and knowledge": his desire and his nostalgia are for the reconciliation of a broken, decolonizing first world. Paradoxically, such reconciliation can only be achieved through stretching and breaking the components of signification in every direction. Any future conciliations of meaning will occur only through a commitment to "sarcasm," he writes, which means the rending of the flesh of the social body. For a white European male enacting a theory capable of decolonizing his own culture and consciousness, sarcasm is the only alternative, the only "condition of truth" left, he believes, the only way, ironically, of actually keeping faith (157). Condemned to enacting satire, the mixture that burns, while longing for new grounds of community and connection between people, Barthes thus embodies, and indeed, he writes, "claims…to the full" the contradictions of his time (12). But Barthes's narrative is not, I think, a tragic one.

True, the semiotic principles of mythology appear to Barthes as terminations, for "the values" of the semiologist's "undertaking" only materialize "as acts of destruction." And more, there is no way of imagining what the world will be like "when the immediate object" under analysis disappears, Barthes writes; the "mythologist is excluded," from the very "history in the name of which he professes to act." Banished from the dominant realities that comprise "history," for the semiologist seeks to destroy them, the practitioner is also exiled from the future: "utopia is an impossible luxury"; the mythologist will "never see the Promised Land" (157);

for just as past orders of dominant thought are undermined under semiotic analysis, so too are the possibilities for projecting any hopeful future. Instead, the future, under the purview of mythology-as-method, acts like "an essence — the essential destruction of the past" (131). Barthes's method, semiology, can only provide a momentary but sublime thrill, when past and future apocalyptically meet to destroy and re-create the present. At the very moment that Barthes becomes exiled from history in his use of semiotic-mythology, however, people of color in de-colonial struggle are released to realms of possibility, reentering history as mutated subjects of social orders undergoing metamorphosis. For these "oppressed," it is the same sublime "apocalypse" of the present (achieved partially through the method of semiotic-mythology), as it fascinates, terrifies, and exiles Barthes from history, that leads subjugated populations to the promised land.

The willingness to take up sign reading in order to examine dominant orders of thought could serve to liberate meaning again to a realm in which hierarchies are undermined, thus releasing Western consciousness into a renewed creativity. Until that time when semiology becomes Barthes's hoped-for "theoretical locus wherein a certain liberation of 'the significant'" (9) in the West can be enacted, Barthes continues to see himself as the lone, idiosyncratic semiologist who decodes: isolated without community; for Barthes is unable to recognize that his work represents a particular version of an emancipatory methodology of the oppressed. And because he does not realize that his own method — which creates his self-imposed banishment from dominant order — places him securely in the subject position of the subordinated, he is unable to recognize his allies. Nevertheless, Barthes's imagination of a semiotic-mythology contains the basis for identifying a new mode of subjectivity, citizenship, and alliance. Under postmodern globalization where all citizen-subjects become decentered, the "promised land" for all such "marginalized" and "dominated" subjects begins at Barthes's "zero degree" of meaning, the place from which resistance to ideology arises in the specific form of dissidence called the methodology of the oppressed (132). It is movement, Barthes's revolutionary action itself, that gives life to this methodology, the technologies of which are designed to act transitively on the world, the self, and others. The moral technology of democratics, that ethical force of "complicity," negotiation, and isolation that fails Barthes, represents the powerful guiding mechanism for honing the effects of the methodology of the oppressed, for energizing and guiding its work and outcome.

Barthes's employment of a process of consciousness self-consciously wending its way through signification is a story linked to my own; both analyses are concerned with demonstrating forms of consciousness in opposition to dominant social hierarchy that can be effective under twenty-first-century and Euro-American cultural conditions. The meeting place for these two methodologies occurs in the movement between signification, form, and concept, between Signifiers, Signifieds, and referents. I call this realm between and through meaning systems a decolonizing "cyberspace," in which alternative realities provide individuals and communities increased and novel means of communication, creativity, productivity, mobility, and a different sense of "control."[11] Unlike Foucault, the Barthes of 1957 could not imagine this new space as a location, a location of resistance, existing as it does in the interstices between de-colonial processes, transnational capitalism, and the forms of consciousness that postmodern cultural conditions make available for appropriation. At this point, Barthes was only certain that it was through semiotic-mythology that human consciousness in the West could once again become connected to history; it is a method for reconnection and rediscovery of reality that, he predicted, will unleash "unimaginable solutions, unforeseeable syntheses" (157). During the late twentieth century, this decolonizing cyberspace was defined, extended, and transcoded by Euro-American scholars, philosophers, and critical and cultural theorists. At the beginning of the twenty-first century we face unprecedented and global forms of *re*colonization under postmodernism. It is crucial to recognize the connections between seemingly contending intellectual communities that are generating similar models for psychic and social transformation that can lead to postcolonial futures.[12] My contribution is to identify a hermeneutics of love that can create social change. I begin this process by examining Barthes's work again, but this time I examine the Barthes who wrote twenty years after *Mythologies*, at the moment he begins insisting on the "something else" that I call "differential consciousness." This something else is not the differential social movement identified in the "theory and method of oppositional consciousness that is U.S. third world feminism, nor is it the differential movement of the methodology of the oppressed. It is the consciousness these require in order that these theories and methods effectively link in a hermeneutics of love in the postmodern world.

IV

Love in the Postmodern World

Differential Consciousness III

S I X

Love as a Hermeneutics of Social Change, a Decolonizing *Movida*

Today I believe in the possibility of love, that is why I endeavor to trace its imperfections, its perversions.

> Frantz Fanon

The true revolutionary is guided by great feelings of love.

> Che Guevara

Love ... is an important source of empowerment when we struggle to confront issues of sex, race, and class.

> bell hooks

To reoccupy *Aztlán*, the oppressed hallucinate — and that practice has no borders.

> Laura Pérez

THE DIFFERENTIAL mode of social movement (that which transforms and allies all other modes of social movement) relies on what I have called a "cyber" consciousness, a "differential" consciousness that operates as process and shifting location.

Differential consciousness is linked to whatever is not expressible through words. It is accessed through poetic modes of expression: gestures, music, images, sounds, words that plummet or rise through signification to find some void—some no-place—to claim their due. This mode of consciousness both inspires and depends on differential social movement and the methodology of the oppressed and its differential technologies, yet it functions outside speech, outside academic criticism, in spite of all attempts to pursue and identify its place and origin. In seeking to describe it, Barthes wrote toward the end of his life that this mode of differential consciousness "can only be reached" by human thought through an unconformable and "intractable" passage—not through any "synthesizing term"—but rather through another kind of "eccentric," and "extraordinary term."[1] This book has demonstrated that this "eccentric" passage toward "differential consciousness" is designed in a multiplicity of forms, from revolt to religious experience, from *rasquache*[2] to punk, from technical achievements like the methodology of the oppressed, to Saussure's sign reading alone; it is a conduit brought about by any system of signification capable of evoking and puncturing through to another site, to that of differential consciousness.

According to the Barthes of *Incidents, The Pleasure of the Text,* or *A Lover's Discourse,*[3] that term, puncture, passage, or conduit can be provided by the process of "falling in love." Third world writers such as Guevara, Fanon, Anzaldúa, Emma Pérez, Trinh Minh-ha, or Cherríe Moraga, to name only a few, similarly understand love as a "breaking" through whatever controls in order to find "understanding and community": it is described as "hope" and "faith" in the potential goodness of some promised land; it is defined as Anzaldúa's *coatlicue* state, which is a "rupturing" in one's everyday world that permits crossing over to another; or as a specific moment of shock, what Emma Pérez envisions as the trauma of desire, of erotic despair.[4] These writers who theorize social change understand "love" as a hermeneutic, as a set of practices and procedures that can transit all citizen-subjects, regardless of social class, toward a differential mode of consciousness and its accompanying technologies of method and social movement.

Toward the end of his life, Barthes was able to provide written descriptions of the passionate, artful, and even unspoken elements of this mode of consciousness, using the example of love. Centering his discussion on language itself, Barthes points out that what we often detect in the shadow of our lover's speech is that which is "unreal," which is to say, meaning when it is unruly, willful, anarchic (90). The language of lovers can puncture through the everyday narratives that tie us to social time and space, to the descriptions, recitals, and plots that dull and order our senses insofar as such social narratives are tied to the law. The act of falling in love can thus function as a "punctum," that which breaks through social narratives to permit a bleeding, meanings unanchored and moving away from their traditional moorings—in what, Barthes writes, brings about a "gentle hemorrhage" of being (12). That is why, for Barthes, this form of romantic love, combined with risk and courage, can make anything possible. In *A Lover's Discourse* Barthes extends his definitions of the "third,"[5] "zero" (19), and "obtuse" (222) meanings—all terms that reach toward the same differential place of possibility without which no other meaning can find its own life. It is love that can access and guide our theoretical and political *"movidas"*—revolutionary maneuvers toward decolonized being. Indeed, Barthes thinks that access to the spectrum from which consciousness-in-resistance emanates might best materialize in a moment of "hypnosis," like that which occurs when one is first overwhelmed or engulfed by love (11).

Romantic Love Can Access Revolutionary Love: Roland Barthes

Romantic love provides one kind of entry to a form of being that breaks the citizen-subject free from the ties that bind being, to thus enter the differential mode of consciousness, or to enter what Barthes perhaps better describes as "the gentleness of the abyss" (12). In this unlimited space, ties to any responsibility are broken such that, Barthes writes, even "the act (of dying) is not up to me: I entrust myself, I transmit myself (to whom? to God, to Nature, to everything)" (11). Indeed, the consciousness that travels through this abyss becomes transformed insofar as it has now moved into and through what Barthes calls the "zero degree" (19) of all meaning, the place from which the obtuse, third meaning emerges to haunt all we think we know. It is initially a painful crossing to this no-place, this chiasmus, this crossroads, for here new kinds of powers imprecate the body as it is dissolved: Barthes warns: "I fall, I flow, I melt" (10). Subjectivity in this abyss also undergoes a sincere form of "bliss," what he calls *"jouissance."*[6] It is a coming to a utopian nonsite, a no-place where everything is possible—but only in exchange for the pain of the crossing.[7]

But access to this unhabituated space and form of being does not altogether depend on a lover; the lover's image only provides one vehicle for the punctum. When one becomes engulfed by love, entry to this other place of meaning is permitted because there is no longer "any PLACE for me anywhere, not even in death." It is at this point that the image of the lover (to which "I had been glued," in "whose image I lived") stops existing (11). The lover's disappearance can be the result of either loss or abundance: On the one hand, some "catastrophe" may seem to "remove" the lover forever, Barthes writes: he "leaves me"; on the other hand, it might be "excessive happiness which enables" one to unite and merge with the lover. In either case, whether "severed or united," whether "discrete or dissolved, I am nowhere gathered together" (ibid.). This now dispersed lover, Barthes continues, this traveler, thus comes to drift "outside the fatal-couple which links life and death by opposing them to each other" (12). Indeed, this trans-forming lover is no longer part of any couple—of any binary—but through some ingress created by love, the traveler ironically comes to lose its "structure as a lover" altogether (11), to instead enter another place of possibility, Barthes insists, signs all around no longer securely anchored.

Revolutionary Love Occurs outside Ideology

To fall in love means that one must submit, however temporarily, to what is "intractable" (19), to a state of being not subject to control or governance. It is at this point that the drifting being is able to pass into another kind of erotics, to the amplitude of Barthes's "abyss." It is only in the "no-place" of the abyss[8] that subjectivity can become freed from ideology as it binds and ties reality; here is where political weapons of consciousness are available in a constant tumult of possibility. But the process of falling in love is not the only entry to this realm, for the "true site of originality and strength" is neither the lover nor the self. Rather, it is the "originality of the relation" between the two actors that inspires these new powers, while providing passage to that which I call the differential (35).

Once one recognizes this abyss beyond dualisms, Barthes insists that any "injury" created by a love relationship can only arise from one's own "stereotypes" that one lives out as citizen-subject. Once subjectified, "I become obliged, to make myself a lover, like everyone else; to be jealous, neglected, frustrated—like everyone else." But when the relation enters the realm of the abyss—of the "original"—then stereotypes are shaken, "transcended, evacuated." And jealousy, abandonment, and frustration, for instance, "have no more room in this relation without a site," without topos, "without discourse" (35–36). This form of love is not the narrative of love as encoded in the West: it is another kind of love, a synchronic process that punctures through traditional, older narratives of love, that ruptures everyday being. In this commitment, "excess and madness" become, Barthes writes, "my truth, my strength" (42). In this formulation, indeed, they are his access to somewhere else; for through this love, insofar as it acts as "a punctum," as a *coatlicue* state, Barthes is transported into an original realm that is beyond jealousy, he insists, "beyond language, i.e. beyond the mediocre, beyond the generic" (55).

The End of Western Love and Narrative

On the other hand, one can allow love to become law, to become narrative. In the narrative form of "falling in love," a Western ethic predominates. Barthes's example: you love someone, and "either you have hope, and then you act, or else you have none, in which case you renounce. This is the discourse of the so-called 'healthy-subject'" who lives in the dominant: "either/or." But there is a third option, another approach to loving. This other course of action ensues when the loving subject instead tries to "slip between the two members" of the either/or alternative by saying, "I have no hope, but all the same . . . , " or "I stubbornly choose *not* to choose; I choose drifting: I continue" (62; my emphasis). This "drifting" is the movement of meanings that will not be governed; it is the intractable itself as it permeates through, in, and outside of power. Drifting occurs "whenever I do not respect the whole," the social scripts that name, drive, and impel us all through "love"—through life. Barthes refuses to be "driven about by language's illusions, seductions and intimidations," he writes. "I remove myself from Narrative."[9] This is because, for Barthes, "narrative is a death": it transforms "life into destiny, a memory into a useful act, a duration into an oriented and meaningful time." Turning thus from narrative's comforts and limits, from love's "Western" modes, Barthes searches for the punctum, he finds what is "obtuse," he gives himself over, he drifts "on the intractable bliss that beckons" in that place of life that survives outside and between narrative forms, where meanings live in some free, yet marked and wounded space, a site of shifting, morphing meanings that transform to let him in.

It is worth examining Barthes's 1977 demonstration of his own release from dominant reality, identity, power, love. He explains: "I experience reality as a system of power . . . everything imposes on me its system of being. The world is full, plenitude is its system, as a final offense this system is presented as a 'nature' with which I must sustain good relations in order to be 'normal'": One should find the films funny, the restaurant good, some painting beautiful, and "the feast of Corpus Christi lively: not only undergo the system of power," he confesses, "but even enter into sympathy with it: 'to love' reality," to be "happy"—to be in love (89). This "enjoyable" system of power dulls human senses with its normalities, its "shoulds," its scripts. But even when Barthes perceives the world as antagonistic to his potential as a being he remains similarly "linked to it," he warns, as if in sympathy. The cynical and alternative position of "at least I AM NOT CRAZY, like all the others," he writes, though perhaps comforting, also drives him back into the "world," inscribes him into dominant social narratives. Sometimes, however, Barthes breaks out of these relationships with power and enters into a third, differential zone: "once my bad temper is exhausted" (and he neither hates what "reality" is nor is engaged by it), then, he continues, "I have no language left at all." The "world is not unreal—I could then utter it, there are arts of the unreal, among them the greatest arts of all—but disreal: reality has fled from it, is nowhere, so that I no longer have any meaning (any paradigm) available to me; I DO NOT MANAGE to define my relations with the film, the restaurant, the painting, the Piazza" (ibid.). Yet what relation *is* left for the drifting citizen-subject? What relation can one have with a system of power when one is "neither its slave, nor its accomplice, nor its witness?" (90). The answer Barthes provides is that the relation of human to power can be that of a constant "drifting" to a somewhere else.

Freedom: This Third Meaning Produces De-Colonial Love

It must be remembered that "drifting" has a technology all its own that is not confined to falling in love. Barthes's postulation is that entrance to that somewhere else of the abyss is constantly invited through the medium of the "third meaning," which is that which always haunts any other two meanings in a binary opposition.[10] This third meaning, he ventures, has "the advantage of referring" not to denoted reality, but "to the field of the *signifier* (and not of signification)" (*Image/Music/Text*, p. 54). Even when this third meaning is perceived, he warns, one's "intellection cannot succeed in absorbing" it, for the third meaning is "at once persistent and fleeting, smooth and elusive." Every exchange can be understood as suffused with this meaning as it shimmers around what appears to be concrete. It is an extra, uncategorizable, unnamable meaning haunting all human need to name, classify, order, and control.

This theorization of the third meaning has much connotative (if not denotative) similarity with the twentieth-century subject position designated for subordinated citizen-subjects in the West; for the third meaning can only be discerned when it is understood as extending, "outside the limits" of dominant culture, knowledge, and information (ibid., p. 55). Both meanings may appear as "limited in the eyes of analytic reason"; thriving in the practices of "carnival," "scandal," "pun," "buffoonery" (ibid., p. 57); both are considered "useless expenditure, and indifferent to oral or aesthetic categories" as is the drift or supplement. Like the politics identified and claimed during the mid-twentieth century as "Third World liberation," Barthes's third meaning demands that human consciousness undo the very forms dominant society depends on in order to "ensure its peace of mind." Once this Western peace of mind is unsettled, he believes, consciousness will have the opportunity to "grasp the magnitude, the detours." And in the lines and planes of this

new magnitude, consciousness engages with logics other than those of the ego, Western law, and narrative order.

We have seen such "other" logics enacted in the example of differential U.S. third world feminist social movement, where differential consciousness repoliticizes subjectivities (such as the equal-rights, revolutionary, supremacist,
or separatist modes) when it works in the same manner as Barthes's third meaning
to blur the lines that separate "expression from disguise" while, at the same time,
allowing that "oscillation succinct denotation" (ibid.). Thus practitioners of the differential mode of social movement develop and mobilize identity as political tactic
in order to renegotiate power: identity is thus both disguised and not disguised in a
form of differential consciousness that thrives on oscillation. The positional subject
is not living a lie, then, but rather in disguise, but a real disguise, as in the example
Black Skin, White Masks, a disguise that enables survival. Such are the features of the
third world liberation active during Barthes's lifetime that recurred under U.S. third
world feminism, and that are being refigured for the twenty-first century in this
version of a differential social-movement theory (which is based on the methodology
of the oppressed).

These features are reiterated in Barthes's analysis as we have followed it so far. Barthes's evocation of "falling in love" summons up an alternative
mode of being, not consciousness in its usual mode, but not unconsciousness either.
Rather, Barthes's work invokes another (differential) consciousness, and it is this
which has made the theory and method of oppositional consciousness (outlined in
chapter 2) *conceivable* as an interrelating set of subjectivities and social movements
in resistance to dominating powers. Each mode of oppositional consciousness, linked
to the others in dialectical relationship, creates an alchemy back and forth between
them. When we choose an oppositional form of social action, however, these modal-
ities of arrangement permit us not simply to, in Barthes's terms, "drift," but to pick,
graze, convert, cruise, low-ride through meanings. Insofar as reality (or what is denotative) corresponds to what Barthes describes as "an anchorage of all the possible
denoted meanings of the object" by recourse to naming them, it is difficult to describe
the content and the shape of differential oppositional consciousness. We might say
that the term *differential consciousness* represents a signifier without any set signifieds
unless it is in direct political engagement through one of its specific tactics.

The demands of these similarly configured politics are thus: that
the oppositional citizen-subject be receptive to the presence of the obtuse third meaning as it shimmers behind all we think we know; that the citizen-subject give up con-

trol over meaning in order to perceive the third meaning, relinquish the peace of mind connected to dominant perception—or the third meaning remains invisible: it will not impinge on consciousness, will not disrupt, will not make meaning vibrant to break it apart through the trauma of the puncture, of love. The third meaning is present and can be recognized, but not by searching for what Barthes calls an "else-where of meaning (another content, added to the obvious meaning,)" a latent meaning as opposed to the manifest. The third meaning is, rather, that which "outplays meaning" altogether; it is that which subverts "not the content, but the whole practice of meaning" itself. In 1977, Barthes wrote that this subversion of meaning is "a new, rare practice, affirmed against a majority practice (that of signification)." Even in the political and strategic quest for nationalist solidification of strength and identity the third meaning is always present, no matter how concretely identity becomes fortified against or within the historical imperatives of nation, culture, race, sex, gender, class—or love. Linked as he was to the de-colonial processes of the twentieth century, Barthes's premonition was that evidence of this third meaning is already a certain cultural and social presence that "does not yet belong to today's politics, but nevertheless already to tomorrow's" (ibid., p. 63).

Tomorrow's Politics: Prophetic Love

Barthes's lifework (from his early thinking on the "science of semiotics" to the work generated toward the end of his life in 1980 when he calls for entrance to the abyss through the third meaning) was aimed toward the cessation of suffering through transforming the powers of domination that cause it. In Barthes's mind this meant that he must detach his own intellectual work from the rationality of dominant Western scholarship.[11] But this disassociation will not take place without Barthes's insistence that his work connect with something else, to another system of knowledge that is capable of replacing the older mechanisms of knowledge and power:

> I want to change systems: no longer to unmask, no longer to interpret, but to make consciousness itself a drug, and thereby to accede to the perfect vision of reality, to the great bright dream, to prophetic love. And if such consciousness were our human future? If by an additional turn of the spiral, someday, most dazzling of all, once every reactive ideology had disappeared, consciousness were finally to become this: the abolition of manifest and the latent, of the appearance and the hidden? If it were asked of analysis not to destroy power (nor even to correct or direct it), but only to *decorate* it, as an artist? (60–61)[12]

"Let us imagine," he continues, that the social and human sciences that examine and analyze human psychic and social life and its errors, "were to discover, one day" their own error, their own slip, or lapse, and that "this lapsus should turn out to be: a new unheard of form of consciousness?" (61).

In Barthes's last book, this new "unheard of form of consciousness" (of "prophetic love") is situated as another system of knowledge and power. In its realm, consciousness, life, aesthetics, and knowledge become something other than what we now live, and power becomes aesthetic, a decoration. Barthes's version of "falling in love" generates this kind of opening, or "lapsus." In this lapse the lover "drifts" toward somewhere else through a passage that accesses differential consciousness. The third meaning in Barthes's work, "theoretically locatable but not describable," he writes, can now be described as a passage from language to process,[13] a passage from narrative to an erotics of being, to "soul," to the differential consciousness proposed by 1980s feminists of color.[14] Every time meaning cannot find a solid signified, escapes from that which is tamed and known, is defiant in the face of any binary opposition, undergoes trauma in relation to the "real," then consciousness is "lapsed" and passage permitted to the realm of differential consciousness.[15]

Differential consciousness is described as the zero degree of meaning, counternarrative, utopia/no-place, the abyss, *amor en Aztlán*, soul. It is accessed through varying passages that can include the differential form of social movement, the methodology of the oppressed, poetry, the transitive proverb, oppositional pastiche, *coatlicue*, the middle voice. These puncta release consciousness from its grounding in dominant language and narrative to experience the meanings that lie in the zero degree of power—of differential consciousness. As discussed in chapters 3, 4, and 5, the methodology of the oppressed is comprised of the technologies of semiotics, deconstruction, meta-ideologizing, democratics, and differential movement. These skills comprise the body of the differential mode of social movement, and guide the deployment of its tactics—which include the equal-rights, revolutionary, supremacist, and separatist forms of resistance. These tactics variously etch upon dominant social reality, language, narrative—upon the neocolonial postmodern global. Together, these processes and procedures comprise a hermeneutic for defining and enacting oppositional social action as a mode of "love" in the postmodern world. This is a complex, multidimensional flow that creates upper and lower bounds. The domains of differential consciousness, that of "reality," and that of the methodology of the oppressed are involved in fluid dynamics, each of which turns to affect the others.

Another Version of the Same Hermeneutic: Jacques Derrida

Literary and cultural theorist Jacques Derrida's stated purpose for writing the 1968 manifesto he titles "*Différance*" was to "aggravate the obtrusive character"[16] of a hidden, but nevertheless irritating, always present meaning that is only perceptible out of the corner of one's eye, a presence that moves, transforms, disappears—but that will never go away. To gaze directly at this location (which is what he wants us to do) would be to enter its realm, he warns. What I have previously identified as "differential consciousness," "*la conciencia de la mestiza*," the "abyss," the "zero degree," or the "third meaning" represents an infinitely extending, internally controlling yet unruly power that Derrida designates *différance*. Both Derrida and Barthes agree that this differential power has remained "silent" and eluded "vision and hearing" within Western cultural orders. But a new "practice of perception" can permit citizen-subjects to identify this form of consciousness and activity. And indeed, this new practice of perception can refer citizen-subjects "happily," Derrida continues, to a new cultural and political order (137).

On its most basic level, the term *différance* signifies that which is other as well as an activity. This simultaneous location and movement operates as "an economic reckoning," for *différance* is an "interval that puts off until later the possible that is presently impossible"; it is the "other" deferred (129). *Différance* is thus a "systematic detour," "respite," or "delay" (129, 136)—a familiar psychic transfer point, or passageway, for citizen-subjects who have internalized what Derrida calls a sense of being different, "of not being identical, of being discernible" (136). But if *différance* represents a kind of difference, it is also a process, turn, trope, movement, or identification that contains the means to shatter any economy of difference—any order (150); for this realm of *différance* refers us beyond every known category: it carries us, writes Derrida, "beyond our language . . . beyond everything that can be named" by language. More, *différance* calls for the "necessarily violent transformation" of dominant languages "*by an entirely different language*" (158; my emphasis).

According to Derrida, *différance* is a realm that will only be expressed through developing a "*new tongue*," one conceived "outside the myth of the purely maternal or paternal languages" that belong "to the lost fatherland" of dominant Western thought (159). This new language of *différance* can be generated only while one is in the grip of "affirmation," Derrida writes—apart from negativity. It is generated through a fresh sign system constructed through "play," he continues, with a "certain laughter and with a certain dance," modes of proceeding that are "foreign" to the Western dialectic (ibid.). To call upon *différance*, then, one must engage with the unsettling pleasures of faith, of "hope," of utopian possibility. These are the meanings that energize and motivate his political and intellectual work; they are what aligns *différance* with differential consciousness and the methodology of the oppressed. Like the unnamed abyss of Barthes's imaginary that he believes will lead to a politics for the future, in Derrida's view it is *différance* (that is not yet "a word nor a concept" with academic credentials) that is "strategically the theme most proper to think out, if not master" in "what is most characteristic of our epoch" (130, 135–36).

The Third Voice

Like Barthes, Derrida is calling for a new order that can defend against the binary oppositions that ground Western philosophy. Ironically, this new order, *différance*, rises from the very location that also precedes and sustains binary oppositions. Further, *différance* represents the fundamental (dis)order against which the very distinction between active and passive is made possible. In this sense, *différance* can be said to represent the activity of the now archaic verb form known as the middle voice (130). This grammatical form employed in ancient Sanskrit and Greek, has disappeared from all known living languages. It is a verb form, neither active nor passive, in which the subject's speech acts both "backwards" on the subject as well as "forward" on its object (as in the oath "I swear to tell the truth, the whole truth, and nothing but the truth" in the ritual of legal discourse). Later in this chapter, I describe the operation of this third voice through my discussion of the work of Hayden White. For now, Derrida's explanation is simply this: that the middle voice of the verb does not represent the action of a subject or an object, and it does not start from an agent or from an object—indeed, he writes, the middle voice cannot be understood according to "any of these" former "*terms*" (137). Instead, he asserts, the middle voice of the verb represents a form of speech unused in any living language today, yet it is capable of transforming both the speaker and its object of speech at the moment it is uttered. Derrida's insight and indictment is this: that Western philosophy has "commenced by distributing the activity of the middle voice of the verb" (which is the differential, that which expresses "a certain intransitiveness") into "the active and passive voice" of being—and then it has "itself been constituted in this repression" (ibid.).

The unique activity of the repressed middle voice once utilized can serve as a transit point, writes Derrida, to that "bottomless chessboard where being is set" into play. Derrida challenges the reader to find her or his way to the realm of *différance*, to "stay within the difficulty of this passage," especially in realities where Western "metaphysics serves as the norm" of behavior, thought, and speech (154). Derrida promises that access to this passage is everywhere, for "everywhere the dominance of being" is continually "solicited by *différance*—in the sense that *sollicitare* means, in old Latin, to shake all over, to make the whole tremble" (153). Like Barthes's sublime abyss that disturbs, agitates, and incites meaning with its zero degree, the work of Derrida's *différance* similarly solicits the structure of every kind of human order. Thus, the ascent of *différance* as that which ruptures older meanings discloses in its activity new openings for reading, writing, interpreting, being.

The concept and methods of *différance* as defined by Derrida are substantively and structurally analogous to aspects of previously examined concepts such as "U.S. Third World feminism," the "differential mode of oppositional consciousness," "*la conciencia de la mestiza*," Barthes's "abyss," "punctum," or "third meaning," as well as to those dynamics that activate and aim the methodology of the oppressed. But Derrida does not explicitly connect the possibilities of *différance* to oppositional social movement. The essay's lacuna is indicated in the passage that follows, yet this same passage also points to the profound linkages his concept of *différance* has to the theory and method of social movement enacted by U.S. women of color, for example, within late-twentieth-century differential feminism. Derrida admits that he does not know how "to begin to mark out" his assemblage, the "graph of *difference*"; he is only "clear that it cannot be EXPOSED" (135). We can "expose only what, at a certain moment, can become PRESENT, manifest," he writes, and *différance* in the West cannot become manifest. As Derrida sees it, the problem is that if *différance* is "what makes the presentation of being-present possible" in the West (though it "never presents itself as such" [134]), how, he worries, can "we conceive of what stands *opposed* to Western metaphysics? (158; my emphasis). If *différance* is the repressed ground upon which Western metaphysics rises, how can we discern *différance* as that which also stands opposed to Western metaphysics? How can *différance* be understood as an alternate order for human consciousness and society? Or are we stuck (as Jameson fears) with only theoretical or poetic inscriptions to consider, such as Derrida's and Barthes's notions of *différance* or the abyss, which can only identify "unnamable" possibilities for social and psychic liberation?

Différance Is a Grammatical Position of Subjugation:
A Third-Force Power

The answer to these questions is, like *différance* itself, paradoxically hidden, yet present in Derrida's text. If, as Derrida argues, Western thought "commences" by distributing *différance* — or the middle voice — onto some binary opposition between what is active and what is passive; if Western philosophy itself has been constituted in this repression; if *différance* is that which makes "being-present" possible, though *différance* is itself invisible; if *difference* cannot be exposed without collapsing the system, then there is much in common between the grammatical position of *différance* within dominant culture and the "grammatical position" assigned to particular subordinated constituencies within the U.S. social order. Conquered and dominated populations can be incorporated into dominant society, even when this happens negatively by distributing their possibilities onto its binary rationality (male/female, heterosexual/ homosexual, white/black, human/nonhuman, active/passive, same/different, etc.). But sometimes this distribution is undermined.[17] There are cultural and human forms that do not easily slip into either side of a dominant binary opposition.[18] They are the remainder — unintelligible to dominant order — that is submerged and made invisible (to recognize them would be to upset the binary order of same and different).

The production of Western culture has been at one with this process: as it rises it divides meaning into binaries, repressing the rest and thus constituting *différance*, which becomes a living presence, grammatically marked, held, embodied, and lived out within the dominant social order by subjugated populations who do not "fit." Both Jameson and Derrida are afraid that no force can emerge in opposition to Western metaphysics, but this fear makes invisible the already-present forms of this third force, which twentieth-century decolonizations have set free upon the world stage.[19] Indeed, this third-force presence is what made the presence of *différance* even conceivable for Derrida in 1968, who at that point remained conceptually blinded, as was Barthes and Jameson, to such (grammatical and material) allies in resistance.

Decolonization released a *transformed* version of Derrida's *différance* into social circulation, transformed because it was *politicized* and *concretely manifested*, first as the "third world liberation" of the 1950s, a liberation that shattered naturalized binaries (first/second, white/black, dominant/subordinate, superior/ inferior) in order to release the repressed. To an even greater extent and more recently, this politicized version of *différance* has found its most material incarnation and development as the explicitly differential oppositional political practice, theory, and method of 1970s and 1980s U.S. third world feminism, which is quickly becoming "third space" feminism. It was in these decades that feminists of color, as well as other similarly displaced gender, race, sex, and class transgressors, became expedient and skillful agents of a political practice that we should perhaps no longer call "*différance*."[20] If we can agree that past U.S. peoples of color have served grammatically as representatives and functionaries of *différance* in the service of dominant relations—surviving in that in-between (silent) space that made social order, alliance, affinity, even love between white skins possible—then today, with *différance* set free, no longer invisible through the uprising presence of subjects out of colonization, the nature of social affinity must change, already has changed: so too, the nature of love in the West is changing. In tracking this hermeneutic of love in what follows, I translate Derrida's language of *différance* in order to make manifest the social movement language embedded within it: the methodology of the oppressed.

The End of Academic Apartheid

A transcoding will help make visible the theoretical, methodological, and practical tools that are capable of aligning critical and cultural theory across disciplines. In the following example connect the theoretical realm of *différance* with U.S. third world feminist theory, method, and criticism. It is important to recognize that in the example of U.S. third world feminist rhetorical figuration (which interrelates liberal, revolutionary, supremacist, separatist, and differential tropes of social movement), differences between any one of the oppositional ideologies are produced and at the same time deferred through the differential mode of social movement, which we can now recognize as a *politicized* and material version of the very process Derrida calls *différance*. Each mode of social movement, whether operating under liberal, revolutionary, supremacist, or separatist terms, retroactively takes on new meaning when it is deployed differentially—deferring its own differences through an alchemy that transforms. This politicized form of *différance* transforms each oppositional ideology into a strategically deployed *tactic* of differential social movement.

In this fashion, Derrida's terminological model of *différance* recodes and translates what I have traced in this book as "U.S. third world feminism," "the differential form of social movement," "differential consciousness-in-opposition," and what Barthes has named the "abyss," or the "third meaning."[21] Reading these theoretical apparatuses together through the lens of Derrida's definition of *différance* simultaneously exposes the activist nature of *différance* and the philosophical aims of the political practice of the differential mode of social movement—where for both (in Derrida's terms) "everything is a matter of strategy and risk." We can read differential U.S. third world feminist practice, then, as an instance of politicized *différance* when we read differential U.S. third world feminism as "hazardous," writes Derrida, "because the strategy is not simply one in the sense that we say that strategy orients the tactics according to a final aim, a TELOS or the theme of a domination, a mastery or an ultimate reappropriation of movement and field. In the end, it is a strategy without finality" (135). Moreover, when oppositional ideologies such as the liberal, revolutionary, supremacist, or separatist modes are enacted strategically and differentially as tactics, each becomes dialectically interrelated in what Derrida (describing *différance*) says is the "structure of an interlacing, a weaving, or a web" that allows "different threads and different lines of sense or force to separate again, as well as being ready to bind others together" (132). There are profound coalitional possibilities in the kind of bringing together proposed here.

In the example of 1970s U.S. third world feminism, this weaving structure permitted alliances between varying oppositional ideologies under the mode of differential consciousness that Anzaldúa named *"la conciencia de la mestiza."* U.S. feminists of color have stubbornly claimed this in-between space as that of the "outsider/within" (Patricia Hill Collins), of "in-appropriated otherness" (Trin Minh-ha), as the "house of difference" (Audre Lorde), or as the unsettled mobility of "strategic essentialism" (Gayatri Spivak). Of this space, Derrida writes that "in presenting itself it becomes effaced; in being sounded it dies away" (133) in just the way that the U.S. third world feminism of this stripe, during the 1990s, fell back into the shadows of social movement. This is because enactment of differential social movement—of the methodology of the oppressed—necessarily creates new modes of resistance, new questions and answers that supersede those that went before; for it is, above all, a theory and method of oppositional consciousness that belongs to no single population, no race, gender, sex, or class except for the subordinated who seek empowerment. The process of *différance*, Derrida continues, "very well may, even one day must, be sublated, and lend itself, if not to its own replacement, at least to its involvement in a series of events in which in fact it never commanded" (135), as is also the case with any outcome triggered through the deployment of differential social movement. Concluding his description of *différance* in the following famous passage, Derrida insists:

> Not only is there no realm of *différance*, but *différance is even the subversion of every realm.* This is obviously what makes it threatening and necessarily dreaded by everything in us that desires a realm, the past or future presence of a realm. And it is always in the name of a realm that, believing one sees it ascend to the capital letter, one can reproach it for wanting to rule. (153; my emphasis)

Différance unsettles every rule; once politicized as differential social movement it can mobilize and transform any tactic, and it is always in the process of transformation. But it also leaves a "trace," Derrida writes, and this can be followed (154).

Interdisciplinary Knowledges across Disciplines: Hayden White

One of Hayden White's most important contributions has been to materialize the presence of *différance* into a method that can be utilized by historians and analysts of the human and social sciences. To briefly summarize White's early argument (see Metahistory [1975]): all scholarship is enclosed, structured, and emplotted by particular modes of perception, "frames of mind" that represent specific "postures" that people assume before historical reality.[22] The radical aim of White's scholarship was to develop a method and "a typology of the modes of understanding" that permit a mediation "between contending ideologues" who regard their own positions as what is real, and of their opponents, whose positions are viewed as "mere ideology" or as "false consciousness."[23] White's protocols for translating between these modes of thought are based on what he identifies as a four-mode schemata-template for understanding and creating human and social relationships—what have since come to be well known as "tropes." White understands a trope not only as a "deviation *from* one possible, proper meaning," but also as a "deviation *towards* another meaning."[24] In this discussion I make one further trope toward *what remains*, that is, toward the form of consciousness that is required and necessary in order to *discern or move between* varying modes of consciousness—or tropes. What is the mode of consciousness that remains both within yet *outside* this "number of possible postures" for constituting scholarship, the position that allowed White to generate and articulate his own metatheory and method of analysis? At the turn of the twenty-first century, nearly twenty years after *Metahistory*, White begins to identify and define the protocols for accessing *this* form of differential consciousness.[25] Of this form of consciousness, White writes that the "human and social sciences [insofar as they are based on or presuppose a specific conception of historical reality] are as blind to the *sublimity* of the historical process and to the *visionary* politics it authorizes as is the disciplinized historical consciousness that informs their investigative procedures."[26] Hayden White does not turn away from this sublime. The scholarship he provides generates a theory and method that create a specifically U.S. model for interdisciplinary historical, political, and cultural studies.

The Reflexive Middle Voice Is Revolutionary

What White is identifying adds up to what can be described as another kind of *morality*, one that permits its practitioner to act both from within and from outside ideology. From this atypical moral, scholarly, and differential positioning, the practitioner breaks with ideology while also speaking in and from within ideology. In both Derrida's and White's terms, this moral positioning and all of its consequences can, once again, be best described through the technical medium of what grammarians call the "middle voice of the verb."[27] Earlier, I pointed out that though the middle voice of the verb is lost to modern languages, there are other routes (as in Barthes's lover-who-does-not-choose) that make available this same mode of consciousness that does not have to choose between the active and the passive in order to be expressed. White's scholarship reinjects this middle-verb form back into social reality.

In the discussion on Derrida, I introduced the metaphorical grammatical equivalence of *différance* that is embodied in the positions of subjectivity permitted U.S. people of color, and I suggested that as subjugated peoples rise from this grammatically enslaved position as the third, repressed presence that facilitates and rationalizes binary oppositions in the West, then the third, middle voice also finds its release in, among other ways, the oppositional form of consciousness I call the differential. This is the form of consciousness that asks the oppositional actor to *think modally* (e.g., from oppositional ideology to oppositional ideology, or, as White would say, from trope to trope), in the way in which native indigenous peoples have been arguing for since the beginning of conquest and colonization.[28] White's work indicates that this ability to think or act modally is not possible without the simultaneous recognition and application of the "third" middle voice of the verb, which can itself be considered a *specific mode of consciousness.*[29]

The third, middle voice of the verb, White explains, works through a "metatransitive relationship between an agent, an act, and an effect" (180), "metatransitive" because these three bodies work across one another to simultaneously affect the others. This means that the middle voice can be understood as "at once productive of an effect on an object" and "constitutive of a particular kind of agent . . . by means of an action" (181). Among the examples he gives are the acts of "promising," "swearing an oath," and "judging," for in doing these "one not only acts on the world, but also changes one's own relation to it" (187). In similar fashion, I have argued that enactment of the differential form of social movement is also designed (in the specifics of its oppositional and ideological tactics) to act upon social reality while at the same time transforming the practitioner's relation to it; for differential social movement can only function through a metatransitivity, "a similar kind of dual action on an object and on oneself," writes White, a similar kind of "enclosure within the action" (181). Just as we can say that an activist is what exists in the interior of resistance—it is only IN action and BY action that the practitioner can be said to exist—so too does the third voice of the verb function: it becomes *constituted* as it "both acts and is acted upon" (182). Differential social movement thus can be considered a *technical effect* where the activist *becomes* in the moment of acting, is "made" in the same way the judge, promiser, or oath taker is "made" in the act of judging, promising, or swearing an oath. To understand this function of the middle voice of the verb in this way is thus also to understand the differential mode of consciousness-in-opposition.

Hayden White provides a very clear example in his discussion of the ancient Greek middle-voice verb form for heterosexual marriage, which demonstrates in significant ways how "a man and a woman are respectively involved." *Gamein* is an active verb form—that is reserved for males—which means "to marry," while *gamesthai*, the same verb but in the *middle* voice, is reserved for women, and means "to wed." The difference between these two verb forms, White explains, is "not a matter of doing something, on the one side, and having something done to one, on the other," a difference we are familiar with in dominant phallogocentric terms as active or passive states. The difference between these two ancient verb forms is rather a matter of "distinguishing between two kinds of *transitivity*, one in which either the subject or the object remains *outside* the action" on the male side, and "one in which the distinction between subject and object is obliterated" on the female (186).

As opposed to active or passive constructions, then, the third voice of the verb represents a form of consciousness in which there is no separation between the subject and the object of the action, which are instead conflated. So too are actions and their effects "conceived to be simultaneous," writes White, and past and present are understood as "integrated" (ibid.). Hovering among and between the movement of active and passive, of past, present, and future, this middle (and third) voice of the verb invokes a specific psychological condition that acts according to whatever precepts best bind the being-of-the-agent to its cause.[30] This unique activity of the middle voice is thus best designed to indicate any action that is informed by what White describes as "a heightened moral consciousness on the part of the subject performing" it: "I promise," "I swear," "I judge that..." (ibid.). The middle voice can be seen as the technical embodiment of what he calls a "*morality of form*": its being is directly inspired and linked to the *social world* inside of which the agent must act, a social world that acts back on the agent, but only through the intercession of the agent's own act. The middle voice thus represents a differential, politicized, and modal form of consciousness.

Unlike a naive use of any previous oppositional mode of consciousness, whether liberal, revolutionary, supremacist, separatist, or other, wherein the activist attempts to exercise power upon *what is* conceived as an object (as in the active verb form), and unlike positions of social subordination such as those of "pet," "game," or "wild," positions permitted the oppressed in which exterior powers exercise domination on the citizen-subject, who can only act in response (as in the passive verb form),[31] the middle voice represents the consciousness required to transform any of these previous modes of resistance out of their active-or-passive incarnations into what White calls a "reflexive," differential form (185). That reflexive mode of consciousness self-consciously deploys subjectivity and calls up a *new* morality of form that intervenes in social reality through deploying an action that re-creates the agent even as the agent is creating the action — in an ongoing, chiasmic loop of transformation. The differential activist is thus made by the ideological intervention that she is also making: the only predictable final outcome is transformation itself.

The technology of the middle voice of the verb provides the specific medium for performing the mode of consciousness in opposition called for by Althusser, one capable of acting both from within ideology and from outside ideology — at the same time. Indeed, the location of the middle voice is similar to the place *exacted* of those "oppressed" citizens who, as Fanon points out, reflexively act to self-consciously effect themselves in acting, always remaining inside the action — and outside the action as well — in the transitive, mobile, middle location of "doubled consciousness." The technology of the middle voice thus politicized represents a mechanism for survival, as well as for generating and performing a higher moral and political mode of oppositional and coalitional social movement. Recognizing these connections of differential consciousness and resistance to the middle voice of the verb repoliticizes and contemporizes White's metatheory of tropes, which becomes one other applied formula intimately linked to the methodology of the oppressed, part and parcel of a hermeneutics toward love, a cosmopolitics for dissidence in the postmodern world.

S   E   V   E   N

Revolutionary Force:
Connecting Desire to Reality

Our language evolves from a culture that abhors anything tending to obscure or delete the fact of the human being who is here and now/the truth of the person who is speaking or listening. Consequently, there is no passive voice construction possible . . . every sentence insists on the living and active participation of at least two human beings, the speaker and the listener.

June Jordan

It may well be that on the plane of "life," there is but a totality where structures and forms cannot be separated. But science has no use for the ineffable: it must speak about "life" if it wants to transform it.

Roland Barthes

The only way we can [fight oppression] is by creating another whole structure that touches every aspect of our existence, at the same time as we are resisting.

Audre Lorde

In our *mestizaje* theories we create new categories for those of us left out or pushed out of the existing ones. We recover and examine non-western aesthetics while critiquing western aesthetics; recover and examine non-rational modes and blanked out realities while critiquing rational consensual reality; recover and examine indigenous languages while critiquing the languages of the dominant cultures.

Gloria Anzaldúa

I feel as if I'm gonna keel over any minute and die. That is often what it feels like if you're really doing coalition work. Most of the time you feel threatened to the core and if you don't, you're not really doing no coalescing.

Bernice Johnson Reagon

New Citizen-Subjects: Michel Foucault

Many twentieth-century prophets predicted a revolutionary form of human who rises from the ruins of previous social orders: from Fanon and Césaire to Bhabha and Said; from Haraway and de Lauretis to Anzaldúa and Lorde, the list goes on.[1] The vision of this new being in the passage that follows emerges from the 1966 mind of Michel Foucault. The psychic landscape Foucault describes in the following passage images the cultural terminations and beginnings that typify postmodernism globalization, the end of "Western man," the homogenization of difference, and some other, utopian, decolonizing zone as well:

> And yet the impression of fulfillment and of end...something we glimpse only as a thin line of light low on the horizon—that feeling and that impression are perhaps not ill founded....It will be said that Hölderlin, Hegel, Feuerbach, and Marx all felt this certainty that in them a thought and perhaps a culture were coming to a close, and that...another was approaching—in the dim light of dawn, in the brilliance of noon, or in the dissension of the falling day. But this close, this perilous imminence whose promise we fear today, whose danger we welcome, is probably not of the same order....In our day...it is not so much the absence or the death of God that is affirmed as the end of man...man has "come to an end," and that by reaching the summit of all possible speech, he arrives not at the very heart of himself but at the brink of that which limits him...new gods, the same gods, are already swelling the future Ocean; man will disappear.[2]

Ten years later (and one year before his death) Foucault challenged historians, philosophers, and critical and cultural scholars alike by asserting that the "most certain" of all contemporary philosophical problems is "the problem of the present time—of what we are, in this very moment."[3] His suggestion for how the citizen-subject should behave in relation to globalizing cultural dynamics was clear: in order to allow for the emergence of a liberatory "something else," Foucault predicted nothing less than the self-deconstitution of (Western) man.[4] The target of our attention under postmodern cultural conditions, he claimed, is "not to discover what we are, but to *refuse* what we are." At the same time, we must learn how to "promote new forms of subjectivity," he advises. But the generation of new kinds of citizen-subjects can happen only when we become capable of refusing "the kind of individuality which has been imposed on us for several centuries."[5] To self-reflexively refuse one's own sense of "individuality," of identity, is not an easy task—but this is the content of the emancipatory work that Foucault believed was necessary.

Such questions of identity have hovered on the academic horizon for decades and determined much scholarly writing in journals and books. Little of this discussion, however, has been accomplished for the sake of bringing about the kind of self-reflexive psychic transformations for which Foucault is agitating.[6] Like Foucault, for example, Fredric Jameson also senses the presence of new subjectivities coalescing under the pressures of postmodern globalizing conditions. Jameson cringes at this new emergence, however, which for him represents another horrifying effect of a world gone mad, a world that produces schizophrenic citizen-subjects who take in every new experience with the exhilaration of difference, but who are not capable of discerning the differences that matter in terms of organizing a more egalitarian and just human order. Jameson's despair is that there is no way to make effective interventions, no way to rechart subjectivity in an advanced capitalist cultural machine that desires our interventions to feed its machinations. Jameson's position is that there are no strategic interventions to be made, only horror to be felt in the recognition of a living cultural pathology—schizophrenic in nature—which we must all partake of eventually, or remain in the netherworld of detachment, unable to feel a part of social life at all. For Jameson, neocolonial postmodernism seduces through a form of insanity appropriate to the twenty-first century that is being generalized to a point of normality. But Foucault at the end of his life is less interested in the desires of the cultural order; his interests are in the desires of the citizen-subject: this shift in focus and interest makes all the difference.

Periodizing Resistance

Resistance is the unspecified term that lies outside the binary configuration of domination and subordination—yet form of resistance is only effective insofar as it is specifically related to the forms of domination and subordination that are currently in place. Foucault and Jameson agree that a new, global decolonizing collective project of resistance can be best advanced through understanding the configurations of power that operated in the historical periods just prior to our own time. According to Jameson, the most important manifestations of power occurred under the two previous moments of capitalism: small-market capitalism and monopoly (or imperialist) capitalism.[7] Jameson considers the transnational, postmodern stage of capitalism we now inhabit as the contemporary and third stage of capitalist development.[8] Crucial to understanding the desperation that drives Jameson's theoretical apparatus is the understanding that the first two stages have culminated in the current sci-fi moment of postmodernism wherein the "underside of culture is death," violence, and horror,[9] and the possibility of resistance lies only as faint hope on the rising "dystopian horizon" of transnational capitalism.[10] For Foucault, alternately, resistance is possible and already present, even if its existence circulates in heretofore unrecognizable forms.

Like Jameson, Michel Foucault situates our present moment in history by outlining its differences from two historical stages that preceded it. But Foucault wants to compare contemporary cultural conditions (which he leaves unnamed) to two more broadly defined previous modes of social organization that matter—feudalism and capitalism. Each of these historical periods expresses its own predominant modes of domination, subordination, and resistance. Today, he believes, citizen-subjects who are interested in generating effective modes of resistance capable of confronting neocolonial postmodernism must first recognize the fact that much of our perceptual apparatuses and tactics for action are based on past, outmoded yet residual conceptions of power and resistance.

The two most previous modes for organizing Western social order—feudalism and capitalism—each generated very different approaches for understanding and resisting power. Under feudalism, for instance, Foucault writes that struggles "against forms of ethnic (religious) or social domination were prevalent."[11] Under capitalism, however, a shift occurs so that "the Marxist struggle against exploitation (e.g., that which separates individuals from what they produce) came into the foreground."[12] In the twentieth century, and primarily in industrialized first world nations, a third form of social organization and its concomitant forms of dominations and subordinations has emerged so that, in Foucault's view, a third form of resistance has necessarily developed. This new predominant mode of resistance occurs, writes Foucault, in the form of a political "struggle against the forms of subjection—against the submission of subjectivity—against that which ties the individual to himself and submits him to others in this way.["13] Foucault wants us to recognize the revolutionary and unique character of this third mode of resistance.

Every social order structured around domination and subordination releases power relations that crush citizen-subjects into positionalities, escape from which only certain kinds of resistances prove effective.[14] But whether a social order is predominantly feudal, market-capitalist, monopoly-capitalist, or postmodern in function, theorists across disciplinary divides can agree generally that the first world during the late twentieth century experienced a great social, economic, and political divide—a mutation that has transfigured the kinds of powers, dominations, subordinations, and resistances that can be constituted. For Jameson, this mutation resulted in a "cultural pathology" that produces in the citizen-subject a hysterical exhilaration akin to schizophrenia, out of which effective forms of oppositional consciousness are unlikely to rise. Foucault, however, perceives this great new cultural and social mutation that is postmodernism as helping to saturate all citizen-subjects with forms of oppositional consciousness that are capable of confronting the most psychically intrusive forms of domination and subordination yet devised. Both thinkers understand that the forces released by this third-stage transmutation of cultural economics are saturating the psyche of the individual citizen-subject in a new kind of power.

Refusing Fascism with Foucault

This new kind of power, Foucault warns, "applies itself to immediate everyday life, categorizes the individual, marks him by his own individuality, attaches him to his own identity, imposes a law of truth on him which he must recognize and which others have to recognize in him."[15] This is how postmodern powers turn individuals into subjects—citizen-subjects. There are two meanings of the word SUBJECT, Foucault continues, "subject to someone else" by control and dependence, or being "tied" to ones' own identity through "conscience or self-knowledge." Both meanings suggest a form of power that "subjugates and makes subject to." But, unlike Jameson (or Althusser, for that matter), Foucault does not recognize this form of power to be fundamentally *de*humanizing—*de*individualizing. Rather, this immersion of the state's apparatus into every aspect of the individual citizen-subject's life and into the very structuring of the psyche has allowed, Foucault thinks, the development of a new kind of resistant and "oppositional" individual who could never have been produced under earlier forms of Western social organization.

Before the citizen-subject's birth into the social world, the intersections of race, culture, sex, gender, class, and social powers are already locating in order to provide a particular space to hold that individual, to pattern the kind of subjectivity it will be permitted. From the moment of its birth, the citizen-subject becomes regulated, branded, and shaped, the first world ideological apparatus imbricated through its subjectivity in a novel and, we might say, more total way than ever before. First world citizen-subjects take pride in their "freedom" of movement and speech, their activities trusted — as "good citizens" — to replicate the social order and its hierarchizations, usually without the necessary imposition of directly brutal state force. From the vantage point of Foucault's analysis, the first world citizen-subject who is wholly incorporated in the (post)modern state might well envy the largely unincorporated subjective spaces that still survive around certain populations living under more feudal or earlier capitalist forms of domination, who, in spite of the subordinations under which they live, are still "free" from the overwhelming determinations that influence the subjective spaces of neocolonized postmodern first world citizen-subjects. The problematics of postmodern transnational globalization are of a special nature in relation to consciousness and the status of first world citizen-subjects, Foucault thinks. That is why he advises such citizen-subjects to recognize that the "political, ethical, social, and philosophical problem of our day is not to try to liberate the individual from the state, and from the state's institutions, but to liberate us . . . from the type of individualization which is linked to the state."

This nature of this "liberation" must be of a different order than that struggled for under previous modes of social organization. It will require, Foucault insists, that we "promote new forms of subjectivity through the refusal of the kind of individuality which has been imposed on us."[16] Citizen-subjects have become so surrounded and "trapped" in our own histories of domination, fear, pain, hatred, and hierarchy that the strategic adversary under postmodern times has become our own sense of self.[17] Unlike "enemies" under feudal or capitalist eras, the major enemy to face during our own time has infiltrated every citizen-subject's body. What we must face, writes Foucault, is that the structure of this internalized form of everyday being is fascist. And there is "fascism in us all," he continues, "in our heads and in our everyday behavior." It is this internalized fascism that "causes us to love power," so that we now "desire the very thing that dominates and exploits us." Foucault challenges all citizen-subjects of every social class who live under neo-colonial postmodernism to answer the following questions: "How does one keep from being fascist, even (especially) when one believes oneself to be a revolutionary militant? How do we rid our speech and our acts, our hearts and our pleasures, of fascism? How do we ferret out the fascism that is ingrained in our behavior?"[18]

Principles of Politically Revolutionary Love and Desire:
Anti-Postmodernism, Deindividualization

These questions can be answered through understanding and applying the principles below, which, in Foucault's view generate access to politically revolutionary love, desire, and resistance. Taken together, these principles represent a new model for political action in resistance that is effective under postmodern cultural conditions: their enactment creates an oppositional and differential form of consciousness. The kinds of affinities and coalition building that these principles promote undo fascism by grounding identity differently than ever before. Foucault was concerned to point out that the forces of transnational capitalism inspired this "developing movement toward political struggle" which "no longer conforms" to any previous struggle for emancipation in history—Marxist or otherwise (xii). This social and identity movement is generating a new form of oppositional consciousness that inspires in its practitioners what Foucault describes as an unprecedented "experience and a technology of desire" (ibid.). Even though today, he continues, "old banners" of political resistance and identity are still "raised," ideological combat has already "shifted and spread" into "new zones" that can undo fascism—new zones of oppositional consciousness (ibid.). The principles below of political desire, love, and resistance should "motivate us to go further," Foucault hopes, in developing this new, "anti-postmodern," antifascist, and anticolonial oppositional consciousness and praxis (xiii). These principles puncture through the contingencies of everyday life, and provide access to that other reality with so many names and technologies, the differential place of consciousness.

This new social movement is infused with what Foucault calls a "desire" capable of driving the body and the will beyond their limits. Desire permeates being of all kinds, he writes, being-in-resistance as well as being in-domination. Indeed, it is desire, Foucault thinks, that drives, focuses, and permeates all human activity. What is required, then, is to reinforce an experience and technology of *desire-in-resistance* that can permit oppositional actors to move—as Audre Lorde puts it—"erotically" through power.[19] Foucault adds this ingredient to the hermeneutic of love we are constructing by asking, and answering, the following question: "How can and must desire deploy its forces within the political domain, and grow more intense in the process of overturning the established order? *Ars erotica, ars theoretica, ars politica*" (xii). He provides the following schema to permit this unprecedented politics of desire, a schema focused and driven by concrete principles that can "guide" oppositional agents in "the art" of countering "all forms" of fascism: "the fascism in our behavior, the fascism in our hearts" (xiii). These principles are Foucault's contribution to a uniquely politicized (and "differential") form of social and psychic opposition to authoritarian postmodern global powers. They cut right to the chase, and are "less concerned with *why* this or that than with *how*" to proceed (xii):

- Free political action from all unitary and totalizing paranoia.

- Develop action, thought, and desires by proliferation, juxtaposition, and disjunction, and not by subdivision and pyramidal hierarchization.

- Withdraw allegiance from the old categories of the Negative (law, limit, castration, lack, lacuna), which Western thought has so long held sacred as a form of power and an access to reality. Prefer what is positive and multiple, difference over uniformity, flow over unities, mobile arrangements over systems. Believe that what is productive is not sedentary but nomadic.

- Do not think that one has to be sad in order to be militant, even though the thing one is fighting is abominable. It is the connection of desire to reality (and not its retreat into the forms of representation) that possesses revolutionary force.

- Do not use thought to ground a political practice in Truth; nor political action to discredit, as mere speculation, a line of thought. Use political practice as an intensifier of thought, and analysis as a multiplier of the forms and domains for the intervention of political action.

- Do not demand of politics that it restore the "rights" of the individual, as philosophy has defined them. The individual is the product of power. What is needed is to "deindividualize" by means of multiplication and displacement, diverse combinations. The group must not be the organic bond uniting hierarchized individuals but a constant generator of *deindividualization*.

- Do not become enamored of power. (xiii; my emphasis)

Oppositional Cyber-Consciousness, Feminists of Color, and
Revolutionary Politics: Donna Haraway

This book ends in its own chiasmus by examining the connections of feminist theory to U.S. third world feminism, theories of globalization, de- and postcoloniality, and all of these are related to the methodology of the oppressed. This chapter studies these theoretical sites as they influence the work by a contemporary philosopher of science. Donna Haraway's "Manifesto for Cyborgs" is one of the most highly circulated essays written in the late twentieth century on the relations between science, technology, and revolutionary feminist politics. The manifesto might best be described its own terms—it is a "theorized and fabricated hybrid," a textual "machine," and a "fiction" that maps and locates "our social and bodily reality." But make no mistake, these are also the terms that Haraway uses in order to describe and ensure the development of a revolutionary form of human being, a creature who lives in both "social reality" and "fiction," and who performs and speaks in a "middle voice" that is forged in the amalgam of technology and biology—a cyborg-poet.[20]

This vision standing at the center of Haraway's imaginary is a "monstrous" image; for this new creature is the "illegitimate" child of human and machine, science and technology, dominant society and oppositional social movement, male and female, "first" and "third" worlds—indeed, of every binary. It is a being whose hybridity challenges all binary oppositions and every desire for wholeness, she claims, in the very way "blasphemy" challenges the body of religion (149). Haraway's blasphemy is a twenty-first-century being that reproaches, challenges, transforms, and shocks. But perhaps the greatest shock in this feminist theory of cyborg politics has taken place in the corridors of women's studies, where Haraway's model has acted as a transcoding device, a technology that has translated the fundamental precepts of differential U.S. third world feminist criticism into categories comprehensible under the jurisdictions of feminist, cultural, and critical theory.

Haraway has been very clear about the intellectual lineages and alliances of the propositions she named "cyborg theory." As she writes in her introduction to *Simians, Cyborgs, and Women* (1991), one primary aim of her work is equivalent to a central aim of U.S. third world feminist criticism, which is the "breakup of versions of Euro-American feminist humanism in their devastating assumptions of master narratives deeply indebted to racism and colonialism."[21] Her second aim is to propose a new technopolitics and form of being. Cyborg feminism will be "more able" than racist feminisms of earlier times, she writes, to "remain attuned to specific historical and political positionings and permanent partialities without abandoning the search for potent connections."[22] Through these aims, the structures of cyborg feminism become one with those of differential U.S. third world feminism.

Indeed, Haraway's cyborg feminism was conceived as a way to join the efforts of U.S. feminists of color in challenging what Haraway herself has identified as hegemonic feminism's "unreflective participation in the logics, languages, and practices of white humanism," insofar as white feminism tended to search "for a single ground of domination" by which to "secure our revolutionary voice" as women (160). The feminist theory produced since 1968 "by women of color," Haraway asserts, has developed "alternative discourses of womanhood," and these discourses have disrupted "the humanisms of many Western discursive traditions."[23] Haraway's statements demonstrate her strong political alliances with feminists of color, so it makes sense that Haraway should turn to differential U.S. third world feminism for help in modeling a revolutionary form of human body and consciousness capable of challenging "the networks" and "informatics" of postmodern social realities.

As she lays the foundations for her theory of science, technology, and oppositional politics in the postmodern world, Haraway thus recognizes and reckons with differential U.S. third world feminist criticism in ways that other scholars have been unable to. Remaining clear on the issue of cyborg feminist theory's intellectual lineages and alliances, Haraway writes:

> White women, including socialist feminists, discovered (that is, were forced kicking and screaming to notice) the non-innocence of the category "woman." That consciousness changes the geography of all previous categories; it denatures them as heat denatures a fragile protein. Cyborg feminists have to argue that "we" do not want any more natural matrix of unity, and that no construction is whole. (157)[24]

But to recognize that "no construction is whole" is not enough to stop internalized and externalized forms of authoritarianism — of fascism. Much of Haraway's work thus has been to identify the technical *skills* required for producing a dissident global movement and human being that are capable of generating egalitarian and just social relations. The skills she identifies are equivalent to the technologies I have identified in this book as the methodology of the oppressed.

Radical *Mestizaje*

It is no accident of metaphor that Haraway's theoretical formulations are woven through with terminologies and techniques from U.S. third world cultural forms, from Native American categories of "trickster" and "coyote" being (199), to *mestizaje*, through to the category of "women of color" itself, until the body of the oppositional cyborg becomes wholly articulated with the material and psychic positionings of differential U.S. third world feminism.[25] Like the "mestiza consciousness" described and defined under U.S. third world feminism, which, as Anzaldúa explains, arises "on borders and in margins" where feminists of color keep "intact shifting and multiple identities" with "integrity" and "love," the cyborg of Haraway's manifesto is also "resolutely committed to partiality, irony, intimacy and perversity" (151). In this equivalent alignment, Haraway's feminist cyborgs can be recognized (like agents of U.S. third world feminism) as the "illegitimate offspring" of militaristic "patriarchal capitalism" (ibid.). So too are feminist cyborg weapons and the weapons of U.S. third world feminism similar: "transgressed boundaries, potent fusions and dangerous possibilities" (154). Indeed, Haraway's cyborg textual machine generates a methodology that runs parallel to that of differential U.S. third world feminist criticism. Thus, insofar as Haraway's work became influential in feminist studies, her oppositional cyborgology helped to bring hegemonic feminist theory into alignment with theories of indigenous resistance, *mestizaje* understood as a critical apparatus, the differential form of U.S. third world feminism, and the methodology of the oppressed.[26]

The alignment between U.S. hegemonic feminism and U.S. third world feminism clicks into place at the point when Haraway provides a doubled vision of a "cyborg world," as seen in the passage below. The "cyborg" world of neocolonial postmodernism, she believes, can be understood either as the culmination of a Euro-American "white," masculinist society in its drive for mastery, on the one side, or, on the other, as the material manifestation of such resistant "indigenous" worldviews as *mestizaje*, U.S. third world feminism, or cyborg feminism.[27] Haraway writes:

> A cyborg world is about the final imposition of a grid of control on the planet, about the final abstraction embodied in Star Wars apocalypse waged in the name of defense, about the final appropriation of women's bodies in a masculinist orgy of war. *From another perspective* a cyborg world might be about lived social and bodily realities in which people are not afraid of their *joint kinship* with animals and machines, not afraid of permanently partial identities and contradictory standpoints. (154; my emphasis)

The important notion of "joint kinship" here is analogous to that called for in contemporary indigenous writings in which tribes or lineages are identified out of those who share, not bloodlines, but rather lines of affinity. Such lines of affinity occur through attraction, combination, and relation carved out of and in spite of difference. They are what comprise the mode of radical *mestizaje* called for in the works of U.S. scholars of color, as in the following 1982 example. Here Alice Walker asks U.S. black liberationists to recognize themselves as mestizos:

> We are the African *and* the trader. We are the Indian *and* the Settler. We are oppressor *and* oppressed...we are the *mestizos* of North America. We are black, yes, but we are "white," too, and we are red. To attempt to function as only one, when you are really two or three, leads, I believe, to psychic illness: "white" people have shown us the madness of that.[28]

The kind of radical *mestizaje* referred to in this passage and elsewhere can be understood as a complex kind of love in the postmodern world, where love is understood as affinity—alliance and affection across lines of difference that intersect both in and out of the body. Walker understands "psychic illness" as the attempt to be "one"—like the singularity of Barthes's narrative love that controls all meanings through the medium of the couple in love. The function of *mestizaje* in Walker's vision is more like that of Barthes's "prophetic love," where subjectivity becomes freed from ideology as it ties and binds reality. Prophetic love undoes the "one" that gathers the narrative, the couple, the race, into a singularity. Instead, prophetic love gathers up the *mezcla*, the mixture that lives through *differential movement* between possibilities of being. This is the kind of "love" that motivates U.S. third world feminist *mestizaje* understood as the differential theory and method of oppositional consciousness, what Anzaldúa has theorized as *la conciencia de la mestiza*, or the consciousness of the "Borderlands."[29]

Haraway weaves these U.S. third world feminist commitments to affinity through difference into her model for an oppositional cyborg feminism. In so doing, she provides yet another mapping of the differential theory and method of oppositional consciousness that is comprised of the technologies of the methodology of the oppressed.[30] In Haraway's version, oppositional cyborgism does not view differences and their corresponding "pictures of the world" relativistically (190), that is, as "allegories of infinite mobility and interchangeability."[31] Such anarchistic mobility is not enough. Instead, Haraway believes, differences should be seen as instances of the "elaborate specificity" and the "loving care people might take to learn how to see faithfully from another point of view" (ibid.). Haraway's example is provided in the differential writings by U.S. feminists of color whose hope and vision is not grounded on their own belief in some "original innocence (or the imagination of a once-upon-a-time wholeness" or oneness). The power of their writings, she continues, is derived from their insistence on the possibilities of affinity through difference — of differential consciousness enacted as a method of racial *mestizaje* — which allows for the guided use of any tool at one's disposal in order to ensure survival and to remake the world. Put differently, translates Haraway, the task of an oppositional cyborg feminism should be to "recode" all tools of "communication and intelligence" with one's aim being the subversion of "command and control" (175). Haraway's analysis of the written work by Chicana activist/intellectual Cherríe Moraga's provides her a primary example.

Women of Color

The passage below reflects the way in which Haraway understands the identities of "women of color" to operate in the same manner as her theory and politics of oppositional cyborgism. It is in this conflation between women of color as identity, and cyborg feminism as theory, that a peculiar elision occurs, as we shall see. Haraway rightly describes Cherríe Moraga's language as one that is not "whole":

> it is self-consciously *spliced*, a chimera of English and Spanish, both conqueror's languages. But it is this *chimeric monster*, without claim to an original language before violation, that crafts the erotic, competent, potent identities of women of color. Sister Outsider hints at the possibility of world survival not because of her innocence, but because of her ability to live on the boundaries, to write without the founding myth of original wholeness, with its inescapable apocalypse of final return to a deathly oneness.... Stripped of identity, the bastard race teaches about the power of the margins and the importance of a mother like *Malinche*. Women of color have transformed her from the evil mother of masculinist fear into the originally literate mother who teaches survival. (175–76)

Unfortunately, differential U.S. third world feminist criticism (which is a set of theoretical and methodological strategies) is often misrecognized and underanalyzed by readers when it is translated as a demographic constituency only (women of color), and not as a theoretical and methodological approach in its own right.[32] The textual problem that becomes a philosophical problem and, indeed, a political problem, is the conflation of U.S. third world feminist criticism — understood as a theory and method of oppositional consciousness — with the demographic or "descriptive" and generalized category of "women of color," thus depoliticizing and repressing the specificity of the politics and form of consciousness developed by "U.S. women of color," or "feminists of color," and erasing the specificity of what is a *particular* form of these: "differential U.S. third world feminism."

Haraway recognizes these problematics, however, and how by gathering up the category "women of color" and identifying it as a "cyborg identity, a potent subjectivity synthesized from fusions of outsider identities" (i.e., "Sister Outsider"), her work inadvertently contributes to the elision of differential U.S. third world feminism by turning its approaches, methods, forms, and skills into examples of cyborg feminism (174). In 1991 she thus amended her position, by saying that today "I would be much more careful about describing who counts as a 'we' in the statement 'we are all cyborgs.'" Indeed, she suggests that the centrality of cyborg theory might be replaced with something else capable of bridging the apartheid of theoretical domains. Why not find a name or concept that can signify "a family of displaced figures, of which the cyborg" is only one, she suggests, and then "ask how the cyborg" can make connections with other nonoriginal people who are also "multiply displaced."[33] Let us imagine a new "family of figures," she continues, who can "populate our imaginations" of "postcolonial, postmodern worlds that will not be quite as imperializing in terms of a single figuration of identity.[34]

At the beginning of the twenty-first century, such aims remain unresolved across the terrain of oppositional discourse, or rather, they remain *multiply answered and divided by academic terrain*. Even within feminist theory, Haraway's cyborg feminism and her later development of the technology of "situated knowledges" (though they come close), cannot bridge the gaps that create the apartheid of theoretical domains identified earlier. So Haraway tries another approach in her argument from a chapter in the Butler and Scott anthology *Feminists Theorize the Political*. Her essay begins by stating that those women who were "subjected to the conquest of the new world faced a broader social field of reproductive unfreedom, in which their children did not inherit the status of human in the founding hegemonic discourses of U.S. society."[35] This is the reason that "feminist theory produced by women of color" in the United States generates "discourses that confute or confound traditional Western standpoints." If dominant feminist theory is to incorporate differential U.S. third world feminist theory and criticism, she asserts, then the focus of feminist theory and politics must shift to that of making "*a place for the different social subject*."[36] This shift could bring women's studies into affinity with theoretical terrains such as postcolonial discourse theory, U.S. third world feminism, postmodernism, global studies, and queer theory, she thinks, and would thus begin to bridge the apartheid of theoretical domains. Here, Haraway's work introduces the cross-disciplinary method I have identified in this book as the methodology of the oppressed.

How can such a shift in feminist theory be accomplished? Haraway proposes this: that feminists become "less interested in joining the ranks of gendered femaleness," to instead become focused on "gaining the INSURGENT ground as female social subject" (95).[37] This means that the focus of "women's studies" must be relocated to examining how power moves through, between, and *outside* the binary divide male/female. Haraway's challenge is that only in this way will feminist theories concerned with sexed and "gendered racial subjectivities" be able to take "affirmative *and* critical account of emergent, differentiating, self-representing, contradictory social subjectivities, with their claims on action, knowledge, and belief."[38] What we are talking about is the development of a new form of "antiracist"—indeed, even antigender—feminism where there will be "no place for women," Haraway asserts, only "geometrics of difference and contradiction crucial to women's cyborg identities" (171). How does one enact this new kind of "feminism"—or oppositional consciousness?

The Science, Technics, and Erotics of the Methodology of the Oppressed

A new feminist oppositional consciousness, Haraway thinks, will require the development of "technologies" that can disalienate and realign the human joint that connects our "technics" (material and technical details, rules, machines, and methods) with our "erotics" (the sensuous apprehension and expression of love as affinity).[39] This new joining can only occur through the methodology of the oppressed, what she calls a "politics of articulation,"[40] which is capable of creating "more powerful collectives in dangerously unpromising times."[41] Haraway's politics of articulation is comprised of "skilled practices," she writes, that are honed and developed within oppressed, or subordinated, classes. Haraway's position is that all peoples who now live under postmodern cultural conditions must learn to act from what she (along with Foucault) calls these "standpoints of the subjugated." Subjugated standpoints are described as being

> savvy to [dominant] modes of denial through repression, forgetting, and disappearing acts—ways of being nowhere while claiming to see comprehensively. The subjugated have a decent chance to be on to this god-trick and all its dazzling—and therefore, blinding—illuminations. "Subjugated" standpoints are preferred because they seem to promise more adequate, sustained, objective, transforming accounts of the world. *But HOW to see from below is a problem requiring at least as much skill with bodies and language, with the mediations of vision, as the "highest" techno-scientific visualizations.* (191; my emphasis)

The key to finding a dissident form of globalization is to develop technologies to "see from below," and, as Haraway points out, learning to do so requires "as much skill" with bodies, language, and vision as learning the most sophisticated forms of "technoscientific" visualization. Haraway's answer is to provide readers her own version of the technologies of the methodology of the oppressed, which, in her view, are the very skills necessary to "see from below." It is these skills that permit the constant, differential repositioning necessary for perception from "subjugated standpoints." Haraway's work develops its own vocabulary for identifying the five technologies of the methodology of the oppressed ("semiotics," "deconstruction," "meta-ideologizing," "democratics," and "differential movement"). In her view, these technologies together comprise the politics of articulation that are necessary for forging an unprecedented mode of feminist methodology.

Haraway describes the first skill of the subjugated/oppressed when she writes that "self-knowledge requires a semiotic-material technology." This initial technology, she states, links "meanings and bodies" in order to open "non-isomorphic subjects, agents, and territories to stories" that are "unimaginable from the vantage point of the cyclopian, self-satiated eye of the master subject" (192). The second and third technologies of concern here, deconstruction and meta-ideologizing, are interventionary vectors that are primary means, asserts Haraway, for "understanding and intervening in the patterns of objectification in the world." In the effort to transform this objectification, "decoding and transcoding plus translation and criticism: all are necessary." The fourth technology, democratics, is that which guides the others. The moral force of this technology is indicated in Haraway's assertion that in all oppositional activity "*we must be accountable*" for the "patterns of objectification in the world" that have become the real. To rise to the level of this accountability, the practitioner of cyborg feminism cannot be "about fixed locations in a reified body." Rather, the practitioner must deploy a fifth and final technology, to move differentially in, with, and about "nodes in fields" and "inflections in orientations." Through such differential mobilities the practitioner engages her and his own ethical approach and "responsibility for difference in material-semiotic fields of meaning," she writes (195). Haraway's cyborg feminism recognizes that all innocent "identity" politics and epistemologies are impossible as strategies for seeing from the standpoints of the subjugated. Thus, in relation to differential consciousness itself, Haraway's cyborg feminism is "committed" in the enactment of all its skills to "mobile positioning," "passionate detachment," and the "kinship" generated by affinity through difference (192). These six locations are the "cyborg skills" that Haraway believes are necessary for developing a feminism for the twenty-first century. They represent another transcodation of the differential consciousness and the five "subjugated stand-points" that are the technologies I have identified in this book as the methodology of the oppressed.

Whether figured in the terms of cyborg feminism, as Foucault's principles for polit-ical desire, as Barthes's punctum to political being, as White's power of the middle voice, as Anzaldúa's *mestizaje*, or as the methodology of the oppressed, these skills, born of de-colonial processes, similarly insist on new kinds of human and social ex-change that have the power to forge a dissident transnational coalitional conscious-ness, or what Haraway calls an "earthwide network of connections." These skills enable a coalitional consciousness that permits its practitioner to "translate knowl-edges among very different—and power-differentiated—communities" (187). They thus comprise the grounds for a different kind of "objectivity"—of science itself—Haraway continues.

New Sciences: Objectivity and Differential Consciousness

Haraway's science for the twenty-first century is one of "interpretation, translation, stuttering, and the partly understood." It is being welded by an oppositional practi-tioner she calls the "multiple subject with at least double vision." From the view-point of this unprecedented science, objectivity becomes transformed into a process Haraway calls "situated knowledges" (188). When scholars transform their conscious-ness of objectivity into a consciousness of situated knowledges, they develop a differ-ent kind of relation to perception, objectivity, understanding, and production that is akin to White's and Derrida's descriptions of the middle voice; for this consciousness demands the practitioner's "situatedness," writes Haraway, "in an ungraspable middle space" (111).[42] Like the mechanism of the middle voice of the verb, Haraway's situated knowledges require that what is an "object of knowledge" also be "pictured as an actor and agent" (198), transformative of itself and its own situation while also being acted upon. Haraway's development of the concept of situated knowledges demands the ability of consciousness to perceive, move, and perform according to a process that is becoming more easily identifiable and nameable: this is the differential form of oppositional consciousness that, through political and technical necessity, depends on the methodology of the oppressed.

      Thus it is no accident that the third chapter of Haraway's book *Simians, Cyborgs, and Women* is named "differential politics for inappropriate/d others." Her chapter defines a coalescing and ever more articulated form of decolonizing global social movement from where, as Haraway puts it, "feminist embodiment" resists "fixation" in order to better ride the "webs of differential positioning" (196). Haraway's thesis is this: theorists who subscribe to this decolonizing postmodern mode of oppositional consciousness must learn to be "more generous and more suspicious—both generous *and* suspicious, exactly the receptive posture" we must all seek in "political semiosis generally." This strategy for identity and social construction is "closely aligned with the oppositional and differential consciousness"[43] of U.S. third world feminism, she writes, that is, with the *theory and method of oppositional consciousness in its differential form* that is outlined in *Methodology of the Oppressed.* The differential politics of 1980s U.S. third world feminism thus was not only a cultural politics. It also represented a technoscience politics sufficient for the next phase of resistance.[44]

Technoscience Politics: The Methodology of the Oppressed Creates a *Decolonizing Cyberspace*

The oppositional and differential politics outlined in this book occur in a realm I first defined in the preceding chapters on the methodology of the oppressed as a "cyberspace." Haraway provides the definition for a neocolonizing postmodern version of cyberspace as follows:

> Cyberspace seems to be the consensual hallucination of too much complexity, too much articulation. It is the virtual reality of paranoia. Paranoia is the belief in the unrelieved density of connection, requiring, if one is to survive, withdrawal and defense unto death. The defended self re-emerges at the heart of relationality. Paradoxically, paranoia is the condition of the impossibility of remaining articulate. In virtual space, the virtue of articulation, the power to produce connection threatens to overwhelm and finally engulf all possibility of effective action to change the world.[45]

This is a harsh, unrelenting, and ruthless cyberspace of infinite dispersion and interfacing. But how does cyberspace alternately come to be understood as the generous and compassionate zone of the zero degree of meaning, prophetic love, or of the form of differential consciousness that is accessed by the methodology of the oppressed?

It has been assumed that the oppressed will behave without recourse to any *particular* method, or rather, that their behavior consists of whatever acts one must commit in order to survive, whether physically or psychically. This is exactly why the methodology of the oppressed can now be recognized as the mode of being best suited to life under neocolonizing postmodern and highly technologized conditions in the first world; for to enter a world where any activity is possible in order to ensure survival is to enter a cyberspace of being. In the past this space was accessible only to those forced into its terrain. As in Haraway's definition above, this cyberspace can be a place of boundless and merciless destruction—for it is a zone where meanings are only cursorily attached and thus capable of reattaching to others depending on the situation to be confronted. Yet this very activity also provides cyberspace its decolonizing powers, making it a zone of limitless possibility, as in the examples of the "gentle abyss" in Barthes's formulation, the realm of *différance*, the processes of the "middle voice," or in Fanon's "open door of every consciousness," and Anzaldúa's "*coatlicue* state." Its processes are closely linked with those of differential consciousness.

This benevolent version of cyberspace is analogous to the harsh cyberspace of computer and even social life under conditions of globalization in Haraway's pessimistic vision. Through the viewpoint of differential oppositional consciousness, the technologies developed by subjugated populations to negotiate this realm of shifting meanings can be recognized as the very technologies necessary to all first world citizens who are interested in renegotiating postmodern first world cultures, with what we might call a sense of their own power and integrity intact. But power, integrity—and morality—as Anzaldúa suggests,[46] will be based on entirely different terms than those identified in the past when, as Jameson writes, individuals could glean a sense of self in opposition to a centralizing dominant power that oppressed them, and then determine how to act. Under global postmodern disobediencies the self blurs around the edges, shifts in order to ensure survival, transforms according to the requisites of power, all the while (under the guiding force of the methodology of the oppressed as articulated by Fanon and the rest) carrying with it the integrity of a self-conscious awareness of the transformations desired, and above all, a sense of the impending ethical and political impact that such transformations will perform.

Haraway's theory of cyborg feminism, her recognition of "subjugated standpoints," her articulation of the skills that comprise these standpoints, and her theory of objectivity as "situated knowledges" constitute a politically articulate and this time feminist version (and another affirmation of the presence across disciplines) of what I refer to as the differential form of social movement and consciousness. When she writes that cyborg feminism is about "nodes in fields, inflections in orientations, a responsibility for difference in material-semiotic fields of meaning" (195), her cyborg feminism calls up the same nexus of affinity, the same technologies of resistance, the same "love" in the postmodern world called up not only by contemporary theorists who have written their way out of dominant first world status, including Barthes, Fanon, Derrida, Foucault, Hayden White, and many others, but also by those who insisted on an internally dissident country within their own nation-state, U.S. "third world" feminists[47] such as (to name only a few) Paula Gunn Allen, Nellie Wong, Audre Lorde, Gloria Anzaldúa, Trin Minh-ha, Joy Harjo, and Janice Gould.

Haraway's theory challenges and weds first world postmodern politics on a transnational world scale with the decolonizing apparatus for global survival I call the methodology of the oppressed. It is in these couplings (where "race, gender, and capital require a cyborg theory of wholes and parts" [181]) that Haraway's work contributes to bridging the gaps between disciplines that create the apartheid of theoretical domains, outlined in chapter 3. What is being suggested here is that the coding necessary to remap the "disassembled and reassembled" post-modern "collective and personal self" (163) must occur according to a guide that is capable of aligning feminist theory with other locations for thought and politics that are aimed at egalitarian social change. This alignment can happen when being and action, knowledge and science, are self-consciously encoded through what Haraway calls subjugated and situated knowledges, and what I call the methodology of the oppressed. This methodology is arising globally from varying locations, through a multiplicity of terminologies and forms,[48] and indomitably from the minds, bodies and spirits of U.S. feminists of color who demanded the recognition of *la conciencia de la mestiza*, womanism, indigenous resistance, and identification with the colonized. Only when feminist theory self-consciously recognizes and applies this methodology can feminist politics become fully synonymous with antiracism; only when global theory, cultural theory, critical theory, and ethnic theory recognize this methodology can they become synchronous with feminism and each other.

By the twentieth century's end, oppositional activists and thinkers had invented new names, indeed, new languages, for what is the purview of the methodology of the oppressed and the *coatlicue*, differential consciousness it demands. Some of these terminologies and technologies, from "signifyin'" to *la facultad*, from U.S. third world feminism to cyborg feminism, from Foucault's principles for political desire to the apparatus of the middle voice, from situated knowledges to strategic feminism, from the abyss to *différance*, have been variously identified. The methodology of the oppressed provides a schema for the cognitive map of power-laden social reality under global postmodern conditions for which oppositional actors and theorists across disciplines, from Fanon to Jameson, from Barthes to Anzaldúa, from Lorde to Haraway, are longing.

Conclusion: Differential Manifesto, Trans-Languages, and Global Oppositional Politics

DIFFERENTIAL SOCIAL movement and the forms of praxis it produces are not simply part and parcel of the cultural superstructure of our age, deeply connected as they are to the methodology developed by the oppressed under previous social formations, and which is now reemerging as useful to all citizen-subjects who must learn to negotiate, survive, and transform present social conditions into better worlds come to life. The self-conscious operation of differential social movement represents the opportunity to engage in social praxis through the constant surveying of social powers and interjection in them by a new kind of repoliticized citizen-warrior. Differential oppositional social movement and consciousness represent constructivist functions that perceive power as their world space, and identity as the monadic unit of power via subjectivity capable of negotiating and transforming power's configurations. Through the deployment of a differential mode of oppositional consciousness, practitioners can self-consciously replace themselves within the circle of moral conceptions defining our current social horizons, for its activity undoes the conscience—the incarnation of the law—thus renewing consciousness itself.

The differential mode of oppositional social movement and consciousness can thus be understood as a *symptom* of transnational capitalism in its neocolonizing postmodern form (insofar as interest in this mode of resistance is arising out of pressures peculiar to this newest form of globalization), as well as a *remedy* for neocolonizing postmodernism both in spite and because of its similarities in structure to power's postmodern configurations. Yet what must be remembered is that the differential resides in the place where meaning escapes any final anchor point, slipping away to surprise or snuggle inside power's mobile contours—it is part and parcel of the undefinable meaning that constantly escapes every analysis.

As we saw in chapter 3, where differential consciousness arises in that space between and through meaning systems I call a "cyberspace," and in chapter 5, which examines some of the "unimaginable solutions and unforeseeable syntheses" predicted by Barthes that lead to a *coatlicue* state, to what is theorized as "love" in the postmodern world in chapters 6 and 7, differential consciousness permits the poetic movement of consciousness both "backwards" through the Sr/Sd/Sign relationship and "forward" to create new levels of metaideology: it represents a cruising, migrant, improvisational mode of subjectivity. This subjectivity is prodded into existence through an outsider's sensibilities: a lack of loyalty to dominant ideological signification, combined with the intellectual curiosity that demands an explosion of meaning (in semiotic and deconstructing activities), or to meaning's convergence and solidification (in meta-ideologizing), for the sake either of survival or of political change toward equality. The politicized differential mode of oppositional consciousness expressed here can be represented as a form of awareness that touches human reality as encoded in ideology on every side: it provides the condition or medium through which difference both arises and is undone; it joins together through *movement*, both in the processes of the perception and semiotic decoding of meaning and in the deployment of units-of-reality in the production of meta-ideologizing; and it provides a social, cultural, political, and psychic means for engaging with reality. In this last sense, differential oppositional consciousness is contingent upon the ways in which reality—as constructed through historical agencies—presents itself as "natural" while being laden with the values, hopes, and desires of the dominant social order.

That is why the differential is subjunctive; it is that which joins together the possible with what is, the place where indirect style or discourse occurs until it finds purposeful, guided, political reason to be through the reconfiguration of units-of-power in the interests of their egalitarian distribution. This form of political subjectivity resides in a state of contingency, of possibility, readying for any event. Dependent on the chances provided by power, the differential mode of oppositional consciousness movement is conditional: subject to the terms of dominant power, yet capable of challenging and changing those very same terms. It is a mode of consciousness and activity that is not necessarily true or false—only possible, active, and present. It promotes social movement with purpose, both subject to the terms of power and capable of transforming them. This social movement generates a different kind of negotiation as it barters meaning systems, using skills accomplished by a new kind of collectivity that attaches strings, makes demands, imposes conditions, negotiates terms.

Differential social movement finds its expression through the methodology of the oppressed. The technologies of semiotic reading, deconstruction of signs, meta-ideologizing, differential movement, and moral commitment to equality are its vectors, its expressions of influence. These vectors meet in the differential mode of consciousness, which carries them through to the level of the "real" where they can impress and guide dominant powers. So too differential oppositional consciousness is itself a force that rhizomatically and parasitically inhabits each of these vectors, linking them in movement, while the pull of each vector creates the ongoing tension and re-formation of the liberal, revolutionary, supremacist, or separatist ideological forces that inscribe social reality. The differential can be thus thought of as a constant reapportionment of space, of boundaries, of horizontal and vertical re-alignments of oppositional powers. Because each vector occurs at different velocities, one of them can realign all the others, creating different kinds of patterns, and permitting entry at different points. These energies revolve around each other, aligning and realigning in a field of force that materializes a hermeneutics of love in the postmodern world that can generate an oppositional cosmopolitics. Each technology of the methodology of the oppressed creates new conjunctural possibilities, produced by ongoing and transforming regimes of exclusion and inclusion. Differential consciousness is thus a crossing network of consciousness, a trans-consciousness that occurs in a register permitting the networks themselves (as we saw in the example of U.S. third world feminism) to be appropriated as ideological weaponry.

This theory and method of oppositional consciousness is a committed and achievable field for mobile and transformable subjectivity; a consciousness (formally demanded only of the oppressed) developed and represented within women-of-color feminism, where it was understood and utilized as an expression of the methodology of the oppressed. Here, differential oppositional consciousness was encoded as *la facultad* (a semiotic vector), the "outsider/within" (a deconstructive vector), "strategic essentialism," (a meta-ideologizing vector), *la conciencia de la mestiza*, "world traveling" or "loving cross-cultures" (differential vectors), and "womanism" (a democratizing, moral vector).[1] Unlike Westerners such as Patrick Moynihan who have argued that "the collapse of (Soviet) Communism" in 1991 proves that "racial, ethnic, and national ties of difference only ultimately divide any society,"[2] the differential technologies of oppositional consciousness, as utilized and theorized by a racially diverse U.S. coalition of women of color, demonstrate the procedures for achieving affinity and alliance across difference; they represent the modes that love takes in the postmodern world.[3] The differential permits the generation of a new kind of coalitional consciousness and warrior-citizenship: countrywomen and country-men of the same psychic terrain. Differential consciousness, the technologies of the methodology of the oppressed, and oppositional differential social movement and its ideological weaponry are part and parcel of a global decolonizing alliance of differ-ence in its drive toward egalitarian social relations and economic well-being for all citizenry: an oppositional global politics, a cosmopolitics for *planeta tierra*.

Postmodern neocolonialism is mitigated by the differential form of oppositional social movement, which etches and transforms it with varying resistant *movidas*. The differential form of social movement is guided by the methodology of the oppressed, which is a set of technologies that grasp meaning—transforming and moving it on both sides, that of social reality, and that of the realm of the "abyss." The methodology of the oppressed acts as a punctum, a courier that accesses the realm of consciousness that is differential. *This* differential consciousness is a practice for identity, a political site for the third meaning, that obtuse shimmering of signification that glances through every binary opposition. Taken together, these processes and procedures comprise a hermeneutic for defining and enacting love in the postmodern world, and a method for generating oppositional global politics.

But the differential is not easily self-consciously wielded, inhab-ited, named, or achieved, as many of our great contemporary thinkers so aptly explain. "Most of the time you feel threatened to the core," states Bernice Johnson Reagon.[4] Louis Althusser puts it this way: because "class instinct is subjective and spontaneous," the class instinct of the middle classes and "*thus of intellectuals*" must undergo a painful and "revolutionary" transformation in order to become oppositional—that is, in order to become aligned with the methodology of the oppressed.[5]

In chapter 2 I schematized the politics of the oppressed into four principal practices, which I argued are the four prevalent rhetorical figures generated within U.S. leftist politics during the late twentieth century. I typified these figures as the equal-rights, revolutionary, supremacist, and separatist forms of oppositional political activity. Each political tactic is generated in order to challenge the dominant ideological/economic/social forms that define and castigate particular social types as inferior. I argued that these four forms of oppositional politics should be understood as differing ideologies, each requiring its own particular subjective life from practi-tioners, and each delimiting the forms of collectivity-in-opposition that it permits.

As in the example of the U.S. women's movement of the 1960s and 1970s, we saw that these ideologies can congeal and solidify within any liberation movement until each comes to represent itself as *the* most effective and moral mode of oppositional behavior and consciousness. This dynamic is the basis on which each of these political practices-become-ideology earned the charge against it of "racism," "sexism," "elitism," or "essentialism."

Barthes warns that when ideologies gather up inside a revolutionary movement (that collective will committed to cathartic acts meant to "reveal the political load of the world"—and then to *make* the world), when oppositional tactics become strategies, metalanguages, ideologies, then what Barthes calls an "ex-nomination" of the revolutionary impulse takes place. Ex-nomination, or unnaming, Barthes explains, is what happens when revolutionary political practice "distorts itself into a 'Nature'" in order to take better control, to be more easily understood, exchanged, and deployed. This form of meta-ideologizing, Barthes warns, if not exercised self-consciously and tactically, will "sooner or later be experienced as a process counter to revolution," as in the way "Stalin" as meta-ideology became the dominant ideology during the 1930s Soviet Union. This revolutionary form of frozen meta-ideologizing, the unhinging of consciousness from its political commitment to the differential mode, permits any oppositional practice to become only another version of dominant ideology, another version of supremacism. This is why the oppressed have only one true mode of revolutionary activity, the ability to perceive and decode dominant-order sign systems in order to move among them with a certain literacy, thus ensuring their survival, and one true mode of revolutionary consciousness, which is the ability of consciousness to differentially move through the being of meaning, and *toward* a possible and utopian world of desire, social and psychic life, *amor en Aztlán*, differential consciousness.

Indeed, my argument is that it is the ability to conceive of the equal-rights, revolutionary, supremacist, and separatist ideologies as *constructed* by the oppressed in liberatory action, to understand them as forms of consciousness that are themselves readable, inhabitable, interpretable, and transformable when necessary, and to recognize their structural relations to one another through an overgirding theory and method of oppositional consciousness, that comprises the fifth and differentially acting form of consciousness and activity in opposition. The differential form of oppositional consciousness is both another mode of these oppositional ideologies and at the same time a transcendence of them. Functioning on an altogether different register, differential oppositional consciousness is what makes it possible to identify the previous modes as the politics of the Other-in-opposition, what permits the practitioner to perceive their structural relatedness, and thus to tactically utilize or move among them. In Barthes's terms, it is a differential form of consciousness that permits the oppositional social actor to use ideology itself as "the departure point" for another semiological chain,[6] a resignification process whose ultimate outcome is then viewed as only another *tactic*—not a strategy—capable of shifting dominant ideological systems. This is a transitive, revolutionary activity born out of a differential political practice, a strategy comprised fully of tactics. It is a self-conscious and transitive movement of mind, of middle-voice reflexivity that is required for this kind of operation, if one is to fully understand and utilize semiology as a practice for the emancipation of the imagination. This manipulation of one's own consciousness through ideological forms and meanings requires the desire and ability to move differentially through one layer of Sr/Sd/Sign relationship and into another artificial or self-consciously manufactured ideological system, according to one's reading of power as it settles inside of ideology—that humanly constructed artifice of meaning itself.

With the transnationalization of capitalism, when elected officials are no longer leaders of singular nation-states but nexuses for multinational interests, it also becomes possible for citizen-subjects to become activists for a new decolonizing global terrain, a psychic terrain that can unite them with similarly positioned citizens-subjects within and across national borders into new, post–Western-empire alliances. Barthes, in spite of his commitments to the metamorphosis of dominant cultures and forms of consciousness, banished himself from this imagined community. But the new countrypeople who fight for egalitarian social relations under neocolonial postmodernism welcome citizenry to a new polity, a new homeland. The means for entry is "the methodology of the oppressed," a set of technologies for decolonizing the social imagination. These technologies—semiotic perception, the deconstruction of supremacy, the meta-ideologizing of signification, the differential perception and deployment of consciousness, are all processes that are guided by democratics, the practitioners' commitment to the equal distribution of power. All these technologies together, when also joined to those of differential social movement and to those of differential consciousness, operate as a single apparatus that I call the physics of love. Love as social movement is enacted by revolutionary, mobile, and global coalitions of citizen-activists who are allied through the apparatus of emancipation.

Notes

Introduction

1. The transnationalization of economies and cultures is transforming first world societies in ways no longer identifiable under any previous rubrics: first world social orders are no longer identifiable as simply "capitalist," whether of the market, monopoly, or multinational varieties, but neither are they "socialist," "primitive communist," "slave," or "feudal." Global economic and cultural expansion is the cause and symptom of completely original economic, political, social, and cultural relations, such that theorists are searching for new names to represent a new era; this is what Jameson has done in his foundational work on postmodernism. See Fredric Jameson, *Postmodernism, or the Cultural Logic of Late Capitalism* (Durham, N.C.: Duke University Press, 1991); *The Geopolitical Aesthetic: Cinema and Space in the World System* (Bloomington: Indiana University Press, 1992); "Cognitive Mapping," in *Marxism and the Interpretation of Culture*, ed. Cary Nelson and Lawrence Grossberg (Urbana: University of Illinois Press, 1988), pp. 347–57; and "Postmodernism, or the Cultural Logic of Late Capitalism," *New Left Review*, 146 (July–August 1984): 53–94. For a thorough and excellent bibliography of Jameson's works (1961–89) (the predecessors of his 1990 formulation of postmodernism), see *Postmodernism/ Jameson/Critique*, ed. Douglas Kellner (Washington, D.C.: Maisonneuve Press, 1989).

2. Rafael Pérez-Torres suggests that there are two forms of postmodernism, one neocolonizing, reactionary, but "multicultural," as in Jameson's formulation, the other also multicultural but effective in "resistance." See "Movements in a 'Minority Literature,'" in *Movements in Chicano Poetry: Against Margins, against Myths* (New York: Cambridge University Press, 1995), p. 14. In *Methodology of the Oppressed*, U.S. third world feminism is articulated as a postmodern resistance movement.

3. Just as the "differential" is the gear of a car that permits a new kind of transmission of power, so too are the differential mode of social movement and the new alliances it propels technologies for transmitting power in new ways. In the analysis of 1970s to 1980s U.S. third world feminism, five forms of resistance and the relations obtaining among them through the medium of differential consciousness are seen to comprise a methodological schema for analyzing, understanding, and explaining varying modes of consciousness in opposition that appear to be distinctly different from one another. Each mode is similar, however, insofar as each comprises one peculiar idiom of resistance, that is, a speech form particular to itself, while functioning *at the same time* as a linked rhetoric or language of resistance. The (1) integrationist, (2) revolutionary, (3) supremacist, (4) separatist, and (5) differential modes of opposition are united under their differential aspect—which functions not only as a fifth form, but as an overall organizing principle. I argue that the differential mode of social movement represents a new kind of generative activity, the step outside of ideology (for which Althusser called) into the realm of movement—the place from which language is generated. Part II of this book identifies five principal categories around which a theory and method of oppositional consciousness under postmodern conditions organized. Each category represents an equally effective means for transforming dominant power relations. But they do not intervene in postmodern powers unless they are deployed through the differential mode of oppositional consciousness and social movement, which is comprised of a methodology described in Part III, "The Methodology of the Oppressed." The methodology of the oppressed is a set of procedures that guide differential social movements in deploying its rhetoric. Thus, U.S. third world feminist criticism is the method used throughout this book for the analysis of all texts.

4. I find this term useful for pointing out that "globalization" includes many forms of "cosmopolitics," from neocolonizing "postmodern" forces to differential practices of resistance. For further definition of this neologism, see Pheng Cheah and Bruce Robbins, eds., *Cosmopolitics, Thinking and Feeling beyond the Nation* (Durham, N.C.: Duke University Press, 1998). For further provocative definitions and descriptions of oppositional postmodern globalization see Guillermo Gómez-Peña's *The New World (B)order: Prophecies, Poems and Loqueras for the End of the Century*, which formulates "*La Gringostroika*," "The Official Transculture," "The *Barrios* of Resistance," "The Mafia's," and "Chicano/a cyberpunk art" as models for constructing decolonizing alternatives to global postmodernism (i.e., the "official transculture") in the form of a postmodern but dissident "Hybrid State." See also Alicia Gaspar De Alba, *Chicano Art: Cultural Politics and the CARA Exhibition* (Austin: University of Texas Press, 1998).

5. What I have prepared in my analysis of Barthes's work is a manifesto on the necessity of radical semiology: a contemporary method for sign reading. Part III, "The Methodology of the Oppressed," and the chapters "On Cultural Studies" and "Semiotics and the Methodology of the Oppressed" argue the importance of radical semiology to all academic studies interested in further developing de-coloniality and human liberation.

6. Helen Tiffin describes decolonization as a "process, not arrival." De-coloniality involves a dialectical relationship, she writes, "between European ontology and epistemology, and the impulse to create or re-create" local reality. My use of the term *de-coloniality* follows her definition. See "Post-Colonial Literature and Counter-Discourse," *Kunapipi* 9 (1987): 17–34. The term *postcolonial* is understood in its most general sense as a utopian site located somewhere beyond authoritarianism and domination. For an excellent examination of this term's problematics, see Anne McClintock, "The Angel of Progress: Pitfalls of the Term 'Post-Colonialism,'" *Social Text* 31–32 (summer 1992): 32–67. The term

neocolonization is understood in its traditional sense to represent the policies through which a powerful force maintains or extends its control over foreign dependencies.

7. Part III furthermore identifies seven ways to negotiate dominant systems of power. These rhetorics include (1) the speech of "legitimated" citizen-subjects; (2) speech utilized by "oppressed" citizen-subjects; (3) revolutionary speech; (4) radical semiological speech; (5) silence as speech; (6) poetic speech; and (7) meta-ideologizing speech. Once this outline of rhetorics is accomplished, the last chapter of Part III identify and develop the rhetoric by which supremacy is developed, maintained, and rationalized in consciousness.

8. For Barthes's definition of the "punctum," see his *A Lover's Discourse: Fragments*, trans. Richard Howard (New York: Hill and Wang, 1978), p. 12. The other terms are defined in Gloria Anzaldúa's Introduction to *Making Face, Making Soul/Haciendo Caras* (San Francisco: Spinsters/Aunt Lute, 1990), pp. xv–xvii; Jacques Derrida, "*Différance*," from *Margins of Philosophy*, trans. Alan Bass (Brighton, Sussex: Harvester Press, 1982), in *A Critical and Cultural Theory Reader*, ed. Antony Easthope and Kate McGowan (Toronto: University of Toronto Press, 1992), pp. 108–32; Hayden White, *The Content of the Form* (Baltimore: Johns Hopkins University Press, 1987), p. 75; and Roland Barthes, *Image/Music/Text*, trans. Stephen Heath (New York: Hill and Wang, 1977), pp. 60–61. In each of these cases, this other and outer zone of consciousness is explicated through varying terminologies.

9. These are only two of many attempts to identify in theory this difficult to discern mode of being and action. See Cornel West, *Prophetic Reflections: Notes on Race and Power in America* (Monroe, Maine: Common Courage Press, 1993, p. 112. For a thorough examination of the middle voice of the verb, see Judith Butler's elegant *Excitable Speech: A Politics of the Performative* (New York: Routledge, 1997). *Methodology of the Oppressed* argues that the colonizing ethic of Western Europe culminated in the great global movements for decolonization of the twentieth century, and these are what undermined the rationality and philosophical moorings of Western man. U.S. third world feminism is one result—a methodological and theoretical form that should not be erased or appropriated by the very allies who are also intent on furthering that same decolonization. An interesting and unfortunate example of this kind of erasure and its effects is found in Butler's earlier *Gender Trouble: Feminism and the Subversion of Identity* (New York: Routledge, 1990), a systemic oversight that Butler attempts to remedy in later work.

The mystery of the academic erasure of U.S. third world feminism is an ongoing disappearing trick. Its exemption from academic canon short-circuits knowledge, but secures the acquittal of a "third," feminist "force." It is out of this terrain that U.S. third world feminism calls up new kinds of people, those with skills to rise out of citizenship to agency: countrypeople of a new territory. For these countrypeople-warriors who are no longer necessarily "U.S. third world feminist," the game is beginning again, new names, new players.

10. In this effort, *Methodologies of the Oppressed* joins the efforts of thinkers such as Ernesto Laclau and Chantal Mouffe, *Hegemony and Socialist Strategy: Towards a Radical Democratic Politics* (London: New Left Books, 1997); Ernesto Laclau, *Emancipation(s)* (London: Verso, 1996); Judith Butler, *Excitable Speech* and *The Psychic Life of Power: Theories in Subjection* (Stanford, Calif.: Stanford University Press, 1997); the "lines of flight" of minority discourse described by Gilles Deleuze and Félix Guattari, *Kafka: For a Minor Literature*, trans. Dana Polan, foreword by Réda Bensmaïa (Minneapolis: University of Minnesota Press, 1986 [1975]); Rafael Pérez-Torres's notion of "radical *mestizaje*" in "Polyglossia and Radical *Mestizaje*," in *Movements in Chicano Poetry*, pp. 208–234, and many others. These works are the inheritors of foundational U.S. third world feminist social texts that articulated differential consciousness, such as Bonnie Thorton Dill's "Race, Class and Gender: Prospects for an All-Inclusive Sisterhood," *Feminist Studies* 9 (1983); Deborah K. King's "Multiple Jeopardy, Multiple Consciousness: The Contents of a Black Feminist Ideology," *Signs Journal of Women in Culture and Society* 14: 1 (1988): 42–72; Alice Yun Chai's "Toward a Holistic Paradigm for Asian Women's Studies: A Synthesis of Feminist Scholarship and Women of Color's Feminist Politics," Working paper no. 54, March 1984; Cherríe Moraga and Gloria Anzaldúa, eds., *This Bridge Called My Back: Writings by Radical Women of Color* (New York: Kitchen Table: Women of Color Press, 1981); Gloria Anzaldúa's *Borderlands/La Frontera: The New Mestiza* (1987), and the many other U.S. third world feminist contributions listed in Part II of this book and in the bibliography, all of which made many of the former texts possible and comprehensible. Today, modes of the methodological apparatus outlined in this book are being developed in academic terrains as diverse as sociology, physics, geography, New Historicism, cultural studies, and literary theory, from feminist theory and sex studies to immigration diaspora and global studies. A selection of these projects is examined in this book.

11. Terry Eagleton, *Literary Theory: An Introduction* (Oxford: Basil Blackwell, 1983), p. 205; my emphasis.

12. Utopia "must be named," writes Jameson, "without which its half-life decays with unbelievable speed on exposure to the smog-filled light and polluted air of current reality" ("On Cultural Studies," *Social Text* 34 [1993]: 17–51).

13. Jacques Derrida, "*Différance*," p. 127; Anzaldúa, *Making Face, Making Soul*; Audre Lorde, "The Erotic as Power," in *Sister Outsider* (New York: Crossing Press, 1984), p. 56. See also Leslie Marmon Silko, *Yellow Woman and a Beauty of the Spirit: Essays on Native American Life Today* (New York: Simon and Schuster, 1996).

14. The decolonizing battles for self-determination waged during the twentieth century form the grammar by which contemporary Western scholarship registers resistance. For examples of how this transformative grammar inspires and generates innovative twentieth-century scholarship, see Antonia I. Castañeda, "Women of Color and the Rewriting of Western History: The Discourse, Politics, and Decolonization of History," *Pacific Historical Review* 61 (November 1992): 501–33, and "Gender, Race, and Culture: Spanish-Mexican Women in the Historiography of Frontier California," *Frontiers* 11:1 (1990): 8–20; David G. Gutiérrez, "Significant to Whom?: Mexican Americans and the History of the American West," *Western Historical Quarterly*, 14:4 (November 1993): 519–39. Other instances of such histories include the works of Gayatri Chakravorty Spivak, such as "Subaltern Studies: Deconstructing Historiography," in *Selected Subaltern Studies*, ed. Ranajit Guha and Gayatri Chakravorty Spivak (New York: Oxford University Press, 1998), pp. 3–32; Ranajit Guha, "On Some Aspects of the Historiography of Colonial India," in *Selected Subaltern Studies*, pp. 72–84; Florencia E. Mallon, "The Promise and Dilemma of Subaltern Studies: Perspectives from Latin American History," *American Historical Review* 99:5 (December 1994): 12–36; Michel Foucault, "Preface," in *The Order of Things: An Archaeology of the Human Sciences*, trans. R. D. Laing (New York: Vintage Books, 1970) pp. xv–xxiv; Teresa Córdova, "Roots and Resistance: The Emergent Writings of Twenty Years of Chicana Feminist Struggle," in *Handbook of Hispanic Cultures in the United States Sociology*, (Houston: Arte Público Press, 1994), pp. 175–202; Aimé Césaire, *Discourse on Colonialism* (New York: Monthly Review Press, 1972); Ward Churchill, ed., *Marxism and Native Americans* (Boston: South End Press, 1983); Frantz Fanon, *The Wretched of the Earth* (New York: Grove Press, 1964); Paulo Freire, *Pedagogy of the Oppressed* (New York: Continuum, 1982); Albert Memmi, *Dominated Man* (Boston: Beacon Press, 1968), and *The Colonizer and the Colonized* (London: Souvenir Press, 1974); and Kwame Nkrumah, *Neo-Colonialism: The Last Stage of Imperialism* (London: Nelson, 1965).

15. This season of twentieth-century de-coloniality has been analytically subsumed and accommodated under the all-embracing conceptual light provided by theories of postmodernism and globalization. But this containment stifles understanding of the economic, social, and cultural dynamics that are critical to mobilizing resistance under twenty-first-century postmodern globalization. For meditations on the problematics of this (politicized) juncture, which is theorized as the difference between "postmodernism" and "postcolonialism," see Homi K. Bhabha, "The Postcolonial and the Postmodern: The Question of Agency," in *The Location of Culture* (New York: Routledge, 1994), pp. 171–97; Anne McClintock, "The Angel of Progress: Pitfalls of the Term 'Post-Colonialism,'" *Social Text* 31–32 (summer 1992): 32–67; S. During, "Postmodernism or Post-Colonialism Today," *Textual Practice* 1:1 (1987): 32–67; Kwame Anthony Appiah, "Is the Post- in Postmodernism the Post- in Postcolonial?" *Critical Inquiry* 17:2 (winter 1991): 336–55; Walter Mignolo, "Are Subaltern Studies Postmodern or Postcolonial? The Politics and Sensibilities of Geo-Cultural Locations," unpublished manuscript, n.d.; R. Radhakrishnan, "Ethnic Identity and Post-Structuralist *Différance*," *Cultural Critique* 6 (spring 1987): 199–220. For readers interested in further pursuing these issues, bibliographic information is provided in this note and in notes 17, 21, and 23. See Rosaura Sánchez, Postmodernism and Chicano Literature, *Aztlán* 18:2 (1992): 1–14; Emma Pérez, *The Decolonial Imaginary: Writing Chicanas into History* (Bloomington: Indiana University Press, 1999); Ella Shohat, "Notes on the Post-Colonial," *Social Text* 31–32 (1990): 99–113; Chandra Talpade Mohanty, "Under Western Eyes: Feminist Scholarship and Colonial Discourses," in *Third World Women and the Politics of Feminism*, ed. Chandra Talpade Mohanty, Ann Russo, and Lourdes Torres (Bloomington: Indiana University Press, 1991); J. M. Blaut, *The Colonizer's Model of the World: Geographical Diffusionism and Eurocentric History* (New York and London: Guilford Press, 1993); Gordon Brotherston, *Book of the Fourth World: Reading the Native Americans through Their Literature* (Cambridge: Cambridge University Press, 1992); Inderpal Grewal and Caren Kaplan, eds., *Scattered Hegemonies: Postmodernity and Transnational Feminist Practices* (Minneapolis: University of Minnesota Press, 1994); James Clifford, *The Predicament of Culture* (Cambridge: Harvard University Press, 1988); Henry A. Giroux and Peter McLaren, *Between Borders: Pedagogy and the Politics of Cultural Studies* (New York: Routledge, 1994); Barbara Harlow, *Resistance Literature* (New York: Methuen, 1987); Dominick LaCapra, ed., *The Bounds of Race* (Ithaca, N.Y.: Cornell University Press, 1991); Ashis Nandy, *The Intimate Enemy: Loss and Recovery of Self under Colonialism* (Delhi: Oxford University Press, 1991); Lawrence Grossberg, Paula A. Treichler, and Cary Nelson, eds., *Cultural Studies* (New York: Routledge, 1992); Mary Louise Pratt, *Imperial Eyes: Travel Writing and Trans-culturation* (New York: Routledge, 1992); Juanita Ramos, ed., *Compañeras: Latina Lesbians* (New York: Latina Lesbian History Project, 1987); Ronald T. Takaki, *From Different Shores: Perspectives on Race and Ethnicity in America* (New York: Oxford University Press, 1988); Tzvetan Todorov, *On Human Diversity: Nationalism, Race*

and Exoticism in French Thought, trans. Catherine Porter (Cambridge: Harvard University Press, 1993); Cornel West, *Beyond Eurocentrism and Multiculturalism*, vols. 1 and 2 (Monroe, Maine: Common Courage Press, 1992); or Robert Young, *White Mythologies: Writing History and the West* (New York: Routledge, 1990).

16. Cherríe Moraga, "Theory in the Flesh," in *This Bridge Called My Back*, p. 23. For an extensive bibliography on this mode of U.S. third world feminism, see Part IV and the bibliography.

17. This argument also has been made by theorists such as E. San Juan, *Beyond Postcolonial Theory* (New York, St. Martin's Press, 1997); Aijaz Ahmad, *In Theory: Classes, Nations, Literatures* (London: Verso, 1992); and Abdul R. JanMohamed and David Lloyd, eds., *The Nature and Context of Minority Discourse* (New York: Oxford University Press, 1990). For further bibliographic information, see Marianna Torgovnick, *Gone Primitive* (Chicago: University of Chicago Press, 1990); Barbara Christian, "The Race for Theory," in *Making Face, Making Soul*, pp. 335–45; Haunani-Kay Trask, *From a Native Daughter: Colonialism and Sovereignty in Hawaii* (Monroe, Maine: Common Courage Press, 1993); Trinh T. Minh-ha, *Woman/Native/Other* (Bloomington: Indiana University Press, 1989), and *When the Moon Waxes Red: Representation, Gender and Cultural Politics* (New York: Routledge, 1991); George Lipsitz, *Dangerous Crossroads* (New York: Verso, 1994); and Lisa Lowe, *Immigrant Acts: On Asian American Cultural Politics* (Durham, N.C.: Duke University Press, 1996).

18. Postcolonial analysis takes for granted the limits of Western thought; Foucauldian analysis examines the demarcations of power; queer theory relies on all these methods in order to name the boundaries of sex and the body itself. The expansion of Western boundary knowledges continues to undergo a period of increase.

19. Including the subversion of any innocent desire for realism in the forms and ethos of Western aesthetics by artists such as Godard in film, Picasso in art, or Sartre in philosophy, all three of whom were profoundly influenced by decolonizing social and cultural activities.

20. For these U.S. intellectual movements, the ethos of the West was no longer considered a universal norm, but rather as only another kind of cultural manifestation, another kind of "imagined community," in Benedict Anderson's terms (*Imagined Communities: Reflection on the Origin and Spread of Nationalism* [London: Verso, 1991]).

21. Influential theorists of capitalist transformation include Paul Sweezy, *Monopoly Capitalism* (New York: Monthly Review Press, 1966); Immanuel Wallerstein, *The Modern World-System*, vol. 1 (New York: Academic Press, 1974); Keith Cowing, *Monopoly Capitalism* (London: Macmillan, 1982); Terry Eagleton, "Capitalism, Modernism and Post-Modernism," *New Left Review* 152

(September 1994): 60–71; Aihwa Ong, *Spirits of Resistance and Capitalist Discipline* (Albany: State University of New York Press, 1987); Richard Appelbaum, "Multiculturalism and Flexibility: Some New Directions in Global Capitalism," in *Mapping Multiculturalism*, ed. Avery Gordon and Christopher Newfield (Minneapolis: University of Minnesota Press, 1996), pp. 297–316. For further bibliographic information, see Edward Said, *Culture and Imperialism* (New York: Knopf, 1993); Michel Foucault, "Governmentality," in *The Foucault Effect: Studies in Governmentality*, ed. Graham Burchell, Colin Gordon, and Peter Miller (London: Wheatsheaf, 1991), pp. 82–98; Frantz Fanon, *A Dying Colonialism*, trans. Haakon Chevalier (New York: Grove Weidenfield, 1965); Jacques Derrida, *Specters of Marx: The State of the Debt, the Work of Mourning, and the New International*, trans. Peggy Kamuf (New York: Routledge, 1995); and Jacqui Alexander and Chandra Talpade Mohanty, eds., *Feminist Genealogies, Colonial Legacies, Democratic Futures* (New York: Routledge, 1997).

22. The "new" right faced this recognition by reaching back to a time when older values, morals, and traditions were held in place (or imagining such a time)—a "traditionalization" of quite radical contemporary politics and moralities.

23. The most circulated works on postmodernism during this period were Fredric Jameson, "Postmodernism, or the Cultural Logic of Late Capitalism"; Jean-François Lyotard, *The Postmodern Condition: A Report on Knowledge*, trans. Geoff Bennington and Brian Massumi (Minneapolis: University of Minnesota Press, 1984); Hal Foster, ed., *The Anti-Aesthetic: Essays on Postmodern Culture* (Port Townsend, Wash.: Bay Press 1983); Jürgen Habermas, "Modernity—An Incomplete Project," trans. Selya Benhabib, in *The Anti-Aesthetic*, pp. 3–15; Linda Hutcheon, *A Poetics of Postmodernism* (New York: Routledge 1988), and "The Politics of Postmodernism," *Cultural Critique* 5 (1986–87): 174–207. Further bibliographic references include David Harvey, *The Condition of Postmodernity: An Enquiry into the Origins of Cultural Change* (Oxford: Basil Blackwell, 1990); Mike Featherstone, "In Pursuit of the Postmodern," *Theory, Culture and Society* 5:2–3 (1988): 195–215; Arthur Kroker and David Cook, *The Postmodern Scene: Excremental Culture and Hyper-Aesthetics* (New York: St. Martin's Press, 1986; Montreal: New World Perspectives, 1986). Other widely cited works include Andrew Ross, *Universal Abandon: The Politics of Postmodernism* (Minneapolis: University of Minnesota Press, 1988); Drucilla Cornell and Sylya Benhabib, *Feminism as Critique: Essays on the Politics of Gender in Late-Capitalist Societies* (Cambridge: Polity Press, 1987); Hal Foster, "(Post)Modern Polemics," in *Recodings: Art, Spectacle, Cultural Politics* (Port Townsend, Wash.: Bay Press 1985, pp. 44–56; Cornel West, "Ethics and Action in Fredric Jameson's Marxist Hermeneutics," in *Postmodernism and Politics*, ed.

Jonathan Arac (Minneapolis: University of Minnesota Press, 1986), pp. 103–19; Richard Wolin, "Modernism vs. Postmodernism," *Telos* 62 (1984): 117–30; and Edward Soja, *Postmodern Geographies: The Reassertion of Space in Critical Social Theory* (London: Verso 1989).

Fredric Jameson's foundational engagements with first world social reality as postmodern made invisible an alternative and necessary approach to the U.S. cultural situation. What Jameson's work did not take into account is the legacy of de-colonial discourse that concurrently permeated the West's inherited cultural moment. In the theoretical intersection between the critical study of colonial discourse, hegemonic feminist theories, contemporary theories of postmodernism, queer theory, and U.S. third world feminist criticism rises a form of oppositional consciousness and activity once only necessary to socially marginalized citizenry, but that contemporary postmodern cultural dynamics made available at the end of the twentieth century—indeed, perhaps unavoidable—for all first world citizen-subjects, a form of consciousness that parallels in its internal structures the very globalizing dynamics it also resists, so that a word other than *oppositional* to describe its activity of resistance and transformation may need to be identified. The content of this form of oppositional consciousness has been partially (and rather naively) celebrated and welcomed by other (primarily white, male) first world theorists of postmodernism, such as Jean-François Lyotard. But whether welcoming or rejecting the variously construed meanings of the new cultural dominant, both theoretical camps of postmodernist thought—represented here by Jameson on the one side, Lyotard on the other—share the longing for a regenerated hope and the creation of new identities that are capable of negotiating the crumbling traditions, values, and cultural institutions of the West (in the first example by celebrating a passing modernist form of unitary subjectivity; in the second by celebrating an identity form whose contours are comparable to the fragmenting status of present Western cultural forms).

24. Charles Long suggested that this methodology generates "a hermeneutics of love." In *Methodology of the Oppressed*, "love" is redefined as a mode of social and psychic activism. For Long's own turn on these matters, see his *Significations: Signs, Symbols and Images in the Interpretation of Religion* (Philadelphia: Fortress Press, 1986).

25. For further work on theoretical apartheid, see M. Annette Jaimes Guerrero, "Academic Apartheid: American Indian Studies and 'Multiculturalism,'" and Michael Omi, "Racialization in the Post-Civil Rights Era," in *Mapping Multiculturalism*, pp. 49–63, 118–86, respectively. See also Gianni Vattimo, "The Truth of Hermeneutics," in *Questioning Foundations*, ed. Hugh Silverman (New York: Columbia University Press, 1993), pp. 92–119. *Methodology of the Oppressed* is calculated to make a contribution to the "human and social sciences" understood as an interacting or interdisciplinary field of investigation, for the book is part of a larger project by Chicanos and Chicanas to understand and write a history of consciousness that does not exclude or deny intellectual contributions from any field, but that opens up, includes, and transforms through insisting on the recognition of shared methods and meanings across disciplines, whether these are named "hybridity," "the third meaning," "womanism," "ghost dancing," "radical democratic politics," "the outsider/within," "New Historicism," "semiotics," *mestizaje*," or *la facultad."

1. Fredric Jameson

1. After years of discussion, rebuttal, and revision, this manifesto became what Gayatri Spivak described in 1989 as the necessary "metonym" for understanding the "late-twentieth-century cultural conjuncture." See Spivak's quote on the front jacket of the collection of essays organized around Jameson's manifesto in *Postmodernism/Jameson/Critique*, ed. Douglas Kellner (Washington, D.C.: Maisonneuve Press, 1989). At the very least, Jameson's work during the 1980s and beyond has established the discursive groundwork by which issues of postmodernism are addressed. Jameson's first essay on postmodernism appeared in 1983 as "Postmodernism and Consumer Society," in *The Anti-Aesthetic*, ed. Hal Foster (Port Townsend, Wash.: Bay Press, 1983), pp. 111–25. His second essay on the matter quickly became one of the most widely circulated academic manuscripts published in the 1980s. This "manifesto" (my term) appeared in the *New Left Review* in 1984 as "Post-modernism, or the Cultural Logic of Late Capital." The final version of what is essentially the same essay appeared in 1991 as "The Cultural Logic of Late Capitalism," and comprises the introductory chapter of Jameson's long-awaited book, *Postmodernism, or the Cultural Logic of Late Capitalism* (Durham, N.C.: Duke University Press, 1991). The aim of Jameson's book on postmodernism, as announced on its own jacket cover, is to "crystallize a definition of this term that has taken on so many meanings it has virtually lost all historical significance."

All further references in the present volume to Jameson's definition of postmodernism will be given in the text, and are derived from his fundamental 1984 version published in the *New Left Review*, "Postmodernism, or the Cultural Logic of Late Capital." For further discussions of the nature of transnationalization in Jameson's work, see Andrew Ross, *Universal Abandon: The Politics of Postmodernism*, (Minneapolis: University of Minnesota Press, 1988); Cornel West, "Postmodern Culture," in *Prophetic Reflections: Notes on Race and Power in America* (London: Routledge, 1993), pp. 251–70, and "Ethics and Action in Jameson's Marxist Hermeneutics," in *Postmodernism and Politics: Theory and History of Literature*, vol. 28, ed. Jonathan Arac (Minneapolis: University of

Minnesota Press, 1986), pp. 59–78, as well as Arac's excellent introduction to the book; Clint Bunham, *The Jamesonian Unconsciousness: The Aesthetics of Marxist Theory* (Durham, N.C.: Duke University Press, 1995); Hayden White, "Getting Out of History: Jameson's Redemption of Narrative," in *The Content of the Form: Narrative Discourse and Historical Representation* (Baltimore: Johns Hopkins University Press, 1987), pp. 142–68; Linda Hutcheon, *A Poetics of Postmodernism: History, Theory, Fiction* (New York: Routledge, 1990); Laura Doan, ed., *The Lesbian Postmodern* (New York: Columbia University Press 1994); and Thomas Docherty, ed., *Postmodernism: A Reader*, which contains excellent essays by Simon During, Nelly Richard, and Rey Chow on postcoloniality versus postmodernism. See also Santiago Colas, "The Third World in Jameson's Postmodernism, or the Cultural Logic of Late Capitalism" (*Social Text* 32 [1992]): 323–42; Homi K. Bhabha, "The Postcolonial and the Postmodern: The Question of Agency," in *Redrawing the Boundary of Literary Study in English*, ed. Giles Gunn and Stephen Greenblatt (New York: Modern Language Association, 1992), pp. 46–57; as well as the following journal collections: *Diacritics* 12 (fall 1982), *Critical Exchange* 14 (fall 1983), *New Orleans Review* 1 (spring 1984). See also note 23 in the Introduction to this book.

2. Karl Marx and Friedrich Engels, *The Communist Manifesto* (Harmondsworth, England: Penguin Books, 1967).

3. Daniel Bell, *The Cultural Contradictions of Capitalism* (New York: Basic Books, 1976), and "Modernism and Capitalism," *Partisan Review* 46 (1978): 206–26; and Jean-François Lyotard, *The Postmodern Condition: A Report on Knowledge*, trans. Geoff Bennington and Brian Massumi (Minneapolis: University of Minnesota Press, 1984).

4. *Methodology of the Oppressed* is about another kind of political function that moves outside of these older political categories.

5. My understanding of postmodern pastiche is unlike Jameson's, who considers it an "insubstantial" depoliticized form—"blank parody," he calls it—the most predominant aesthetic of our time (65). I view postmodern pastiche as an aesthetic form that is both empty *and* full at the same time, a site of active possibility. It is a mode of production and perception that expanded in the late twentieth century to the point where all first world citizen-subjects are faced with the dissolution of subjectivity's wholeness—not into the fragmentation of Jameson's horror—but into the possibilities of an empty form capable of constantly refilling. The extremities of life lived in the regions of social subjugation, war, and postmodernism unlock the shackles of perception, and provide the methods by which postmodern being can fill with resistance. The form of differential consciousness described in this book represents one example of an actively politicized, ethical, decolonizing, and *oppositional* form of postmodern pastiche in action.

6. This architectural model for oppositional consciousness is being represented through the strategies, tactics, and methods developed under domination and subjugation, and identified in the academy as "strategic essentialism," "*différance*," "hybridity," "*mestizaje*," and so on. The affective positionings required by social marginality have transformed academic critical strategies insofar as these deny linguistic normality, celebrate pastiche, and demand transformative identities. Parts II and III of this book examine these processes and procedures in depth. Here I am only indicating their dimensions insofar as they define the term *differential*. In the epigram to this chapter, Rafael Pérez-Torres begins to indicate the relations between subaltern and academic consciousness this way: "Chicanos, as *los de abajo*, know all too intimately the reality of decentered subjectivity and the violence that results from the pursuit of master narratives—progress, expansion, Manifest Destiny.... Chicanos have lived and survived (which is a form of triumph over) the disparities made plain by the critical light of postmodernism" (*Movements in Chicano Poetry: Against Margins, against Myths* (New York: Cambridge University Press, 1995), p. 9.

7. As Roland Barthes proposes, any text can be analyzed "through several entrances none of which can be said to be the main one. (*S/Z: An Essay*, trans. Richard Miller [New York: Hill and Wang], 1974), p. 12.

8. Note that this quotation slowly generates a perceptual system in the first paragraph that then congeals—hammerlike—to become a binary breaker in the second (Michael Herr, *Dispatches* [New York: Random House, 1978], p. 89).

9. Explicit references to Chicano/a gang life, the war zone of *la vida loca*, include Luis Rodriquez's *Always Running: La Vida Loca, Gang Days in L.A.* (New York: Simon and Schuster, 1994), and the film *Mi Vida Loca*.

10. Louis Althusser, "Ideology and Ideological State Apparatuses (Notes Toward an Investigation)," in *Lenin and Philosophy and Other Essays* (London: New Left Books, 1970), p. 135.

11. See Gloria Anzaldúa's work on "masks, interfaces, and masquerade" in "Haciendo Caras, Una Entrada," the "Introduction" to *Making Face, Making Soul/Haciendo Caras*, ed. Gloria Anzaldúa (San Francisco: Spinsters/ Aunte Lute, 1990). In Anzaldúa's example, the radical U.S. third world feminist practitioner of survival under domination comes already immersed in the variability and possibility of power's potential locations, as we see in Part II of this book. This submersion can become transformative; practitioners learn to operate through whole new navigational and collective principles.

12. To understand present globalization as a move from "modernism" to "postmodernism" makes invisible the de-colonial processes of the last five hundred years, especially those that occurred during the twentieth century. That is why there has been a movement to understand contemporary globalization that shifts from mapping the global against a "modernism/postmodernism mode" to a "colonial/postcolonial model." *Methodology of the Oppressed* generates something in between: it seeks a cosmopolitics that can analyze neocolonial postmodernism at the same time that it maps dissident and postcolonial dynamics active globally.

13. This third form of consciousness, identity, and practice was developed and enacted by subjugated peoples who employed a differential survival skill that allowed them to center, decenter, and recenter in discourse according to demand, necessity, or moral aim. Recognition of this differential practice generates another model for imagining what "critical distance," "resistance," and "social movement" can look like under postmodern cultural and economic conditions, and clears space for understanding the dissident postcolonial (Gayatri Spivak), feminist (Donna Haraway), U.S. third world feminist (Gloria Anzaldúa), and queer (Audre Lorde) theoretical challenges to postmodernism that have arisen since 1984.

14. In its beginning shows, *The X-Files* imaged the once centered first world subject negotiating the new postmodern space of the first world, his allies a white woman and a black man, his enemies the networks of power that catch all citizens in their rationality, his only weapon the determination to find the "truth" of being in what was a conspiracy of domination, oppression, and meaninglessness.

15. The processes of this third view of the subject have become of interest to academics across disciplines since the 1980s, encoded under the theoretical aegis of "postcolonial studies," "diaspora studies," "*différance*" (Derrida), "borderlands theorizing" (Chicano/a studies), "ex-centric subjectivity" (Teresa de Lauretis and Linda Hutcheon), "cyborg feminism" (Donna Haraway), "in/appropriated otherness" (Trin T. Minh-ha), "the third space" (Homi Bhabha), or "*la conciencia de la mestiza*" (Gloria Anzaldúa), for example.

16. Moreover, regardless of social position, who among us has not experienced that span of psychic shattering, when all the world and its past shift and dissolve into meaninglessness, if only for a moment's time?

17. Toni Morrison, *Sula* (New York: Bantam Books, 1980), p. 44.

18. This is not to say that, as Octavio Paz argues, "we are all on the margin because there is no center." Rather, as Santiago Colas has clarified, human societies recognize, perhaps for the first time, that center-margin relations are allocated via diverse structures, practices and discourses, and that every human body is subject to these new power relations. See Santiago Colas, "The Third World in Jameson's *Postmodernism, or the Cultural Logic of Late Capitalism*," *Social Text* 31/32 (1989): 258–70; and Octavio Paz, *The Labyrinth of Solitude: Life and Thought in Mexico*, trans. Lysander Kemp (New York: Grove Press, 1962).

2. U.S. Third World Feminism

1. The phrases "third world" and "first world" are not capitalized in my writings as in older uses of such designations. This is because these terms are so frayed around the edges that they can no longer "mean" in the geographic and economic ways they were used in previous academic thinking. In this chapter, "U.S. third world feminism" refers to a deliberate politics organized to point out the so-called third world *in* the first world. The very effort of this 1970s naming by U.S. feminists of color was meant to signal a *conflagration* of geographic, economic, and cultural borders in the interests of creating a new feminist and internationalist consciousness and *location*: not just the third world *in* the first world, but a new global consciousness and terrain that challenges the distinctions of nation-state. This usage also prepared the way for the contemporary phase of U.S. feminist of color politics that is called "third *space* feminism." For other examples of similar uncapitalized usages of "first," "second," and "third" worlds, see the essays in Fredric Jameson and Masao Miyoshi, eds., *The Cultures of Globalization* (Durham, N.C.: Duke University Press, 1998). For the most recent example of third space feminism, see Emma Pérez, *The De-Colonial Imaginary* (Bloomington: Indiana University Press, 1999).

The theory and method of oppositional consciousness outlined in this chapter became visible in the activities of a political unity variously named "U.S. third world feminism," "womanism," or "the practices of U.S. feminist women of color." In this chapter, U.S. third world feminism represents the political alliance made during the 1960s and 1970s between a generation of feminists of color who were separated by culture, race, class, sex, or gender identifications but who became allied through their similar positionings in relation to race, gender, sex, and culture subordinations. Their newfound unity coalesced across these and other differences. These differences nevertheless were painfully manifest in any of their gatherings: materially marked physiologically or in language, socially value-laden, and shot through with power. Such differences confronted feminists of color at every gathering, constant reminders of their undeniability. These constantly speaking differences became the crux of another, mutant unity. This unity did not occur in the name of all "women," nor in the name of race, class, sex, culture, or "humanity" in general, but in a location heretofore unrecognized. As

Cherríe Moraga put it in 1981, alliances between U.S. feminists of color occurred "between the seemingly irreconcilable lines — class lines, politically correct lines, the daily lines we run to each other to keep difference and desire at a distance"; it is *between* such lines, she wrote, "that the truth of our connection lies." This political connection constantly weaves and reweaves an interaction of differences into coalition. This chapter demonstrates how differences within this coalition became understood and utilized as political tactics constructed in response to dominating powers. See Cherríe Moraga, "Between the Lines: On Culture, Class and Homophobia," in *This Bridge Called My Back: Writings by Radical Women of Color*, ed. Cherríe Moraga and Gloria Anzaldúa (New York: Kitchen Table: Women of Color Press, 1981), p. 106. For excellent histories of U.S. women of color in struggle, see Antonia I. Casteñeda's prizewinning essay "Women of Color and the Rewriting of Western History: The Discourse, Politics, and Decolonization of History," *Pacific Historical Review* 61 (November 1992); Asian Women United of California, ed., *Making Waves: An Anthology of Writings by and about Asian Women* (Boston, 1989); Paula Giddings, *Where and When I Enter: The Impact of Black Women on Race and Sex in America* (Toronto, 1984); Ellen Dubois and Vicki Ruiz, eds., *Unequal Sisters: A Multicultural Reader in U.S. Women's History* (New York, 1990); Gretchen Bataille and Kathleen Mullen Sands, eds., *American Indian Women: Telling Their Lives* (Lincoln, Nebr., 1984); Rayna Green, ed., *Native American Women* (New York, 1985); Paula Gunn Allen, ed., *Spider Woman's Granddaughters* (New York, 1989); Albert Hurtado, *Indian Survival on the California Frontier* (New York 1989); Tsuchida, ed., *Asian and Pacific American Experiences* (San Francisco, 1989); Toni Cade Bambara, "Preface," in *This Bridge Called My Back*; Angela Davis, *Women, Race and Class* (New York: Random House, 1983 [1st ed.]); and Bettina Aptheker, *Tapestries of Life* (Amherst: University of Massachusetts Press, 1989). Other foundational U.S. third world feminist writings include Toni Cade Bambara, ed., *The Black Woman: An Anthology* (1970); Velia Hancock, *Chicano Studies Newsletter* (1971); Frances Beale, *Third World Women* (1971); Toni Morrison, *Sula* (1975); Janice Mirikitani, ed., *Third World Women* (1973); Shirley Hill Witt, "Native Women Today: Sexism and the Indian Woman," *Civil Rights Digest* 6 (spring 1974); Janice Mirikitani, *Time to Greez! Incantations from the Third World* (1975); Anna Nieto-Gomez, "Sexism in the Movimiento," *La Gente* 6:4 (1976); Jane Katz, *I Am the Fire of Time — Voices of Native American Women* (1977); Dexter Fisher, ed., *The Third Woman: Minority Women Writers of the United States* (1980); Norma Alarcón, ed., *Journal of the Third Woman* (1980–); Moraga and Anzaldúa, eds., *This Bridge Called My Back* (1981); Audre Lorde, *Sister Outsider* (1984); bell hooks, *Ain't I a Woman* (1981); Cherríe Moraga and Amber Hollibaugh, "What

We're Rollin' around in Bed With," *Heresies* (1981); Paula Gunn Allen, "Beloved Women: The Lesbian in American Indian Culture," *Conditions* 7 (1981); Gloria Hull, Patricia Bell Scott, and Barbara Smith, eds., *All the Women Are White, All the Blacks Are Men, but Some of Us Are Brave: Black Women's Studies* (1982); Audre Lorde, *Zami* (1982); Cherríe Moraga, *Loving in the War Years* (1983); Bernice Johnson Reagon, "Coalition Politics: Turning the Century," in Barbara Smith, ed., *Home Girls* (1983); Gloria Anzaldúa, *Borderlands/La Frontera: The New Mestiza* (1987); Beth Brant, ed., *A Gathering of Spirit: A Collection by North American Indian Women* (1988); Aida Hurtado, "Reflections on White Feminism: A Perspective from a Woman of Color," unpublished manuscript (1985); Trinh T. Minh-ha, *Woman/Native/ Other: Writing Postcoloniality and Feminism* (1989); Gloria Anzaldúa, ed., *Making Face, Making Soul/Haciendo Caras* (1990).

The definition of "U.S. third world feminism" appears in the *Oxford Companion to Women's Writing in the United States*, ed. Cathy Davidson and Linda Wagner-Martin (New York: Oxford University Press, 1995), pp. 880–82. For an excellent discussion and analysis of this definition, see Katie King, *Theory in Its Feminist Travels: Conversations in U.S. Women's Movements* (Bloomington: Indiana University Press, 1994). The most cited examples of U.S. feminists of color arguing for a specific method called "U.S. third world feminism" can be found in Moraga and Anzaldúa, *This Bridge Called My Back*. See also Chandra Talpade Mohanty's renowned collection and her essay "Cartographies of Struggle: Third World Women and the Politics of Feminism," in *Third World Women and the Politics of Feminism*, ed. Chandra Talpade Mohanty, Anne Russo and Lourdes Torres (Bloomington: Indiana University Press, 1991). See also Chela Sandoval, "Comment on Susan Krieger's 'Lesbian Identity and Community,'" *Signs* (spring 1983): 324.

During the infamous conference of the National Women's Studies Association (NWSA) in 1981, three hundred feminists of color agreed that: "1) It is white men who have access to the greatest amount of freedom from necessity in this culture, 2) white women who serve as their 'helpmates' and chattel, with people of color as their women's servants. 3) People of color form a striated social formation that allows men of color to call upon the circuits of power which charge the category of (white) 'male' with its privileges 4) which leaves women of color as the final chattel, the ultimate servant in a racist and sexist class hierarchy. U.S. third world feminism seeks to undo this hierarchy first by reconceptualizing the first category (of 'freedom') and who can inhabit its realm." See Chela Sandoval, "The Struggle Within: A Report on the 1981 N.W.S.A. Conference," published by the Center for Third World Organizing, 1982; reprinted by Gloria Anzaldúa, ed., in *Making Face, Making Soul/ Haciendo Caras* (San Francisco: Spinsters/Aunt Lute, 1990), pp. 55–71.

2. Gayatri Spivak, "The Rani of Sirmur," in *Europe and Its Others*, ed. F. Barker, vol. 1 (Essex: University of Essex Press, 1985), p. 147.

3. The most well circulated example of the writings of U.S. third world feminists is found in the 1981 collection *This Bridge Called My Back*, but many other articles were published during the previous decade. See note 1 and the bibliography.

4. The factors that permit this subjectivity and political practice to be called into being and the explanations for how one lives out its imperatives are laid out in Part III of this book.

5. Fredric Jameson's "Postmodernism, or the Cultural Logic of Late Capitalism," *New Left Review* 146 (July–August 1984): 53–92, defines and positions post-modernism as neocolonial (imperialist) in function, as I argued in chapter 1.

6. Louis Althusser, "Ideology and Ideological State Apparatuses (Notes Towards an Investigation)," in *Lenin and Philosophy and Other Essays* (London: New Left Books, 1970), pp. 123–73.

7. Ibid., p. 147.

8. In the essay "Uneffective Resistance," I identify the forms of consciousness encouraged within subordinated classes that are resistant (but not self-consciously in *political* opposition to the dominant order). "Resistant" forms of consciousness can be understood in Althusser's terms, that is, the repressive state apparatus and the ideological state apparatus create subordinated forms of *resistant* consciousness, as opposed to the politicized and self-conscious forms of *oppositional* consciousness described in this chapter. Resistant forms of consciousness developed by subordinated citizen-subjects seem to coalesce around the following four subject positions: (1) the "human," (2) the "pet," (3) the "game," and (4) the "wild." The value of each of these subject positions is measured by its proximity to the category of the most human: each position delimits its own kinds of freedoms, privileges, and resistances. Their final outcome, however, only supports the social order as it already functions. The rationality of this four-category schema depends on the work of the anthropologist Edmund Leach, who demonstrates through his examples of English and Tibeto-Burman language categories that human societies tend to organize individual identity according to perceived distance from the "most human" and male self and then into relations of exchange that Leach characterizes as those of the "sister," "cousin," or "stranger." He suggests that these relationships of value and distance are replicated throughout myriad cultures and serve to support and further the beliefs, aims, and traditions of whatever social order is dominant. See Edmund Leach, "Anthropological Aspects of Language: Animal Categories and Verbal Abuse," in *New Directions in the Study of Language*, ed. Eric Lenneberg (Cambridge: MIT Press, 1964), p. 62.

9. Differential consciousness is becoming recognized and theorized across academic disciplines, and under many rubrics. See, for example, *Living Chicana Theory*, ed. Carla Trujillo (Berkeley: Third Woman Press, 1998), and Ernesto Laclau, *Emancipations* (London: Verso, 1996). For other examples, see note 61 in this chapter and note 10 in chapter 1.

10. Frances Beale, "Double Jeopardy: To Be Black and Female," in *Sisterhood Is Powerful: An Anthology of Writings from the Women's Liberation Movement*, ed. Robin Morgan (New York: Random House, 1970), p. 136; my emphasis.

11. Sojourner Truth, "Ain't I a Woman?" in *The Norton Anthology of Literature by Women*, ed. Sandra M. Gilbert and Susan Gubar (New York: Norton, 1985), p. 252.

12. Paula Gunn Allen, "Some like Indians Endure," in *Living the Spirit* (New York: St. Martin's Press, 1987), p. 9.

13. Toni Morrison, in Bettye J. Parker, "Complexity: Toni Morrison's Women—An Interview Essay," in *Sturdy Black Bridges: Visions of Black Women in Literature*, ed. Roseanne Bell, Bettye Parker, and Beverly Guy-Sheftall (New York: Anchor/Doubleday, 1979), pp. 32–43.

14. Velia Hancock, "La Chicana, Chicano Movement and Women's Liberation," *Chicano Studies Newsletter*, University of California, Berkeley (February–March 1971): 3–4.

15. Gloria Hull, Patricia Bell Scott, and Barbara Smith, eds., *All the Women Are White, All the Blacks Are Men, but Some of Us Are Brave: Black Women's Studies* (New York: Feminist Press, 1982). The sense that people of color occupy an "in-between/outsider" status is a frequent theme among third world liberationists writing both inside and outside the United States. Reverend Desmond Mpilo Tutu, on receiving the Nobel Prize, for example, said he faced a "rough passage" as intermediary between ideological factions, because he has chosen to become "detribalized." He is thus difficult to racially or culturally "locate," he says. Rosa Maria Villafane-Sisolak, a West Indian from the Island of Saint Croix, expands on this theme: "I am from an island whose history is steeped in the abuses of Western imperialism, whose people still suffer the deformities caused by Euro-American colonialism, old and new. Unlike many third world liberationists, however, I cannot claim to be descendent of any particular strain, noble or ignoble. I am, however, 'purely bred'—descendent of all the parties involved in that cataclysmic epoch. I . . . despair, for the various parts of me cry out for retribution at having been brutally uprooted and transplanted to fulfill the profit-cy of

'white' righteousness and dominance. My soul moans that part of me that was destroyed by that callous righteousness. My heart weeps for that part of me that was the instrument—the gun, the whip, the book. My mind echos with the screams of disruption, desecration, destruction." Alice Walker, in a controversial letter to an African-American friend, told him she believes that "we are the African and the trader. We are the Indian and the Settler. We are oppressor and oppressed. . . . we are the mestizos of North America. We are black, yes, but we are 'white,' too, and we are red. To attempt to function as only one, when you are really two or three, leads, I believe, to psychic illness: 'white' people have shown us the madness of that." Gloria Anzaldúa continues this theme: "You say my name is Ambivalence: Not so. Only your labels split me." Desmond Tutu as reported by Richard N. Osting, "Searching for New Worlds," *Time*, October 29, 1984; Rosa Maria Villafane-Sisolak, from a 1983 journal entry cited in *Making Face, Making Soul*, p. xviii; Alice Walker, "In the Closet of the Soul: A Letter to an African-American Friend," *Ms.*, 15 (November 1986): 33; Gloria Anzaldúa, "La Prieta," in *This Bridge Called My Back*, p. 201.

16. bell hooks, *Ain't I a Woman: Black Women and Feminism* (Boston: South End Press, 1981); Amy Ling, *Between Worlds* (New York: Pergamon Press, 1990); Norma Alarcón, ed., *The Third Woman* (Bloomington, Ind.: Third Woman Press, 1980).

17. See Walker, "Letter to an African-American Friend," Anzaldúa, *Borderlands/La Frontera*; Maxine Hong Kingston, *The Woman Warrior* (New York: Vintage Books, 1977); and Moraga and Anzaldúa, *This Bridge Called My Back*.

18. Audre Lorde, *Sister Outsider* (New York: Crossing Press, 1984).

19. Maxine Baca Zinn, Lynn Weber Cannon, Elizabeth Higginbotham, and Bonnie Thornton Dill, "The Costs of Exclusionary Practices in Women's Studies," *Signs: Journal of Women in Culture and Society* 11:2 (winter 1986): 296. Note here already the implication of another "third space" gender, which in the 1990s was theorized as the category of the decolonizing "queer" as conceived by scholars of color. See the works of Cherríe Moraga, Gloria Anzaldúa, Emma Pérez, Audre Lorde, Kitty Tsui, Makeda Livera, Paula Gunn Allen, Jacqueline Martinez, and Yvonne Yarbro-Bejarano for examples: Moraga, *The Last Generation* (Boston: South End Press, 1995); Pérez, "Sexuality and Discourse: Notes From a Chicana Survivor," in *Chicana Lesbians*, ed. Carla Trujillo (Berkeley: Third Woman Press, 1991); Lorde, *Sister Outsider*; Kitty Tsui, Nellie Wong, and Barbara Noda, "Coming Out, We Are Here in the Asian Community: A Dialogue with Three Asian Women," *Bridge* (spring 1979): 34–38; Asian Women United of California, *Making Waves*; Makeda Livera, ed., *A Lesbian of Color*

Anthology: Piece of My Heart (Toronto, Ontario: Sister Vision Press, 1991); Allen, "Beloved Women"; Deena Gonzáles, *Chicana Identity Matters*, forthcoming; Sandoval, "Comment on Susan Krieger's 'Lesbian Identity and Community.'" Here we can see how Judith Butler's work on the performative developed parallel structures to those of U.S. third world feminism (and its differential *mestiza* consciousness).

20. Alison Jaggar, *Feminist Politics and Human Nature* (New York: Rowman and Allenheld, 1983), p. 11.

21. Hester Eisenstein, *The Future of Difference* (New Brunswick, N.J.: Rutgers University Press, 1985), p. xxi.

22. The mystery of the academic erasure of U.S. third world feminism is a disappearing trick. Its exemption from academic canon short-circuits knowledge but secures the acquittal of a "third," feminist "force" about which Derrida suggested "it should not be named." Not named, he hoped, in order that what is performative and mobile never be set into any place: freedom resides, thus, everywhere. It is out of this terrain that U.S. third world feminism calls up new kinds of people, those with skills to rise out of citizenship to agency: countrypeople of a new territory. For these countrypeople-warriors who are no longer "U.S. third world feminist," the game is beginning again, new names, new players.

23. Elaine Showalter, ed., *The New Feminist Criticism: Essays on Women, Literature and Theory* (New York: Pantheon Books, 1985). See especially the following essays: "Introduction: The Feminist Critical Revolution," "Toward a Feminist Poetics," and "Feminist Criticism in the Wilderness," pp. 3–18, 125–43, and 243–70.

24. Gayle Greene and Coppélia Kahn, eds., *Making a Difference: Feminist Literary Criticism* (New York: Methuen, 1985). See the chapter "Feminist Scholarship and the Social Construction of Woman," pp. 1–36.

25. Showalter, *The New Feminist Criticism*, p. 128.

26. Eisenstein, *The Future of Difference*, p. xvi.

27. Greene and Kahn, *Making a Difference*, p. 13.

28. Jaggar, *Feminist Politics*, p. 37.

29. Showalter, *The New Feminist Criticism*, p. 138.

30. Eisenstein, *The Future of Difference*, p. xviii.

31. Greene and Kahn, *Making a Difference*, p. 13.

32. Jaggar, *Feminist Politics*, p. 52.

33. Showalter, *The New Feminist Criticism*, p. 139.

34. Eisenstein, *The Future of Difference*, p. xviii.

35. Greene and Kahn, *Making a Difference*, p. 14.

36. Jaggar, *Feminist Politics*, p. 88. Like U.S. hegemonic feminism, European feminist theory replicates this same basic structure. For example, Toril Moi and Julia Kristeva argue that feminism has produced "three main strategies" for constructing identity and oppositional politics. They represent feminist consciousness as a hierarchically organized historical and political struggle, which they schematically summarize as follows:

1. Women demand equal access to the symbolic order. Liberal feminism. Equality.

2. Women reject the male symbolic order in the name of difference. Radical feminism. Femininity extolled.

3. (This is Kristeva's own position.) Women reject the dichotomy between masculine and feminine as metaphysical. (Toril Moi, *Sexual/Textual Politics: Feminist Literary Theory* [New York: Methuen, 1985], p. 12.

Note that the second category combines both the second and third categories of U.S. feminism, and the third category dissolves "the dichotomy between masculine and feminine" altogether. Luce Irigaray is considered a "radical feminist," according to this schema.

37. Lydia Sargent, *Women and Revolution: A Discussion of the Unhappy Marriage of Marxism and Feminism* (Boston: South End Press, 1981), p. xx. The hegemonic typology of feminist consciousness we have just analyzed—(1) that women are the same as men, (2) that women are different from men, and (3) that women are superior—was challenged at its every phase by feminists of color. If women were seen as "the same as men"—differing only in form, not in content—then feminists of color challenged white women for striving to represent themselves as only other versions of the dominant white male. When women's liberationists were thus forced to recognize and claim their differences from "men," then feminists of color pointed out that the most valued differences were recognized and ranked according to the codes and values of the dominant class, race, culture, and sex. In attempting to ethically respond to this new challenge to a unified women's movement for liberation, the movement constructed its third phase, which saw any feminist expression as being as valid as any other as long as it expressed a higher moral and spiritual position: that of "woman." But U.S. feminists of color did not feel comfortable with the "essence" (of woman) being formulated. If ethical and political leadership should arise only from that particular location, then for U.S. feminists of color, who did not see themselves easily inhabiting any form of female subjectivity identified so far, Sojourner Truth's lingering question "Ain't I a woman?" sounded even more loudly. This schema of three phases does not provide the opportunity to recognize the existence of another kind of woman—to imagine another, aberrant form of subjectivity, aesthetics, politics, feminism. That is why U.S. feminists of color argued that each hegemonic feminist phase tended to generate its own equivalent forms of racist ideology.

38. Eisenstein, *The Future of Difference*, p. xix; my emphasis.

39. Jaggar, *Feminist Politics*, p. 123.

40. Cora Kaplan, "Pandora's Box: Subjectivity, Class and Sexuality in Socialist Feminist Criticism," in Greene and Kahn, *Making a Difference*, pp. 148–51.

41. Jaggar, *Feminist Politics*, p. 123; my emphasis.

42. This shift in paradigm requires a fresh mapping, the creation of another kind of typology that would prepare the ground for a new theory and method of feminist consciousness in resistance. This other typology brings into view new sets of alterities and another way of understanding "otherness." It demands that oppositional actors claim alternative grounds for generating identity, ethics, and political activity across lines of gender, race, sex, class, psychic, or cultural differences; it makes visible another method for understanding oppositional consciousness in a transnational world.

43. Sheila Radford-Hill, "Considering Feminism as a Model for Social Change," in *Feminist Studies/Critical Studies*, ed. Teresa de Lauretis (Bloomington: Indiana University Press, 1986), p. 160.

44. bell hooks, *Feminist Theory: From Margin to Center* (Boston: South End Press, 1984), p. 9.

45. Gayatri Chakravorty Spivak, "Three Women's Texts and a Critique of Imperialism," *Critical Inquiry* 12 (autumn 1985): 245.

46. As Katie King points out in her analysis of social movement histories in *Theory in Its Feminist Travels*.

47. Anzaldúa writes that she lives "between and among" cultures in "La Prieta," p. 209.

48. Aida Hurtado, "Reflections on White Feminism: A Perspective from a Woman of Color" (1985), from an unpublished manuscript, p. 25. Another version of this quotation appears in Hurtado's essay "Relating to Privilege: Seduction and Rejection in the Subordination of White Women and Women of Color," *Signs* (summer 1989): 833–55.

49. In Moraga and Anzaldúa, *This Bridge Called My Back*, pp. xix, 106. See also the beautiful passage from Margaret Walker's *Jubilee* that similarly outlines and enacts this mobile mode of consciousness from the viewpoint of the female protagonist (New York, Bantam Books, 1985), pp. 404–7.

50. Anzaldúa, "La Prieta," p. 209.

51. Audre Lorde, "Comments at 'The Personal and Political Panel,'" Second Sex Conference, New York, September 1979. Published in *This Bridge Called My Back*, p. 98. See also Audre Lorde, "The Uses of the Erotic," in *Sister Outsider*, pp. 58–63, which calls for challenging and undoing authority in order to enter a utopian realm only accessible through a processual form of consciousness that Lorde names the "erotic."

52. Anzaldúa refers to this survival skill as "*la facultad*, the capacity to see in surface phenomena the meaning of deeper realities" (*Borderlands/La Frontera: The New Mestiza* (San Francisco: Spinsters/Aunt Lute, 1987), p. 38. The consciousness that typifies *la facultad* is not naive to the moves of power: it is constantly surveying and negotiating its moves. Often dismissed as "intuition," this kind of "perceptiveness," "sensitivity," consciousness, if you will, is not determined by race, sex, or any other genetic status; neither does its activity belong solely to the "proletariat," the "feminist," or the oppressed, if the oppressed is considered a unitary category, but it is a learned emotional and intellectual skill that is developed amid hegemonic powers. It is the recognition of *la facultad* that moves Lorde to say that it is marginality, "whatever its nature . . . which is also the source of our greatest strength" (*Sister Outsider*, p. 53), for the cultivation of *la facultad* creates the opportunity for a particularly effective form of opposition to the dominant order within which it is formed. The skills required by *la facultad* are capable of disrupting the dominations and subordinations that scar U.S. culture. But it is not enough to utilize them on an individual and situational basis. Through an ethical and political commitment, U.S. third world feminism requires the technical development of *la facultad* to a methodological level capable of generating a political strategy and identity politics from which a new citizenry arises. In Part III, we examine this technique in greater detail under a rubric I call the "methodology of the oppressed."

Movements of resistance have always relied on the ability to read below the surfaces—a way of mobilizing—to re-vision reality and call it by different names. This form of *la facultad* inspires new visions and strategies for action. But there is always the danger that even the most revolutionary of readings can become bankrupt as a form of resistance when it becomes reified, unchanging. The tendency of *la facultad* to end in frozen, privileged "readings" is the most divisive dynamic inside any liberation movement. In order for this survival skill to provide the basis for a differential and coalitional methodology, it must be remembered that *la facultad* is a process. Answers located may be only temporarily effective, so that wedded to the process of *la facultad* is a flexibility that continually woos change.

53. Alice Walker coined the neologism "womanism" as one of many attempts by feminists of color to find a name that would signal their commitment to egalitarian social relations, a commitment that the women's movement and the name "feminism" had, by 1980, betrayed. See Alice Walker, *In Search of Our Mother's Gardens: Womanist Prose* (New York: Harcourt Brace Jovanovich, 1983), pp. xi–xiii.

54. Allen, "Some like Indians Endure"; in Anzaldúa, *Borderlands/La Frontera*; Maria Lugones, "Playfulness, 'World'-Traveling, and Loving Perception," *Hypatia* 2 (1987): 123–50; Patricia Hill Collins, *Black Feminist Thought: Knowledge, Consciousness, and the Politics of Empowerment* (New York: Routledge, 1990); Gayatri Chakravorty Spivak, "Criticism, Feminism and the Institution," *Thesis Eleven* 10/11 (1984–85): 19–32, and "Explanations of Culture," in *The Post-Colonial Critic* (New York: Routledge, 1990), p. 156; and Walker, *In Search of Our Mother's Gardens*. Analysis of these writings reveals that each posits the following technologies: (1) sign reading-constructing-deconstructing; (2) commitment to differential movement and location, and (3) ethical commitment to social justice and democratic egalitarianism. Together, these technologies enable the differential form of social movement introduced in chapters 1 and 2. The content and form of these self-consciously produced modes of counterknowledge are examined in Part III of this book.

55. Barbara Christian, "Creating a Universal Literature: Afro-American Women Writers," *KPFA Folio*, special African History Month edition, February 1983, front page; reissued in *Black Feminist Criticism: Perspectives on Black Women Writers* (New York: Pergamon Press, 1985), p. 163.

56. Hooks, *Feminist Theory*, p. 9; Audre Lorde, "An Interview: Audre Lorde and Adrienne Rich," held in August 1979, *Signs* 6:4 (summer 1981): 323–40; and Barbara Smith, ed., *Home Girls: A Black Feminist Anthology* (New York: Kitchen Table: Women of Color Press, 1983), p. xxv.

57. Merle Woo, "Letter to Ma," in *This Bridge Called My Back*, p. 147.

58. Chandra Talpade Mohanty "Cartographies of Struggle," in *Third World Women and the Politics of Feminism*, ed. Chandra Talpade Mohanty, Ann Russo, and Lourdes Torres (Bloomington: Indiana University Press, 1991).

59. These strategies were understood and utilized as tactics for intervention by U.S. women of color in 1960s–70s ethnic liberation movements as well as in women's liberation movements. For explication of these usages, see Adaljiza Sosa Riddell, "Chicanas en el Movimiento," *Aztlán* 5 (1974): Moraga and Anzaldúa, *This Bridge Called My Back*; Barbara Smith, "Racism in Women's Studies," in Hull, Scott, and Smith, *All the Women Are White*; Bonnie Thorton Dill, "Race, Class and Gender: Perspectives for an All-Inclusive Sisterhood," *Feminist Studies* 9 (1983): 19–26; Mujeres en Marcha, ed., "Chicanas in the '80's: Unsettled Issues" (Berkeley: 1983) pp. 3–4; hooks, *Feminist Theory*; Alice Chai, "Toward a Holistic Paradigm for Asian American Women's Studies: A Synthesis of Feminist Scholarship and Women of Color's Feminist Politics," *Women's Studies International Forum* 8 (1985): 26–48; Cynthia Orozco, "Sexism in Chicano Studies and the Community," in Teresa Córdova, Norma Cantú, Gilberto Cardenas, Juan Garcia, and Christine Sierra, eds., *Chicano Voices: Intersections of Class, Race, and Gender* (Austin: CMAS Publications, (1986), pp. 29–41; Chela Sandoval, "Feminist Agency and U.S. Third World Feminism," in *Provoking Agents: Theorizing Gender and Agency*, ed. Judith Kegan Gardiner (Bloomington: Indiana University Press, 1995).

60. Such stratagems generate aesthetic works marked by disruption *and* by taking place, by immigrations, diasporas, and border crossings; by traveling style, politics, poetics, and procedures; by tactics, strategies, movement, and position — all produced with the aim of, as U.S. third world feminist Merle Woo put it in "Letter to Ma," equalizing power on behalf of the colonized, the nation-, class-, race-, gender-, and sexually subordinated.

61. Differential consciousness is composed of difference and contradictions, which then serve as tactical interventions in the other mobility that is power. Entrance into the realm "between and among" the others demands a mode of consciousness once relegated to the province of intuition and psychic phenomena, but which now must be recognized as a specific practice. I define differential consciousness as a kind of anarchic activity (but with method), a form of ideological guerrilla warfare, and a new kind of ethical activity that is discussed here as the way in which opposition to oppressive authorities is achieved in a highly technologized and disciplinized society. Inside this realm resides the only possible grounds for alliance across differences. Entrance into this new order requires an emotional commitment within which one experiences the violent shattering of the unitary sense of self as the skill that allows a mobile identity to form takes hold. As Bernice Reagon has written, "most of the time you feel threatened to the core and if you don't, you're not really doing no coalescing" ("Coalition Politics: Turning the Century"). Within the realm of differential consciousness there are no ultimate answers, no terminal utopia (though the imagination of utopias can motivate its tactics), no predictable final outcomes. Its practice is not biologically determined, restricted to any class or group, nor must it become static. Although it is a process capable of freezing into a repressive order, or of disintegrating into relativism, these dangers should not shadow its radical activity.

To name the theory and method made possible by the recognition of differential consciousness "oppositional" refers only to the ideological effects its activity can have. It is a naming that signifies a realm with constantly shifting boundaries that serve to delimit. Indeed, like Derrida's "*différance*," this form of oppositional consciousness participates in its own dissolution as it comes into action. Differential consciousness under postmodern conditions is not possible without the creation of another ethics, a new morality, and these will bring about a new subject of history. Movement into this realm was heralded by the claims of U.S. third world feminists. This movement made manifest the possibility of ideological warfare in the form of a theory and method, a praxis of oppositional consciousness. But to think of the activities of U.S. third world feminism thus is only a metaphorical avenue that allows one conceptual access to the threshold of this other realm, a realm accessible to *all* people.

62. Today, debates among U.S. feminists of color continue over how effective forms of resistance should be identified, valued, distinguished, translated, enacted, and/or named. Contending possibilities include "transnational" or "transcultural" feminisms, where issues of race and ethnicity are sublimated; to approaches that include "the differential," "*la conciencia de la mestiza*" (which deploys the technologies of *la facultad, coatlicue,* and *nepantla*), "womanism," and/or "third-space feminism," which together signify the activities of the specific 1980s form of "U.S. third world feminism" identified here; to "U.S. women-of-color feminism," which emphasizes the exclusion of its population from legitimate state powers by virtue of color, physiognomy, and/or social class. U.S. women-of-color feminism tends to commit to one or more of the five technologies of power outlined earlier: the equal-rights, revolutionary, supremacist, or separatist forms are means of increasing and reinforcing racial and tribal loyalties and self-determination. This focus is more specific than that of the differential, third space, or "U.S. third world" form of feminism, however, which, when understood as a technical and critical term, is focused, above all else, on the poetic deployment of each of these mechanisms for mobilizing power. As such, the U.S. third world form of feminism identified here is not inexorably gender-, nation-, race-, sex-, or class-linked. It represents, rather, *a theory and method of oppositional consciousness* that rose out of a specific deployment, that is, out of a particular tactical expression of 1980s U.S. third world feminist politics. This tactic that became an overriding strategy is guided, above all else, by imperatives of social justice that can engage a hermeneutics of love in the postmodern world, as we shall see in Parts III and IV.

3. On Cultural Studies

1. See Rosa Linda Fregoso's excellent chapter on differential consciousness as expressed in film in *The Bronze Screen: Chicano and Chicana Film Culture* (Minneapolis: University of Minnesota Press, 1993). The comic book series the *X-Men* first appeared in September 1963. In December 1970, the title was revived in reprint form. See the *World Encyclopedia of Comics*, 1976.

2. See, for example, Homi K. Bhabha, "DissemiNation: Time, Narrative, and the Margins of the Modern

Nation," in *Nation and Narration*, ed. Homi K. Bhabha (New York: Routledge, 1990), pp. 291–320; Gilles Deleuze and Félix Guattari, *Anti-Oedipus: Capitalism and Schizophrenia*, trans. Robert Hurley, Mark Seem, and Helen R. Lane (Minneapolis: University of Minnesota Press, 1983), and *Kafka: Toward a Minor Literature*, trans. Dana Polan (Minneapolis: University of Minnesota Press, 1986); Gayatri Spivak, "Explanation and Culture: Marginalia," in *In Other Worlds: Essays in Cultural Politics* (New York: Methuen, 1987), pp. 103–18, and "In a Word, Interview," *differences, essentialism issue* (summer 1989): 124–56; Gloria Anzaldúa, "*La conciencia de la mestiza:* Towards a New Consciousness," in *Borderlands/ La Frontera: The New* Mestiza (San Francisco: Spinsters/ Aunt Lute, 1987), pp. 77–102; Judith Butler, *Gender Trouble: Feminism and the Subversion of Identity* (New York: Routledge, 1990); Donna Haraway, "Situated Knowledges: The Science Question in Feminism and the Privilege of Partial Perspective," in *Simians, Cyborgs, and Women: The Reinvention of Nature* (New York: Routledge, 1991), pp. 183–203, and "The Actors Are Cyborg, Nature Is Coyote, and the Geography Is Elsewhere: Postscript to "'Cyborgs at Large,'" in *Technoculture*, ed. Constance Penley and Andrew Ross (Minneapolis: University of Minnesota Press, 1991), pp. 21–27; Henry Louis Gates Jr., "The Blackness of Blackness: A Critique of the Sign and the Signifying Monkey," in *Black Literature and Literary Theory* (New York: Methuen, 1984), pp. 286–323; Patricia Hill Collins, *Black Feminist Thought: Knowledge, Consciousness, and the Politics of Empowerment* (Boston: Unwin Hyman, 1990); Teresa de Lauretis, "Eccentric Subjects: Feminist Theory and Historical Consciousness," *Feminist Studies* (spring 1990): 115–49; Jacques Derrida, *Writing and Difference*, trans. Alan Bass (Chicago: University of Chicago Press, 1978); Hayden White, "Writing in the Middle Voice," *Stanford Literature Review* 9:2 (1992): 179–87; Trinh T. Minh-ha, ed., "She the Inappropriate/d Other," *Discourse* 8 (special issue) (winter 1986–87): 32–50; see also her *Woman/ Native/Other: Writing Postcoloniality and Feminism* (Bloomington: Indiana University Press, 1989); and Gerald Vizenor, *Crossbloods: Bone Courts, Bingo, and Other Reports* (Minneapolis: University of Minnesota Press, 1990).

3. This inability to recognize common ground for coalition between scholarly communities is especially surprising in the developing field of cultural studies (including poststructuralism, feminist theory, queer theory, postcolonial criticism, third world feminism, and the concomitant histories, sociologies, philosophies, anthropologies, and political sciences associated with each). The problem is the inability to recognize and name the shared methodology (outlined in the next chapter) that links each of these endeavors.

4. Barthes, Derrida, and Foucault are the usual examples of poststructuralist theorists. Influential white feminist theorists include de Beauvoir, Millet, Kolodny, Kristeva, Rich, Gubar, Choderow, and Butler. Postcolonial thinkers include Edward Said, Homi Bhabha, Cornel West, Stuart Hall, Abdul Jan Mohamed, José Saldívar, Michael Omi, and Gerald Vizenor. U.S. third world feminist theorists include Lorde, Anzaldúa, Lugones, Minh-ha, Spivak, Moraga, Baca Zinn, Collins, Gunn Allen, and Pérez. Of course, these are general tendencies, and border crossers always arise, as evinced by those whose work has emerged out of the volatile boundary between U.S. third world and white feminist theoretical domains, such as Donna Haraway, Teresa de Lauretis, and Gayatri Spivak. And provocative bridges across theoretical divides were made during the 1990s in the domains of "postmodern," "postcolonial," and "transnational" feminisms. But, overall, the stubborn boundaries that divide these theoretical domains continue regenerating.

Global studies represents the most current effort to subsume this apartheid under a broader conceptual understanding. Issues of colonization, decolonization, and emancipatory forms of consciousness tend to be put under erasure through the conceptual elisions the category of "global studies" tends to effect, however. What is the mode of conceptual unification that can imagine and connect the world in the interests of a (dissident) globalization?

5. Cornel West, *Prophet Reflections: Notes on Race and Power in America* (Monroe, Maine: Common Courage Press, 1993), p. 54.

6. In the chapters to come, I have found it most provocative to detail the methodology of the oppressed first by reading its effects in the works of two theorists who are poised on the cusp between the end of the colonial era and the beginning of the postmodern (Frantz Fanon and Roland Barthes made their contributions during the mid-twentieth century) before I track its manifestations through a plethora of Western theorists who follow, the effects of which all finally circle back to U.S. third world feminism.

7. Michel Foucault, "The Subject and Power," in *Michel Foucault: Beyond Structuralism and Hermeneutics*, ed. Hubert Dreyfus and Paul Rabinow (Chicago: University of Chicago Press, 1993), p. 213.

8. The film *Freejack* (1991) images this shift in morality thus: the corporate head, a kindly, older, white patriarchal male played by Anthony Hopkins, who wants to live forever, is transformed into a living memory with only four days of existence left on the net of a computer brain. Once he disappears from the computer matrix, his position of power will be refilled by new forms of subjectivity, which are imaged as youth, the underclasses, and woman, all of whom possess mystically transcendental powers. In those four days, this living memory tragically crosses every moral boundary in order to stop his own

death and replacement, but, in spite of his own almost mystical computer-enhanced powers, nothing works.

9. The "paradigmatic" refers to the vertical axis of language, one of the two relationships signs can have to other signs. It designates a set of signs that can be substituted for each other in the same position within any sequence, because replacing one with another has no effect on the overall syntax of a meaning. The "syntagmatic," on the other hand, refers to the sequential and diachronic relations of signs, to the horizontal-metonymic axis of language.

10. This is another alternative to the dynamics of neocolonial postmodernism—a transnationalization without the postmodern flattening effect—a multidimensional cosmopolitics.

11. Roman Jakobson, *Fundamentals of Language* (The Hague: Mouton, 1956).

12. Engagement with life in this locale requires emotional tolerance for that which is not easily categorized, for difficult speech out of place, for what is nonnarrative, the undomesticated, the untamed; for language, speech, and activity in this domain do not naively repeat the authoritative laws of the social order: these forms of being are, rather, guided by a purposive drive for equality. Differential consciousness, the methodology of the oppressed, and the differential form of social movement are art-form knowledges, not easily scientized or narrativized, for they are in constant flux, in continual revolution. What the dominant order views as a "riot" of behavior, as "conflagrations" of difference, as turbulent lawlessness, when understood through a differential consciousness, become enactments of a self-conscious commitment to consciousness untamed through movement from habitual subjugation . . . toward freedom itself. See the Conclusion of *Methodology of the Oppressed.*

13. *Theory Uprising* was the original title of this book.

4. Semiotics and Languages of Emancipation

1. The texts selected in order to identify the methodology of the oppressed at work within them are written by Frantz Fanon and Roland Barthes, two theorists writing at the outset of our global postmodern age—that is, they are situated historically at a key point when the issues forming postmodernism (and against which Jameson writes) first become visible.

2. Roland Barthes, *Mythologies*, trans. Richard Miller (New York: Hill and Wang, 1972), pp. 109–59. Further references to this work will be given in the text.

3. See, for example, Merle Woo, "Letter to Ma," *This Bridge Called My Back*; Maria Lugones, "World-Traveling"; Patricia Hill Collins, *Black Feminist Thought*; and June Jorden, "Where Is the Love?" in *Making Face, Making Soul/Haciendo Caras.*

4. This use of the term *differential* differs from its use in chapter 2, which describes the "differential form of social movement" utilized by U.S. third world feminists. The term *differential* is used in this chapter to signify *one specific technology* of the methodology of the oppressed. In Part IV, the term will be put to a third and final use. For further explanation of the varying uses of the term in this book, see the Introduction.

5. The thinking of this Caribbean psychologist living in an Algeria struggling for independence during the mid-twentieth century is particularly relevant to understanding how to create twenty-first-century modes of decolonizing cosmopolitics. Fanon is one of the first theorists in the post–World War II *postcolonial* period to articulate the failure of Western ideology, which he does by employing the very philosophical, rationalist tradition on which Western civilization was asserting its mastery and dominance. At the same time, Fanon deconstructs the psychological, epistemological, and economic bases of European colonialism through his evocation of and intervention in Freudian, Kantian, and Marxist thought. In what follows, I demonstrate how he accomplishes all this through deploying a subaltern theory and method, the methodology of the oppprressed.

6. Frantz Fanon, *Black Skin, White Masks*, trans. Charles Markmann (New York: Grove Press, 1967). Further references to this work will be given in the text.

7. See Anzaldúa's meditation on the vertigo of this interspace which she calls an "interface," in *Haciendo Caras/Making Face, Making Soul*.

8. See, for example, W. E. B. Du Bois, *The Souls of Black Folk*, reprinted in *Three Negro Classics* (New York: Avon, 1965), pp. 214–215; Jameson Weldon Johnson, *The Autobiography of an Ex-Colored Man*, reprinted in ibid., p. 403; Audre Lorde, *Sister Outsider*, pp. 114–15; Gloria Anzaldúa, *Borderlands/La Frontera*, p. 194; Trinh T. Minh-ha, *Woman/Native/Other*, p. 90; Paula Gunn Allen, "Making Sacred, Making True" in *Grandmothers of the Light* (Boston: Beacon Press, 1991), p. 71.

9. It must be understood that for the hegemonic white and colonizing population of the time, the soul was understood as an essence: unattested being produced not by human interests but by godly insight. This essence of the soul was thought to express itself in mind, action, emotion, culture, spirit, and even physical appearance. It was this essence theory of the soul that underlay white policies justifying the conquest and colonization of people of color who were judged as inferior by virtue of a soul that expressed its different and subordinate nature through the colors and shapes of bodies, cultures, and languages. If, as Fanon insisted, the soul was not an essence, but instead an "artifact" crafted by the "white man," then the ideologies through which economically fruitful social policies as conquest and colonization were

set into place and harvested would be defeated. Fanon's heresy proposed an intervention, then, not only into the realm of the spirit, but into ideological, economic, social, and political arenas.

By 1960, the term *soul* was reappropriated by the black community as follows: "Soul is bein' true to your self . . . is . . . that uninhibited self-expression that goes into practically every Negro endeavor" (Claude Brown, quoted in the *American Heritage Dictionary of the English Language* [New York: Houghton Mifflin, 1975]). Here *soul* becomes the product not of God but of a racialized (and essentialized) human concern for "truth."

10. See Sojourner Truth, "Ain't I a Woman?" and Tracy Chapman, "All That You Have Is Your Soul," *Crossroads* (Elektra Records, 1989).

11. Barthes's own identity construction at this time is no small matter: he is an outsider, a gay man, a social exile, a Marxist, and an academic whose stakes in articulating a radical and utilitarian methodology of the oppressed that can both ally with the subject positions accorded and/or demanded by the colonized, and extend beyond them to include others as well, are crucial to his own sense of hope, community, and of a continuing utopian social history.

12. Nancy Hartsock, "The Feminist Standpoint: Developing the Ground for a Specifically Feminist Historical Materialism," in *Discovering Reality: Feminist Perspectives on Epistemology, Metaphysics, Methodology, and Philosophy of Science*, ed. Sandra Harding and Merrill B. Hintikka (Dordrecht, Holland: D. Reidel, 1983), pp. 53–65; Donna Haraway, "A Manifesto for Cyborgs: Science, Technology, and Socialist Feminism in the 1980s," *Socialist Review 80:2* (March 1985): 12–39.

13. This chapter reviews Barthes's argument regarding the "speech of the oppressed," in order to separate his category from the category of the "methodology of the oppressed."

14. Nevertheless, in the following pages I argue that embedded in Barthes's analysis is a methodology that erases and goes beyond all such distinctions: a queer formulation that wobbles in between.

15. Barthes himself argued the importance of coining new terms in order to make a fluctuating reality more comprehendible. He did this with the term *myth* itself when he defined it as "a mode of signification, a form." He added, "innumerable other meanings of the word 'myth' can be cited against" this one. "But," he wrote, "I have tried to define things, not words" (109).

Naming the liberatory mode of consciousness in opposition "mythology" or "mythologies" was, however, an unfortunate mistake. Given the many other meanings of the term *myth*, and of *mythologies* itself in his own work, leftist activists and thinkers over the last thirty years have all but overlooked the centrality of Barthes's manifesto for developing new modes of praxis in resistance. Referring to "myth" as "ideology" helps clarify the importance of Barthes's findings.

16. Henry Louis Gates Jr., "The Signifyin' Monkey"; and Anzaldúa, *Borderlands/La Frontera*, p. 25.

17. Indeed, Barthes argues, not only ideology, but all meanings — and consciousness itself — are structured according to this same "form," which we examine in what follows.

18. His proposal was that this could occur through a differential movement of signification. As we shall see, this differential movement among Signifiers in Barthes's emancipatory praxis prefigures the poststructuralist insistence on the movement of meaning from Signifier to Signifier posited by theorists of meaning such as Derrida Kristeva, Baudrilland, and so on.

19. If Part III examines this prison house of meaning, Part IV investigates its modes of release.

20. In chapter 5 we watch how this process creates the consciousness and politics of supremacism.

21. Two technologies used to identify, survive, and bridge that chasm are "semiology," which involves taking in an image with all the emotional consequences of such consumption, and "mythology," which is the deconstruction of that image in a process that releases consciousness from loyalties to the pleasures or defects which that image demands. Although somewhat conflated in Barthes's own descriptions, these two processes are two of the five technologies that are fundamental to the methodology of the oppressed. In the reverberation from colonial margins to colonial centers occurring toward the end of Western expansion, this methodology and its technologies became available for tracking, and this to a large extent is what Western theorists, from Peirce and Saussure at the turn of the century to Barthes, Foucault, Derrida, and other theorists of meaning at its end have been doing.

22. From today's vantage point, using the example of U.S. third world feminism, I can add what Barthes was unable to as yet imagine: a fifth, tactical form of perception that moves from one "focus" to another in order to ensure survival. This fifth form requires another kind of perception altogether that understands and demands a different relationship of signifier to signified; it is an apparatus I call the methodology of the oppressed.

23. How is it possible to perceive both as a dominant consumer, at the same time that one is perceiving the *routes through perception* demanded by ideology, from the perspective of some other, third consciousness? Barthes's method maps the formal routes to developing this third mode of consciousness demanded of oppressed citizenry in order to ensure one's survival under colonization.

24. Unlike Barthes's primary audience (the favored middle-class and white citizens of the 1950s) who must *learn* to unjoin perception from its object in the process of a "de-ideologizing semiotic-mythology," the colonized were often forcibly and unwillingly ripped out of the comforts of dominant ideology, out of legitimized social narratives, in a process of power that placed these constituencies in a very different position to view objects-in-reality than other kinds of citizen-subjects. Surviving the horrors of colonization, these citizen-subjects learned to ride the razor edge between what is, and what might be, between a purely signifying and a purely imagining consciousness as means to survival, *self-consciously navigating* Western forms of dominant consciousness — through to the very being of meaning itself.

25. In 1957, Barthes's third, "dominant" mode of perceiving and deciphering represents the consciousness of the "bourgeois" white colonizer. This "dominant" mode of consciousness generates an identity that rests in a vision of reality made up of naturalized Signified-concepts, a cohesive and apparently grounded reality, held fast, in which to believe. The outsider citizenship of Barthes's "mythologist," however, arises in a realm in which every object and being is a "Signifier," every form is scrutinized, read, and interpreted, and every action is understood as unleashing a further tumult of Signifiers, all of which are understood as pieces of the body-of-power. But Barthes cannot recognize that subjugated social actors, who are cast under dominant rule as "insane," "possessed," "animal-like" — who are forced to live in this world of multiplying Signifiers — have also developed technologies for survival that are at one with the techniques of his "semiotic-mythology." Fanon had recognized in his study of the bodies and minds of peoples of color under colonial rule that for the conquered citizen-subject dominant significations are, unfortunately, only all too distinguishable as a combination of some form (Sr), with an imposed meaning (Sd), and the deformation one imposes on the other is all too clearly apprehended. Had Barthes asked what the techniques and technologies of resistance were that guided opposition among oppressed constituencies, he would have enabled his own theory as a coalitional praxis for advancing oppositional social movement, as he had hoped. Barthes did not ask this question, though, and was unable to make these connections. Indeed, the economy of dominant theory in the academy makes such coalitions and accountabilities all but impossible, *unless struggled for collectively.*

26. When the oppressed do not *theorize* what they see, as do the cynic, the semiologist, or the dominant consumer, when one simply "acts," one becomes separated from the practice of "semiotic-mythology" in a primary way. This is the central problem with Barthes's understanding of what happens to consciousness under oppression. The rest of this chapter describes Barthes's understanding of the speech of the oppressed, revolutionary speech, and the last three technologies of the methodology of the oppressed, in order to demonstrate how Barthes's conceptualization of the "speech of the oppressed" is only one element of what I have described as the methodology of the oppressed emancipation.

27. We must insist on the nonisomorphic simultaneity, co-constructions, and competitions that exist between the categories of "the proletariat" and "the colonized." Indeed, it will be when thinkers and activists stop *replacing* one position of oppression with another — "proletariat," "colonized," "women," "the oppressed" — and start recognizing their complicated *simultaneity* and heterogeneity that the theory of differential oppositional social movement and consciousness will become most applicable and enabling.

28. It is at this point that we can challenge Barthes's notion of "the speech of the oppressed" (his example of the "zero degree of language"), that we can refuse the idealization of a speech outside language that is fully action (though this form of speech does exist, it does not belong only to the "oppressed"), to argue instead that the speech of the "oppressed" is fully semiological. Indeed, this chapter has argued that this "speech" also can be understood as being composed of the tactics, strategies, and technologies that we have identified as "the methodology of the oppressed," and which I am tracking through Barthes's work.

29. Differential movement was not proposed by the marginalized as an end in and of itself for, as we have seen in the example of U.S. third world feminism, people of color are also deeply committed to very *particular* ideological standpoints from which they act on behalf of liberation. Fanon gives examples of how colonial imposition can shatter a sense of self; physiological and cultural denigration can shatter identity into pathological psychic forms, on the one side, but, on the other, such denigrations can enforce the generation of other survival skills as well. Differential consciousness in opposition depends on what Henry Louis Gates Jr. refers to as "signifyin'" and what Anzaldúa calls "*la facultad*," both terms referring to the skill of reading power in signs, and the slipping of identity/ideology into a position most likely to ensure survival, a meta-ideologizing tactic of opposition that Gayatri Spivak calls "strategic essentialism." When incorporated into the methodology of the oppressed, differential movement becomes an applied political technology that works on other ideological possibilities as materials at hand for self-consciously pressing against authoritarian structures of order and power.

Differential consciousness is the basis that makes ideological deconstructions, whether in the form of semiology, mythology, or revolutionary ex-nomination, possible. What have recently come to be known as the "postmodern forms" that work to release the lone, isolated subjectivities of a Fredric Jameson or a Roland Barthes into a kind of "schizophrenic" enjoyment of perceptual play — a freedom from cultural classifications (a "freedom" forced upon subjugated citizens) — also represents for previously centered subjects a liberation of the self from its subjection to the law of the social order. The theoretical contributions of certain scholars of critical and cultural studies can become strangely depoliticized in their development and exchange within Western academia. These works are repoliticized when they are recontextualized and understood as symptoms of a new, postcolonial/transnational situation. Part and parcel of a worldwide movement toward decolonization, a post-empire condition, these works provide grounds for the emancipation of consciousness when they are recognized as containing technologies identifiable as those previously utilized in order to ensure survival under first world conditions within subordinated and colonized communities.

30. For the Western theorist to give up the figural pose of being *alone* is no mean feat. Barthes's inability to theoretically recognize the coalitional consciousness connecting his own theory of semiology and the methodology of the oppressed did not arise through any personal or idiosyncratic lack on his part, at the level of psychological maturation, for example. Rather, his inability to make these connections occurs at the level of glitches in the technology of theory itself, and, above all, glitches in the structures of accountability — who one talks to, and writes for and with: that is, at the level of the material apparatus of theory production at a sociological and institutional level.

31. Barthes does not acknowledge the methods of alterity, yet he imposes his jurisdiction on their realm, and in the process the technologies of alterity, the methodology of the oppressed, are made invisible. That is why Barthes's discovery and articulation of the "new," liberatory category of perception and deciphering, semiotic-mythology, belongs to the praxis of his heroic mythologist, alone. This unfortunate theoretical strategy makes the articulation of a coalitional consciousness in social struggle impossible to imagine or enact. In this way, Barthes participates in a double movement. His terminologies appropriate the technologies of the oppressed for use by academic classes, while his schema erases the category of the "oppressed" from the realm of theoretical production altogether. Sadly, the conclusion of Barthes's essay is all about his own similar "exile" and banishment from dominant reality.

32. This turn from annihilation to assimilation is represented in such contemporary Hollywood films as *Thunderheart* (1992), for example, which images a white man who, over the course of the narrative, is transformed into a man of color, a warrior for aboriginal rights.

5. The Rhetoric of Supremacism as Revealed by the Ethical Technology

1. How can cultural, critical, and literary theorists of whiteness use, learn from, and build on Barthes, Fanon, and the lessons of their juxtapositioning? Have scholars genericized Barthes, taking him up only as a critic of the "human" condition (also known as the unmarked-dominant-posing-as-universal) in its drive to signify, at the same time that they ignore his substantial contributions toward undoing colonial, middle-class, "white," and supremacist forms of consciousness? Simultaneously, have we marginalized Fanon by reading him only as a critic of the subjecthood of the colonized and oppressed while failing to engage him as a critic of dominant subject formation? Indeed, are these tendencies symptoms of an apartheid of theoretical domains that keeps knowledges in the academy developing separate versions of the methodology of the oppressed—under varying terminologies—while they at the same time seek a method for transdisciplinarity that works?

2. Which it can never admit; all finally depends on the effectiveness of ideology/naturalization.

3. As reflected in the anti–affirmative-action position that states: We want neither white people nor people of color, we only want the "best," and in the late-1990s controversy involving University of California regent Ward Connerly and his desire to undo affirmative action, versus the pro–affirmative-action stance of large percentages of students, faculty, and staff: neither position is judged to be "rational" by certain University of California professionals, who insist on taking an "independent, objective, and neutral" pose.

4. Donna Haraway pointed out to me that this rhetorical figure, the quantification of quality, also is crucial to the affect of postmodernism globalization—the subject immersed in sensation, in stimulation, in the hyperreal. The quantification of quality is not only a liberal, figural pose, then, as in Barthes's original formulation. It is a figure of the "new world" postmodern order in its neocolonial mode. This book seeks to make the postmodern de- and postcolonial.

5. Western thinkers such as Hegel (1770–1831), Marx (1818–83), Nietszche (1844–1900), Saussure (1857–1913), and Freud (1856–1939), of course, considered consciousness in its supremacist forms. Their clarity of insight was generated through their ability to compare Western forms of being with those that insistently appeared as profoundly "other" during the imperialist expansion of the West, but none of these thinkers explicitly drew upon the survival techniques of colonized and oppressed classes, by turning those techniques into a "science," as Barthes attempted to do. Barthes does refer to statements by both Marx and Gorki in order to guide his own definition of the rhetoric of supremacy. He

quotes Marx as saying: "what makes [people] representative of the petit-bourgeois class, is that their minds, their consciousness do not extend beyond the limits which this class has set to its activities" (*The Eighteenth Brumaire of Louis Bonaparte*); and Gorki: "the petit-bourgeois is the man who has preferred himself to all else" (151).

6. Ruth Frankenberg, *White Women, Race Matters* (Berkeley: University of California Press, 1997); Bernice Johnson Regon, "Coalition Politics, Turning the Century," in *Home Girls: A Black Feminist Anthology*, ed. Barbara Smith (New York: Kitchen Table: Women of Color Press, 1983), pp. 356–59; bell hooks, "Representations of Whiteness," in *Black Looks* (Boston: South End Press, 1992), pp. 165–79; Vron Ware, *Beyond the Pale* (London: Verso, 1992); Cherríe Moraga, *Loving in the War Years* (Boston: South End Press, 1983).

7. This supremacism is capable of transforming a black African soldier saluting the French national flag (in Barthes's famous 1957 example) into an example of the goodness of colonialism; or, in Fanon's famous 1951 example, of modifying "black skin" to signify only through a "white mask" so that what is seen, or enacted, is a white mask—in blackface.

8. Carl Jung, Fanon writes, asserts that the "collective unconscious" of the dominating class, "its mythologies and archetypes," are "permanent engrams of the race" of humans and rooted in "spirit" itself (188). But, for Fanon, the "collective unconscious" only represents Jung's naturalization and theorization of the dominant order. Fanon reiterates that any "collective unconscious" discovered by science is only an artifact, like consciousness itself—both are produced by an "unreflected imposition of culture." But mind formed through the imperatives of culture is transformable through self-conscious reflection, Fanon believes. It is this *possibility of transformation* and self re-formation that makes possible Fanon's hope for creating a definition and practice of liberty and justice that can ally and connect differing categories of the human (191).

9. Homi Bhabha's article on Fanon is worth looking at in this regard: "Remembering Fanon: Self, Psyche, and the Colonial Position," in *Remaking History*, ed. Barbara Kruger and Phil Mariani (Seattle: Bay Press, 1989), pp. 131–48.

10. Oswald Ducrot and Tzvetan Todorov, *Encyclopedic Dictionary of the Sciences of Language* (Baltimore: Johns Hopkins University Press, 1983), p. 362, my emphasis.

11. This form of decolonizing cyberspace is difficult to mold, manage, manipulate, or govern, or rather, "governing" and control take place on altogether different terms. The term *cybernetics* was coined by Norbert Wiener from the Greek word *Kubernan*, meaning to steer, guide, and govern. In 1989, the term *cybernetics* was split in two, and its first half, "cyber" (which is a neologism with no earlier root), was broken from its "control" and "govern" meanings to represent the possibilities of travel and existence in the new space of computer networks, a space negotiated by the human mind in new kinds of ways. This uncontrolled cyberspace is imaged in virtual-reality films such as *Freejack*, *Lawnmower Man*, and *Tron*. But it was first named "cyberspace" and explored by the science-fiction writer William Gibson in his 1984 book *Neuromancer*. This Gibsonian history, however, passes through and makes invisible 1970s feminist science fiction and theory, including the works of Russ, Butler, Delany, Piercy, Haraway, Sofoulis, and Sandoval. In all cases, this cyberspace best describes the new kind of location and movement possible of "differential" consciousness, as we see in Part IV.

12. This is what we investigate in Part IV. The theorists examined in the next two chapters put forth a series of propositions that I intend to convey in all their provocative force. However different their propositions may be, each theorist, from Foucault and Hayden White to Derrida and Donna Haraway, is allied through a similar commitment to transform the networks perm-eating our time by developing and articulating forms of consciousness-in-resistance to the powers that hier-archize all meanings. In chapters 6 and 7, I cruise through the proposals and models generated differently by each of these thinkers. More than the destination, the pleasure is in the (differential) transit.

6. Love as a Hermeneutics of Social Change, a Decolonizing *Movida*

1. Roland Barthes, *A Lover's Discourse: Fragments*, trans. Richard Howard (New York: Hill and Wang, 1978), p. 55. Unless indicated, all quotations in this chapter will be from this book.

2. The Chicana/o term *rasquache* as defined by Tomás Ybarra-Frausto is "the outsider viewpoint" that stems from "a funky, irreverent stance that debunks convention and spoofs protocol. To be *rasquache* is to post a bawdy, spunky consciousness, to seek to subvert and turn ruling paradigms upside down. It is a witty, irreverent, and impertinent posture that recodes and moves outside established boundaries." *Rasquachismo* is, he writes, "rooted in Chicano structures of thinking, feeling, and aesthetic choice. It is one form of a Chicano vernacular, the verbal-visual codes we use to speak to each other among ourselves" ("*Rasquachismo*: A Chicano Sensibility," in *Chicano Art: Resistance and Affirmation* (Los Angeles: UCLA Wight Art Gallery, 1991), p. 155.

3. Roland Barthes, *Incidents*, trans. Richard Howard (Berkeley: University of California Press, 1992); *The Pleasure of the Text*, trans. Richard Miller (New York: Noonday Press, 1975).

4. Gloria Anzaldúa, *Borderlands/La Frontera*, 41; Emma Pérez, "Sexuality and Discourse: Notes from a Chicana Survivor," in *Chicana Lesbians: The Girls Our Mothers Warned Us About*, ed. Carla Trujillo (Berkeley: Third Woman Press, 1992), pp. 159–84; Trinh T. Minh-ha, *Woman/Native/Other*, p. 86; June Jordan "Where Is the Love?" in Gloria Anzaldúa, ed., *Making Face, Making Soul/Haciendo Caras*, p. 174. See also Jesse Jackson, "Service and a New World Order," in *Straight from the Heart*, ed. Roger Hatch and Frank Watkins (Phila-delphia: Fortress Press, 1987), pp. 76–86; and Audre Lorde, "Uses of the Erotic: The Erotic as Power," in *Sister Outsider*, pp. 53–60.

5. Roland Barthes, "The Third Meaning: Research Notes on Some Eisenstein Stills," in *Image/Music/Text*, trans. Stephen Heath (New York: Hill and Wang, 1977), pp. 52–69.

6. Barthes, *The Pleasure of the Text*, p. 4.

7. The well-known film and culture theorist Stephen Heath explains in his introduction to *Image/Music/Text* the distinctions in Barthes's earlier work between the terms *pleasure* and *jouissance*, or "bliss." The term *pleasure*, he writes, is linked to "cultural enjoyment and identity, to the cultural enjoyment of identity, to a homogenizing movement of the ego," to desire and love once they have entered into the realm of law. On the other side, writes Heath, Barthes uses the term *jouissance* to signify the "radically violent pleasure which shatters, dissipates — loses that cultural identity, that ego." Even in these early writings it is clear that it is through *jouissance* or "bliss" that reality is punctured, perhaps always traumatically, and one is enabled to enter the interzone, the abyss, that location of the "zero degree" where meaning moves, is generated, and deconstructed (9).

8. That place we know, but that continually defies definition by words and signs. For a full discussion of these terms, see Barthes, *The Pleasure of the Text*, pp. 18–19.

9. Ibid., p. 18.

10. See Barthes, *Image/Music/Text*, pp. 52–69.

11. In tracing Barthes's lifework, narrative released epiphany as he turned from the semiotic and structural analyses of the minutiae that comprise the signs of everyday experience, to examine the meanings that cannot be categorized, tamed, or even, as he wrote, "named." His final work in *Incidents* and *A Lover's Discourse* provides a poetic prose that moves toward that moment when the ground disappears from beneath one's feet, the abyss rises, confuses, subverts with poetic inspiration, illumination, and revelation — calling up a moment of no origin nor primary authority. Ironically, however, this form subverts the traditional academic authority of his own discourse as literary theorist.

12. Barthes's footnote here is worth repeating because he finds it necessary to provide us the following clarification in the form of an etymology for his version of "prophetic love." He writes that "the Greeks opposed... (onar), the vulgar dream, to...(hypar), *the prophetic (never believed) vision*" (60; my emphasis).

13. Barthes, *Image/Music/Text*, p. 65.

14. This process of social action, identity, and consciousness transformation that is understood as "prophetic love" or "soul" is the meaning behind the title of Anzaldúa's book *Making Face/Making Soul/Haciendo Caras*, and the reason for so much attention by U.S. feminists of color to matters related to "spirit," "soul," and "love." For recent examples of this, see Kathleen Alcalá, *Spirits of the Ordinary: A Tale of Casa Grandes* (San Francisco: Chronicle, 1997); Paula Gunn Allen, *The Sacred Hoop: Recovering the Feminine in American Indian Traditions* (Boston: Beacon Press, 1986); Gloria Anzaldúa, ed., *Borderlands/La Frontera: The New Mestiza*; Amalia Mesa-Bains, "Curatorial Statement," in *Ceremony of Spirit: Nature and Memory in Contemporary Latino Art*; Tey Diana Rebolledo, *Women Singing in the Snow: A Cultural Analysis of Chicano Literature*; and Laura E. Pérez, "Spirit Glyphs: Reimagining Art and Artist in the World of Chicana *Tlamatinime*," *MFS Modern Fiction Studies* (spring 1998): 54–63.

15. And to differential social movement, love in the postmodern world, or to *amor en Aztlán*. Laura Pérez defines *Aztlán* thus: "*Aztlán* exists as an invisible nation within the engulfing 'imagined community' of dominant U.S. discourse. The day-to-day practices in this invisible collective zone are disordering to the dominant culture's *migra* (border patrol agents) ("*El desorden*, Nationalism, and Chicana/o Aesthetics" [1993], unpublished manuscript, p. 1).

16. Jacques Derrida, "*Différance*," in *Speech and Phenomena and Other Essays on Husserl's Theory of Signs* (Evanston: Northwestern University Press, 1973), p. 131. Further references to this book will be given in the text. Derrida is of "third world" origin, born in Algeria in 1930, educated in France. Like the work of all the thinkers examined in this book, Derrida's scholarship was greatly impacted by the end of Western colonial expansion and by worldwide de-colonial political practices.

17. There are also social constituencies who hold the place in society of the repressed middle voice, of *différance*. Their release would release as well the psychic and social chains that hold the two sides of the binary opposition together—no more hierarchy, no more domination.

18. It is this inability to "fit" that prompted Sojourner Truth to ask ironically, "Ain't I a woman?" which helped create the cultural promise of *la conciencia de la mestiza*,

and the position held by U.S. Indians, Chicanos/as, Asians, and mestizo/as, who remained until recently members of unmarked, invisible colors and cultures—neither white nor black.

19. The decolonization, generally speaking, not only of nations but of women, sexualities, genders, races, ethnicities, students—of social orders and their categories such as "love."

20. Yet *différance* can still be usefully comprehended as that space that circulates around, through, and outside of some Grammasian square white men/white women/men of color/women of color. See Fredric Jameson, "Preface to Greimas," unpublished manuscript, 1988.

21. We could list other theoretical namings of this apparatus, from Homi Bhabha's "third space" to the "minority discourse" and "lines of flight" proposed by Deleuze and Guattari. I am not seeking to add up instances, however, but to point out a common metatheoretical structure that motivates such efforts across disciplines, and to link these similar theoretical and political efforts to the historical reality of decolonization—that is, to the contributions made by subordinated subjects (queers, women, peoples of color, slaves, children, students) to the evolution of human knowledge, and social, psychic, and spiritual freedom.

22. See Hayden White, *Metahistory: The Historical Imagination in Nineteenth-Century Europe* (Baltimore: Johns Hopkins University Press, 1975), p. xii. White's proposed method permits scholars to learn how to *self-consciously* choose between alternative postures for translating reality into discourse. In utilizing this method, the researcher comes to understand that every representation constructed, every scholar's "strategy for constituting reality" contains "its own ethical implications." Ascertaining the ethical implications of scholarly productions is, according to White, as important to its construction as is the content of the research itself, and this can be determined by reading the "content of the form" in which the research has been organized and presented. White's method allows scholarly "frames of mind" to be identified and analyzed as ideologies—each bound differently in and by power to create and circumscribe differing forms of knowledge, ethics, history, and reality. White's method has provided the human and social sciences with new analytic bearings, and has also provided the basis by which to generate a particularly U.S. version of cultural studies.

23. Ibid., p. 22.

24. Ibid., p. 12.

25. Beginning with Hayden White, "Writing in the Middle Voice," *Stanford Literature Review* 9:2 (fall 1992): 179–87. Further references to this work will be given in the text.

26. Hayden White, *The Content of the Form* (Baltimore: Johns Hopkins University Press, 1987), p. 75; my emphasis.

27. The third voice is neither active nor passive, nor is it gendered, raced, or rule-governed. Indo-European discourses do not have an agreed-upon name or language for identifying what is the production in Western discourse of the Greek or Sanskrit middle voice. That is one reason why theorists across disciplines continually attempt to reinvent its terms.

28. See, for example, the forms of consciousness argued for by Paula Gunn Allen in *Grandmothers of the Light: A Medicine Woman's Source Book* (Boston: Beacon Press, 1991) and by Ramón A. Gutiérrez in *When Jesus Came, the Corn Mothers Went Away: Marriage, Sexuality, and Power in New Mexico, 1500–1846* (Stanford, Calif.: Stanford University Press, 1991).

29. White himself indicates this in his discussion of Freud in "Writing in the Middle Voice." Judith Butler has theorized this middle voice of the verb and the radical consciousness it implies as "performativity." See her excellent work on this theoretical location in *Excitable Speech: A Politics of the Performative* (New York: Routledge, 1997).

30. We could thus say that the agent of the third voice is *bound* to the process of differential consciousness and its oppositional technologies.

31. For further description of this persistent, but "passive" verb form, see chapter 2, note 8.

7. Revolutionary Force

1. My analyses of postmodernism, U.S. third world feminism, the methodology of the oppressed, and oppositional consciousness have permitted me to identify a mutant form of resistance. It has developed in the maw of an unprecedented postmodern and especially urban first world space that moves across the globe with an appetite for novelty capable of engulfing every untouched sector. In order to rise to this new occasion, a mutant and morphing form of differential oppositional consciousness demands the construction of an original mode of subjectivity, and the construction of an extraordinary citizen-subject capable of confronting the powers that work to insist themselves within and throughout its body. Should this new form of resistance be developed, no form of subjectivity, no social order, no human action can ever be considered as it once was in any previous moment of Western history.

Under such imperatives, new social actors are being born, extraterritorials who live on the borders of a strange, new hallucinatory and technologically constructed world and who are capable of using that technology on behalf of a new collective ideal. This presence is posttraditional, post-postmodern, de-colonial, posttechnological and possible only *after* the dream of "Western man" has morphed into a nightmare that is populated by new subjects of history—a re-originary vision. The social subjects of this unprecedented vision reflexively recognize themselves as metamorphizing creatures. As categories of the human blur and fuse, this creature rising from the opening gaps is not the postmodern schizophrenic citizen-subject of Jameson's nightmare, for Jameson is still blinded to the existence, originality, activity, and power of such extraterritorial subjectivities, their powers and possibilities.

2. Michel Foucault, *The Order of Things: An Archaeology of the Human Sciences*, trans. R. D. Laing (New York: Vintage Books, 1973), pp. 383–85.

3. Michel Foucault, "The Subject and Power," in *Michel Foucault: Beyond Structuralism and Hermeneutics*, ed. Hubert Dreyfus and Paul Rabinow (Chicago: University of Chicago Press, 1983), p. 216.

4. In any of its gendered, raced, or sexed incarnations, whether as female, colored, or homosexual.

5. Foucault, "The Subject of Power," p. 216.

6. With the exception of U.S. third world feminist writings. See, for example, Cherríe Moraga and Gloria Auzaldúa, eds., *This Bridge Called My Back*.

7. Jameson follows Ernest Mandel in this formulation (Jameson, "Postmodernism, or the Cultural Logic of Late Capitalism," *New Left Review* 146 [July–August 1984]: 78).

8. In Jameson's analysis, each of these three phases of capitalism also corresponds to stages in Western modes of aesthetic representation, so that the period of market capitalism is linked to realism, monopoly (imperialist) capitalism generates modernism, and the evolution of multinational capitalism brings about postmodern aesthetic and psychic production. Jameson also links these three evolutionary stages to stages in the development of technology, from the steam engine under realism and market capitalism, to the railroad under modernism and monopoly capitalism, to the electronic computer chip under postmodernism and global capitalism.

9. Jameson, "Postmodernism," p. 57.

10. Ibid., p. 77.

11. Even though economic exploitation may also have been very important among the revolts' causes.

12. This refers to nineteenth-century capitalism. Foucault, "The Subject and Power," pp. 212, 213.

13. Ibid., p. 213.

14. South Africa until the late 1980s was a political regime that, though encompassing both other forms of subjection, primarily depended on those power relations that operated within a feudal mode. This social order set into effect dominations and subordinations—explicit, direct, and brutal—that were feudal in nature, insofar as it operated on a raced hierarchy grounded on ethnic, culture, religion, and gender distinctions. Such feudal conditions have an immediate and palpable side benefit for any organizing resistance movement, which is that there are easily identifiable oppressor and oppressed classes. (When feudal orders change to capitalist orders, a shift in how oppression is generated and resisted occurs.) This "benefit" also helped to keep the U.S. civil rights movement and other race liberation movements of the 1950s–80s in coalition (resulting in "third world liberation movements," for example): What was being resisted was a legalized form of ethnic, race, and culture domination against which one could morally organize for equal rights. The tactics and strategies generated by resistance movements operating under such conditions take into account very different kinds of power relations from those experienced under the cultural conditions of transnational postmodernism.

Marx was the great analyst of capitalist forms of domination and subordination and of the resistances its activity released from imagination. Struggles against that which separates workers from their own labor power (ibid., p. 212) can exist at the same time as struggles against a more direct and brutal form of racialized power, but when economic relations are the main form of power against which citizen-subjects resist, then tactics and strategies of opposition must be generated accordingly.

15. Ibid.

16. Ibid., p. 216. Foucault poses the problem of resistance under first world cultural conditions. But how do we go about "refusing what we are"? New power relations demand that we develop supplementary forms of resistance. The twenty-first century, Foucault thinks, will be known for the articulation and development of new theories and practices of resistance. The oppositional speech and resistance of the 1960s and 1970s made it possible to examine the locations in discourse and activity where an antagonism of strategies within the hierarchy of power occurred. It is at these points that one can view the contours of dominant power and hear it speak. Foucault proposes such activity because it is the only way in which the first world citizen-subject can perceive the ways in which Westerners are trapped in our own histories of domination. We then might better locate more effective modes for emancipation.

17. Ibid., p. 210.

18. Michel Foucault, "Preface" to Gilles Deleuze and Félix Guattari, *Anti-Oedipus: Capitalism and Schizophrenia*, trans. Robert Hurley, Mark Seem, and Helen R. Lane (Minneapolis: University of Minnesota Press, 1983 [1972]), p. xiii. Further references to this work will be given in the text.

19. Audre Lorde, "The Erotic as Power," in *Sister Outsider*, p. 53.

20. Donna Haraway, *Simians, Cyborgs, and Women: The Reinvention of Nature* (New York: Routledge, 1991), p. 150. Unless otherwise noted, all quotations in this section are from this text (especially chapters 8 and 9, "A Cyborg Manifesto: Science, Technology, and Socialist-Feminism in the Late Twentieth Century" and "Situated Knowledges: The Science Question in Feminism and the Privilege of Partial Perspective"). Describing the function of the cyborg-poet's middle voice, Haraway writes: "If we are imprisoned by language, then escape from that prison-house requires language poets."

21. It should be noted that this same challenge, if uttered through the lips of a feminist scholar of color, is often indicted, or worse, dismissed as "an example of separatism" that "undermines potential for coalitional politics."

22. Haraway, *Simians, Cyborgs, and Women*, p. 1.

23. Donna Haraway, "Ecce Homo, Ain't (Ar'n't) I a Woman, and Inappropriate/d Others: The Human in a Post-Humanist Landscape," in *Feminists Theorize the Political*, ed. Judith Butler and Joan Scott (New York: Routledge, 1992), p. 95.

24. This quotation refers its readers to the historical impact of those 1970s U.S. third world feminist propositions that significantly revised the women's liberation movement by, among other things, renaming it with the ironic emphasis "the *white* women's movement." And perhaps all uncomplicated belief in the righteous benevolence of U.S. liberation movements can never return after Audre Lorde summarized 1970s women's liberation by saying that "when white feminists call for 'unity'" among women, "they are only naming a deeper and real need for homogeneity." By the 1980s, the central political problem on the table was how to go about imagining and constructing a feminist liberation movement that might bring women together across and through their differences. Haraway's first principle for action in 1985 was to call for and then teach a new hoped-for constituency—"cyborg feminists"—that "'we' do not want any more natural matrix of unity, and that no construction is whole."

25. See Haraway's "The Promises of Monsters," in *Cultural Studies* (New York: Routledge, 1992), p. 328, where the woman of color becomes the emblematic figure, a "disturbing guide figure," for the feminist cyborg, "who promises information about psychic, historical and bodily formations that issue from some other semiotic processes than the psychoanalytic in modern and postmodern guise" (306).

26. This alignment has been difficult to achieve, as represented, for example, in the citation practices of

Judith Butler's early book *Gender Trouble*. See Gloria Anzaldúa, *Borderlands/La Frontera: The New Mestiza*. See also Sonia Saldívar-Hull's excellent proposal for Chicana *mestizaje*, "Feminism on the Border: From Gender Politics to Geopolitics," in *Criticism in the Borderlands: Studies in Chicano Literature, Culture, and Ideology*, ed. Héctor Calderón and José David Saldívar (Durham, N.C.: Duke University Press, 1991), pp. 203–21. For excellent discussions of *mestizaje* as a methodological apparatus, see Rafael Pérez-Torres, *Movements in Chicano Poetry: Against Myths, against Margins* (New York: Cambridge University Press, 1995); Carmen Huaco-Nuzum, "Reconstructing Chicana, Mestiza Representation"; and Alicia Gaspar de Alba, "The Alter-Native Sign." See also Chela Sandoval, "New Sciences: Cyborg Feminism and the Methodology of the Oppressed," in *The Cyborg Handbook*, ed. Chris Gray (New York: Routledge, 1995). For recent and succinct overviews of "diasporic" and borderlands theorizing, see Carl Gutiérrez-Jones, "Desiring B/orders," *Diacritics* (spring 1995): 13–29, and James Clifford, "Diasporas," *Cultural Anthropology* 9:3 (1994): 302–39. See also Ramón Saldívar, essay "The Borderlands of Culture: Americo Paredes's *George Washington Gomez* and Chicano Literature at the End of the Twentieth Century," *American Literary History* 5:2 (1993): 263–85; José Saldívar, *Border Matters: The Multiple Routes of Cultural Studies* (Berkeley: University of California Press, 1997); Antonia Casteñeda, "Indias, Españolas, Mestizas" (forthcoming); John Rechy, *The Miraculous Day of Amalia Gomez* (New York: Arcade 1991); Norma Alarcón, "Chicana Feminism: In the Tracks of 'the' Native Woman," *Cultural Studies* 4 (1990): 269–300, and "The Theoretical Subjects of *This Bridge Called My Back* and Anglo American Criticism," in Calderón and Saldívar, eds., *Borderlands: Studies in Chicano Literature, Culture, and Ideology*, pp. 99–129; Mary Louise Pratt, *Imperial Eyes: Travel Writing and Transculturation* (London: Routledge, 1992); Audre Lorde, *Zami: A New Spelling of My Name* (Freedom, Calif.: Crossing Press, 1982); Aiwah Ong, "On the Edge of Empires: Flexible Citizenship among Chinese in Diaspora," *Positions 1* (1993): 326–50; Homi K. Bhabha, "DissemiNation: Time, Narrative, and the Margins of the Modern Nation," in *Nation and Narration* (London: Routledge, 1990), pp. 201–30; Deleuze and Guattari, *Anti-Oedipus*; Roland Barthes, *Image/Music/Text* trans. Richard Miller (New York: Hill and Wang, 1977); Donna Haraway, "Situated Knowledges: The Science Question and the Privilege of Partial Perspective," in *Simians, Cyborgs, and Women*, pp. 183–203. U.S. feminists of color recognize an alliance understood as "indigenous *mestizaje*," a term that underlines the kinship between peoples of color similarly subjugated by race in U.S. colonial history (including, but not limited to, Native peoples, colonized Chicanos/as, blacks, and Asians), and viewing them, in spite of their differences, as "one people."

27. The attempt here is to define cyberspace culture as either a *colonizing* or a *decolonizing* space and activity. Haraway's contribution to understanding a decolonizing "cyborg world" is to extend the notion of *mestizaje* so that not only does the mixture, or "affinity," includes and connect human, animal, physical, spiritual, emotional, and intellectual being, as it is currently understood under U.S. third world feminism, but also a connection occurs between all these and the machines of dominant culture. This is one model for a cosmopolitics that can challenge postmodern globalization.

28. Alice Walker, "In the Closet of the Soul: A Letter to an African-American Friend," *Ms.* 15 (November 1986): 33; my emphasis.

29. Anzaldúa, *Borderlands/La Frontera*, p. 77. Also, see chapter 2 on U.S. third world feminism.

30. Although this book ends with her example, it could be extended with many other provocative examples, including Judith Butler's meditation on "performativity"; the work on *mestizaje* being accomplished in Chicano studies; the example of Zapatista politics; and the notion of a "cosmopolitics" that can function oppositionally to globalizing postmodernism.

31. Mobility without purpose is not enough, as Spivak asserts in her example of "strategic essentialism," which requires mobility and identity consolidation at the same time in order to bring about political change.

32. When this happens, the category "women of color" becomes used as an example to advance new theories of what have been identified in the academy as "postmodern feminisms," but it is not itself recognized as a critical apparatus. But even when Haraway's category "women of color" is understood "as a cyborg identity (a potent subjectivity synthesized from fusions of outsider identities and in the complex political-historical layerings of her biomythography)" (174), as she does, feminist, critical and cultural theory across disciplines has yet to recognize either the methods of "cyborg feminism" or of those differential U.S. third world feminism as critical apparatuses capable of allying oppositional agents across ideological, racial, gender, sex, or class differences, even though the nonessentializing identity demanded by U.S. third world feminism in its differential mode creates what Haraway calls for, an indigenous *mestiza*, and cyborg identity. Are not these kinds of elisions and absences yet further symptoms of an active apartheid of theoretical domains?

33. Constance Penley and Andrew Ross, "Cyborgs at Large: Interview with Donna Haraway," in *Technoculture* (Minneapolis: University of Minnesota Press, 1991), p. 12.

34. Ibid., p. 13.

35. Haraway, "Ecce Homo," p. 95.

36. Ibid.; my emphasis.

37. The theoretical grounds necessary for under-standing postmodern cultural conditions in the first world and globally, as well as the theories necessary for understanding the nature of resistance within post-modernism, are inadequate, according to Haraway. Scholars, she writes, "lack sufficiently subtle connections for collectively building effective theories of experience. Present efforts — Marxist, psychoanalytic, feminist, anthropological — to clarify even "our" experience are rudimentary" (173).

38. Ibid., p. 96.

39. Haraway, "The Promises of Monsters," p. 329.

40. Ibid.

41. Ibid., p. 319.

42. This redefinition and the migrant processes of consciousness and analysis it refers to are especially useful in a discipline such as women's studies, Haraway asserts, where "even the simplest matters" demand "contradictory moments and a wariness of their resolution."

43. Haraway, "The Promises of Monsters," p. 326; my emphasis.

44. Ibid., p. 319.

45. Ibid., p. 325.

46. In many places, see, for example, "*En Rapport: In Opposition: Cobrando Cuentas a Las Nuestras,*" in *Making Face, Making Soul/Haciendo Caras,* pp. 142–51.

47. Understood as "*feministas de la planeta tierra*" — those who break apart *national* borders.

48. See the lecturing work of Haunani-Kay Trask, Cornel West, and the performance pieces of Guillermo Gómez-Peña, Monica Palacios, and John Lugizamo for contemporary examples of globalizing "third world" politics enacted within first world nation-states.

Conclusion

1. These figures and technologies are what enable narrative to transform the moment, to change the world with new stories. Utilized together, these technologies create trickster histories: stratagems of magic, deception, and truth for healing the world, like rap or cybercinema, which work through the reapportionment of dominant powers.

2. *MacNeil/Lehrer NewsHour,* November 23, 1991.

3. The writings by U.S. feminists of color on the matter of love are profuse. See, for example, June Jordan, "Where Is the Love?" in *Making Face, Making Soul/ Haciendo Caras,* ed. Gloria Anzaldúa; Merle Woo, "Letter to Ma," in *This Bridge Called My Back*; Patricia Hill Collins, *Black Feminist Thought*; Maria Lugones, "Play-fulness, 'World-Traveling,' and Loving Perception"; and Audre Lorde, *Sister Outsider.*

4. Bernice Johnson Reagon, "Coalition Politics: Turning the Century," p. 356.

5. Louis Althusser, "Ideology and the Ideological State Apparatuses," p. 130; my emphasis.

6. Roland Barthes, *Mythologies,* trans. Richard Miller (New York: Hill and Wang, 1972), p. 135.

Bibliography

Critical and Cultural Theory

Ahmad, Aijaz. *In Theory: Classes, Nations, Literatures*. London: Verso, 1992.

Althusser, Louis. *For Marx*. Trans. Ben Brewster. New York: Random House, 1970.

———. "The Object of *Capital*. In Louis Althusser and Étienne Balibar, *Reading Capital*. Trans. Ben Brewster. London: New Left Books, 1970. 103–49.

———. "Ideology and Ideological State Apparatuses (Notes towards an Investigation)." In Louis Althusser, *Lenin and Philosophy and Other Essays*, trans. Ben Brewster. New York: Monthly Review Press, 1971: 121–73.

———. *Lenin and Philosophy and Other Essays*. Trans. Ben Brewster. New York: Monthly Review Press, 1971.

Althusser, Louis and Étienne Balibar. *Reading Capital*. Trans. Ben Brewster, New Left Books, 1970.

American Journal of Semiotics 4: 3–4, (1986).

Anderson, Benedict. *Imagined Communities: Reflections on the Origins and Spread of Nationalism*. London: Verso, 1983.

Arendt, Hannah. *The Origins of Totalitarianism*. New York: Harvest Books, 1973.

Attali, Jacques. *Noise: The Political Economy of Music*. Trans. Brian Massumi. Minneapolis: University of Minnesota Press, 1985.

Auerbach, Erich. *Mimesis: Scenes from the Drama of European Literature*. 1959. Reprint, Minneapolis: University of Minnesota Press, 1984.

———. *Mimesis: The Representation of Reality in Western Literature*. Trans. Willard Trask. Princeton, N. J.: Princeton University Press, 1974.

Bachelard, Gaston. *The Poetics of Space*. Trans. Maria Jolas. Boston: Beacon Press, 1969.

———. *The Politics of Reverie: Childhood, Language and the Cosmos*. Trans. Daniel Russell. Boston: Beacon Press, 1969.

Baran, Paul, and Paul Sweezy. *Monopoly Capitalism*. New York: Monthly Review Press, 1966.

Barthes, Roland. *Writing Degree Zero*. Trans. Annette Lavers and Colin Smith. New York: Noonday Press, 1953, 1968 with Susan Sontag Preface.

———. *Elements of Semiology*. Trans. Annette Lavers and Colin Smith. New York: Hill and Wang, 1967.

———. *Mythologies*. Trans. Richard Miller. New York: Hill and Wang, 1972.

———. "Myth Today." In Roland Barthes (1972 [1957]). 109–59.

———. *S/Z: An Essay*. Trans. Richard Miller. New York: Hill and Wang, 1974.

———. *The Pleasure of the Text*. Trans. Richard Miller. New York: Hill and Wang, 1975.

———. *Image/Music/Text*. Trans. Stephen Heath. New York: Hill and Wang, 1977.

———. *Sade/Fourier/Loyola*. Trans. Richard Miller. New York: Hill and Wang, 1977.

———. *A Lover's Discourse: Fragments*. Trans. Richard Howard. New York: Hill and Wang, 1978.

———. *Barthes par Roland Barthes*. Paris: Éditions du Seuil, 1980.

———. *Empire of Signs*. Trans. Richard Howard. New York: Hill and Wang, 1982.

———. *The Fashion System*. Trans. Matthew Ward and Richard Howard. New York: Hill and Wang, 1983.

———. *Michelet*. Trans. Richard Howard. New York: Hill and Wang, 1987.

———. *Roland Barthes*. Trans. Richard Howard. New York: Noonday Press, 1989.

———. *Incidents*. Trans. Richard Howard. Berkeley: University of California Press, 1992.

Bateson, Gregory. *Steps to an Ecology of Mind*. Frogmore: Paladin, 1973.

Baudrillard, Jean. *For a Critique of the Political Economy of the Sign*. Trans. Charles Levin. St. Louis, Mo.: Telos Press, 1981.

———. *Simulations*. Trans. Paul Foss, Paul Patton, and Philip Beitchman. New York: Semiotext(e), 1983.

Bell, Daniel. *The Cultural Contradictions of Capitalism*, New York: Basic Books, 1976.

———. "Modernism and Capitalism," *Partisan Review*, 46 (1978), 206–26.

Benjamin, Walter. *Illuminations*. New York: Schocken Books, 1968.

———. "Theses on the Philosophy of History." In *Illuminations*, ed. Hannah Arendt, trans. Harry Zohn. New York: Schocken Books, 1969 [1940]: 253–64.

Benveniste, Emile. *Problems of General Linguistics*. Trans. Mary Elizabeth Meek. Coral Gables, Fla.: University of Miami Press, 1971.

Berger, John. *Ways of Seeing*. London: British Broadcasting Corporation and Penguin Books, 1978, 1982, 1988.

Bloom, Allan. *The Closing of the American Mind*. New York: Simon and Schuster, 1987.

Bloom, Harold. *The Anxiety of Influence: A Theory of Poetry*. Oxford: Oxford University Press, 1973.

———. *A Map of Misreading*. Oxford: Oxford University Press, 1975.

Bloom, Harold, Paul de Man, Jacques Derrida, Geoffrey H. Hartman and J. Hillis Miller. *Deconstruction and Criticism*. New York: Continuum, 1979.

Brown, Norman O. *Life against Death: The Psychological Meaning of History*. Middletown, Conn: Wesleyan University Press, 1977.

Bruce-Novoa, J. "History as Content, History as Act: The Chicano Novel." *Aztlán*, 18:1 (1987).

Bunham, Clint. *The Jamesonian Unconsciousness: The Aesthetics of Marxist Theory*. Durham, N.C.: Duke University Press, 1995.

Burke, Kenneth. *A Grammar of Motives*. Berkeley and Los Angeles: University of California Press, 1969.

Calderón, Héctor, and José David Saldívar, eds. *Criticism in the Borderlands: Studies in Chicano Literature, Culture, and Ideology*. Durham, N.C.: Duke University Press, 1991.

Calvino, Italo. *Cosmicomics*. Trans. William Weaver. San Diego: Harcourt Brace Jovanovich, 1968.

Cassirer, Ernst. *Language and Myth*. Trans. Susanne K. Langer (1925). New York: Harper and Bros., 1946.

Cheah, Pheng, and Bruce Robbins, eds. *Cosmopolitics, Thinking and Feeling beyond the Nation*. Minneapolis: University of Minnesota Press, 1998.

Chipp, Herschel B. *Theories of Modern Art: A Source Book by Artists and Critics*. Berkeley: University of California Press, 1968.

Clifford, James. *The Predicament of Culture: Twentieth-Century Ethnography, Literature, and Art*. Cambridge: Harvard University Press, 1988.

———. "The Transit Lounge of Culture." *Times Literary Supplement*, May 5, 1991. 1–3.

———. "Borders and Diasporas." Unpublished manuscript. 1992.

———. *Person and Myth: Maurice Leenhardt in the Melanesian World*. Durham, N.C.: Duke University Press, 1992.

———. "Traveling Culture." In *Cultural Studies*, ed. Lawrence Grossberg, Cary Nelson, and Paula Treichler. New York: Routledge, 1992: 96–116.

Clifford, James, and George E. Marcus, eds. *Writing Culture: The Poetics and Politics of Ethnography*. Berkeley: University of California Press, 1986.

Collingwood, R. G. *The Idea of History*. 1936. Reprint, London: Oxford University Press, 1976.

Coward, Rosalind, and John Ellis. *Language and Materialism: Developments in Semiology and the Theory of the Subject*. London: Routledge and Kegan Paul, 1977.

Cowling, Keith. *Monopoly Capitalism*. London: Macmillan, 1982.

Culler, Jonathan. *Structuralist Poetics: Structuralism, Linguistics, and the Study of Literature*. Ithaca, N. Y.: Cornell University Press, 1976.

———. *On Deconstruction*. London: Routledge and Kegan Paul, 1983.

de Certeau, Michel. *The Practice of Everyday Life*. Berkeley: University of California Press, 1984.

DeGeorge, Richard and Fernanade deGeorge, eds. *The Structuralist from Marx to Lévi-Strauss*. Garden City, N. Y.: Doubleday, 1972.

de Lauretis, Teresa, ed. *Feminist Studies/Critical Studies*. Bloomington: Indiana University Press, 1986.

Deleuze, Gilles, and Félix Guattari. *Anti-Oedipus: Capitalism and Schizophrenia*. Trans. Robert Hurley, Mark Seem, and Helen R. Lane. Preface by Michel Foucault. Minneapolis: University of Minnesota Press, 1983 (1972).

———. *Kafka: For a Minor Literature*. Trans. Dana Polan. Foreword by Réda Bensmaïa. Minneapolis: University of Minnesota Press, 1986 (1975).

Derrida, Jacques. "Structure, Sign and Play in the Discourse of the Human Sciences." In *The Structuralist Controversy*, ed. Richard Macksey and Eugenio Donato. Baltimore: Johns Hopkins University Press, 1972. 247–64.

———. *Speech and Phenomena*. Trans. David B. Allison. Evanston, Ill.: Northwestern University Press, 1973.

———. *Of Grammatology*. Trans. Gayatri Chakravorty Spivak. Baltimore: Johns Hopkins University Press, 1978.

———. *Spurs: Nietzsche's Styles*. Trans. Barbara Harlow. Chicago: University of Chicago Press, 1978.

———. *Writing and Difference*. Translated by Alan Bass. Chicago: University of Chicago Press, 1978.

———. *Dissemination*. Trans. Barbara Johnson. Chicago: University of Chicago Press, 1981.

———. *Positions*. Trans. Alan Bass. Chicago: University of Chicago Press, 1981.

———. *Specters of Marx: The State of the Debt, the Work of Mourning, and the New International*. Trans. Peggy Kamuf. New York: Routledge, 1995.

Douglas, Mary. *Purity and Danger: An Analysis of the Concepts of Pollution and Taboo*. London: Routledge and Kegan Paul, 1966.

Dreyfus, Hubert L., and Paul Rabinow. *Michel Foucault: Beyond Structuralism and Hermeneutics*. 2d. ed. Chicago: University of Chicago Press, 1983.

Ducrot, Oswald, and Tzvetan Todorov. *Encyclopedic Dictionary of the Sciences of Language*. Baltimore: John Hopkins University Press: 1983.

Eagleton, Terry. *Literary Theory: An Introduction*. Minneapolis: University of Minnesota Press, 1983.

———. "Capitalism, Modernism and Post-modernism," *New Left Review*, 152: 60–71.

Easthope, Antony, and Kate McGowan, eds. *A Critical and Cultural Theory Reader*. Toronto and Buffalo: University of Toronto Press, 1992.

Easton, Loyd D., and Kurt H. Guddat, eds. and trans. *Writings of the Young Marx on Philosophy and Society*. Garden City, N. Y.: Anchor Books, 1967.

Eco, Umberto. *The Role of the Reader: Exploration in the Semiotics of Text*. Bloomington: Indiana University Press, 1979.

———. *A Theory of Semiotics*. Bloomington: Indiana University Press, 1979.

———. *Semiotics and the Philosophy of Language*. Bloomington: Indiana University Press, 1984.

Fabian, Johannes. *Time and the Other: How Anthropology Makes Its Object*. New York: Columbia University Press, 1983.

Featherstone, Mike. "In Pursuit of the Postmodern." *Theory, Culture and Society*, 5:2–3 (1988): 195–215.

Foster, Hal. *The Anti-Aesthetic*. Port Townsend, Wash.: Bay Press, 1983.

———. "(Post)Modern Polemics," in *Recodings: Art, Spectacle, Cultural Politics*. Port Washington, Wash.: Bay Press, 1985.

Foucault, Michel. *Madness and Civilization: A History of Insanity in the Age of Reason*. Trans. Richard Howard. New York: Pantheon Books, 1965.

———. *The Order of Things: An Archaeology of the Human Sciences*. Trans. R. D. Laing. New York: Vintage, 1970.

———. *The Archaeology of Knowledge*. Trans. A. M. Sheridan Smith. New York: Harper and Row, 1972.

———. *The Birth of the Clinic*. London: Tavistock, 1973.

———. *I, Pierre Rivière, Having Slaughtered My Mother, My Sister, and My Brother . . . : A Case of Parricide in the 19th Century*. Trans. Frank Jellinek. Lincoln: University of Nebraska Press, 1975.

———. *Language, Counter-Memory, Practice: Selected Essays and Interviews*. Trans. Donald Bouchard and Sherry Simon. Ithaca, N. Y.: Cornell University Press, 1977.

———. *The History of Sexuality, Vol. 1, An Introduction*. Trans. Robert Hurley. New York: Pantheon Books, 1978.

———. *Discipline and Punish: The Birth of the Prison.* Harmondsworth, England: Penguin Books, 1979.

———. "What Is an Author?" *Screen* 20:1 (1979): 13–33.

———. *Power/Knowledge: Selected Interviews and Other Writings, 1972–1977.* Trans. and ed. Colin Gordon. Brighton, Sussex: Harvester Press, 1980.

———. "The Subject and Power," in *Michel Foucault: Beyond Structuralism and Hermeneutics,* ed. Hubert Dreyfus, Paul Rabinow. Chicago: University of Chicago Press, 1983. 216.

———. *The History of Sexuality, Vol. 2, The Use of Pleasure.* Harmondsworth, England: Viking Press, 1986.

———. "Of Other Spaces." *Diacritics* 16 (1987): 22–27.

———. "Clarifications on the Question of Power." An interview with Pasquale Pasquine. In *Foucault Live.* New York: Semiotext(e), 1989.

———. "Governmentality." In *The Foucault Effect: Studies in Governmentality,* ed. Graham Burchell, Colin Gordon, and Peter Miller. London: Harvester Wheatsheaf, 1991.

Fowler, Roger. *A Dictionary of Modern Critical Terms.* London: Routledge and Kegan Paul, 1973.

Freud, Sigmund. *Beyond the Pleasure Principle.* Trans. James Strachey. New York: Norton, 1975.

Frye, Northrop. *The Anatomy of Criticism: Four Essays.* Princeton, N. J.: Princeton University Press, 1957.

Gauquelin, Michel. *The Cosmic Clocks: From Astrology to a Modern Science.* Chicago: Henry Regnery, 1967.

Geetz, Clifford. "Sociosexology." *New York Review of Books* 26 (January 24, 1980): 27B.

Girard, René. *Violence and the Sacred.* Trans. Patrick Gregory. Baltimore: Johns Hopkins University Press, 1977.

Giroux, Henry A., and Peter McLaren. *Between Borders: Pedagogy and the Politics of Cultural Studies.* New York: Routledge, 1994.

Giroux, H., D. Shumway, P. Smith and J. Sosnoski. "The Need for Cultural Studies: Resisting Intellectuals and Oppositional Public Spheres." *Dalhousie Review* 64:2 (1984): 472–86.

Gombrich, E. H. *Art and Illusion: A Study in the Psychology of Pictorial Representation.* London and New York: Phaidon Books, 1960.

Gramsci, Antonio. "The Study of Philosophy." In *Selections from the Prison Notebooks,* trans. Quintin Hoare and Geoffrey Nowell. New York: International Publishers, 1971. 321–43.

Greenblatt, Stephen. *Shakespearean Negotiations: The Circulation of Social Energy in Renaissance England.* Berkeley: University of California Press: 1988.

Grossberg, Lawrence, Cary Nelson and Paula A. Treichler, eds. *Cultural Studies.* New York: Routledge, 1992.

Guiraud, Pierre. *Semiology.* Trans. George Gross. London: Routledge and Kegan Paul, 1975.

Habermas, Jürgen. "Modernity–An Incomplete Project." Trans. Selya Benhabib. In *The Anti-Aesthetic: Essays on Postmodern Culture,* ed. Hal Foster. Port Townsend, Wash.: Bay Press, 1983. 3–15.

Hall, Stuart. "The Emergence of Cultural Studies and the Crisis of the Humanities." *October* 53 (1990): 11–90.

———. "The Local and the Global: Globalization and Ethnicity." In *Culture, Globalization and the World System.* State University of New York, Binghamton, Department of Art History, 1991: 41–68.

Harari, Josue V., ed. *Textual Strategies: Perspectives in Post-Structuralist Criticism.* Ithaca, N. Y.: Cornell University Press, 1979.

———. "The Heart of Africa: Nations, Dreams, and Apes." *Inscriptions* 2 (1986): 9–15.

Hartman, Geoffrey H. *Criticism in the Wilderness: The Study of Literature Today.* New Haven: Yale University Press, 1980.

Harvey, David. *The Condition of Postmodernity.* Oxford: Basil Blackwell, 1990.

Hawkes, Terence. *Structuralism and Semiotics.* Berkeley: University of California Press, 1977.

Hayles, N. Katherine. *Chaos Bound: Orderly Disorder in Contemporary Literature and Science.* Ithaca, N. Y.: Cornell University Press, 1990.

Heath, Stephen. "The Turn of the Subject." *Cine-Tracts.* 8 (1976): 32–48.

Hebdige, Dick. *Subculture: The Meaning of Style.* New York: Routledge, 1979.

Heidegger, Martin. *What Is Philosophy?* Trans. W. Kluback and J. T. Wilde. New Haven: New College and University Press, 1958.

Herr, Michael. *Dispatches.* New York: Avon Books, 1987.

Hutcheon, Linda. "A Poetics of Postmodernism?" *Diacritics* 13:4 (1983): 33–42.

———. *A Poetics of Postmodernism: History, Theory, Fiction.* New York: Routledge, 1990.

Jackson, Jesse. "Service and a New World Order." In *Straight from the Heart,* ed. Roger Hatch and Frank Watkins. Philadelphia: Fortress Press, 1987.

Jakobson, Roman. "The Twofold Character of Language." In *The Fundamentals of Language.* The Hague: Mouton, 1956: 58–62.

———. "Closing Statement: Linguistics and Poetics." In *Style and Language*, ed. Thomas A. Sebeok. Cambridge: MIT Press, 1960. 350–77.

———. Poetry of Grammar and Grammar of Poetry." *Lingua* 21 (1968): 597–609.

Jakobson, Roman and Lawrence G. Jones. *Shakespeare's Verbal Art in the Expense of Spirit*. The Hague: Mouton, 1970.

Jakobson, Roman and M. Hale. "The Metaphoric and Metonymic Poles." In *The Fundamentals of Language*. The Hague: Mouton, 1956: 76–82.

Jameson, Fredric. *The Prison-House of Language: A Critical Account of Structuralism and Russian Formalism*. Princeton, N. J.: Princeton University Press, 1972.

———. *Marxism and Form: Twentieth-Century Dialectical Theories of Literature*. Princeton, N. J.: Princeton University Press, 1974.

———. "Postmodernism and Consumer Society." In *The Anti-Aesthetic: Essays on Postmodern Culture*, ed. Hal Foster. Port Washington, Wash: Bay Press, 1983.

———. "Postmodernism, or the Cultural Logic of Late Capitalism." *New Left Review* 146 (July–August 1984): 53–92.

———. *The Political Unconscious: Narrative as a Socially Symbolic Act*. Ithaca, N. Y.: Cornell University Press, 1985.

———. "Third-World Literature in the Era of Multinational Capitalism." *Social Text* 15 (1986): 65–88.

———. *Postmodernism, or the Cultural Logic of Late Capitalism*. Durham: Duke University Press, 1991.

———. *The Geopolitical Aesthetic: Cinema and Space in the World System*. Bloomington: Indiana University Press, 1992.

———. "On Cultural Studies," *Social Text* 34: 17–51.

Jung, Carl G. *Man and His Symbols*. New York: Dell, 1964.

———. "Literary Criticism Review Essay." *Signs* 2 (winter 1976): 404–21.

Kellner, Douglas, ed. *Postmodernism/Jameson/Critique*, Washington, D.C.: Maisonneuve Press, 1989.

Kristeva, Julia. *Powers of Horror: An Essay on Abjection*. Trans. Léon S. Roudiez. New York: Columbia University Press, 1982.

Kroker, Arthur, and David Cook. *The Postmodern Scene*. New York: St. Martin's Press, 1986.

Kuhn, Thomas S. *The Structure of Scientific Revolutions*. 2d ed. V 2 N 2 International Encyclopedia of Unified Science. Chicago: University of Chicago Press, 1970.

Laclau, Ernesto. *Emancipation(s)*. London: Verso, 1996.

Laclau, Ernesto, and Chantal Mouffe. *Hegemony and Socialist Strategy: Towards a Radical Democratic Politics*. London: Verso, 1985.

Lane, Michael, ed. *Introduction to Structuralism*. New York: Basic Books, 1970.

Latour, Bruno, and Steve Woolgar. *Laboratory Life: The Social Construction of Scientific Facts*. V. 80 Sage Library of Social Research. Beverly Hills, Calif.: Sage Publications, 1979.

Leach, Edmund. "Anthropological Aspects of Language: Animal Categories and Verbal Abuse." In *New Directions in the Study of Language*, ed. Eric Lenneberg. Cambridge: MIT Press, 1964. 62.

Lemert, Charles C., and Garth Gillan. *Michel Foucault: Social Theory and Transgression*. New York: Columbia University Press, 1982.

Lévi-Strauss, Claude. *Structuralist Anthropology*. Trans. Claire Jocobson and Brooke Grundfest. New York: Basic Books, 1963.

———. *The Savage Mind*. Chicago: University of Chicago Press, 1966.

———. "Overture to Le Cru et le cuit." In *Structuralism*, ed. Jacques Ehrmann. New York: Doubleday, 1970.

———. *The Raw and the Cooked*. Trans. John Weightman and Doreen Weightman. New York: Harper and Row, 1970.

Lichtheim, George. *The Phenomenology of Mind*. Trans. J. B. Baillie. New York: Harper and Row, 1976.

Lipsitz, George. "Buscando America (Looking for America): Collective Memory in an Age of Amnesia." In *Time Passages: Collective Memory and American Popular Culture*. Minneapolis: University of Minnesota Press, 1990. 257–71.

———. "Rocking around the Historical Bloc." In *Time Passages: Collective Memory and American Popular Culture*. Minneapolis: University of Minnesota Press, 1990. 133–60.

———. *Time Passages: Collective Memory and American Popular Culture*. Minneapolis: University of Minnesota Press, 1990.

———. *Dangerous Crossroads: Popular Music, Postmodernism, and the Poetics of Place*. New York: Verso, 1994.

Lloyd, David. "Adulteration and the Nation." In *An Other Tongue: Nation and Ethnicity in the Linguistic Borderlands*, ed. Alfred Arteaga. Durham, N.C.: Duke University Press, 1994. 53–92.

Long, Charles. *Significations: Signs, Symbols and Images in the Interpretation of Religion*. Philadelphia: Fortress Press, 1986.

Lotman, Jurif. *The Structure of the Artistic Text*. Trans. Ronald Vroon. Michigan *Slavic Contributions*, no. 7. Ann Arbor: University of Michigan Press, 1977.

Lukács, Georg. *The Meaning of Contemporary Realism*. London: Merlin Press, 1963.

———. *Studies in European Realism*. Introduction by Alfred Kazin. New York: University Library, 1964.

———. *History and Class Consciousness: Studies in Marxist Dialectics*. Trans. Rodney Livingstone. Cambridge: MIT Press, 1976.

Lyotard, Jean-François. *The Postmodern Condition: A Report on Knowledge*. Trans. Geoff Bennington and Brian Massumi. Minneapolis: University of Minnesota Press, 1984.

Macksey, Richard, and Eugenio Donato. *The Structuralist Controversy: The Languages of Criticism and the Sciences of Man*. Baltimore: Johns Hopkins University Press, 1972.

Manheim, Karl. *Ideology and Utopia*. Trans. Louis Wirth and Edward Shils. New York: Harvest/Harcourt Brace Jovanovich, 1936.

Marcuse, Herbert. *Eros and Civilization: A Philosophical Inquiry into Freud*. Boston: Beacon Press, 1955.

———. *Counterrevolution and Revolt*. Boston: Beacon Press, 1972.

———. *The Aesthetic Dimension: Toward a Critique of Marxist Aesthetics*. Trans. Herbert Marcuse and Erica Sherover. Boston: Beacon Press, 1978.

Marx, Karl. *Capital: A Critique of Political Economy*. Vol. 1. Ed. Frederick Engels, trans. Samuel Moore and Edward Aveling. London: Lawrence and Wishart, 1954.

Marx, Karl, and Frederick Engels. *Selected Writings in Sociology and Social Philosophy*. Trans. T. B. Bottomore. New York: McGraw-Hill, 1956.

———. *Basic Writings on Politics and Philosophy*. Ed. Lewis S. Feuer. Garden City, N. Y.: Doubleday, 1959.

———. *Capital*. Trans. Eden Paul and Cedar Paul. London: Dent and Sons, 1962.

———. *The Eighteenth Brumaire of Louis Bonaparte*. New York: International Publishers, 1963.

———. *The German Ideology*. English translations cited in the text are from T. B. Bottomore, ed., *Karl Marx: Selected Writings*. New York: McGraw-Hill, 1964.

———. *The Communist Manifesto*. Introduction by A. J. P. Taylor. Harmondsworth, England: Penguin, 1967.

Matthews, Robert J. "How is Criticism Possible?" *Diacritics* 20 (spring 1972): 23–28.

McClellan, David, ed. *Karl Marx: Selected Writings*. Oxford: Oxford University Press, 1977.

Miller, D. A. *Bringing Out Roland Barthes*. Berkeley: University of California Press, 1992.

Mitchell, W. J. T., ed. *The Politics of Interpretation*. Chicago: University of Chicago Press, 1983.

———. *New German Critique: An Interdisciplinary Journal of German Studies*. "Modernity and Postmodernity," no. 33 (fall 1984).

Nelson, Cary, and Lawrence Grossberg, eds. *Marxism and the Interpretation of Culture*. Urbana: University of Illinois Press, 1988.

Nelson, Cary, Paula A. Treichler and Lawrence Grossberg, eds. *Cultural Studies*. New York: Routledge, 1992.

Nietzsche, Friedrich. *The Use and Abuse of History*. Trans. Adrian Collins. Indianapolis: Bobbs-Merrill, 1957.

O'Connor, Alan. "The Problem of American Cultural Studies." *Critical Studies in Mass Communication* 6 (1989): 405–13.

Ollman, Bertell. *Alienation: Marx's Conception of Man in Capitalist Society*. Cambridge: Cambridge University Press, 1975.

Owens, Craig. "The Discourse of Others: Feminists and Postmodernism." In *The Anti-Aesthetic*, ed. Hal Foster. Port Townsend: Bay Press, 1983. 57–82.

Penley, Constance, and Andrew Ross, eds. *Technoculture*. Minneapolis: University of Minnesota Press, 1991.

Pfeil, Fred. "Postmodernism and Our Discontent." *Socialist Review* 87 (1986): 125–35.

Plato. *Timaeus and Critias*. Trans. Desmond Lee. New York: Penguin Books, 1977.

———. *The Last Days of Socrates*. Trans. Hugh Tredenniek. New York: Penguin Books, 1983.

Propp, Vladimir. *Morphology of the Folktale*. 2d ed. Trans. Laurence Scott. Ed. Louis A. Wagner. Austin: University of Texas Press, 1968.

Rabinow, Paul, ed. *The Foucault Reader*. New York: Pantheon Books, 1984.

Ricoeur, Paul. "The Model of the Text: Meaningful Action Considered as a Text." *Social Research* 38 (autumn 1971): 302–39.

———. *The Conflict of Interpretations: Essays in Hermeneutics*. Ed. Don Ihde. Evanston, Ill.: Northwestern University Press, 1974.

———. *Interpretation Theory: Discourse and the Surplus of Meaning*. Fort Worth: Texas Christian University Press, 1976.

Ross, Andrew, ed. *Universal Abandon: The Politics of Postmodernism*. Minneapolis: University of Minnesota Press, 1988.

Said, Edward W. "Eclecticism and Orthodoxy in Criticism." *Diacritics* 20 (spring 1972): 2–13.

Sartre, Jean-Paul. *Nausea.* Trans. Lloyd Alexander. New York: New Directions Books, 1964.

———. *Search for a Method.* Trans. Hazel E. Barnes. New York: Vintage Books, 1968.

Saussure, Ferdinand de. *A Course in General Linguistics.* London: Fontana, 1974.

Scholes, Robert. *Textual Power: Literary Theory and the Teaching of English.* New Haven: Yale University Press, 1985.

Smith, Barbara Hernstein. *Contingencies of Value: Alternative Perspectives for Critical Theory.* Cambridge: Harvard University Press, 1988.

Sofia, Zoe (also Zoe Sofoulis). "Exterminating Fetuses: Abortion, Disarmament, and the Sexo-Semiotics of Extra-Terrestrialism." *Diacritics* 14:2 (1984): 47–59.

Soja, E. W. *Postmodern Geographies: The Reassertion of Space in Critical Social Theory.* London: Verso, 1989.

Spivak, Gayatri Chakravorty. *In Other Worlds: Essays in Cultural Politics.* New York: Routledge, 1987.

Sturrock, John, ed. *Structuralism and Since: From Lévi-Strauss to Derrida.* New York: Oxford University Press, 1981.

Sweezy, Paul. *Monopoly Capitalism.* New York: Monthly Review Press, 1966.

Taussig, M. *Shamanism, Colonialism, and the Wild Man: A Study in Terror and Healing.* Chicago: University of Chicago Press, 1987.

Traweek, Sharon. *Beam Times and Life Times: The World of High Energy Physicists.* Cambridge: Harvard University Press, 1988.

Valesio, Paolo. "The Practice of Literary Semiotics: A Theoretical Proposal." February 1978. Urbino: Università. Centro Internazionale di Semiotica e di Linguistica. Working Papers and Prepublications, Series D, no. 71.

Vattimo, Gianni. "The Truth of Hermeneutics." In *Questioning Foundations: Truth/Subjectivity/Culture,* ed. Hugh J. Silverman. New York: Routledge, 1993.

Vico, Giambattista. *The New Science.* Trans. of 3d ed. (1744) by Thomas Goddard Bergin and Max Harold Fisch. Ithaca, N.Y.: Cornell University Press, 1968.

Wallerstein, Immanuel. *The Modern World-System.* Vol. 1. New York: Academic Press, 1974.

———. *The Modern World-System: Capitalist Agriculture and the Origins of the European World-Economy in the Sixteenth Century.* New York: Academic Press, 1976.

———. "The Construction of Peoplehood: Racism, Nationalism, Ethnicity." In *Race, Nation, Class: Ambiguous Identities,* ed. Étienne Balibar and Immanuel Wallerstein: trans. of Étienne Balibar by Chris Turner, London: Verso, 1991.

Watney, Simon. "Taking Liberties: An Introduction." In *Talking Liberties: AIDS and Cultural Politics.,* ed. E. Carter and Simon Watney. London: Serpent's Tail, 1989.

West, Cornel. "Ethics and Action in Fredric Jameson's Marxist Hermeneutics." in *Postmodernism and Politics,* ed. Jonathan Arac. Minneapolis: University of Minnesota Press, 1986.

White, Hayden. *Metahistory: The Historical Imagination in Nineteenth-Century Europe.* Baltimore: Johns Hopkins University Press, 1975.

———. "Criticism as Cultural Politics." Review of *Beginning: Intention and Method* by Edward Said. *Diacritics* 6:3 (1976): 8–23.

———. "The Absurdist Moment in Contemporary Literary Alternatives." In *Direction for Criticism: Structuralism and Its Alternatives,* ed. Murray Krieger and L. S. Dembo. Madison: University of Wisconsin Press, 1977.

———. "The Historical Text as Literary Artifact." In *The Writing of History: Literary Form and Historical Understanding,* ed. Robert H. Canary and Henry Kozicki. Madison: University of Wisconsin Press, 1978.

———. *Topics of Discourse: Essays in Cultural Criticism.* Baltimore: Johns Hopkins University Press, 1978.

———. "The Value of Narrativity in the Representation of Reality." *Critical Inquiry* 7 (autumn 1980): 5–27.

———. "Literature and Social Action: Reflections on the Reflection Theory of Literary Art." *New Literary History* 20 (winter 1980): 363–80.

———. *The Content of the Form: Narrative Discourse and Historical Representation.* Baltimore: Johns Hopkins University Press, 1987.

———. "Writing in the Middle Voice," *Stanford Literature Review,* 9:2 (1992), 179–87.

———. *Figural Realism.* Baltimore: Johns Hopkins University Press, 1999.

Williams, Raymond. *The Country and the City.* New York: Oxford University Press, 1976.

———. *Marxism and Literature.* Oxford: Oxford University Press, 1978.

———. *Keywords: A Vocabulary of Culture and Society.* New York: Oxford University Press. Rev. ed. 1976, 1983, 1986.

Wolin, Richard. "Modernism vs. Postmodernism." *Telos,* 62 (1984): 117–130.

Zejowski, Arlene. *Image Breaking Images: A New Mythology of Language.* New York: Horizon Press, 1976.

U.S. Third World Feminism

Al-Hibri, Azizah. "Capitalism Is an Advanced Stage of Patriarchy, but Marxism Is Not Feminism." In *Women and Revolution*, ed. Lydia Sargent. Boston: South End Press, 1981.

Alarcón, Norma, ed. *The Third Woman.* Bloomington, Ind.: Third Woman Press, 1980.

———. "Interview with Pat Mora." *Third Woman* 3 (1986): 121–26.

———. "Making *Familia* from Scratch: Split Subjectivities in the Work of Helena María Viramontes and Cherríe Moraga." In *Chicana Creativity and Criticism: Charting New Frontiers in American Literature*, ed. María Herrera-Sobek and Helena María Viramontes. Houston: Arte Público Press, 1988. 14–59.

———. "Traddutora, Traditora: A Paradigmatic Figure of Chicana Feminism." *Cultural Critique* 13 (Fall 1989): 57–87.

———. "The Sardonic Powers of the Erotic in the Work of Ana Castillo." In *Breaking Boundaries: Latina Writing and Critical Readings*, ed. Asunción Harno-Delgado, Eliana Ortega, Nina M. Scott, and Nancy Saporta Sternbach. Amherst: University of Massachusetts Press, 1989. 94–107.

———. "Chicana Feminism: In the Tracks of 'the' Native Woman." *Cultural Studies* 4:3 (October 1990): 248–56.

———. "The Theoretical Subject(s) of *This Bridge Called My Back* and Anglo-American Feminism." In *Criticism in the Borderlands: Studies in Chicano Literature, Culture, and Ideology*, ed. Héctor Calderón and José David Saldívar. Durham, N.C.: Duke University Press, 1991. 28–39.

———. "Conjugating Subjects: The Heteroglossia of Essence and Resistance." In *An Other Tongue: Nation and Ethnicity in the Linguistic Borderlands*, ed. Alfred Arteaga, Durham, N.C.: Duke University Press, 1994. 125–39.

Alexander, M. Jacqui, and Chandra Talpade Mohanty, eds. *Feminist Genealogies, Colonial Legacies, Democratic Futures.* New York: Routledge, 1997.

Alexander, Vicki, and Grace Lyu-Volckhausen. "Black/Asian Conflict: Where Do We Begin?" *Ms.* (November–December 1981): 63–67.

Allen, Paula Gunn. "Beloved Women: The Lesbian in American Indian Culture." *Conditions* 7 (1981): 203–20.

———. *The Sacred Hoop: Recovering the Feminine in American Indian Traditions.* Boston: Beacon Press, 1986.

———. "Some like Indians Endure." In *Living the Spirit.* New York: St. Martin's Press, 1987. 9–20.

———, ed. *Spider Woman's Granddaughters.* Boston: Beacon Press, 1989.

———. *Grandmothers of the Light: A Medicine Woman's Source Book.* Boston: Beacon Press, 1991.

Anzaldúa, Gloria. "La Prieta." In *This Bridge Called My Back: Writings by Radical Women of Color.* Ed. Cherríe Moraga and Gloria Anzaldúa. New York: Kitchen Table: Women of Color Press, 1981. 148–209.

———. *Borderlands, La Frontera: The New Mestiza.* San Francisco: Spinsters/Aunt Lute, 1987.

———. "*La conciencia de la mestiza*: Towards a New Consciousness." In *Borderlands/La Frontera: The New Mestiza.* San Francisco: Spinsters/Aunt Lute, 1987. 77–91.

———, ed. *Making Face, Making Soul/Haciendo Caras.* San Francisco: Spinsters/Aunt Lute, 1990.

Aptheker, Bettina. *Tapestries of Life.* Amherst: University of Massachusetts Press, 1989.

Asian Women United of California, ed. *Making Waves: An Anthology of Writings by and about Asian Women.* Boston: Beacon Press, 1989.

Baca, Judith Francisca. "Our People Are the Internal Exiles." In *Cultures in Contention.* Seattle, Wash.: Real Comet Press, 1984. 42–50.

Bambara, Toni Cade. *The Salt Eaters.* New York: Random House, 1980.

———, ed. *The Black Woman: An Anthology.* New York: New American Library, 1970.

Bataile, Gretchen, and Kathleen Mullen Sands, eds. *American Indian Women: Telling their Lives.* Lincoln: University of Nebraska Press, 1984.

Beale, Frances. "Double Jeopardy: To Be Black and Female." In *Sisterhood Is Powerful: An Anthology of Writings from the Women's Liberation Movement*, ed. Robin Morgan. New York: Random House, 1970. 136–43.

Bethel, Lorraine, and Barbara Smith, eds. "The Black Women's Issue." *Conditions* 5 (1979).

Bhavnani, Kum-Kum, and Margaret Coulson. "Transforming Socialist-Feminism: The Challenge of Racism." *Feminist Review* 23 (February 1986): 81–92.

Brady, Mary Patricia. "Extinct Lands, Scarred Bodies: Chicana Literature and the Reinvention of Space." Ph.D. diss., University of California, Los Angeles, 1996.

Brant, Beth, ed. *A Gathering of Spirit: A Collection by North American Indian Women.* New York: Firebrand Books, 1988.

Brixton Black Women's Group. "Black Women Organizing." *Feminist Review* 17 (July 1984): 84–89.

Bulkin, Elly, Minnie Bruce Pratt and Barbara Smith, eds. *Yours in Struggle: Three Feminist Perspectives on Anti-Semitism and Racism.* New York: Long Haul Press, 1984.

Bush, Avtar. "*Différance*, Diversity and Differentiation." In *"Race," Culture and Difference*, ed. James Donald and Ali Rattansi, London: Sage Publications, 1992.

Carby, Hazel V. *Reconstructing Womanhood: The Emergence of the Afro-American Woman Novelist.* New York: Oxford University Press, 1987.

———. "The Politics of Difference." *Ms.*, (September–October 1989): 84–85.

Carmen, Gail, Shaila and Pratibha. "Becoming Visible: Black Lesbian Discussions." *Feminist Review* 17 (July 1984): 53–72.

Castaneda, Antonia. "Gender, Race, and Culture: Spanish-Mexican Women in the Historiography of Frontier California." *Frontiers*, 11:1 (1990): 8–20.

———. "Women of Color and the Rewriting of Western History: The Discourse, Politics, and Decolonization of History." *Pacific Historical Review*, (November 1992): 501–33.

Cervantes, Lorna Dee. "Poem for the Young White Man Who Asked Me How I, an Intelligent, Well-Read Person, Could Believe in the War between Races." In *Emplumada.* Pittsburgh: University of Pittsburgh Press, 1981. 35–7.

———. "Astro-no-mía." In *Chicana Creativity and Criticism: Charting New Frontiers in American Literature*, ed. María Herrera-Sobek and Helena María Viramontes. Houston: Arte Público Press, 1988. 44.

Chabram-Dernersesian, Angie. "I Throw Punches for My Race, but I Don't Want to Be a Man: Writing Us—Chica-nos (Girl, Us)/Chicanas—into the Movement Script." In *Cultural Studies*, ed. Lawrence Grossberg, Cary Nelson, and Paula Treicher. New York: Routledge, 1992. 81–95.

Chai, Alice Yun. "Toward a Holistic Paradigm for Asian American Women's Studies: A Synthesis of Feminist Scholarship and Women of Color's Feminist Politics." *Women's Studies International Forum* 8 (1985).

Christian, Barbara. "Creating a Universal Literature: Afro-American Women Writers, *KPFA Folio*, special African History Month edition, February 1983, front page. Reissued in *Black Feminist Criticism: Perspectives on Black Women Writers.* New York: Pergamon Press, 1985. 163.

———. *Black Feminist Criticism: Perspectives on Black Women Writers.* New York: Pergamon Press, 1985.

———. "The Race for Theory." In *Making Face, Making Soul/Haciendo Caras*, ed. Gloria Anzaldúa. San Francisco: Spinsters/Auntie Lute, 1990.

Cisneros, Sandra. "You Bring Out the Mexican in Me." In *Loose Woman.* New York: Knopf, 1994. 4–6.

Cliff, Michelle. *Claiming an Identity They Taught Me to Despise.* Watertown, Mass.: Persephone Press, 1980.

Collins, Patricia Hill. "Third World Women in America." In *The Women's Annual*, ed. Barbara K. Haber. Boston: G. K. Hall, 1982.

———. *Black Feminist Thought: Knowledge, Consciousness, and the Politics of Empowerment.* New York: Routledge, 1990.

Combahee River Collective. "A Black Feminist Statement." In *Capitalist Patriarchy and the Case for Socialist Feminism*, ed. Zilla Eisenstein. New York: Monthly Review Press, 1979. 83–88.

Córdova, Teresa, Norma Cantár, Gilberto Cardenas, Juan Garcia, and Christine Sierra, eds. *Chicano Voices: Intersections of Class, Race, and Gender.* Austin: Center for Mexican-American Studies Publications, 1986.

———. "Roots and Resistance: The Emergent Writings of Twenty Years of Chicana Feminist Struggle." In *Handbook of Hispanic Cultures in the United States Sociology.* Houston: Arte Público Press, 1994. 175–202.

Cornell, Drucilla, and Sylya Benhabib. *Feminism as Critique: Essays on the Politics of Gender in Late Capitalist Societies.* Cambridge: Polity Press 1987.

Cotera, M. "Feminism: The Chicana and the Anglo Versions." In *Twice a Minority*, ed. M. Melville. Saint Louis: Mosby, 1980. 217–34.

Crenshaw, Kimberle. "Demarginalizing the Intersection of Race and Sex: A Black Feminist Critique of Antidiscrimination Doctrine, Feminist Theory and Antiracist Politics." *University of Chicago Legal Forum* (1989): 139–67.

Crow Dog, Mary, and Richard Erdoes. *Lakota Woman.* New York: HarperCollins, 1990.

Datta, Manjira. "Interview with Independent Filmmaker Manjira Datta" by Helen Lee. *Awakening Thunder: Asian Canadian Women Fireweed.* 30 (1990): 116–20.

Davies, Miranda, ed. *Third World, Second Sex.* London: Zed Books, 1990.

Davis, Angela. *Women, Race and Class.* New York: Random House, 1983.

de la Torre, Adela, and Beatriz Pesquera, eds. *Building with Our Hands.* Berkeley: University of California Press, 1993.

Del Castillo, Adelaida. "La Vision Chicana." *La Gente* (1974): 8.

Dill, Bonnie Thorton. "Race, Class and Gender: Perspectives for an All-Inclusive Sisterhood." *Feminist Studies* 9, 1983.

Din, Mutriba, and Ravida Din. "Sisters in the Movement," *Awakening Thunder: Asian Canadian Women. Fireweed* 30 (winter 1990): 35–39.

Dubois, Ellen, and Vicki Ruiz, eds. *Unequal Sisters: A Multicultural Reader in U.S. Women's History.* New York: Routledge, 1990.

Eisenstein, Hester. *The Future of Difference.* New Brunswick, N.J.: Rutgers University Press, 1985.

Elsasser, Nan, Kyle MacKenzie, and Yvonne Tixier y Vigil. *Las Mujeres: Conversations from a Hispanic Community.* New York: Feminist Press, 1980.

Escamill, Edna. *Daughter of the Mountain.* San Francisco: Spinsters/Aunt Lute, 1991.

Fallis, Guadalupe Valdes. "The Liberated Chicana — a Struggle against Tradition." *Women: A Journal of Liberation* 3:20 (1974).

Fisher, Dexter, ed. *The Third World Woman: Minority Women Writers of the United States.* Boston: Houghton, Mifflin, 1980.

Fong, Katheryn M. "Feminism is Fine, but What's It Done for Asia America?" *Bridge* 6:21–22, (1978).

Fregoso, Rosa Linda, and Angie Chabram-Dernersesian. "Chicana/o Cultural Representations: Reframing Alternative Critical Discourses." *Cultural Studies* 4:3 (1990): 203–12.

———. *The Bronze Screen: Chicana and Chicano Film Culture.* Minneapolis: University of Minnesota Press, 1993.

Gaspar De Alba, Alicia. *Chicano Art Inside/Outside the Master's House: Cultural Politics and the CARA Exhibition.* Austin: University of Texas Press, 1998.

Giddings, Paula. *Where and When I Enter: The Impact of Black Women on Race and Sex in America.* New York: Morrow, 1984.

Gomez, Alma, Cherríe Moraga and Mariana Romo-Carmona, eds. *Cuentos: Stories by Latinas.* New York: Kitchen Table: Women of Color Press, 1983.

Gonzales, Sylvia. "The Chicana in Literature." *La Luz.* (January 1973) Available from *La Luz*, 1000 Logan St., Denver, CO 80203.

González, Nancie L. *The Spanish-Americans of New Mexico: A Heritage of Pride.* Albuquerque: University of New Mexico Press, 1969.

Gould, Janice. *Beneath My Heart.* Ithaca, N.Y.: Firebrand Books, 1990.

Guerrero, M. Annette Jaimes. "Academic Apartheid: American Indian Studies and 'Multiculturalism,'" in *Mapping Multiculturalism*, eds. Avery Gordon, Christopher Newfield. Minneapolis: University of Minnesota Press, 1996. 49–63.

Hancock, Veila. "La Chicana, Chicano Movement and Women's Liberation," *Chicano Studies Newsletter* (February–March 1971).

Harlow, Barbara. *Resistance Literature.* New York: Methuen, 1987.

Herrera-Sobek, María, ed. "The Politics of Rape: Sexual Transgression in Chicano Fiction." In *Chicana Creativity and Criticism: Charting New Frontiers in American Literature*, ed. María Herrera-Sobek and Helena María Viramontes. Houston: Arte Público Press, 1988. 171–81.

Heresies 8. "Third World Women: The Politics of Being the Other." 1979.

hooks, bell. *And There We Wept.* Los Angeles: Polemics, 1978.

———. *Ain't I a Woman: Black Women and Feminism.* Boston: South End Press, 1981.

———. *Feminist Theory: From Margin to Center.* Boston: South End Press, 1984.

———. "Talking Back." *Discourse.* 8 (1986): 123–28.

———. "Out of the Academy and into the Streets." From "Theory as Liberatory Practice." *Yale Journal of Law and Feminism* 4:1 (1990): 1–12.

———. *Black Looks: Race and Representation.* Boston: South End Press, 1992.

Hull, Gloria. "Reading Literature by U.S. Third World Women." Working paper no. 141, Wellesley College, 1984.

Hull, Gloria, Patricia Bell Scott, and Barbara Smith, ed. *All the Women Are White, All the Blacks Are Men, but Some of Us Are Brave: Black Women's Studies.* New York, Feminist Press, 1982.

Hurston, Zora Neale. *Their Eyes Were Watching God.* Urbana: University of Illinois Press, 1978.

Hurtado, Aida. "Reflections on White Feminism: A Perspective from a Woman of Color." 1985, unpublished manuscript.

———. "Relating to Privilege: Seduction and Rejection in the Subordination of White Women and Women of Color." *Signs* 14:4 (summer 1989): 833–55.

Hurtado, Albert. *Indian Survival on the California Frontier.* New York: Columbia University Press, 1989.

Jaggar, Alison. *Feminist Politics and Human Nature.* New York: Rowman and Allanheld, 1983.

Jhabvala, Ruth Prawer. *Heat and Dust.* New York: Harper and Row, 1977.

Joanne, Primila, and Anau. "Lesbians of Colour: Loving and Struggling." *Women of Colour Fireweed* 16 (spring 1983): 66–72.

Jordan, June. *Passion.* Boston: Beacon Press, 1980.

Katrak, Ketu H. "Decolonizing Culture: Toward a Theory for Postcolonial Women's Texts." *Modern Fiction Studies* 35 (spring 1989): 157–59.

Katz, Jane. *I Am the Fire of Time—Voices of Native American Women.* New York: Dutton, 1977.

King, Deborah K. "Multiple Jeopardy, Multiple Consciousness: The Context of a Black Feminist Ideology." *Signs* 14:1 (1988): 42–72.

King, Katie. *Theory in Its Feminist Travels: Conversations in U.S. Women's Movements.* Bloomington: Indiana University Press, 1994.

Kingston, Maxine Hong. *The Woman Warrior.* New York: Vintage Books, 1977.

——. *China Men.* New York: Ballantine Books, 1981.

Lanser, Susan S. "Feminist Criticism, 'The Yellow Wallpaper,' and Politics of Color in America." *Feminist Studies* 15:3 (fall 1989): 415–41.

La Rue, Linda. "The Black Movement and Women's Liberation." *Black Scholar* 1 (1976): 36–42.

Ling, Amy. *Between Worlds.* New York: Pergamon Press, 1990.

Livera, Makeda, ed. *A Lesbian of Color Anthology: Piece of My Heart.* Ontario: Sister Vision Press, 1991.

Longauex y Vasquez, Enriqueta. "Soy Chicana Primero." *El Grito del Norte,* April 26, 1972, 11.

Lorde, Audre. *The Cancer Journals.* Argyle, N.Y.: Spinsets, Ink, 1980.

——. "An Interview: Audre Lorde and Adrienne Rich." *Signs: Journal of Women in Culture and Society* 6:4. (summer 1981): 81–109.

——. *The Black Unicorn.* New York: Iridian Press, 1981.

——. "Comments at 'The Personal and Political Panel.'" Second Sex Conference, New York, September 1979. In *This Bridge Called My Back: Writings by Radical Women of Color,* ed. Cherríe Moraga and Gloria Anzaldúa. New York: Kitchen Table: Women of Color Press, 1981: 98.

——. *Zami: A New Spelling of My Name.* Freedom, Calif.: Crossing Press, 1982.

——. "The Uses of the Erotic." In *Sister Outsider.* New York: Crossing Press, 1984. 58–63.

——. *Sister Outsider.* New York: Crossing Press, 1984.

Lorenzana, Noemi. "Hijas de Aztlán." *De Colores,* 1:3 (1974): 39–43.

Lowe, Lisa. "Heterogeneity, Hybridity, Multiplicity: Marking Asian American Differences." *Diaspora* 1 (spring 1991): 24–44.

——. *Immigrant Acts: On Asian American Cultural Politics.* Durham, N.C.: Duke University Press, 1996.

Lugones, Maria. "Playfulness, World-Traveling, and Loving Perception." *Hypatia: A Journal of Feminist Philosophy* 2 (1987): 85–99.

Malveaux, Julianne. "What You Said about Race: Analysis of the *Ms.* Survey on Race and Women." *Ms.* (May–June 1992): 24–30.

Mama, Amina. "Black Women, the Economic Crisis and the British State." *Feminist Review* 17 (July 1984): 21–35.

Mani, Lata. "Multiple Mediations: Feminist Scholarship in the Age of Multi-National Reception." *Feminist Review* 35 (July 1990): 32–38.

Marquez, Evelina, and Margarita Ramirez. "Women's Task Is to Gain Liberation." In *Essays on La Mujer,* ed. Rosaura Sanchez and Rosa Martinez Cruz. Los Angeles: UCLA Chicano Studies Center Publication, 1977. 188–94.

Martin, Biddy, and Chandra Talpade Mohanty. "Feminist Politics: What's Home Got to Do with It?" In *Feminist Studies/Critical Studies,* ed. Teresa de Lauretis. Bloomington: Indiana University Press, 1986. 191–212.

Medicine, Bea. "The Roles of Women in Native American Societies: A Bibliography." *Indian Historian* 8 (1975): 89–100.

Minh-ha, Trinh T. "Difference: A Special Third World Women Issue." *Discourse* 8 (1986): 11–38.

——. "'Introduction' and 'Difference': A Special Third World Women Issue." *Discourse: Journal for Theoretical Studies in Media and Culture* 8 (1986–1987): 3–38.

——. "Not You/Like You: Post-Colonial Women and the Interlocking Questions of Identity and Difference." *Inscriptions* 3/4 (1988): 71–76.

——. *Woman/Native/Other: Writing Postcolonial and Feminism.* Bloomington: Indiana University Press, 1989.

——. ed. *She, the Inappropriate/d Other. Discourse* 8 (1986–1987). 32–50.

——. *When the Moon Waxes Red: Representation, Gender and Cultural Politics.* New York: Routledge, 1991.

Mirandé, Alfredo and Evangelina Enriquez. *La Chicana: The Mexican-American Woman.* Chicago: University of Chicago Press, 1979.

Mirikitani, Janice, ed. *Third World Women.* San Francisco: Third World Communications, 1973.

——. *AYUMI: A Japanese American Anthology.* San Francisco: Japanese American Anthology Committee, 1980.

Mirikitani, Janice, et al., eds. *Time to Greez! Incantations from the Third World.* San Francisco: Third World Communications, 1975.

Mohanty, Chandra Talpade. "Under Western Eyes: Feminist Scholarship and Colonial Discourses," in *Third World Women and the Politics of Feminism*, ed. Chandra Talpade Mohanty, Ann Russo, and Lourdes Torres. Bloomington: Indiana University Press, 1991.

Moraga, Cherríe. "Between the Lines: On Culture, Class and Homophobia." In *This Bridge Called My Back: Writings by Radical Women of Color*, ed. Cherríe Moraga and Gloria Anzaldúa. New York: Kitchen Table: Women of Color Press, 1981. 23–33.

———. *Loving in the War Years*. Boston: South End Press, 1983.

———. "From a Long Line of Vendidas: Chicanas Feminism." In *Feminist Studies/Critical Studies*, ed. Teresa de Lauretis. Bloomington: Indiana University Press, 1986. 173–90.

———. *Giving Up the Ghost: Teatro in Two Acts*. Los Angeles: West End Press, 1986.

———. *The Last Generation*, Boston, Mass.: South End Press, 1995.

Moraga, Cherríe, and Amber Hollibaugh, "What We're Rollin' around in Bed With: Sexual Silences in Feminism, a Conversation toward Ending Them." *Heresies* 12 (spring 1981): 46–58.

Moraga, Cherríe, and Gloria Anzaldúa, eds. *This Bridge Called My Back: Writings by Radical Women of Color*. New York: Kitchen Table: Women of Color Press, 1981.

Morrison, Toni. "Complexity: Toni Morrison's Women—An Interview Essay." In *Sturdy Black Bridges: Visions of Black Women in Literature*, ed. Roseanne Bell, Bettye Parker, and Beverly Guy-Shetfall. New York: Anchor/Doubleday, 1979.

———. *Sula*. New York: Bantam Books, 1980.

Nieto, Consuelo. "Consuelo Nieto on the Women's Rights Movement." *La Luz* 3 (September 1972): 10–11, 32.

Nieto-Gomez, Anna. "Chicanas Identify." *Hijas de Cuauhtémoc* (April 1971): 9.

———. "La Chicana." *Women Struggle* 9 (1976): 24–30.

———. "Sexism in the Movimento." *La Gente* 6: 4 (1976): 8–11.

Noda, Barbara. *Strawberries*. San Francisco: Shameless Hussy Press, 1980.

Noda, Barbara, Tsui, and Z. Wong. "Coming Out. We Are Here in the Asian Community. A Dialogue with Three Asian Women." *Bridge* (spring 1979): 24–34.

Ochoa, Maria, and Teresia Teaiwa, eds. "Enunciating Our Terms: Women of Color in Collaboration and Conflict." *Inscriptions* 7 (1994): 1–8.

Orozco, Cynthia. "Sexism in Chicano Studies and the Community." In *Chicana Voices: Intersections of Class, Race, and Gender*, ed. Teresa Cordova, Norma Cantú, Gilberto Cardenas, Juan Garcia and Christine Sierra. Austin, Tex.: CMAS Publications, 1986.

Orozco, Yolanda. "La Chicana and 'Women's Liberation.'" *Voz Fronteriza*, January 5, 1976, 6, 12.

Paredes, Milagros. "From the Inside Out." *Awakening Thunder: Asian Canadian Women. Fireweed* 30 (winter 1990): 77–81.

Pérez, Emma. "Sexuality and Discourse: Notes from a Chicana Survivor." In *Chicana Lesbians, the Girls Our Mothers Warned Us About*, ed. Carla Trujillo. Berkeley: Third Woman Press, 1991. 159–84.

———. *The Decolonial Imaginary: Writing Chicanas into History*. Bloomington: Indiana University Press, 1999.

Quintana, Alvina. *Home Girls: Chicana Literary Voices*. Philadelphia: Temple University Press, 1996.

Radford-Hill, Sheila. "Considering Feminism as a Model for Social Change." In *Feminist Studies/Critical Studies*, ed. Teresa de Lauretis. Bloomington: Indiana University Press, 1986. 125–42.

Reagon, Bernice Johnson. "Coalition Politics, Turning the Century." In *Home Girls: A Black Feminist Anthology*, ed. Barbara Smith. New York: Kitchen Table: Women of Color Press, 1983. 356–69.

Rebolledo, Tey Diana. "The Politics of Poetics: Or, What Am I, a Critic, Doing in This Text Anyhow?" In *Chicana Creativity and Criticism: Charting New Frontiers in American Literature*, ed. María Herrera-Sobek and Helena María Viramontes. Houston: Arte Público Press, 1988. 129–38.

Riddell, Adaljiza Sosa. "Chicanas en el Movimiento," *Aztlán* 5 (1974).

Rodriguez, Raquel. "Yo soy mujer." *Comadre* 18 (1978) 8–11.

Salazar, Claudia, ed. *Third World Feminism*. Special issue of *Women and Language* 11:2 (1989).

Saldívar-Hull, Sonia. "Feminism on the Border: From Gender Politics to Geopolitics." In *A Criticism in the Borderlands: Studies in Chicano Literature, Culture, and Ideology*, ed. Héctor Calderón and José David Saldívar. Durham, N.C.: Duke University Press, 1991. 203–21.

Sanchez, Carol Lee. "Sex, Class, and Race Intersections/Visions of Women of Color." In *A Gathering of Spirit: Writing and Art by North American Indian Women*, ed. Beth Brant. Rockland, Maine: Sinister Wisdom Books, 1984. 163–67.

Sandoval, Chela. "Comment on Susan Krieger's 'Lesbian Identity and Community,'" *Signs* (spring 1983).

———. "The Struggle Within: A Report on the 1981 N.W.S.A. Conference." In *Making Face, Making Soul— Haciendo Caras*, ed. Gloria Anzaldúa. San Francisco: Spinsters/Aunt Lute: 1990. 55–71.

———. "U.S. Third World Feminism." In *Oxford Companion to Women's Writing in the United States*, ed. Cathy Davidson, Linda Wagner-Martin, New York: Oxford University Press, 1995. 880–82.

———. "Feminist Agency and U.S. Third World Feminism," in *Provoking Agents: Theorizing Gender and Agency*, ed. Judith Kegan. Gardiner: Indiana University Press, 1995.

———. "New Sciences: Cyborg Feminism and the Methodology of the Oppressed," in *The Cyborg Handbook*, ed. Chris Gray. New York: Routledge, 1995.

Showalter, Elaine, ed. *The New Feminist Criticism: Essays on Women, Literature and Theory*. New York: Pantheon Books, 1985.

Silko, Leslie Marmon. *Yellow Woman and a Beauty of the Spirit: Essays on Native American Life Today*. New York: Simon and Schuster, 1996.

Silvera, Makeda, and Nila Gupta. "We Were Never Lost." Editorial. *Fireweed*, 16 (May 1983): 5–7.

Smith, Barbara. ed. *Home Girls: A Black Feminist Anthology*. New York: Kitchen Table: Women of Color Press, 1983.

———. "Toward a Black Feminist Criticism." In *The New Feminist Criticism: Essays on Women, Literature and Theory*, ed. Elaine Showalter. New York: Pantheon Books, 1985. 168–85.

Spivak, Gayatri Chakravorty. "Explanation and Culture: Marginalia." *Humanities in Society* 2 (summer 1979): 201–21.

———. "French Feminism in an International Frame." *Yale French Studies* 62 (1981): 154–84.

———. "Criticism, Feminism and the Institution." *Thesis Eleven* 10–11 (1984–1985).

———. "The Rani of Sirmur." In *Europe and its Others*, ed. F. Barker. Essex: University of Essex, 1985. 147.

———. "Three Women's Texts and a Critique of Imperialism." *Critical Inquiry* 12 (autumn 1985): 243–61.

———. "Explanation and Culture: Marginalia." In *In Other Worlds: Essays in Cultural Politics*, New York, Methuen, 1987. 103–18.

———. "In a Word, Interview." *differences* (summer 1989): 124–56.

———. "Explanations of Culture." In *The Post-Colonial Critic: Interviews, Strategies, Dialogues*. New York: Routledge, 1990.

Torres, Lourdes and Chandra Talpade Mohanty, eds. *Third World Women and the Politics of Feminism*. Bloomington: Indiana University Press, 1991.

Trujillo, Carla, ed. *Chicana Lesbians: The Girls Our Mothers Warned Us About*. Berkeley: Third Woman Press, 1991.

Truth, Sojourner. "Ain't I a Woman?" In *The Norton Anthology of Literature by Women*. New York: Norton, 1985.

Tsui, Kitty, Nellie Wong, and Barbara Noda, "Coming Out, We are Here in the Asian Community: A Dialogue with Three Asian Women," *Bridge* (spring 1979).

Vidal, Mirta. "New Voices of La Raza: Chicanas Speak Out." *International Socialist Review* 32 (1971): 31–33.

Villafañe-Sisolak, Rosa María. 1983 journal entry cited in *Making Face, Making Soul/Haciendo Caras: Creative and Critical Perspectives by Feminists of Color*, ed. Gloria Anzaldúa. San Francisco: Spinsters/Aunt Lute, 1990. xviii.

Walker, Alice. "In the Closet of the Soul: A Letter to an Afro-American Friend." *Ms.* 15 (November 1966): 32–35.

———. *Meridian*. New York: Harcourt Brace Jovanovich, 1970.

———. *The Third Life of Grange Copeland*. New York: Harcourt, 1970.

———. *In Love and Trouble: Stories of Black Women*. New York: Harcourt, 1971.

———. *You Can't Keep a Good Woman Down*. New York: Harcourt, 1981.

———. *The Color Purple*. New York: Pocket Books, 1982.

———. *In Search of Our Mother's Gardens: Womanist Prose*. New York: Harcourt Brace Jovanovich, 1983.

Walker, Margaret. *Jubilee*. New York: Bantam Books, 1985.

Wallace, Michele. "A Black Feminist's Search for Sisterhood." *The Village Voice*, July 28, 1975, 58D.

Ware, Vron. *Beyond the Pale: White Women, Racism, and History*. New York: Verso, 1992.

Welty, Eudora. *The Golden Apples*. New York: Harvest/ Harcourt Brace Jovanovich, 1977.

Witt, Shirley Hill. "Native Women Today: Sexism and Indian Women." *Civil Rights Digest* 6 (spring 1974): Available from the U.S. Commission on Civil Rights, 1121 Vermont Ave. NW, Washington, D.C. 10010.

Wong, Germaine Q. "Impediments to Asian-Pacific-American Women Organizing." In *Conference on the Educational and Occupational Needs of Asian Pacific Women*. Washington, D.C.: National Institute of Education, 1980.

Wong, Nellie, Merle Woo, and Yamada Mitsuye. "Three Asian American Writers Speak Out on Feminism." 1974. Available from *Radical Woman*, 2661 21st St., San Francisco, CA 94110.

Wong, Shelley Sunn. "Unnaming the Same: Thersa Hak Kyung Cha's Dictée." In *Writing Self, Writing Nation*, ed. Norma Alarcón and Elaine Kim. Berkeley: Third Woman Press, 1994. 103–40.

Woo, Merle, "Letter to Ma." In *This Bridge Called My Back: Writings by Radical Women of Color*, ed. Cherríe Moraga and Gloria Anzaldúa. New York: Kitchen Table: Women of Color Press, 1981. 140–47.

Wynter, Sylvia. "Sambos and Minstrels." *Social Text* 1:1 (1979): 149–58.

Yamada, Mitsuye. *Camp Notes and Other Poems*. San Francisco: Shameless Hussy Press, 1976.

Yarbro-Bejarano, Yvonne. "The Female Subject in Chicano Theatre: Sexuality, 'Race,' and Class." *Theatre Journal* 38:4 (1986): 389–407.

———. "Chicana Literature from a Chicana Feminist Perspective." In *Chicana Creativity and Criticism: Charting New Frontiers in American Literature*, ed. María Herrera-Sobek and Helena María Viramontes. Houston: Arte Público Press, 1988. 139–45.

———. "Gloria Anzaldúa's *Borderlands/La Frontera*: Cultural Studies, 'Difference,' and the Non-Unitary Subject." *Cultural Critique* 28 (Fall 1994): 5–28.

Zinn, Maxine Baca, Lunn Weber Cannon, Elizabeth Higginbotham, and Bonnie Thornton Dill. "The Costs of Exclusionary Practices in Women's Studies." In *Signs: Journal of Women in Culture and Society* 11:2 (winter 1986): 296–320.

Feminist Theory

Alcalá, Kathleen. *Spirits of the Ordinary: A Tale of Casa Grandes*. San Francisco: Chronicle, 1997.

Albrecht, Lisa, and Rose M. Brewer, eds. *Bridges of Power: Women's Multicultural Alliances*. Santa Cruz, Calif.: New Society Publishers, 1990.

Benstock, Shari, ed. *Feminist Issues in Literary Scholarship*. Bloomington: Indiana University Press, 1987.

Bloom, Lisa. *Gender on Ice: American Ideologies of Polar Expeditions* Minneapolis: University of Minnesota Press, 1993.

Burke, Carolyn. "Irigaray through the Looking Glass." *Feminist Studies* 7:2 (summer 1981): 288–306.

Butler, Judith. "The Force of Fantasy: Feminism, Mapplethorpe, and Discursive Excess." *Differences: A Journal of Feminist Cultural Studies* 2:2 (1990): 105–25.

———. *Gender Trouble: Feminism and the Subversion of Identity*. New York: Routledge, 1990.

———. *Bodies That Matter: On the Discursive Limits of "Sex."* New York: Routledge, 1993.

———. *The Psychic Life of Power: Theories in Subjection*, Stanford, Calif.: Stanford University Press, 1997.

Butler, Judith, and Joan W. Scott. *Feminists Theorize the Political*. New York: Routledge, 1992.

Califia, Pat. *Sapphistry: The Book of Lesbian Sexuality*. Naiad Press, 1980.

———. *Macho Sluts*. Boston: Alyson Publications, 1988.

Cixous, Hélène. "The Laugh of the Medusa." *Signs* 1:4 (autumn 1976): 875–93.

Daly, Mary. *Gyn/Ecology: The Metaethics of Radical Feminism*. Boston: Beacon Press, 1978.

de Beauvoir, Simone. *The Second Sex*. Trans. H. M. Parshley. New York: Vintage Books, 1974.

de Lauretis, Teresa. *Alice Doesn't: Feminism, Semiotics, Cinema*. Bloomington: Indiana University Press, 1984.

———. "The Violence of Rhetoric: Considerations on Representation and Gender." *Semiotica* 54 (1985): 11–31.

———. *Technologies of Gender: Essays on Theory, Film and Fiction*. Bloomington: Indiana University Press, 1987.

———. *Feminist Studies/Critical Studies*. Bloomington: Indiana University Press, 1986. 102–20.

———. "Eccentric Subjects: Feminist Theory and Historical Consciousness." *Feminist Studies* 1 (spring 1990): 115–49.

Dinnerstein, Dorothy. *The Mermaid and the Minotaur: Sexual Arrangements and Human Malaise*. New York: Harper Colophon, 1976.

DuPlessis, Rachel Blau. "For the Etruscans." Revised version of essay first published in *The Future of Difference*, ed. Hester Eisenstein and Alice Jardine. Boston: G. K. Hall, 1980.

Eagleton, Mary, ed. *Feminist Literary Theory*. Oxford: Basil Blackwell, 1986.

Echols, Alice. *Daring to Be Bad: Radical Feminism in America 1967–1975*. Minneapolis: University of Minnesota Press, 1989.

Eisenstein, Hester, and Alice Jardine, eds. *The Future of Difference: The Scholar and the Feminist*. Boston: G. K. Hall, 1980.

———. *Contemporary Feminist Thought*. Boston: G. K. Hall, 1983.

Eisenstein, Zillah R., ed. *Capitalist Patriarchy and the Case for Socialist Feminism*. New York: Monthly Review Press, 1979.

———. *The Radical Future of Liberal Feminism*. New York: Longman, 1981.

Felman, Shoshana. "Women and Madness: The Critical Phallacy." *Diacritics* 5 (winter 1975): 2–10

Frankenberg, Ruth. *White Women, Race Matters: The Social Construction of Whiteness*. Minneapolis: University of Minnesota Press, 1993.

Fregoso, Rosa Linda. *The Bronze Screen*. Minneapolis: University of Minnesota Press, 1993.

Fuss, Diana. *Essentially Speaking: Feminism, Nature and Difference*. New York: Routledge, 1989.

Gelpi, Barbara Charlesworth. *Signs: Journal of Women in Culture and Society*. Chicago: University of Chicago Press, 1984.

Gilbert, Sandra M., and Susan Gubar. *The Norton Anthology of Literature by Women*. New York: Norton, 1985.

Gordon, Linda. *Woman's Body, Woman's Right: A Social History of Birth Control in America*. New York: Penguin Books, 1980.

Greene, Gayle and Copelia Kahn, eds. *Making a Difference: Feminist Literary Criticism*. New York: Methuen 1985.

Griffin, Susan. *Woman and Nature: The Roaring inside Her*. New York: Harper Colophon, 1978.

———. *Rape: The Power of Consciousness*. San Francisco: Harper and Row, Publishers, 1979.

Haraway, Donna. "Animal Sociology and a Natural Economy of the Body Politic, Part 1: A Political Physiology of Dominance." *Signs* 4:1 (autumn 1978): 21–36.

———. "Animal Sociology and a Natural Economy of the Body Politic, Part II: The Past Is the Contested Zone: Human Nature and Theories of Production and Reproduction in Primate Behavior Studies." *Signs* 4:1 (autumn 1978): 37–60.

———. "In the Beginning Was the Word: The Genesis of Biological Theory." *Signs* 6:3 (spring 1981): 469–81.

———. "A Manifesto for Cyborgs: Science, Technology, and Socialist Feminism in the 1980's." *Socialist Review* 80:2 (March 1985): 65–108.

———. "The Heart of Africa: Nations, Dreams, and Apes." *Inscriptions* 2 (1986): 9–15.

———. *Simians, Cyborgs and Women: The Reinvention of Nature*. New York: Routledge, 1991.

———. "Ecce Homo, Ain't (Ar'n't) I a Woman, and Inappropriate/d Others: the Human in a Post-Humanist Landscape." In *Feminists Theorize the Political*, ed. Judith Butler and Joan Scott. New York: Routledge, 1992, 95.

Harding, Sandra. "Is Gender a Variable in Conceptions of Rationality?" In *Beyond Domination*, ed. Carol Gould. Totowa, N.J.: Roman and Allenheld, 1984. 112–38.

———. *The Science Question in Feminism*. Ithaca, N.Y.: Cornell University Press, 1986.

———. "Feminism, Science, and the Anti-Enlightenment Critiques." In *Feminism/Postmodernism*, ed. Linda J. Nicholson. New York: Routledge, 1990. 83–106.

Harding, Sandra, and Merrill B. Hintikka. *Discovering Reality: Feminist Perspectives on Epistemology, Metaphysics, Methodology and Philosophy of Science*. Dordrecht, Holland: D. Reidel, 1983.

Hartsock, Nancy. "The Feminist Standpoint: Developing the Ground for a Specifically Feminist Historical Materialism" In *Discovering Reality: Feminist Perspectives on Epistemology, Metaphysics, Methodology, and Philosophy of Science*, ed. Sandra Harding and Merrill B. Hintikka. Dordrecht: Reidel, 1983.

Hayles, N. Katherine. "Text Out of Context: Situating Postmodernism within an Information Society." *Discourse* 9, (1987): 24–36.

Hirsch, Marianne, and Evelyn Fox Keller, eds. *Conflicts in Feminism*. New York: Routledge, 1990.

Hutcheon, Linda. "The Post-Modern Ex-centric: The Center That Will Not Hold." In *Feminism and Institutions: Dialogues on Feminist Theory*, ed. Linda Kaufman. Cambridge, England: Basil Blackwell, 1989. 151–65.

Irigaray, Luce. "The Sex Which Is Not One." In *Language, Sexuality and Subversion*, ed. Paul Foss and Meeghan Morris Darlington, Sydney, Australia: Feral, 1978. 161–67.

———. "When Our Lips Speak Together." Trans. Carolyn Burke. *Signs: Journal of Women in Culture and Society* 6:1 (autumn 1980): 69–79.

———. "And the One Doesn't Stir without the Other." Trans. Hélène Vivienne Wenzel *Signs* 7:2 (summer 1981): 247–63.

———. *Speculum of the Other Woman*. Trans. Gillian C. Gill. Ithaca, N. Y.: Cornell University Press, 1985.

Jaggar, Alison. *Feminist Politics and Human Nature*. Brighton, Sussex: Harvester Press, 1983.

Jaggar, Alison, and Susan Bordo, eds. *Gender/Body/Knowledge: Feminist Reconstructions of Being and Knowing*. New Brunswick, N.J.: Rutgers University Press, 1989.

Kaplan, Cora. "Pandora's Box: Subjectivity, Class and Sexuality in Socialist Feminist Criticism." In *Making a Difference: Feminist Literary Criticism*, ed. Gayle Green and Copelia Dahn. New York: Methuen, 1985.

Kaplan, E. Ann. *Women and Film*. London: Methuen, 1983.

Keller, Evelyn Fox. *Reflections on Gender and Science*. New Haven: Yale University Press, 1985.

King, Katie. "Gender and Genre: Investigating the Epistemology of Criticism." Ph.D. diss. prospectus. History of Consciousness, University of California, Santa Cruz. March 26, 1981

———. *Theory in Its Feminist Travels*. Bloomington: Indiana University Press, 1997.

Kolodny, Annette. "Dancing through the Minefield: Some Observations on the Theory, Practice, and Politics of a Feminist Literary Criticism." *Feminist Studies* 6 (1980): 1–25.

———. "A Map for Rereading: Or, Gender and the Interpretation of Literary Texts." *New Literary History* 11 (spring 1980): 451–65.

Kristeva, Julia. "Women's Time." *Signs* 7:1 (summer 1981): 363–400.

———. *Powers of Horror: An Essay on Abjection*. Trans. Léon S. Roudiez. New York: Columbia University Press, 1982.

———. *Revolution in Poetic Language*. New York: Columbia University Press, 1984.

———. *The Kristeva Reader*. Ed. Toril Moi. Oxford: Basil Blackwell, 1986.

Lakoff, Robin. *Language and Woman's Place*. New York: Harper Colophon, 1975.

Linden, Robin Ruth, Darlene R. Pagano, Diana H. Russel, and Susan Leigh Star, eds. *Against Sadomasochism: A Radical Feminist Analysis*. East Palo Alto, Calif.: Frog in the Well, 1982.

MacKinnon, Catharine A. "Feminism, Marxism, Method and the State: An Agenda for Theory." *Signs* 7:3 (spring 1982): 515–44.

Mani, Lata. "Multiple Mediations: Feminist Scholarship in the Age of Multinational Reception." *Feminist Review* 35 (1990): 24–41.

Marks, Elaine, and Isabelle de Courtiuron, eds. *New French Feminisms: An Anthology*. Amherst: University of Massachusetts Press, 1980.

Meese, Elizabeth A. *Crossing the Double-Cross: The Practice of Feminist Criticism*. Chapel Hill: University of North Carolina Press, 1986.

Merchant, Carolyn. *The Death of Nature: Women, Ecology and the Scientific Revolution*. San Francisco: Harper and Row, 1980.

Meyerowitz, Patricia. *Gertrude Stein: Look at Me Now and Here I Am, Writings and Lectures 1909–1945*. Baltimore: Penguin Books, 1971.

Miller, Nancy K. *Subject to Change: Reading Feminist Writing*." New York: Columbia University Press, 1988.

Millett, Kate. *Sexual Politics*. New York: Avon Books, 1970.

———. *Flying*. New York: Knopf, 1974.

Modleski, Tania. "Feminism and the Power of Interpretation: Some Critical Readings." In *Feminist Studies/Critical Studies*, ed. Teresa de Lauretis. Bloomington: Indiana University Press, 1986. 121–38.

Moi, Toril. *Sexual/Textual Politics: Feminist Literary Theory*. New York: Methuen, 1985.

Morgan, Robin, ed. *Sisterhood Is Powerful: An Anthology of Writings from the Women's Liberation Movement*. New York: Vintage Books, 1970.

Off Our Backs. Reports of the Ninth Barnard Conference on the theme "The Scholar and the Feminist," titled "Towards a Politics of Sexuality." June–July 1982.

Ortner, Sherry B. "Is Female to Male as Nature Is to Culture?" In *Women, Culture and Society*, ed. M. Z. Rosaldo and L. Lamphere, Stanford, Calif.: Stanford University Press, 1974. 67–87.

Penley, Constance and Andrew Ross, eds. *Technoculture*. Minneapolis: University of Minnesota Press, 1991.

Piercy, Marge. *Woman on the Edge of Time*. Greenwich, Conn.: Fawcett Publications, 1976.

Rich, Adrienne. *Poems, Selected and New, 1950–1974*. New York: Norton, 1975.

———. *Of Woman Born: Motherhood as Experience and Institution*. New York: Norton, 1976.

———. *Women and Honor: Some Notes on Lying*. Pittsburgh: Motheroot Publications, Women Writers, 1977.

———. *The Dream of a Common Language, Poems 1974–1977*. New York: Norton, 1978.

———. *On Lies, Secrets and Silence: Selected Prose 1966–1978*. New York: Norton, 1979.

———. "Compulsory Heterosexuality and Lesbian Existence." *Signs* 5:4 (winter 1980): 631–60.

———. *A Wild Patience Has Taken Me This Far. Poems 1978–1981*. New York: Norton, 1981.

———. "Notes toward a Politics of Location." In *Blood, Bread, and Poetry: Selected Prose, 1979–85*. New York: Norton, 1986. 210–31.

Riley, Denise. *"Am I That Name?"Feminism and the Category of "Women" in History.* Minneapolis: University of Minnesota Press, 1988.

Rosaldo, Michelle Zimbalist, and Louise Lamphere, eds. *Woman, Culture and Society.* Stanford, Calif.: Stanford University Press, 1974.

Rubin, Gayle. "The Traffic in Women: Notes toward a 'Political Economy of Sex,'" In *Toward an Anthropology of Women*, ed. Rayne Reiter. New York: Monthly Review Press, 1975. 157–211.

———. "Thinking Sex: Notes for a Radical Theory of the Politics of Sexuality." In *Pleasure and Danger: Exploring Female Sexuality*, ed. Carole Vance. Boston and London: Routledge and Kegan Paul, 1984. 267–319.

Russ, Joanna. *The Female Man.* New York: Bantam Books, 1975.

Sargent, Lydia. *Women and Revolution: A Discussion of the Unhappy Marriage of Marxism and Feminism.* Boston: South End Press, 1981.

Sawicki, Jana. *Disciplining Foucault: Feminism, Power, and the Body.* New York: Routledge, 1991.

Scott, Joan Wallach. *Gender and the Politics of History.* New York: Columbia University Press, 1988.

Scott, Jody. *I, Vampire.* New York: Ace Science Fiction Books, 1984.

Sheba Collective, ed. *Serious Pleasure: Lesbian Erotic Stories and Poetry.* Pittsburgh: Cleis Press, 1989.

Showalter, Elaine. *A Literature of Their Own: Women Novelists from Brontë to Lessing.* Princeton, N.J.: Princeton University Press, 1977.

———. *Toward a Feminist Poetics: Women Writing and Writing about Women*, ed. Mary Jacobus. London: Croom Helm, 1979.

———, ed. *The New Feminist Criticism: Essays on Women, Literature and Theory.* New York: Pantheon Books, 1985.

Signs: Journal of Women in Culture and Society, 9:4 (1984).

Sofia, Zoe. "Exterminating Fetuses: Abortion, Disarmament, and the Sexo-semiotics of Extraterrestrialism." *Diacritics* 14:2 (1984): 47–59.

Sontag, Susan. *Illness as Metaphor.* New York: Vintage Books, 1979.

Stacey, Judith. "Sexism by a Subtler Name? Postindustrial Conditions and Postfeminist Consciousness." *Socialist Review* 96 (1987): 7–28.

Weedon, Chris. *Feminist Practice and Poststructuralist Theory.* Cambridge: Basil Blackwell, 1987.

Wittig, Monique. *The Lesbian Body.* New York: William Morrow, 1979.

———. "The Straight Mind." *Feminist Issues* 1 (1980): 103–12.

———. "One Is Not Born a Woman." *Feminist Issues* 1:2 (1981): 47–54.

Woolf, Virginia. *Between Acts.* New York: Harcourt Brace Jovanovich, 1941.

———. *A Room of One's Own.* New York: Harcourt Brace Jovanovich, 1957.

Zimmerman, Bonnie. "What Has Never Been: An Overview of Lesbian Feminist Criticism." *Feminist Studies* 7:3 (1981): 202–35.

De-Colonial Theory

Achebe, Chinua. *Things Fall Apart.* New York: Fawcett Crest Books, 1959.

Acuña, Rodolfo. *Occupied America: A History of Chicanos.* 2d ed. New York: Harper and Row, 1981.

Ahmad, Aijaz. "Jameson's Rhetoric of Otherness and the 'National Allegory.'" *Social Text* 17 (fall 1987): 3–25.

———. " 'Third World Literature' and the national ideology." *Journal of Arts and Ideas.* 17–18 (June 1989): 117–35.

Alarcón, Daniel. "The Aztec Palimpsest: Toward a New Understanding of Aztlán." in *Aztlán* 19:2 (1992): 33–68.

Alarcón, Francisco X. *Quake Poems.* Santa Cruz, Calif.: We Poems, 1989.

Alloula, Malek. *The Colonial Harem.* Trans. Myrna Godzich and Wlad Godzich. Minneapolis: University of Minneapolis Press, 1986.

Anaya, Rudolfo A. *Bless Me, Ultima.* Berkeley: Tonatiuh International, 1978.

Appelbaum, Richard. "Multiculturalism and Flexibility: Some New Directions in Global Capitalism." In *Mapping Multiculturalism*, ed. Avery Gordon and Christopher Newfield. Minneapolis: University of Minnesota Press, 1996.

Arteaga, Alfred. *An Other Tongue: Nation and Ethnicity in the Linguistic Borderlands.* Durham, N.C.: Duke University Press, 1994.

Appiah, Kwame Anthony. "Is the Post- in Postmodernism the Post- in Postcolonial?" *Critical Inquiry* 17:2 (winter 1991): 336–55.

Baker, Houston A. *Black Studies, Rap, and the Academy.* Chicago: University of Chicago Press, 1993.

Baldwin, James. *The Fire Next Time.* New York: Dess Publishing, 1963.

Bhabha, Homi K. "Of Mimicry and Man: The Ambivalence of Colonial Discourse." *October* 28 (1984): 125–33.

———. "Remembering Fanon: Self, Psyche, and the Colonial Position." In *Remaking History*, ed. Barbara Kruger and Phil Mariani. Seattle: Bay Press, 1989. 131–48.

———. "DissemiNation: Time, Narrative, and the Margins of the Modern Nation." In *Nation and Narration*, ed. Homi K. Bhabha. New York: Routledge, 1990. 291–322.

———. "The Postcolonial and the Postmodern: The Question of Agency." In *Redrawing the Boundaries: The Transformation of English and American Literary Studies*, ed. Giles Gunn and Stephen Greenblatt. New York: Modern Languages Association, 1992.

———. "The Postcolonial and the Postmodern: The Question of Agency," in *The Location of Culture*. New York: Routledge 1994. 171–97.

Blaut, J. M. *The Colonizer's Model of the World: Geographical Diffusionism and Eurocentric History*. New York and London: Guilford Press, 1993.

Brotherston, Gordon. *Book of the Fourth World: Reading the Native Americas through Their Literature*. Cambridge: Cambridge University Press, 1992.

Brown, Wesley, and Amy Ling, eds. "Homosexuality and the Chicano Novel." In *European Perspectives on Hispanic Literature of the United States*, ed. Genevieve Fabre. Houston: Arte Público Press, 1988. 98–106.

———. *Imagining America: Stories from the Promised Land*. New York: Persea Books, 1991.

Calderón, Héctor, and José David Saldívar. *Criticism in the Borderlands: Studies in Chicano Literature, Culture, and Ideology*. Durham, N.C.: Duke University Press, 1991.

Césaire, Aimé. *Discourse on Colonialism*. Trans. Joan Pinkham. New York: Monthly Review Press, 1972.

Chabram-Dernersesian, Angier, and Rosa Linda Fregosa, eds. "Chicana/o Cultural Representations: Reframing Alternative Critical Discourses." *Cultural Studies*, 4:3 (1990): 203–12.

Chinweizu. *The West and the Rest of Us: White Predators, Black Slavers and the American Elite*. New York: Vintage Books, 1975.

Churchill, Ward, ed. *Marxism and Native Americans*. Boston: South End Press, 1983.

Clifford, James. "Diasporas," *Cultural Anthropology* 9:3 (1994): 302–39.

Colas, Santiago. "The Third World in *Jameson's Postmodernism, or the Cultural Logic of Late Capitalism*." In *Social Text* 32 (1992): 323–42.

Coles, Robert. *The Old Ones of New Mexico*. New York: Anchor Books, 1975.

Deleuze, Gilles, and Félix Guattari. *Kafka: Toward a Minor Literature*. Trans. Dana Polan. Minneapolis: University of Minnesota Press, 1986.

Dhareshwar, Vivek. "Toward a Narrative Epistemology of the Postcolonial Predicament." *Inscriptions* 5 (1989): 135–57.

Dubois, W. E. B. *The Souls of Black Folk*, in *Three Negro Classics*. New York: Avon, 1965.

During, S. "Postmodernism or Post-Colonialism Today," *Textual Practice*, 1:1 (1987): 32–67.

Eagleton, Terry, Fredric Jameson, and Edward W. Said. *Nationalism, Colonialism, and Literature*. Minneapolis: University of Minnesota Press, 1990.

Fanon, Frantz. *The Wretched of the Earth*. New York: Grove Press, 1964.

———. *A Dying Colonialism*. Trans. Haakon Chevalier. New York: Grove Weidenfield, 1965.

———. *Black Skin, White Masks*. New York: Grove Press, 1967.

Foner, Phillip, ed. *The Black Panthers Speak*. Philadelphia: Lippincott, 1970.

Foster, Hal, ed. *The Anti-Aesthetic: Essay on Postmodern Culture*. Port Townsend, Wash.: Bay Press, 1983.

Freire, Paulo. *Pedagogy of the Oppressed*. New York: Continuum, 1982.

García, Mario T. "Internal Colonialism: A Critical Essay." *Revista Chicano–Riqueña* 6 (1978): 37–41.

Gaspar de Alba, Alicia. "The Alter-Native Sign." In *Chicano Art*. Austin: University of Texas Press, 1998.

Gates, Henry Louis Jr. "The Blackness of Blackness: A Critique of the Sign and the Signifying Monkey." In *Black Literature and Literary Theory*, ed. Henry Louis Gates Jr. New York: Methuen, 1984. 285–322.

———. ed. *Black Literature and Literary Theory*. New York: Methuen, 1984.

———. *"Race," Writing, and Difference*. Chicago: University of Chicago Press, 1986.

Gilroy, Paul. *"There Ain't No Black in the Union Jack": The Cultural Politics of Race and Nation*. Chicago: University of Chicago Press, 1991.

Gómez-Peña, Guillermo. "Border Culture: A Process of Negotiation toward Utopia." *La Línea Quebrada* 1:1 (June 1986): 1–6.

———. "Border Culture and Deterritorialization." *La Línea Quebrada* 2:2 (March 1987): 1–10.

———. "Border Brujo: A Performance Poem." *Drama Review* 35:3 (fall 1991): 49–66.

———. *The New World (B)order: Prophecies, Poems and Laqueras for the End of the Century*. University of California, Santa Cruz, Performing Arts Theater, April 13, 1993.

Grewal, Inderpal, and Caren Kaplan, eds. *Scattered Hegemonies: Postmodernity and Transnational Feminist Practices*. Minneapolis: University of Minnesota Press, 1994.

Guha, Ranajit. "On Some Aspects of the Historiography of Colonial India." In *Selected Subaltern Studies*, ed. Ranajit Guha and Gayatri Chakravorty Spivak. New York: Oxford University Press, 1998.

Gunew, Sneja. "The Mother Tongue and Migration." *Australian Feminist Studies* 1 (summer 1985): 134–50.

Gutiérrez, David G. "Significant to Whom? Mexican Americans and the History of the American West." *Western Historical Quarterly*, 14: 4 (November 1993): 519–39.

Gutiérrez, Ramón A. *When Jesus Came, the Corn Mothers Went Away: Marriage, Sexuality, and Power in New Mexico, 1500–1846*. Stanford, Calif.: Stanford University Press, 1991.

Gutiérrez-Jones, Carl. "Desiring (B)orders." *Diacritics* 25:1 (spring 1995): 99–112.

———. *Rethinking the Borderlands: Between Chicano Culture and Legal Discourse*. Berkeley: University of California Press. 1995.

Hall, Stuart. "The Local and the Global: Globalization and Ethnicity." In *Culture, Globalization and the World System*, State University of New York, Binghamton, Department of Art History, 1991. 41–68.

Huyssen, Andreas. "Mapping the Postmodern." *New German Critique* 33 (fall 1984): 5–52.

Inscriptions 5 (1989). "Traveling Theories Traveling Theorists."

Jackson, George. *Blood in My Eye*. New York: Bantam Books, 1972.

Jaimes, Annette. "American Indian Studies: Towards an Indigenous Model." *American Indian Culture and Research Journal* 11:3 (1987): 1–16.

JanMohamed, Abdul R. *Maintain Aesthetics: The Politics of Literature in Colonial Africa*. Amherst: University of Massachusetts Press, 1983.

JanMohamed, Abdul R., and David Lloyd, eds. "The Nature and Context of Minority Discourse II." Special issue. *Cultural Critique* 7 (fall 1987).

John, M. E. "Discrepant Dislocations: Feminism, Theory, and the Post–Colonial Condition." Qualifying essay, History of Consciousness Board. University of California, Santa Cruz, 1990.

Johnson, James Weldon. *The Autobiography of an Ex-Coloured Man*. New York: Hill and Wang, 1978.

LaCapra, Dominick, ed. *The Bounds of Race*. Ithaca, N.Y.: Cornell University Press, 1991.

Lauter, Paul, ed. *Reconstructing American Literature: Courses, Syllabi, Issues*. Old Westbury, N.Y.: Feminist Press, 1983.

Leonardo, Micaela di. *The Varieties of Ethnic Experience: Kinship, Class, and Gender among California Italian-Americans*. Ithaca, N.Y.: Cornell University Press, 1984.

Limón, José E. *Dancing with the Devil: Society and Cultural Poetics in Mexican-American South Texas*. Madison: University of Wisconsin Press, 1994.

Lowe, Lisa. *Immigrant Acts: On Asian American Cultural Politics*. Durham, N.C.: Duke University Press, 1996.

Mallon, Florencia E. "The Promise and Dilemma of Subaltern Studies: Perspectives from Latin American History." *American Historical Review*. 99:5 (December 1994).

Mani, Lata. "Notes on Colonial Discourse." *Inscriptions* 2 (1986): 3–4.

McClintock, Anne. "The Angel of Progress: Pitfalls of the Term 'Post-Colonialism.'" *Social Text* 31–32 (summer 1992).

Memmi, Albert. *Dominated Man*. Boston: Beacon Press, 1968.

———. *The Colonizer and the Colonized*. London: Souvenir Press, 1974.

Mignolo, Walter. "Are Subaltern Studies Postmodern or Postcolonial? The Politics and Sensibilities of Geo-Cultural Locations." Unpublished essay.

Mirandé, Alfredo, and Evangelina Enríquez. *La Chicana: The Mexican American Woman*. Chicago: University of Chicago Press, 1979.

Mullen, Harryette. "The Psychoanalysis of Little Black Sambo." *Inscriptions* 2 (1986) 22–28.

Nandy, Ashis. *The Intimate Enemy: Loss and Recovery of Self under Colonialism*. Delhi: Oxford University Press, 1991.

Neihardt, John G. *Black Elk Speaks: Being the Life Story of a Holy Man of the Oglala Sioux*. As told through John G. Neihardt. New York: Washington Square Press, 1972.

Newton, Huey P. *Revolutionary Suicide*. London: Wildwood House, 1973.

Nkrumah, Kwame. *Neo-Colonialism: The Last Stage of Imperialism*. London: Nelson, 1965.

Omi, Michael. "Racialization in the Post-Civil Rights Era," in *Mapping Multiculturalism*. Ed. Avery Gordon,

Christopher Newfield. Minneapolis: University of Minnesota Press, 1996.

Omi, Michael, and Howard Winant. *Racial Formation in the United States from the 1960s to the 1980s.* New York: Routledge and Kegan Paul, 1986.

Ong, Aiwah. "On the Edge of Empires: Flexible Citizenship among Chinese in Diaspora," *Positions* 1 (1993).

———. *Spirits of Resistance and Capitalist Discipline.* Albany: State University of New York Press, 1987.

Osting, Richard N. "Searching for New Worlds." *Time,* October 29, 1984, 62.

Paredes, Americo. *With His Pistol in His Hand: A Border Ballad and Its Hero.* Austin: University of Texas Press, 1958.

Patterson, Orlando. "Migration in Caribbean Societies: Socioeconomic and Symbolic Resource." In *Human Migration: Patterns and Policies,* ed. William McNeill and Ruth Adams. Bloomington: Indiana University Press, 1978. 106–45.

———. "The Emerging West Atlantic System: Migration, Culture, and Underdevelopment in the United States and the Cricum-Caribbean Region." In *Population in an Interacting World,* ed. William Alonso. Cambridge: Harvard University Press, 1987. 227–60.

Paz, Octavio. *The Labyrinth of Solitude: Life and Thought in Mexico,* trans. Lysander Kemp. New York: Grove Press, 1962.

Pérez, Emma. *The Decolonial Imaginary: Writing Chicanas into History.* Bloomington: Indiana University Press, 1999.

Pérez, Laura "*El desorden,* Nationalism, and Chicana/o Aesthetics." Unpublished manuscript. 1993.

———. "Spirit Glyphs: Reimagining Art and Artist in the World of Chicana *Tlamatinime.*" *Modern Fiction Studies* (spring 1998).

Pérez-Torres, Rafael. *Movements in Chicano Poetry: Against Margins, against Myths.* New York: Cambridge University Press, 1995.

Pietz, William. "The 'Post-Colonialism' of Cold War Discourse." *Social Text* 19–20 (spring 1988): 55–75.

Pratt, Mary Louise. *Imperial Eyes: Studies in Travel and Transculturation.* London: Routledge, 1992.

Rabasa, José. "Dialogue as Conquest: Mapping Spaces for Counter-Discourse." *Cultural Critique* 6 (1987): 131–60.

———. "Pre-Columbian Pasts and Indian Presents in Mexican History." In *Subaltern Studies in the Americas,* ed. Robert Carr, José Rabasa, and Javier Sanjines. Special issue. *Dispositio/n* 46 (1994): 245–70.

———. "Porque soy Indio: Subjectivity in *La Florida del Inca.*" *Poetics Today* 16:1 (1995): 79–108.

Rabasa, José, and Javier Sanjinés. "Introduction: The Politics of Subaltern Studies." In *Subaltern Studies in the Americas,* ed. Robert Carr, José Rabasa, and Javier Sanjinés. Special issue. *Dispositio/n* 46 (1994): v–xi.

Radhakrishnan, R. "Ethnic Identity and Post-Structuralist *Différance.*" *Cultural Critique* 6 (1987): 187–200.

Radical History Review 39 (September 1987): 117–23.

Ramos, Juanita, ed. *Compañeras: Latina Lesbians.* New York: Latina Lesbian History Project, 1987.

Rebolledo, Tey Diana. *Women Singing in the Snow: A Cultural Analysis of Chicano Literature.* Albuqurque: University of New Mexico Press, 1993.

Rechy, John. "El Paso del Norte." *Evergreen Review* 2 (1958): 127–40.

———. *City of Night.* New York: Grove Press, 1963.

———. *The Miraculous Day of Amalia Gomez.* New York: Arcade 1991.

Rodriguez, Luis. *Always Running: La Vida Loca, Gang Days in L.A.* New York: Simon and Schuster, 1994.

Rodriguez, Richard. *Hunger of Memory: The Education of Richard Rodriguez.* Boston: David R. Godine, 1982.

Román, David. "¡Teatro Viva! Latino Performance and the Politics of AIDS in Los Angeles." In *¿Entiendes? Queer Readings, Hispanic Writings,* ed. Emile L. Bergmann and Paul Smith. Durham, N.C.: Duke University Press, 1995. 346–69.

Said, Edward. *Orientalism.* New York: Vintage Books, 1979.

———. *After the Last Sky: Palestinian Lives.* With photographs by Jean Mohr. New York: Pantheon Books, 1986.

———. *Culture and Imperialism.* New York: Knopf, 1993.

Saldaña, María Josefina. "The Discourse of Development and Narratives of Resistance." Ph.D. diss., Stanford University, 1993.

Saldívar, Jose. *Border Matters: The Multiple Routes of Cultural Studies.* Berkeley: University of California Press, 1998.

Saldívar, Ramón. *Chicano Narrative: The Dialectics of Difference.* Madison: University of Wisconsin Press, 1990.

———. "The Borderlands of Culture: Americo Paredes's *George Washington Gomez* and Chicano Literature at the End of the Twentieth Century." *American Literary History* 5:2 (1993).

Sánchez, Ricardo. "Spanish Codes in the Southwest." In *Modern Chicano Writers: A Collection of Critical Essays*, ed. Joseph Sommers and Tomás Ybarra-Frausto. Englewood Cliffs, N.J.: Prentice Hall, 1979. 41–53.

Sánchez, Rosaura, "Postmodernism and Chicano Literature," *Aztlán* 18:2 (1987): 1–14.

Sangari, Kum Kum. "The Politics of the Possible." *Cultural Critique* 7 (1987): 157–86.

San Juan, E. *Beyond Postcolonial Theory*, New York: St. Martins Press, 1997.

Shohat, Ella. "Notes on the Post-Colonial," *Social Text* 31–32 (1990): 99–113.

Spivak, Gayatri Chakravorty. "The Rani of Sirmur." In *Europe and Its Others*, vol. 1, ed. F. Barker Essex: University of Essex, 1985. 147.

———. "Subaltern Studies: Deconstructing Historiography." In *Selected Subaltern Studies*, ed. Ranajit Guha and Gayatri Chakravorty Spivak. New York: Oxford University Press, 1998. 3–32.

Takaki, Ronald T. *From Different Shores: Perspectives on Race and Ethnicity in America*. New York: Oxford University Press, 1988.

———. *A Different Mirror: A History of Multicultural America*. Boston: Little, Brown, 1993.

Tiffin, Helen. "Post-Colonial Literatures and Counter-Discourse." *Kunapipi* 9 (1987): 17–34.

Todorov, Tzvetan. *The Conquest of America: The Question of the Other*. Trans. Richard Howard. New York: Harper and Row, 1984.

———. *On Human Diversity: Nationalism, Race and Exoticism in French Thought*. Trans. Catherine Porter. Cambridge, Mass.: Harvard University Press, 1993.

Toomer, Jean. *Cane*. New York: Norton, 1975.

Torgovnick, Marianna. *Gone Primitive*. Chicago: University of Chicago Press, 1990.

Trask, Haunani-Kay. *From a Native Daughter: Colonialism and Sovereignty in Hawaii*. Monroe, Maine: Common Courage Press, 1993.

Vizenor, Gerald. *Crossbloods: Bone Courts, Bingo, and other Reports*. Minneapolis: University of Minnesota Press, 1990.

Washington, Booker T. *Up from Slavery: An Autobiography*. New York: Bantam Books, 1977.

West, Cornel. "Minority Discourse and the Pitfalls of Canon Formation." *Yale Journal of Criticism* 1 (fall 1987): 193–201.

———. "Black Culture and Postmodernism." In *Remaking History*, ed. B. Kruger and Phil Mariani. Seattle: Bay Press, 1989. 87–96.

———. *Beyond Eurocentrism and Multiculturalism*. 2 vols. Monroe, Maine: Common Courage Press, 1992.

———. *Prophet Reflections: Notes on Race and Power in America*. Monroe, Maine: Common Courage Press, 1993.

Winant, Howard. "Gayatri Spivak and the Politics of the Subaltern." *Socialist Review* 20 (1990): 89–91.

Wright, Richard. *Black Boy: A Record of Childhood and Youth*. New York: Harper and Row, 1966.

———. *Native Son*. New York: Harper and Row, 1966.

X, Malcolm with Alex Haley. *The Autobiography of Malcolm X*. New York: Grove Press, 1966.

Ybarra-Frausto, Tomás. "Rasquachismo: A Chicano Sensibility." In *Chicano Art, Resistance and Affirmation: An Interpretive Exhibition of the Chicano Art Movement, 1965–1985*, ed. Richard Griswold del Castillo, Teresa McKenna, and Yvonne Yarbo-Bejarano. Los Angeles: Wright Art Gallery, UCLA, 1991. 155–62.

Young, Robert. *White Mythologies: Writing History and the West*. New York: Routledge, 1990.

Queer Theory

Abelove, Henry. "Freud, Male Homosexuality, and the Americans." In *The Lesbian and Gay Studies Reader*, ed. Henry Abelove, Michèle Aina Barale, and David Halperin. New York: Routledge, 1993. 381–93.

Bad Object-Choices, eds. *How Do I Look? Queer Film and Video*. Seattle: Bay Press, 1991.

Beinstein, Krista. *Obszöne Frauen*. Vienna: Promedia, 1986.

Benjamin, Jessica. *The Bonds of Love: Psychoanalysis, Feminism, and the Problem of Domination*. New York: Pantheon Books, 1988.

Brown, Rita Mae. *Rubyfruit Jungle*. New York: Bantam, 1977.

Brownworth, Victoria. "Dyke S/M Wars Rage in London: Racism and Fascism Alleged." *Coming Up!* 10 (October 1988): 14–15.

Burgin, Victor. "Perverse Space." In *Interpreting Contemporary Art*, ed. Stephen Bann and William Allen. New York: Icon Editions [HarperCollins], 1991. 124–38.

Butler, Judith. "The Force of Fantasy: Feminism, Mapplethorpe, and Discursive Excess." *differences: A Journal of Feminist Cultural Studies* 2:2 (summer 1990): 105–25.

Case, Sue-Ellen. "Towards a Butch-Femme Aesthetic." *Discourse: Journal for Theoretical Studies in Media and Culture* 11:1 (1988–1989): 55–73.

———. "Tracking the Vampire." *differences: A Journal of Feminist Cultural Studies* 3:2 (summer 1991): 1–20.

————, ed. *Performing Feminisms: Feminist Critical Theory and Theatre*. Baltimore: Johns Hopkins University Press, 1990.

Colapietro, Vincent M. *Peirce's Approach to the Self: A Semiotic Perspective on Human Subjectivity*. Albany: State University of New York Press, 1989.

Creet, Julia. "Daughter of the Movement: The Psychodynamics of Lesbian S/M Fantasy." *differences: A Journal of Feminist Cultural Studies* 3:2 (summer 1991): 135–59.

Crimp, D., ed. *AIDS: Cultural Analysis/Cultural Activism*. Cambridge: MIT Press, 1988.

Doane, Mary Ann. "Responses." *Camera Obscura* 20–21 (1989): 142–47.

————. *Femmes Fatales: Feminism, Film Theory, Psychoanalysis*. New York: Routledge, 1991.

Dolan, Jill. "The Dynamics of Desire: Sexuality and Gender in Pornography and Performance." *Theatre Journal* 39:2 (May 1987): 157–74.

Dworkin, Andrea. *Pornography: Men Possessing Women*. New York: Seal, 1981.

Erhart, Julia. "Representation and the Female Symbolic: What's Lesbianism Got to Do with It?" Ph.D. qualifying essay in History of Consciousness, University of California, Santa Cruz, 1992.

Faderman, Lillian. *Surpassing the Love of Men: Romantic Friendship and Love between Women from the Renaissance to the Present*. New York: William Morrow, 1981.

Foucault, Michel. *The History of Sexuality. Vol. 1, An Introduction*. Trans. Robert Hurley. New York: Pantheon Books, 1978.

Freud, Sigmund. "The Economic Problem of Masochism." In *General Psychological Theory*, ed. P. Reiff. New York: Collier, 1963. 190–201.

Fuss, Diana. *Inside/Out: Lesbian Theories, Gay Theories*. New York: Routledge, 1991.

————, ed. "Fashion and the Homospectatorial Look." *Critical Inquiry* 18 (summer 1992): 713–37.

Gilman, Sander L. "Black Bodies, White Bodies: Toward an Iconography of Female Sexuality in Late Nineteenth-Century Art, Medicine, and Literature." In *"Race," Writing, and Difference*, ed. Henry Louis Gates Jr. Chicago: University of Chicago Press, 1986. 223–61.

Grosz, Elizabeth A. "The Hetero and the Homo: The Sexual Ethics of Luce Irigaray." *Gay Information* (Australia) 17–18 (March 1988): 37–44.

————. "Lesbian Fetishism?" *differences: A Journal of Feminist Cultural Studies* 3:2 (summer 1991): 39–54.

Holmlund, Christine. "I Love Luce: the Lesbian, Mimesis, and Masquerade in Irigaray, Freud, and Mainstream Film." *New Formations* 9 (winter 1989): 105–23.

Keller, Yvonne. "Tracking Lesbian Pulp Novels of the 1950s and Early 1960s." Ph.D. qualifying essay in History of Consciousness, University of California, Santa Cruz, 1992.

Lorde, Audre. *Zami: A New Spelling of My Name*. Trumansburg, N. Y.: Crossing Press, 1982.

————. *Sister Outsider: Essays and Speeches*. Trumansburg, N. Y.: Crossing Press, 1984.

Miriam, Kathy. "Thanks for the Memory: Revisioning Lesbian-Feminism in the Age of Post-Feminism." Ph.D. qualifying essay in History of Consciousness, University of California, Santa Cruz, 1992.

Moraga, Cherríe. *Giving Up the Ghost: Teatro in Two Acts*. Los Angeles: West End Press, 1986. Reprinted with revisions in *Heroes and Saints and Other Plays*. Albuquerque: West End Press, 1994. 3–35.

Nestle, Joan. "The Fem Question." In *Pleasure and Danger: Exploring Female Sexuality*, ed. Carole Vance. Boston and London: Routledge and Kegan Paul, 1984. 232–41.

————. *A Restricted Country*. Ithaca, N. Y.: Firebrand Books, 1987.

Newton, Esther. *Mother Camp: Female Impersonators in America*. Englewood Cliffs, N.J.: Prentice Hall, 1972.

————. "The Mythic Mannish Lesbian: Radclyffe Hall and the New Woman." *Signs* 9:4 (summer 1984): 557–75.

O'Higgins, James. "Sexual Choice, Sexual Act: An Interview with Michel Foucault." *Salmagundi* 58–59 (fall 1982–winter 1983): 10–24.

Pérez, Emma. "Sexuality and Discourse: Notes from a Chicana Survivor." In *Chicana Lesbians: The Girls Our Mothers Warned Us About*, ed. Carla Trujillo. Berkeley: Third Woman Press, 1991. 159–84.

Roof, Judith. "The Match in the Crocus: Representations of Lesbian Sexuality." In *Discontented Discourses: Feminism/Textual Intervention/Psychoanalysis*, ed. Marleen S. Barr and Richard Feldstein. Urbana: University of Illinois Press, 1989. 100–16.

————. *A Lure of Knowledge: Lesbian Sexuality and Theory*. New York: Columbia University Press, 1991.

Rubin, Gayle. "Thinking Sex: Notes for a Radical Theory of the Politics of Sexuality." In *Pleasure and Danger: Exploring Female Sexuality*, ed. Carole Vance. Boston and London: Routledge and Kegan Paul, 1984. 267–319.

Terry, Jennifer. "Theorizing Deviant Historiography." *differences: A Journal of Feminist Cultural Studies* 5:2 (summer 1991): 55–74.

Trask, Haunani-Kay. *Eros and Power: The Promise of Feminist Theory*. Philadelphia: University of Pennsylvania Press, 1986.

Traub, Valerie. "Ambiguities of 'Lesbian' Viewing Pleasure: The (Dis)articulations of *Black Widow*." In *Body Guards: The Cultural Politics of Gender Ambiguity*, ed. Julia Epstein and Kristian Straub. New York: Routledge, 1991. 305–28.

Trujillo, Carla, ed. *Chicana Lesbians: The Girls Our Mothers Warned Us About*. Berkeley: Third Woman Press, 1991.

Watney, Simon. "Taking Liberties: An Introduction." In ed. E. Carter and Simon Watney. *Talking Liberties: AIDS and Cultural Politics*, London: Serpent's Tail, 1989.

White, Patricia. "Governing Lesbian Desire: *Nocturne*'s Oedipal Fantasy." In *Feminisms in the Cinema*, ed. Ada Testaferri and Laura Pietropaolo. Bloomington: Indiana University Press, 1994.

Wittig, Monique. *The Lesbian Body*. New York: William Morrow, 1979.

———. *The Straight Mind and Other Essays*. Boston: Beacon Press, 1992.

Yarbro-Bejarano, Yvonne. "Cherríe Moraga's *Giving Up the Ghost:* The Representation of Female Desire." *Third Woman* 3:1–2 (1986): 113–20.

Film and Television

Barnouw, Erik. *Documentary: A History of the Non-Fiction Film*. London: Oxford University Press, 1977.

Barsam, Richard Meran, ed. *Non-Fiction Film Theory and Criticism*. New York: Dutton, 1976.

Beasley, Maurine, and Sheila Silver. *Women in Media: A Documentary Source Book*. Washington, D.C.: Women's Institute for Freedom of the Press, 1977.

Bobo, Jacqueline. " 'The Color Purple': Black Women as Cultural Readers." In *Female Spectators: Looking at Film and Television*, ed. E. Deirdre Pribram. London: Verso, 1988.

Cox, Alex. *Repo Man*. Boston: Faber and Faber, 1984.

de Lauretis, Teresa. *Alice Doesn't: Feminism, Semiotics, Cinema*. Bloomington: Indiana University Press, 1984.

———. *Technologies of Gender: Essays on Theory, Film and Fiction*. Bloomington: Indiana University Press, 1987.

———, ed. *Feminist Studies/Critical Studies*. Bloomington: Indiana University Press, 1986.

Deleuze, Gilles. *Cinema 1: The Movement-Image*. Trans. Hugh Tomlinson and Barbara Habberjam. Minneapolis: University of Minnesota Press, 1986.

Fiske, John. *Television Culture*. New York: Routledge, 1987.

Hedges, Elaine and Ingrid Wendt. *In Her Own Image: Women Working in the Arts*. New York: Feminist Press, 1980.

Kuhn, Annette. *Women's Pictures: Feminism and Cinema*. London: Routledge and Kegan Paul, 1982.

Mast, Gerald, and Cohen Marshall. *Film Theory and Criticism*. 2d. ed. New York: Oxford University Press, 1979.

Mellencamp, Patricia, ed. *The Logics of Television*. Bloomington: Indiana University Press, 1990. 193–221.

Mercer, Kobena. "Diaspora Culture and the Dialogic Imagination." In *Blackframes: Critical Perspectives on Black Independent Cinema*, ed. M. Cham and C. Watkins. Cambridge: MIT Press, 1988. 48–70.

Minh-ha, Trinh T. "Reassemblage (Sketch of Sound Track)." *Camera Obscura* 13 (1982): 105–12.

Mulvey, Laura. *Visual and Other Pleasures*. London: Macmillan, 1989.

Penley, Constance. *The Future of an Illusion: Film, Feminism, and Psychoanalysis*. Minneapolis: University of Minnesota Press, 1989.

———. "Brownian Motion: Women, Tactics and Technology." In *Technoculture*, ed. Constance Penley and Andrew Ross. Minneapolis: University of Minnesota Press, 1991. 89–129.

———, ed. *Feminism and Film Theory*. New York and London: Routledge and BFI Publishing, 1988.

Pines, Jim, and Paul Willemen, eds. *Third Cinema*. London: British Film Institute, 1989.

Rosenthal, Alan. *The New Documentary in Action: A Casebook in Film Making*. Berkeley: University of California Press, 1972.

Ryan, Michael, and Douglas Kellner. *Camera Politica: The Politics and Ideology of Contemporary Hollywood Film*. Bloomington: Indiana University Press, 1988.

Spigel, Lynn. "Installing the Television Set: Popular Discourses on Television and Domestic Space, 1948–1955." *Camera Obscura* 16 (1988): 11–46.

Treichler, Paula A., and Ellen Wartella. "Interventions: Feminist Theory and Communication Studies." *Communication* 9:1 (1986): 1–18.

Tuchman, Gaye, ed. *The TV Establishment: Programming for Power and Profit*. Englewood Cliffs, N.J.: Prentice Hall, 1974.

Tunstall, Jeremy. *The Media Are American: Anglo-American Media in the World*. New York: Columbia University Press, 1977.

Ulmer, Gregory. *Teletheory: Grammatology in the Age of Video*. New York: Routledge, Chapman and Hall, 1989.

Wallis, Brian, and Cynthia Schneider, eds. *Global Television*. Cambridge: MIT Press and Wedge, 1989.

Willett, John, ed. and trans. *Brecht on Theatre: The Development of an Aesthetic*. New York: Hill and Wang, 1964.

Williams, Raymond. *Television: Technology and Cultural Form*. New York: Schocken Books, 1974.

Index

Chela Sandoval is associate professor of critical and cultural theory
for the Department of Chicano Studies at
the University of California, Santa Barbara.
She is the author of many articles on third space feminism,
cybercinema, and millennial studies.

Angela Y. Davis is professor in the History of Consciousness Program at
the University of California, Santa Cruz. She is the author of
Women, Race, and Class and *Blue Legacies and Black Feminism:
Gertrude "Ma" Rainey, Bessie Smith, and Billie Holiday.*